Mastering JBoss Enterprise Application Platform 7

Create modular scalable enterprise-grade applications with JBoss Enterprise Application Platform 7

Francesco Marchioni
Luigi Fugaro

[PACKT]
PUBLISHING

BIRMINGHAM - MUMBAI

Mastering JBoss Enterprise Application Platform 7

First published: August 2016

Production reference: 1300816

Published by Packt Publishing Ltd.
Livery Place
35 Livery Street
Birmingham
B3 2PB, UK.
ISBN 978-1-78646-363-0

www.packtpub.com

Credits

Authors

Francesco Marchioni
Luigi Fugaro

Reviewer

Mauro Vocale

Commissioning Editor

Amarabha Banerjee

Acquisition Editor

Reshma Raman

Content Development Editor

Samantha Gonsalves

Technical Editor

Jayesh Sonawane

Copy Editor

Safis Editing

Project Coordinator

Devanshi Doshi

Proofreader

Safis Editing

Indexer

Rekha Nair

Graphics

Jason Monteiro

Production Coordinator

Melwyn D'sa

About the Authors

Francesco Marchioni is a Red Hat Certified JBoss Administrator (RHCJA) and Sun Certified Enterprise Architect working at Red Hat in Rome, Italy. He started learning Java in 1997, and since then he has followed the path to the newest Application Program Interfaces released by Sun. In 2000, he joined the JBoss community when the application server was running the 2.X release.

He has spent years as a software consultant, where he has envisioned many successful software migrations from vendor platforms to open source products, such as JBoss AS, fulfilling the tight budget requirements of current times.

Over the last 10 years, he has authored many technical articles for OReilly Media and ran an IT portal focused on JBoss products (http://www.mastertheboss.com).

He has authored multiple books for Packt Publishing such as *JBoss AS 5 Development* (http://www.packtpub.com/jboss-as-5-development/book), *JBoss AS 5 Performance Tuning* (http://www.packtpub.com/jboss-5-performance-tuning/book), *JBoss AS 7 Configuration Deployment Administration* (http://www.packtpub.com/jboss-as-7-configuration-deployment-administration/book), *JBoss 7 Development* (https://www.packtpub.com/application-development/jboss-7-development), and *MongoDB Java Developers* (https://www.packtpub.com/application-development/mongodb-java-developers).

I would like to express my gratitude to the many people who helped me write this book and assisted in editing and proofreading. So, in strict alphabetical order, I'd like to thank Alessandro Arrichiello, who shared his valuable experience on the Red Hat infrastructure and gave the installation chapter a deep cut. Many thanks to the engineers at Red Hat who provided helpful insights on the new server release, in particular Josef Cacek for the awesome Kerberos stuff published on GitHub and Pedro Igor Silva for the elytron bits. A warm thanks to Luigi Fugaro, who launched the idea of writing this book together along with a nice cup of espresso and scaled this wall with me. This book would not be complete without the careful reviews of Mauro Vocale, who shared a valuable amount of his time to help us on it. And last but not least, thanks to Samantha Gonsalves, our content editor from Packt Publishing, for her patience and professionalism demonstrated in this bleeding-edge project.

Luigi Fugaro had his first encounter with computers back in the early 80s when he was still a kid. He started with a Commodore Vic-20, passing through a Sinclair, a Commodore 64, and an Atari ST 1040, where he spent days and nights giving breath mints to Otis. Then he took a big jump to a 486DX2 66MHz and started programming in Pascal and Basic.

In 1998, he started his career as a webmaster doing HTML, JavaScript, Applets, and some graphics with Paint Shop Pro. He then switched to Delphi, Visual Basic, and finally, started working on Java projects.

While working on Java, he met a lot of people who helped him get more and more hard and soft skills. Luigi has been developing in Java, all kinds of web applications, dealing with both backend and frontend frameworks, for various system integrators.

During his years in Red Hat, Luigi met extraordinary people, both for personal and professional reasons, who believed in him and helped him in his carrier.

He is still working with Red Hat, where he can count on a wide group of highly talented people who help him daily. He would like to mention all of them, but a few of them need special recognition: Ugo, Grande Marinelli, Nonno, Mr. Bernacchi, Frank, 3A, Vocal, eljeko, Scardy, Rinaldo (don't mind the order).

He has authored *WildFly Cookbook* by Packt Publishing.

A special thanks goes to the content editor, Samantha Gonsalves, who helped me a lot with her talent and patience.

A very very big THANK YOU goes to my friend and colleague, Mauro Vocale, for his precious work of reviewing and testing all the technical aspects of the book!

About the Reviewer

Mauro Vocale was born on March 25, 1980 in Venaria Reale, Italy.

He started working on Java and Linux OS in 2001, and he is currently working with Red Hat, which gives him the opportunity to interact with some open source communities.

He is certified Oracle Master Java SE Developer and Oracle Web Component and EJB Developer for JEE 6 also over the last 10 years he worked as a Java consultant to tried to spread the open source technologies and the idea of free software.

I would like to thank my wife, Silvia, for her help and support during the challenge of my work, and my beautiful children, Alessio and Fabrizio.

www.PacktPub.com

For support files and downloads related to your book, please visit www.PacktPub.com.

Did you know that Packt offers eBook versions of every book published, with PDF and ePub files available? You can upgrade to the eBook version at www.PacktPub.com and as a print book customer, you are entitled to a discount on the eBook copy. Get in touch with us at service@packtpub.com for more details.

At www.PacktPub.com, you can also read a collection of free technical articles, sign up for a range of free newsletters and receive exclusive discounts and offers on Packt books and eBooks.

PACKTLiB

https://www2.packtpub.com/books/subscription/packtlib

Do you need instant solutions to your IT questions? PacktLib is Packt's online digital book library. Here, you can search, access, and read Packt's entire library of books.

Why subscribe?

- Fully searchable across every book published by Packt
- Copy and paste, print, and bookmark content
- On demand and accessible via a web browser

Free access for Packt account holders

If you have an account with Packt at www.PacktPub.com, you can use this to access PacktLib today and view 9 entirely free books. Simply use your login credentials for immediate access.

Yesterday I was a writer. Today I'm a writer. Tomorrow I'll probably still be a writer. Sigh! There's so little hope for advancement in this world.

- Francesco Marchioni (inspired by C.Schultz's masterpiece)

I'd like to dedicate this book to my Dad, who passed away this year. I'd also like to dedicate this book to my daughter Giada, the love of my life.

-Luigi Fugaro

Table of Contents

Preface

JBoss Application Server has been, de facto, the open source platform to provision enterprise Java applications. The commercial platform that supported the release of the application server is JBoss Enterprise Application Platform (JBoss EAP), which has just hit its 7th release.

This release contains the advanced features developed for the upstream project—now called WildFly Application Server (currently at version 10)—such as the newly designed web subsystem, Undertow, which uses the latest non-blocking I/O features of Java to provide improved scalability and performance. Undertow also supports the latest standards for web applications, such as HTTP/2, HTTP Upgrade, and WebSockets.

Another change in the application server platform is the messaging subsystem, which is now based on the unified messaging technology for Red Hat products, called Apache ActiveMQ Artemis. Active MQ Artemis enables customers to exchange messages between JBoss EAP 6 and 7, while preserving the performance, scalability, and reliability of the EAP 6's HornetQ.

JBoss EAP 7 also features several significant management updates by giving administrators the ability to see and manage the configuration of JBoss EAP servers offline, or using the new server suspend mode to gracefully shut down the servers only after completing the in-flight transactions.

The preceding list is a non-exhaustive collection of features that will be discussed throughout this book, which will guide you through the core aspects of the Enterprise server, focusing on practical use cases and describing how to solve common issues.

What this book covers

Chapter 1, *Installation and Configuration*, introduces you to the application server platform and provides details about the installation, available server modes, and the management instruments (Web console and CLI).

Chapter 2, *The CLI Management Tool*, describes how you can configure and manage your JBoss EAP 7 platform using the CLI, using its auto completion feature, offline mode, and script files.

Chapter 3, *Managing EAP in Domain Mode*, goes in depth with the application server management using the domain mode, showing how to design advanced domain configurations and handle disaster and recovery scenarios.

Chapter 4, *Deploying Applications*, explains the different ways you can deploy your applications. Either by CLI, Web console, or filesystem, all a deployment's life cycle is managed by the platform itself and for both standalone and domain mode.

Chapter 5, *Load Balancing*, is about balancing requests to EAP 7 servers from a Web frontend layer.

Chapter 6, *Clustering EAP 7*, goes in depth to support and better configure your environment by providing a fault tolerant system with failover capabilities.

Chapter 7, *Logging*, provides a comprehensive description of the logging services available in the application server, teaching you how to build a scalable logging system.

Chapter 8, *Configuring Database Connectivity*, explains how to configure a datasource using the CLI. Adding a JDBC driver, defining a connection pool, choosing between an XA and a non-XA Datasource, and hardening the configuration is all described in depth.

Chapter 9, *Configuring EAP 7 for Java EE Applications*, describes how to configure the services needed for server-side applications through the application server subsystems.

Chapter 10, *Messaging Administration*, goes in detail about message-oriented middleware and how the JBoss EAP 7 platform can help rely on Apache Artemis as its default implementation.

Chapter 11, *Securing the Application Server*, discusses securing the application server infrastructure, including the applications running on top of it.

Chapter 12, *New Security Features of EAP 7*, is a preview of the upcoming security features available in the EAP 7.1 release and how to centralize security concerns of Web applications with the Red Hat Single Sign-On (SSO) server.

Chapter 13, *Using EAP 7 with Docker*, shows how to use the Docker technology to provision EAP 7 in the Enterprise.

Chapter 14, *Running EAP 7 on the Cloud Using OpenShift*, shows how applications leverage the new Red Hat PaaS (based on Docker and Kubernetes) to scale automatically and in any environment.

What you need for this book

To fully benefit from this book, you first need a PC, possibly running a Linux-like system, with at least 4 GB of RAM and around 10 GB of free disk space. Also, an Internet connection is a must.

From a software point of view, you will need JDK 8 and, of course, JBoss EAP 7.x. Furthermore, you should install Git and Maven.

Who this book is for

Java system administrators, developers, and application testers will benefit from this book. You are not expected to have accumulated a lot of experience on the earlier versions of the application server, though you must know the basic concepts of the Java and Linux operating system.

Conventions

In this book, you will find a number of text styles that distinguish between different kinds of information. Here are some examples of these styles and an explanation of their meaning.

Code words in text, database table names, folder names, filenames, file extensions, pathnames, dummy URLs, user input, and Twitter handles are shown as follows: "We can include other contexts through the use of the `include` directive."

A block of code is set as follows:

```
<?xml version="1.0" encoding="UTF-8"
standalone="no"?><AutomatedInstallation
langpack="eng"><productName>EAP</productName><productVersion>7.0.0</product
Version><com.izforge.izpack.panels.HTMLLicencePanel id="HTMLLicencePanel"/>
```

When we wish to draw your attention to a particular part of a code block, the relevant lines or items are set in bold:

```
import socket
socket.setdefaulttimeout(3)
newSocket = socket.socket()
newSocket.connect(("localhost",22))
```

Any command-line input or output is written as follows:

```
cd jboss-eap-7.0
cd bin
$ ./standalone.sh
```

New terms and **important words** are shown in bold. Words that you see on the screen, for example, in menus or dialog boxes, appear in the text like this: "In the next window, select the correct JBoss EAP version from the Version combobox and click **Download.**"

> Warnings or important notes appear in a box like this.

> Tips and tricks appear like this.

Reader feedback

Feedback from our readers is always welcome. Let us know what you think about this book—what you liked or disliked. Reader feedback is important for us as it helps us develop titles that you will really get the most out of.

To send us general feedback, simply e-mail feedback@packtpub.com, and mention the book's title in the subject of your message.

If there is a topic that you have expertise in and you are interested in either writing or contributing to a book, see our author guide at www.packtpub.com/authors.

Customer support

Now that you are the proud owner of a Packt book, we have a number of things to help you to get the most from your purchase.

Downloading the example code

You can download the example code files for this book from `https://github.com/mjbeap7` or from your account at `http://www.packtpub.com`. If you purchased this book elsewhere, you can visit `http://www.packtpub.com/support` and register to have the files e-mailed directly to you.

You can download the code files by following these steps:

1. Log in or register to our website using your e-mail address and password.
2. Hover the mouse pointer on the **SUPPORT** tab at the top.
3. Click on **Code Downloads & Errata**.
4. Enter the name of the book in the **Search** box.
5. Select the book for which you're looking to download the code files.
6. Choose from the drop-down menu where you purchased this book from.
7. Click on **Code Download**.

Once the file is downloaded, please make sure that you unzip or extract the folder using the latest version of:

- WinRAR / 7-Zip for Windows
- Zipeg / iZip / UnRarX for Mac
- 7-Zip / PeaZip for Linux

We also have other code bundles from our rich catalog of books and videos available at `https://github.com/PacktPublishing/`. Check them out!

Downloading the color images of this book

We also provide you with a PDF file that has color images of the screenshots/diagrams used in this book. The color images will help you better understand the changes in the output. You can download this file from `http://www.packtpub.com/sites/default/files/downloads/MasteringJBossEnterpriseApplicationPlatform7_ColorImages.pdf`.

Errata

Although we have taken every care to ensure the accuracy of our content, mistakes do happen. If you find a mistake in one of our books-maybe a mistake in the text or the code-we would be grateful if you could report this to us. By doing so, you can save other readers from frustration and help us improve subsequent versions of this book. If you find any errata, please report them by visiting http://www.packtpub.com/submit-errata, selecting your book, clicking on the **Errata Submission Form** link, and entering the details of your errata. Once your errata are verified, your submission will be accepted and the errata will be uploaded to our website or added to any list of existing errata under the Errata section of that title.

To view the previously submitted errata, go to https://www.packtpub.com/books/content/support and enter the name of the book in the search field. The required information will appear under the **Errata** section.

Piracy

Piracy of copyrighted material on the Internet is an ongoing problem across all media. At Packt, we take the protection of our copyright and licenses very seriously. If you come across any illegal copies of our works in any form on the Internet, please provide us with the location address or website name immediately so that we can pursue a remedy.

Please contact us at copyright@packtpub.com with a link to the suspected pirated material.

We appreciate your help in protecting our authors and our ability to bring you valuable content.

Questions

If you have a problem with any aspect of this book, you can contact us at questions@packtpub.com, and we will do our best to address the problem.

1
Installation and Configuration

Red Hat JBoss Enterprise Application Platform 7.0 (JBoss EAP 7) is a middleware platform built on open standards and compliant with the Java EE 7 specification.

It is derived from the upstream project **Wildfly 10** and provides ready-to-use features such as high-availability clustering, messaging, and distributed caching.

JBoss EAP 7 is designed with a modular structure that allows on-demand services, thus greatly improving startup speed. Thanks to its web based management console and its powerful **Command Line Interface (CLI)**, editing XML configuration files is unnecessary (and is even discouraged!). The CLI also adds the ability to script and automate management tasks. Internally, JBoss EAP includes APIs and development frameworks for quickly developing fast, secure, and scalable Java EE applications compliant with the Java EE 7 specification.

The first part of this book will let you conquer the management instruments and the EAP 7 domain configuration. When you have completed all green bars, we will concentrate on advanced topics, showing the improvements from the earlier release of the server.

As far as this chapter is concerned, we will now have a quick tour of its technology covering these topics:

- What the installation options are and how to choose the one that works better for your context
- How to perform the basic administration steps
- The essentials of the server configuration

What's new in EAP 7?

If you are arriving from a JBoss EAP 6 environment you will be eager to know about the highlights of the new platform. Broadly speaking, the changes encompass both the server administration area and the Java Enterprise APIs that can help to provide applications on it. We will start by introducing the new administrative features and then we will briefly mention the API highlights.

The administrative features are described as follows:

- **Undertow web server**: JBoss Web has for quite a long time been the face of the web application server. Although compatible with Servlet/JSP Specifications it has kept the long-term legacy with Tomcat. The new Undertow web server has been built from scratch using the best-of-breed Java IO API. Some of its core features include non-blocking NIO based APIs, a lightweight and fully embeddable architecture based on pluggable handlers, and support for WebSockets, including JSR-356 and the HTTP Upgrade mechanism. Besides this, Undertow is capable of working as a reverse proxy or load balancer for a clustered application server, opening the door to the full JBoss clustering platform.

- **Simpler server management**: Thanks to the HTTP upgrade mechanism available in Undertow, now you can reduce the number of ports in the default installation to just two:

  * 8080 for applications with JNDI and EJB multiplexed

  * 9990 for management, for both HTTP/JSON and native API

- **Support for HTTP/2**: The new web server architecture supports the new version of the HTTP protocol, named HTTP/2. HTTP/2 aims to reduce latency and make efficient use of the TCP connection by means of binary framing, request/response multiplexing, header compression (HPACK) and more.

- **New life cycle modes**: It is now possible to suspend and resume the execution of the application server. This allows active `sessions/requests/in-flight-txs` to complete and can be used for a graceful server shutdown scenario.

- **Enhanced server management**: The administration web console has been revamped with a new graphical layout and new availabilities such as the Datasource wizard that will let you quickly create database connections with a few touches.

- **ArtemisMQ Messaging Broker**: In the new server version, the messaging broker has changed to ArtemisMQ which is directly derived from the former HornetQ.

Former HornetQ clients will be supported out of the box, while offering compatibility to Apache's ActiveMQ 5.0 clients as well.

- **ORB Switch**: The new version of the application server has switched to OpenJDK ORB which provides better interoperability with other vendors compared with the earlier JacORB implementation.

The Java EE 7 API highlights are related to the the Java EE 7 (JSR 342) specification is an *umbrella* specification which encompasses 33 single specifications. There have been brand new technologies and improvements of existing ones.

Here is a short list of Java EE 7 drivers:

- JSR-352 batch applications for the Java platform, featuring a new API for an XML-based job specification language and a runtime API.
- JSR-236 concurrency utilities for JavaEE, providing a simple and standard API for using multiple threads from Java Enterprise components.
- JSR-353 Java API for JSON Processing (JSON-P). This API can be used to parse, transform, and query JSON data.
- JSR-356 WebSockets support, featuring a full-duplex communication channel between the client and the server by means of simple annotations and life cycle callbacks.

Besides the new additions, some updates have been released to existing services. The most notable ones are as follows:

- JSR-345, which includes EJB 3.2, plus Interceptors 1.2 and Annotations 1.2
- JSR-340, featuring Servlet 3.1: non-blocking I/O, HTTP upgrade, and so on
- JSR-342, including the JMS 2.0 API that delivers a JMSContext resource as a wrapper for JMS resources
- JSR-344 JSF 2.2: HTML 5, FaceFlows, Stateless views, Resource lib contracts

Installing EAP 7

Installing the application server can be done in several ways. For the purpose of learning we will start with the basic unzipping installation which will produce a vanilla installation ready to be used. In real-world scenarios with dozens of customized installations to be completed, you will probably want to learn some advanced installation tactics. Don't worry, we have been trained for it and you will be too in a while.

Installing from the ZIP file

The first one we will detail is also the simplest, which merely requires unzipping a file. The JBoss EAP 7 ZIP file is available from the **Red Hat Customer Portal**. This method of installation is platform-independent and requires the following steps:

1. Open a browser and log into the **Customer Portal** at `https://access.redhat.com`.
2. Click **Downloads**.
3. Select **Red Hat JBoss Enterprise Application Platform** in the Product list and click on it.
4. In the next window, select the correct JBoss EAP version from the Version combobox and click **Download.**

JBoss EAP 7 is now downloaded to your target machine, ready for installation. Execute the following command in order to unzip the archive:

```
unzip jboss-eap-7.0.0.zip
```

Now you can test that the installation was successful by executing the `standalone.sh` shell script (Windows users will launch the `standalone.cmd` equivalent).

```
cd jboss-eap-7.0
cd bin
$ ./standalone.sh
```

> **When to use ZIP installation:**
> The ZIP installation can be used for developers or simple environments where it's just fine to provide a basic default installation of the server, with all the configuration and libraries in the standard folders. Therefore, it's not the best choice for large enterprise systems where you want to automate and customize installations.

Installing EAP from RPM

This method of installation is peculiar of JBoss EAP and can be a practical solution if you want to manage your application ecosystem through **Red Hat Packet Manager** (**RPM**) archives.

Installing JBoss EAP 7 via RPM requires a subscription to the official Red Hat's repositories. You can either subscribe to the current JBoss EAP channel or a minor channel that provides a specific minor release and all applicable patches. This allows you to maintain the same minor version of JBoss EAP 7, while still staying current with high severity and security patches.

Let's see in practice how the installation can be done on a RHEL 7 operating system. First of all, we have to register our brand new server to the **Red Hat Network (RHN)**, using our credentials (username/password) for accessing to all needed subscriptions.

The command will ask for username or password, or in case we've planned to use an internal **RH Satellite 6 system**, we can use a preconfigured **Activation Key** as an option:

```
# subscription-manager register
```

After a successful registration we need to figure out to which Pool we need to attach for downloading the EAP 7 packages. We can use the subscription-manager list command followed by the *less* one for searching through multiple subscriptions:

```
# subscription-manager list --available|less
Subscription Name:    Client SKU
Provides:             Oracle Java (for RHEL Server) - AUS
                      Oracle Java (for RHEL Client)
                      Red Hat Enterprise Linux 7 High
                      Availability
                      Red Hat Enterprise Linux High Availability
                      Red Hat EUCJP Support (for RHEL Server)
                      Red Hat Enterprise Linux for Power
                      Red Hat Enterprise Linux EUS Compute Node
                      Red Hat Enterprise Linux for Power, big
                      endian -
                      Red Hat OpenShift Enterprise JBoss EAP
                      add-on
                      Oracle Java (for RHEL Server) - Extended
                      Update
                      dotNET on RHEL Beta (for RHEL Server)
                      Red Hat Enterprise Linux Load Balancer
                      JBoss Enterprise Web Server
                      JBoss Enterprise Application Platform -
                      ELS

                      . . . . . . . . . . . . . . . . .
```

As soon as we find the right subscription (you should choose something like: **JBoss Enterprise Application Platform**) we have to take note of the **pool ID** and run the following:

```
# subscription-manager attach --pool
844aff014485be8a85f8d058bf198144
```

After that we can explore the available repositories:

```
# subscription-manager repos --list
```

We won't list here all the available repositories which is quite large; however, you have to enable only EAP, RHEL7 base rpms, extras, and optional repository, and disable all the others with the following command:

```
# subscription-manager repos --disable="*" --enable jb-eap-7.0-
for-rhel-7-server-rpms --enable rhel-7-server-rpms --enable
rhel-7-server-extras-rpms --enable rhel-7-server-optional-rpms
```

You can verify that the process worked as expected by simply running the following:

```
# yum repolist
```

The list should look like this:

```
Loaded plugins: search-disabled-repos
repo id
name
!jb-eap-7.0-for-rhel-7-server-rpms/7Server/x86_64  (RPMs)
!rhel-7-server-extras-rpms/x86_64                  (RPMs)
!rhel-7-server-optional-rpms/7Server/x86_64        (RPMs)
!rhel-7-server-rpms/7Server/x86_64                 (RPMs)
repolist: 19,727
```

Complete the installation by executing the following:

```
# yum groupinstall jboss-eap7
```

> **When to use RPM installation:**
> The RPM installation makes things a lot easier in terms of installation because you can use all the tools that know how to deal with RPMs, and upgrading is simpler because you can use **yum** to do it, especially for security errata. The JBoss RPMs put things where many RHEL system administrators would expect them: config files under /etc, content and libraries under /var, and so on.
> Most of the downsides come from being forced to do things the way RHN/RPMs want to do them. You cannot install multiple version of JBoss in parallel, which may not be an issue if you spin up a new VM per instance, but can be for some people. It is also difficult to install non-current versions, since you either need to manually specify the versions of several hundred packages or use satellite with a date cutoff on a custom cloned channel to hide any packages from newer releases.

Installing from the JAR installer

The JBoss EAP 7 installer archive is also available from the Red Hat Customer Portal (`https ://access.redhat.com`). The `.jar` archive can be used to run either the graphical or text-based installers.

In order to complete the JAR installation, follow these steps:

1. Open a terminal and navigate to the directory containing the downloaded installation program JAR.
2. Type the following command:

    ```
    java -jar jboss-eap-7.0.0-installer.jar
    ```

3. As an alternative, if you have just a terminal available, use the text only mode by launching the following command:

    ```
    java -jar jboss-eap-7.0.0-installer.jar -console
    ```

We will not detail the single steps of the installation which are quite intuitive and covered by the EAP installation guide. Rather we would like to stress that the installer produces an XML script; you can reuse it for multiple installations, as you can see from the following picture:

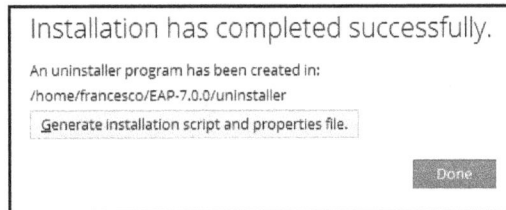

Installation has completed successfully.

An uninstaller program has been created in:
/home/francesco/EAP-7.0.0/uninstaller

Generate installation script and properties file.

Done

If you open the generated XML file, then you can pinpoint some custom elements in the installation:

```
<?xml version="1.0" encoding="UTF-8" standalone="no"?>
<AutomatedInstallation langpack="eng">
<productName>EAP</productName>
<productVersion>7.0.0</productVersion>
<com.izforge.izpack.panels.HTMLLicencePanel id="HTMLLicencePanel"/>
<com.izforge.izpack.panels.TargetPanel id="DirectoryPanel">
<installpath>/home/francesco/EAP-7.0.0</installpath>
. . . . .
</AutomatedInstallation>
```

Then you can repeat the installation with the following command:

```
java -jar jboss-eap-7.0.0-installer.jar -xml yourxml
```

> **When to use the JAR installer**:
> We would recommend using the JAR installer for medium to large sized environments where you have some common defaults for networks, database connectivity, or security settings. Another advantage of this approach is that it can be used for any operating system as it's completely Java based.

Installing from the source

Downloading the source code can be used if you need low-level details about the single modules of the application server. Once you have downloaded the `jboss-eap-7.0.0-src.zip` file, unzip it to your disk at first. Next you can build the server in two ways:

- Executing the batch script (`build.sh` or `build.bat` for Windows)
- If you have Maven 3.2.5 (or newer) installed you can use it directly as follows:

```
$ mvn install
```

Change to the bin directory after a successful build:

```
$ cd build/target/jboss-eap/bin
```

Verify that the application server boots successfully:

```
$ ./standalone.sh
```

Other installation options

The amount of installation options for EAP could well deserve one or more chapters; however, that would take us away from the scope of this book. We will just mention **Ansible**, which is an excellent configuration management and provisioning tool that uses SSH to perform administrative tasks on your machines. This has the evident advantage that nothing needs to be installed on the machines you are targeting as Ansible only runs on your main control machine, which could even be your laptop!

The steps used by Ansible to provision and configure machines are described in a kind of template called **Playbooks**, which are Ansible's configuration, deployment, and orchestration language.

You can find a large list of example Playbooks in the Ansible documentation, available at `http://docs.ansible.com/ansible`. Besides this, for testing purposes we have provided a sample EAP 7 playbook which is attached to the sources of this book. (Read the instructions contained in the `README.txt` file packaged in `ansible.zip`.)

Besides this, if you want a user interface for your provisioning activities, **Ansible Tower** is a web-based solution that makes Ansible even more easy to use for IT teams of all kinds. It's designed to be the hub for all of your automation tasks.

Starting the application server

The scripts for starting the server are contained in the `JBOSS_HOME/bin` folder:

- `standalone.sh` starts the server in standalone mode
- `domain.sh` starts the server in domain mode

An equivalent BAT file is also included for Windows users.

In order to check that your installation was successful, execute one of the startup scripts:

```
$ ./standalone.sh
```

Next surf to `localhost:8080` and check the welcome page of the application server:

Stopping the application server

Stopping the application server can be done in several ways. Sending an interrupt signal (*Ctrl* + *C*) will interrupt the server abruptly, so it's not a recommended option.

So it is sending a kill -9 signal from the terminal against the application server process which is an extreme option to be used when the application server is not responsive through management channels.

The recommended approach is to connect through the Command Line Interface and execute the shutdown command:

1. Execute `jboss-cli.sh` from `JBOSS_HOME/bin`.

2. Once in the command line prompt, execute the connect command:

    ```
    [disconnected /] connect 127.0.0.1:9990
    Connected to 127.0.0.1:9990
    ```

3. Now issue the shutdown command that will stop the application server:

    ```
    [127.0.0.1:9990 /] shutdown
    ```

4. The shutdown command can be also executed with the `restart=true` parameter which will cause the application server to restart:

    ```
    [127.0.0.1@localhost:9990 /] shutdown --restart=true
    ```

> **Two things to know!**
> The first one is that if you don't provide any parameter to the connect command, it will use the defaults contained in the `jboss-cli.xml` that will attempt to connect to localhost on port `9990`.
> Next, if you are connecting to a remote host controller, a username/password challenge will be prompted. See the next section (*Basic server administration*) to learn how to create a management user.

Basic server administration

Once the installation has been completed, it's about time to complete some basic administration tasks. The most obvious one involves creating one or more users for managing your platform. Out of the box, a script called `add-user.sh` is provided along with your installation. The purpose of this script is to manage two different types of user:

- Management users: users in charge of administrating your application server
- Application users: users in charge of accessing your applications

> **Important notice!**
> The add-user script uses a very simple file-based mechanism to store the users' information. This can be acceptable for basic security requirements. Real-world scenarios, however, would need to use more appropriate security polices as detailed in `Chapter 11`, *Securing the Application Server*, of this book.

You can execute the add-user script both in an interactive way and in an automatic way.

In order to execute the add-user script in an interactive way, just execute it as follows and provide the requested information:

```
$ ./add.user.sh
What type of user do you wish to add?
 a) Management User (mgmt-users.properties)
 b) Application User (application-users.properties)
(a): a
Enter the details of the new user to add.
Using realm 'ManagementRealm' as discovered from the existing
property files.
Username : administrator1
. . . . .
Password :
Re-enter Password :
What groups do you want this user to belong to? (Please enter a
comma separated list, or leave blank for none)[  ]:
About to add user 'administrator1' for realm 'ManagementRealm'
Is this correct yes/no? yes
To represent the user add the following to the server-
identities definition <secret value="UGFzc3dvcmQxIQ==" />
```

We have removed some negligible information from the output so that you can focus on the required arguments of the script. The previous information can be filled in also in a non-interactive way by providing the username with the –u parameter, the password with the –p, and the group (if needed) with –g. You can discriminate between management users and application users with the –m and –a parameters.

Here is how to create a management user:

```
$ ./add-user.sh -m -u administrator1 -p Securepassword1!
```

Once you have created the management user, you can verify that the login correctly lets you through the management console, which is available at `http://localhost:9990`.

On the other hand, here is the shell script to create an application user belonging to the `guest` group:

```
$ ./add-user.sh -a -u demouser -p Securepassword1! -g guest
```

Beware that creating users in a non-interactive way exposes your user/password information across the shell history system process table if you are a Linux user.

Once you have created your users the following files (contained in the configuration folder of your server base directory) will be updated:

```
-rw-rw-r--. 1 francesco francesco    711 Oct 26 06:13
application-roles.properties
-rw-------. 1 francesco francesco    935 Oct 26 06:13
application-users.properties
-rw-rw-r--. 1 francesco francesco    646 Nov 24 16:11 mgmt-
groups.properties
-rw-------. 1 francesco francesco   1111 Nov 24 16:11 mgmt-
users.properties
```

The `application-roles.properties` holds the list of roles granted to application users. The file `application-users.properties` contains the list of application users and their hashed passwords. Conversely, `mgmt-groups.properties` contains the list of roles granted to management users and `mgmt-users.properties` holds the management users and their hash passwords. As a final note, the password contained in `*-users.properties` files is in hash using this format:

```
username=HEX( MD5( username ':' realm ':' password))
```

How to recover the password

Being an MD5 based hash means that the password is not reversible. On the other hand, consider that most hashes are also non-unique; rather, they're unique *enough*, so a collision is highly improbable, but still possible.

EAP 7 basic configuration

JBoss EAP provides two operating modes for the servers: the **standalone** mode and the **domain** mode. A standalone server is a Java process which is governed by a single management point using a configuration file. A domain server, on the other hand, is a group of Java processes which are managed through a single point called the Domain Controller and its configuration file.

The difference between the two operating modes is related to management capabilities rather than functionalities: a clear example of this is the high availability (HA) functionality that is available both in the standalone mode and in the domain mode; you will just use different configuration files to manage your cluster. Let's see more in detail the specific server configuration.

Standalone configuration

A standalone server is an independent server process which uses a single configuration file. The configuration, by default, is stored in the JBOSS_HOME/standalone/configuration folder. Within this directory, some built-in configurations are available. Here is a short description of them:

- standalone.xml: This is the default standalone configuration file used by the application server. It does not include the messaging subsystem and is not able to run in a cluster.
- standalone-full.xml: This configuration adds to the default configuration the messaging provider and iiop-openjdk libraries.
- standalone-ha.xml: This configuration enhances the default configuration with clustering support (JGroups/mod_cluster).
- standalone-full-ha.xml: This configuration adds both clustering capabilities and the messaging / iiop openjdk libraries.

If you want to start a non-default configuration, then you can use the -c parameter. Here's, for example, how to start the server using the ha server configuration:

```
$ ./standalone.sh -c standalone-ha.xml
```

Domain configuration

When running in domain mode the configuration is maintained in a single file named domain.xml that resides on the domain controller. This file contains a set of profiles, each one corresponding to the configuration seen earlier in the standalone mode, so you will be able to find the following XML structure within it:

```
<profiles>
        <profile name="default">. . .</profile>
        <profile name="ha"> . . . </profile>
        <profile name="full"> . . .</profile>
        <profile name="full-ha">. . .</profile>
</profiles>
```

Each domain is logically divided into server groups that contain the single server instances. The server groups are bound to the profiles described so far:

```
<server-groups>
        <server-group name="main-server-group" profile="full">
            <socket-binding-group ref="full-sockets"/>
        </server-group>
        <server-group name="other-server-group" profile="full-ha">
            <socket-binding-group ref="full-ha-sockets"/>
        </server-group>
</server-groups>
```

The single server instances are defined in the host.xml file that is included in every host controller. Within this file you will find the list of servers that will be available on that host:

```
<servers>
       <server name="server-one" group="main-server-group">
       </server>
       <server name="server-two" group="main-server-group"
       auto-start="true">
            <socket-bindings port-offset="150"/>
       </server>
       <server name="server-three" group="other-server-group"
       auto-start="false">
            <socket-bindings port-offset="250"/>
       </server>
</servers>
```

We will discuss more in detail about the domain core components in Chapter 3, *Managing EAP in Domain Mode*, of this book. Whatever your server mode, a number of common configuration concepts apply; in the next sections of this chapter we will describe them.

Application server core building blocks

The whole server configuration is XML based and it is strictly ruled by a set of XML schemas. The configuration schemas are located in the JBOSS_HOME/docs/schema/ directory of your installation. Each configuration file has a set of mandatory elements which include the following.

Extensions

Every Java library that is installed into the application server is called a module. An extension is a special kind of module that is strictly bound to the application server life cycle and is managed through the core server configuration. The configuration of the extension, if any, is declared in a subsystem section. Here is an excerpt of the server configuration which declares a set of extensions (such as the logging extension), that is later configured through the logging subsystem:

```
<server xmlns="urn:jboss:domain:4.1">
    <extensions>
        <extension module="org.jboss.as.clustering.infinispan"/>
        <extension module="org.jboss.as.connector"/>
        <extension module="org.jboss.as.deployment-scanner"/>
        <extension module="org.jboss.as.ee"/>
        <extension module="org.jboss.as.ejb3"/>
        <extension module="org.jboss.as.jsf"/>
        <extension module="org.jboss.as.logging"/>
        . . . . .
    </extensions>
    . . . . .
    <profile>
        <subsystem xmlns="urn:jboss:domain:logging:3.0">
        . . . . .
    </profile>
</server>
```

Paths

The path is a logical name for a filesystem path. You can declare a path element in your configuration so that you can reference them using a logical unit, instead of the physical one which may vary on different machines. Out of the box, for example, the logging subsystem includes a reference to the jboss.server.log.dir path.

This in turn points to the server's `log` directory:

```
<file relative-to="jboss.server.log.dir" path="server.log"/>
```

Although you will not find them in the default configuration, some standard paths are available with the application server. Here is a list of them:

Path	Description
jboss.home	Root directory of the JBoss AS distribution
user.home	User's home directory
user.dir	User's current working directory
java.home	Java installation directory
jboss.server.base.dir	Root directory for an individual server instance
jboss.server.data.dir	Directory the server will use for persistent data file storage
jboss.server.log.dir	Directory the server will use for log file storage
jboss.server.tmp.dir	Directory the server will use for temporary file storage
jboss.domain.servers.dir	Directory under which a host controller will create the working area for individual server instances (managed domain mode only)

Here is an example of a custom path definition:

```
[standalone@localhost:9990 /] /path=secure:add(path=securedata,relative-
to=jboss.server.data.dir)
```

This will generate the following output in the server's configuration:

```
<path name="secure" path="securedata" relative-to="jboss.server.data.dir"/>
```

The attributes of the path element are as follows:

- **name**: this is the name of the path.
- **path**: this is the actual filesystem path. It is meant to be an absolute path, unless the relative-to attribute is specified.
- **relative-to**: this can optionally include the name of another path expression.

Interfaces

An interface is a logical name for a network interface / hostname / IP address to which the application server sockets can be bound. The server configuration includes a section where the interfaces are declared. Other parts of the configuration will reference the network interfaces so that you can specify the bindings for the single services.

The most relevant entries in the interfaces section are the management and public interfaces:

```
<interface name="management">
    <inet-address    value="${jboss.bind.address.management:127.0.0.1}"/>
</interface>
<interface name="public">
    <inet-address value="${jboss.bind.address:127.0.0.1}"/>
</interface>
```

As you can guess, the management interface defines the bindings for the administration instruments like the CLI and the web interface. The public interface relates to application-related services like HTTP, HTTPS, AJP, and so on.

The value of an interface is typically exposed using a BeanShell expression which contains in the left section the binding (also as a system property) and optionally in the right side a default value for it, separated by a colon (:).

```
/interface=public/:write-attribute(name=inet-address,
value=${jboss.bind.address:192.168.10.1})
{
    "outcome" => "success",
    "response-headers" => {
        "operation-requires-reload" => true,
        "process-state" => "reload-required"
    }
}
```

The preceding command needs a reload of the server configuration to propagate changes, hence the need to issue the reload command afterwards:

```
[standalone@localhost:9990 /] reload
```

That being said, the best practice for setting interface attributes is by means of system properties; this way you will not introduce any dependency against your environment.

Here is, for example, how you can start the standalone server binding the management interfaces and public interfaces to the loopback address:

```
./standalone.sh -Djboss.bind.address.management=192.168.10.1 -
Djboss.bind.address=127.0.0.1
```

> Please note that you can still use the 0.0.0.0 expression in this server release to indicate a binding towards all available IP addresses.

Socket bindings and socket binding groups

A socket binding is a named configuration for a socket. Both the `domain.xml` and `standalone.xml` configurations include a section where socket configurations can be declared. Other parts of the configuration can then reference those sockets by their logical name, rather than having to include details of the actual socket configuration.

This is an excerpt from the default socket bindings in standalone mode:

```
<socket-binding-group name="standard-sockets" default-interface="public"
port-offset="${jboss.socket.binding.port-offset:0}">
      <socket-binding name="management-http" interface="management"
port="${jboss.management.http.port:9990}"/>
      <socket-binding name="management-https" interface="management"
port="${jboss.management.https.port:9443}"/>
      <socket-binding name="ajp" port="8009"/>
      <socket-binding name="http" port="8080"/>
      <socket-binding name="https" port="8443"/>
      <outbound-socket-binding name="mail-smtp">
          <remote-destination host="localhost" port="25"/>
      </outbound-socket-binding>
</socket-binding-group>
```

Just like the network interfaces, it is a good practice to vary them using shell parameters. This is how you can set a port offset of 100 at startup:

```
./standalone.sh -Djboss.socket.binding.port-offset=100
```

System properties

System property values can be used to customize some aspects of the server configuration. When running in the standalone mode, the properties set in `standalone.xml` will be part of the server boot process.

For example, the following property named `org.apache.cxf.logging.enabled` can be used to set the enable logging of web services deployed on the application server:

```
<system-properties>
  <property name="org.apache.cxf.logging.enabled" value="true"/>
</system-properties>
```

You can achieve this result through the CLI with the following command:

```
[standalone@localhost:9990 /] /system-property=
org.apache.cxf.logging.enabled:add(value=true)
{"outcome" => "success"}
```

You can conversely read the property using the read-resource command:

```
[standalone@localhost:9999 /] /system-property=
org.apache.cxf.logging.enabled:read-resource {      "outcome" =>
"success",      "result" => {"value" => "true"} }
```

When running in the domain mode, properties can be set at different levels. We will discuss this in more detail in Chapter 3, *Managing EAP in Domain Mode*, of this book, which is about the domain mode.

Profiles and subsystems

The most significant part of the server configuration is about defining one (in `standalone.xml`) or more (in `domain.xml`) *profiles*. A profile is nothing but a named set of subsystem configurations. A subsystem in turn is a set of services added to the core server by means of extensions.

For example, the following fragment is an example of a subsystem which controls the capabilities of the JPA server implementation:

```
<subsystem xmlns="urn:jboss:domain:jpa:1.1">
   <jpa default-datasource="" default-extended-
   persistence-inheritance="DEEP"/>
</subsystem>
```

The content of an individual profile configuration looks largely the same in the domain mode and in the standalone mode. The main difference is that in the standalone mode the `standalone.xml` file is only allowed to have a single profile element (the profile the server will run), whereas in the domain mode the `domain.xml` file can have many profiles, each of which can be mapped to one or more groups of servers.

There are two main instruments for managing the subsystems of the application server. The basic approach is to use the web console that is available by default on the port `9990` of the management interface (hence, the default is `http://localhost:9990`).

Once logged in with the management user, you can navigate through the **Configuration** upper tab and choose the subsystem you want to edit by clicking on its **View** button, as depicted by the following picture:

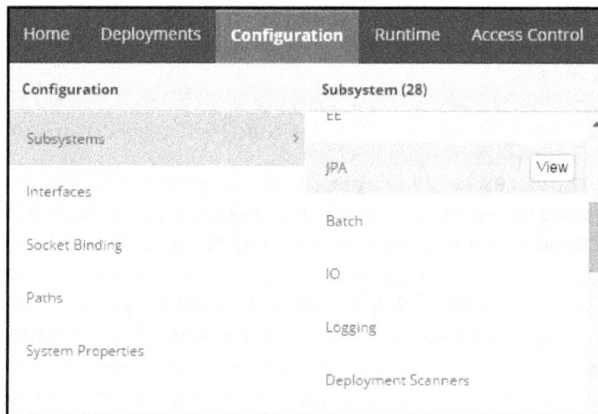

Although pretty simple and powerful, across this book we will use the CLI as the main configuration tool. The CLI is apparently more complex but it offers many advantages such as batch execution of commands in scripts, parameterization of the attributes to be used in scripts, and consistency between different server releases, to mention just a few.

Summary

In this chapter we have covered the required steps to install the application server on your machine, with special focus on provisioning the application server in large enterprise contexts. Then we learnt some basic aspects of the server configuration, going through your first administration tasks. In the next chapter we will dig deeply into the CLI that will be your Swiss Army Knife for managing the application server like a ninja!

2
The CLI Management Tool

In this chapter, we will describe the **Command Line Interface(CLI)** management tool, which can and should be used to control your entire application server, that is, the JBoss Enterprise Application Platform (also JBoss or just EAP).

The application server itself comes with two different management tools: the CLI and the admin console (also called the web console). The latter lets you manage the platform mostly at high-level operations, such as starting, stopping, and restarting JBoss instances, and configuring datasources. Thus, the web console is best for viewing the overall configuration and server instances topology (especially when dealing with the domain mode).

On the other hand, CLI is the best tool to manage your application server in depth, as per its features, your deployments, and JVM settings.

A deep knowledge of the CLI gives you full control over your platform. Despite the management aspect of the CLI, you should concentrate on some of its features, such as the following:

- Atomic operations
- Repeatable operations
- Batching operations
- Execute commands reading a file

Another important aspect of the JBoss EAP configuration is its two main concepts: subsystems and profiles.

A subsystem is a particular set of capabilities that extend the application server core, such as EJB3, CDI, Infinispan, JGroups, and Transaction Manager, just to mention a few.

A profile is a set of subsystem configurations. A standalone server runs a single profile. Managed domain servers can have many profiles, with different servers running different profiles.

The CLI is your Swiss Army Knife, and because it is such a powerful tool, it integrates with the JBoss EAP security system, which supports different authentication stores. But let's start from the basics.

Connecting to the CLI

To start a CLI session, you need to launch a shell script located in the `$JBOSS_HOME/bin` folder, named `jboss-cli.sh` (or `jboss-cli.bat` if you are running Windows).

As you execute the script, you will start a disconnected session, as shown here:

```
./bin/jboss-cli.sh
You are disconnected at the moment. Type 'connect' to connect to the server
or 'help' for the list of supported commands.
[disconnected /]
```

As suggested by the shell, you need to hit the `connect` command to connect to a running EAP instance, as follows:

```
./bin/jboss-cli.sh
You are disconnected at the moment. Type 'connect' to connect to the server
or 'help' for the list of supported commands.
[disconnected /] connect
[standalone@localhost:9990 /]
```

By default, the host and port coordinates are `localhost:9990`, so the `connect` command is the same:

```
./bin/jboss-cli.sh
You are disconnected at the moment. Type 'connect' to connect to the server
or 'help' for the list of supported commands.
[disconnected /] connect localhost:9990
[standalone@localhost:9990 /]
```

Those default settings are specified in the `jboss-cli.xml` file available under the `$JBOSS_HOME/bin` folder.

You can have an already connected session by enabling the flag connection while invoking the script via shell, as follows:

```
./bin/jboss-cli.sh --connect
[standalone@localhost:9990 /]
```

And if you need to provide different schema, host, and port values, you can use the `controller` directive, as follows:

```
./bin/jboss-cli.sh --connect --controller=http-remoting://localhost:9990
[standalone@localhost:9990 /]
```

To close the CLI session you can just invoke the `quit` command. There are also aliases, such as `exit` and `q`, to close the CLI.

Using the CLI

Within the CLI shell, there is a common and useful way to obtain the list of available commands and resources: the *Tab* key.

By hitting the *Tab* key on your keyboard, you can see all available commands and resources, with regard to the current context/resource you are in.

But first, let's define a resource for you.

Everything manageable is exposed via a tree of addressable resources. Resources expose attributes and operations. The concept is very similar to JMX Open MBeans, but note the following:

- Resources are organized in a tree
- Atomic multi-step operations are supported
- Operations across servers are supported

Hit the *Tab* key to see all the available commands and resources, as shown in the screenshot here:

```
● ● ●                    2. root@dev:/opt/rh/jboss-eap-7.0 (ssh)
[standalone@localhost:9990 /]
;                    deploy              ls            set
alias                deployment-info     module        shutdown
batch                deployment-overlay  patch         try
cd                   echo                pwd           unalias
clear                echo-dmr            quit          undeploy
command              help                read-attribute unset
connect              history             read-operation version
connection-info      if                  reload        xa-data-source
data-source          jdbc-driver-info    run-batch
[standalone@localhost:9990 /]
```

The *Tab* key is also used for auto completion of commands and parameters.

You can navigate through the resources, as you would do with your filesystem, by invoking the cd command followed by the resource name, as depicted here:

```
● ● ●                    2. root@dev:/opt/rh/jboss-eap-7.0 (ssh)
[standalone@localhost:9990 /] cd
--help               deployment-overlay    socket-binding-group
--no-validation      extension             subsystem
core-service         interface             system-property
deployment           path
[standalone@localhost:9990 /] cd subsystem=
batch-jberet         io              logging        sar
bean-validation      jaxrs           mail           security
datasources          jca             naming         security-manager
deployment-scanner   jdr             pojo           transactions
ee                   jmx             remoting       undertow
ejb3                 jpa             request-controller webservices
infinispan           jsf             resource-adapters weld
[standalone@localhost:9990 /] cd subsystem=datasources/
data-source   jdbc-driver   xa-data-source
[standalone@localhost:9990 /] cd subsystem=datasources/data-source=
[standalone@localhost:9990 data-source]
```

As you can see from the previous example, the *Tab* key is very important to find your desired context or command.

There are also two special characters: the forward slash (/) and the colon (:). The first one is used to navigate through the context, as you do for folders. The second one, the colon, is used to invoke operations available for the resource you are in.

You don't need to first position in a context and then invoke methods in it, as follows:

```
● ● ●                    2. root@dev:/opt/rh/jboss-eap-7.0 (ssh)
[standalone@localhost:9990 /] cd subsystem=logging
[standalone@localhost:9990 subsystem=logging] :
add                              read-attribute-group-names
list-add                         read-children-names
list-clear                       read-children-resources
list-get                         read-children-types
list-log-files                   read-log-file
list-remove                      read-operation-description
map-clear                        read-operation-names
map-get                          read-resource
map-put                          read-resource-description
map-remove                       remove
query                            undefine-attribute
read-attribute                   whoami
read-attribute-group             write-attribute
[standalone@localhost:9990 subsystem=logging] :list-log-files()
{
    "outcome" => "success",
    "result" => [{
        "file-name" => "server.log",
        "file-size" => 35477L,
        "last-modified-date" => "2016-01-08T20:22:47.000+0100"
    }]
}
[standalone@localhost:9990 subsystem=logging]
```

You could just navigate through the resources and invoke resource methods in line with the CLI, as follows:

```
● ● ●                    2. root@dev:/opt/rh/jboss-eap-7.0 (ssh)
[standalone@localhost:9990 /] /subsystem=logging:list-log-files()
{
    "outcome" => "success",
    "result" => [{
        "file-name" => "server.log",
        "file-size" => 35477L,
        "last-modified-date" => "2016-01-08T20:22:47.000+0100"
    }]
}
[standalone@localhost:9990 /]
```

Now we will take a look at those commands that execute common tasks.

Basic operations

The first thing you may want to know is what version of JBoss EAP is running and which JVM it's using; to gather this information you can rely on the version command, whose result is as follows:

```
[standalone@localhost:9990 /] version
JBoss Admin Command-line Interface
```

```
JBOSS_HOME: /opt/rh/jboss-eap-7.0
JBoss AS release: 2.1.2.Final-redhat-1 "Kenny"
JBoss AS product: JBoss EAP 7.0.0.GA
JAVA_HOME: null
java.version: 1.8.0_65
java.vm.vendor: Oracle Corporation
java.vm.version: 25.65-b01
os.name: Linux
os.version: 4.2.5-300.fc23.x86_64
[standalone@localhost:9990 /]
```

Furthermore, to know the exact state of a JBoss instance, you need to rely on the `read-attribute` method followed by the attribute name, as follows:

As mentioned previously in this chapter, method invocations are bound to resources by the colon
(:) symbol. In this case, the resource is the root, that is, the server. To know where you are, just use the `pwd` command, as follows:

```
[standalone@localhost:9990 /] pwd
/
[standalone@localhost:9990 /]
```

Just to get you a better idea, see the following example:

```
[standalone@localhost:9990 /] cd subsystem=datasources/data-source
[standalone@localhost:9990 data-source] pwd
/subsystem=datasources/data-source
[standalone@localhost:9990 data-source]
```

Managing server state

A JBoss EAP instance, as you have read in the first chapter, can be stopped and restarted by invoking the `shutdown` command (to restart, you need to append the `--restart=true` directive to the command).

Nonetheless, there is one more command that might be helpful, which is `reload`.

The `reload` command stops and starts the JVM, without creating a new one; thus the process ID (also the **PID**) of the EAP instance remains the same – this is particularly handy for monitoring tools that might bind particular metrics to PIDs.

Let me show you an example. First let's grab the **PID** of our EAP, as follows:

```
● ● ●                          3. root@dev:/opt/rh/jboss-eap-7.0 (ssh)
[root@dev jboss-eap-7.0]# ps -efa | grep java
root      7347  7339  2 20:19 pts/2    00:04:24 java -Djboss.modules.system.pkgs=com.sun.java.swing -Dlogging.configuration=f
ile:/opt/rh/jboss-eap-7.0/bin/jboss-cli-logging.properties -jar /opt/rh/jboss-eap-7.0/jboss-modules.jar -mp /opt/rh/jboss-eap
-7.0/modules org.jboss.as.cli --connect
root      7591 25202  0 20:22 pts/0    00:00:44 java -D[Standalone] -server -verbose:gc -Xloggc:/opt/rh/jboss-eap-7.0/ch02/lo
g/gc.log -XX:+PrintGCDetails -XX:+PrintGCDateStamps -XX:+UseGCLogFileRotation -XX:NumberOfGCLogFiles=5 -XX:GCLogFileSize=3M -
XX:-TraceClassUnloading -Xms1303m -Xmx1303m -Djava.net.preferIPv4Stack=true -Djboss.modules.system.pkgs=org.jboss.byteman -Dj
ava.awt.headless=true -Dorg.jboss.boot.log.file=/opt/rh/jboss-eap-7.0/ch02/log/server.log -Dlogging.configuration=file:/opt/r
h/jboss-eap-7.0/ch02/configuration/logging.properties -jar /opt/rh/jboss-eap-7.0/jboss-modules.jar -mp /opt/rh/jboss-eap-7.0/
modules org.jboss.as.standalone -Djboss.home.dir=/opt/rh/jboss-eap-7.0 -Djboss.server.base.dir=/opt/rh/jboss-eap-7.0/ch02 -Dj
boss.server.base.dir=ch02
root     14459  7201  0 23:20 pts/3    00:00:00 grep --color=auto java
[root@dev jboss-eap-7.0]#
```

The PID is 7591. Now let's get into the CLI and reload the server instance, as follows:

```
[standalone@localhost:9990 /] reload
[standalone@localhost:9990 /]
```

If you now check the PID again, as we did before, you should find the same PID associated with the JBoss EAP instance.

On the other hand, a restart will stop and destroy the current JVM and create a new JVM process with a new PID. Let's try it, as follows:

```
[standalone@localhost:9990 /] shutdown --restart=true
[standalone@localhost:9990 /]
```

Now check the PID, as follows:

```
● ● ●                        3. root@dev:/opt/rh/jboss-eap-7.0 (ssh)
[root@dev jboss-eap-7.0]# ps -efa | grep java
root      7347  7339  2 20:19 pts/2    00:04:30 java -Djboss.modules.system.pkgs=com.sun.java.swing -Dlogging.configuration=f
ile:/opt/rh/jboss-eap-7.0/bin/jboss-cli-logging.properties -jar /opt/rh/jboss-eap-7.0/jboss-modules.jar -mp /opt/rh/jboss-eap
-7.0/modules org.jboss.as.cli --connect
root     14623 25202 99 23:24 pts/0    00:00:09 java -D[Standalone] -server -verbose:gc -Xloggc:/opt/rh/jboss-eap-7.0/ch02/lo
g/gc.log -XX:+PrintGCDetails -XX:+PrintGCDateStamps -XX:+UseGCLogFileRotation -XX:NumberOfGCLogFiles=5 -XX:GCLogFileSize=3M -
XX:-TraceClassUnloading -Xms1303m -Xmx1303m -Djava.net.preferIPv4Stack=true -Djboss.modules.system.pkgs=org.jboss.byteman -Dj
ava.awt.headless=true -Dorg.jboss.boot.log.file=/opt/rh/jboss-eap-7.0/ch02/log/server.log -Dlogging.configuration=file:/opt/r
h/jboss-eap-7.0/ch02/configuration/logging.properties -jar /opt/rh/jboss-eap-7.0/jboss-modules.jar -mp /opt/rh/jboss-eap-7.0/
modules org.jboss.as.standalone -Djboss.home.dir=/opt/rh/jboss-eap-7.0 -Djboss.server.base.dir=/opt/rh/jboss-eap-7.0/ch02 -Dj
boss.server.base.dir=ch02
root     14734  7201  0 23:24 pts/3    00:00:00 grep --color=auto java
[root@dev jboss-eap-7.0]#
```

As you can see, we have a different PID (for me, it is 14623 – obviously you may have a different one).

Deploying and undeploying an application using CLI

We will now take a look at how to deploy and undeploy an application using the CLI. It will be just a brief introduction as we will have a dedicated chapter later on in the book.

One of the main tasks you want to do with your application server is deploy an application. Without going further, let's grab the JBoss EAP quickstarts. The quickstarts are a set of projects to show you and explain how to use most of the Java EE specification to run inside JBoss EAP.

Open a browser of your choice and point to the following URL: `http://www.jboss.org/products/eap/download/`.
The previous link connects you to a page where you can download the JBoss EAP 7 installer, its Maven repository, and its quickstarts – while writing this book the available version was 7.0.0.GA; the final version is expected some day around spring or summer 2016.

Download the quickstart bundle and open the archive in a folder of your choice. For convenience, we will refer to that folder as `$JBOSS_QUICKSTARTS`.

Let's start by deploying the `helloworld` project. To build the project, do as follows:

```
cd $JBOSS_QUICKSTARTS
cd helloworld
mvn clean package
```

This will create a WAR bundle in the target folder of the `helloworld` project. Now we are ready to deploy the application.

Get into the CLI and execute the deploy command followed by the bundle's name, as follows:

```
[standalone@localhost:9990 /] deploy target/jboss-helloworld.war
[standalone@localhost:9990 /]
```

Let's check the application by opening the browser and pointing it to the following URL: `http://localhost:8080/jboss-helloworld`.

You should land on a page similar to the one depicted as follows:

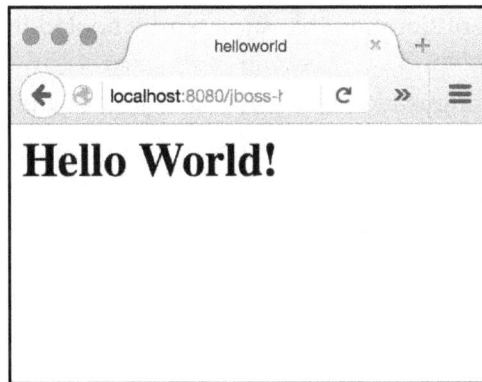

To undeploy the application, you can rely on the undeploy command followed by the runtime name of the application, as shown in the screenshot here:

If you now go back to the browser and refresh the page, you will no longer see the helloworld main page.

Creating a configuration snapshot

Often times, you are required to change your configuration, and when you are dealing with production environments, you surely need to take a backup of what is about to be updated. Configuration needs a backup as well. Despite the JBoss EAP configuration being based on just one or two files, there is a handy command to take a snapshot of your current configuration; that is `take-snapshot`.

Nonetheless, the application server on its own already backs up three temporally different configurations for you:

- **initial** – The initial configuration provided by the application folder is saved in the file named `standalone.initial.xml`
- **boot** – The last configuration that successfully booted the application server is saved in the file named `standalone.boot.xml`
- **last** – The last configuration that was committed by the application server itself is saved in a file named `standalone.last.xml`

All these files are saved in the `standalone_xml_history` folder, placed under `jboss.server.config.dir` (described in Chapter 1, *Installation and Configuration*).

The same criteria apply when running the domain mode, except that you will have a folder named `domain_xml_history` (containing the `initial`, `boot`, and `last` files of the `domain.xml`) and a folder named `host_xml_history` (containing the `initial`, `boot`, and `last` files of the `host.xml`).

Let's now start a standalone JBoss instance and take a snapshot via CLI, as follows:

```
$JBOSS_HOME/bin/jboss-cli.sh
```

You are disconnected at the moment. Type `connect` to connect to the server or `help` for the list of supported commands:

```
[disconnected /] connect
[standalone@localhost:9990 /] :take-snapshot()
{
    "outcome" => "success",
    "result" =>
    "standalone/configuration/standalone_xml_history/snapshot/
     20160110-041508107standalone.xml"
}
[standalone@localhost:9990 /]
```

As you can see from the preceding code, taking a snapshot of the configuration is very easy. Furthermore, you should have noticed that the configuration is saved in an additional folder named snapshot, under the usual `standalone_xml_history` folder. Also, the file configuration file is named by prefixing the timestamp of the date when invoking the command, then appending the `standalone.xml` string. This way, you can easily order and recognize the file that has the configuration you took the snapshot for.

> The timestamp notation used to name a snapshot has the following format: `yyyyMMdd-HHmmssssss`.
> The format should be read as follows:
> **yyyy** – four digits for the year
> **MM** – two digits for the month
> **dd** – two digits for the day
> **–** (the minus sign) – to separate date and time
> **HH** – two digits for the hours
> **mm** – two digits for the minutes
> **ss** – two digits for the seconds
> **sss** – three digits for the milliseconds

Features of the CLI

The CLI offers you some neat features such as executing operations as an atomic operation – which is called batch mode – scripting all the commands into a file (commonly named `.cli` files), and also the opportunity to do configuration tasks offline, which means without a running JBoss EAP instance… or better, there is one, but it's embedded into the CLI and it's not invisible outside.

Let's start gradually.

Batch mode

Batch mode allows you to run multiple CLI commands and operations in sequence, and commit the whole set of statements as one. The all-or-nothing commit pattern is applied, which means that all tasks must run successfully in order to complete correctly, otherwise if just one task goes in error, the whole batch sequence rolls back.

To enable batch mode, first you need to invoke the `batch` directive, since all future commands and operations will not be executed until you invoke the end of the batch sequence by invoking the `run-batch` command.

Suppose you have an application that needs to connect to a MySQL database via JNDI. You will first need to add the JDBC driver, then add datasource configuration, and then deploy the application. All these tasks can be done in batch mode, as follows:

```
[standalone@localhost:9990 /] batch
[standalone@localhost:9990 /] /subsystem=datasources/jdbc-
driver=mysql:add(driver-module-name=jdbc.mysql, driver-name=mysql)
[standalone@localhost:9990 /] /subsystem=datasources/data-source=MySQL-
DS:add(jndi-name="java:jboss/datasources/MySQL-DS", connection-
url="jdbc:mysql://localhost:3306/MJB7", driver-name="mysql", user-
name="mjb7", password="mjb7", prepared-statements-cache-size=128, share-
prepared-statements=true, blocking-timeout-wait-millis=60000, idle-timeout-
minutes=20)
[standalone@localhost:9990 /] deploy mjb7.war
[standalone@localhost:9990 /] run-batch
```

The preceding CLI script actually means the following:

- Start a new batch atomic transaction
- Add the JDCB driver
- Create a data-source
- Deploy the application
- Execute all the statements

There is also a nice feature to use while running batch mode, which is to label a set of batch statements and recall them when needed. The command to achieve such a feature is `holdback-batch`. Improving the preceding example, we could remove the default H2 driver, the default ExampleDS datasource, and split the rest of the example in two, as follows:

```
[standalone@localhost:9990 /] batch
[standalone@localhost:9990 /] /subsystem=datasources/data-
source=ExampleDS:remove
[standalone@localhost:9990 /] /subsystem=datasources/jdbc-driver=h2:remove
[standalone@localhost:9990 /] holdback-batch remove-default-data-source
[standalone@localhost:9990 /] batch
[standalone@localhost:9990 /] /subsystem=datasources/jdbc-
driver=mysql:add(driver-module-name=jdbc.mysql, driver-name=mysql)
[standalone@localhost:9990 /] holdback-batch add-mysql-jdbc-driver
[standalone@localhost:9990 /] batch
[standalone@localhost:9990 /] /subsystem=datasources/data-source=MySQL-
DS:add(jndi-name="java:jboss/datasources/MySQL-DS", connection-
url="jdbc:mysql://localhost:3306/MJB7", driver-name="mysql", user-
name="mjb7", password="mjb7", prepared-statements-cache-size=128, share-
prepared-statements=true, blocking-timeout-wait-millis=60000, idle-timeout-
```

```
minutes=20)
[standalone@localhost:9990 /] holdback-batch add-mysql-data-source
[standalone@localhost:9990 /] batch
[standalone@localhost:9990 /] deploy mjb7.war
[standalone@localhost:9990 /] holdback-batch deploy-mjb7
```

We can now run each batch, as follows:

```
[standalone@localhost:9990 /] batch remove-default-data-source
[standalone@localhost:9990 /] run-batch
[standalone@localhost:9990 /] batch add-mysql-jdbc-driver
[standalone@localhost:9990 /] run-batch
[standalone@localhost:9990 /] batch add-mysql-data-source
[standalone@localhost:9990 /] run-batch
[standalone@localhost:9990 /] batch deploy-mjb7
[standalone@localhost:9990 /] run-batch
```

This feature is quite useful when you have a repeatable task to execute on demand.

Commands in batch mode

There are also other commands available in batch mode. The following table describes all available command when running batch mode:

Command	Description
batch	This starts a batch of commands. Also used to call a holdback-batch.
list-batch	This lists the commands added since the currently active batch.
run-batch	This runs the commands added since the currently active batch.
holdback-batch	This saves the commands added since the currently active batch and stores into a label. It actually closes the batch mode.
clear-batch	This clears all commands added since the currently active batch.
discard-batch	This discards the currently active batch. It actually closes the batch mode.
edit-batch-line	This replaces the specified batch line with the current one.
remove-batch-line	This removes the specified batch line from the currently active batch.
move-batch-line	This moves the specified batch line to the new position, from the currently active batch.

Scripting in the CLI

Scripting the CLI is intended to have interaction with the CLI itself, thus making more sophisticated tasks, read and elaborate the output of a command and make decisions on it. Typically, this is done in Unix-like environments, where there is a massive use of scripts. The first thing you need to know is that you can invoke commands outside of the CLI, as follows:

```
$JBOSS_HOME/bin/jboss-cli.sh --connect --command=":read-
attribute(name=server-state)"
    {
        "outcome" => "success",
        "result" => "running"
    }
```

As mentioned, you can elaborate the output of the command for further use as you prefer. For example, from the previous output we just want to know if the server is in a running state or not, and we can achieve this as follows (only in Linux environments):

```
$JBOSS_HOME/bin/jboss-cli.sh --connect --command=":read-
attribute(name=server-state)" | awk 'NR==3 { print $3 }'
"running"
```

Another feature is executing a list of commands (including batch as well) stored in a file, typically a `.cli` file. Suppose that the previous example is stored in a file named `server-state.cli`:

```
connect
:read-attribute(name=server-state)"
```

You can invoke the commands within the file, as follows:

```
$JBOSS_HOME/bin/jboss-cli.sh --file="ch02/server-state.cli"
    {
        "outcome" => "success",
        "result" => "running"
    }
```

As shown before, you can elaborate the output as you prefer. Eventually, you can redirect the output to a file, if you don't need it printed on the screen. Both Windows and Unix-like environments can redirect an output using the **>** operator, as follows:

```
$JBOSS_HOME/bin/jboss-cli.sh --file="ch02/server-state.cli" > output.log
```

Using the CLI in offline mode

In previous versions, such as JBoss EAP 6, if you wanted to configure your server using the CLI, you needed a running JBoss instance. Now, with the new JBoss EAP 7, you have the feature to set up your entire environment directly from within the CLI without a running server, or better, running a server directly from the CLI as an embedded server.

The embedded server is a fully running EAP instance, except that it does not deploy applications, it does not open network ports, and it has to be considered for *internal use only*.

To run an embedded server, just do as follows:

```
[root@foogaro eap7]# ./bin/jboss-cli.sh
You are disconnected at the moment. Type 'connect' to connect to the server
or 'help' for the list of supported commands.
[disconnected /] embed-server --std-out=echo
12:09:11,779 INFO  [org.jboss.modules] (AeshProcess: 1) JBoss Modules
version 1.5.1.Final-redhat-1
12:09:11,992 INFO  [org.jboss.msc] (AeshProcess: 1) JBoss MSC version
1.2.6.Final-redhat-1
12:09:12,112 INFO  [org.jboss.as] (MSC service thread 1-7) WFLYSRV0049:
JBoss EAP 7.0.0.GA (WildFly Core 2.1.2.Final-redhat-1) starting
12:09:13,827 INFO  [org.jboss.as] (Controller Boot Thread) WFLYSRV0025:
JBoss EAP 7.0.0.GA (WildFly Core 2.1.2.Final-redhat-1) started in 2025ms -
Started 35 of 47 services (18 services are lazy, passive or on-demand)
[standalone@embedded /]
```

This kind of feature is very useful when you want to automate a configuration process to spread to different servers.

Once the configuration is done, you can reload the server and run it as fully operative with the following command:

```
[standalone@embedded /] reload --admin-only=false
```

The output should look like the following:

```
[standalone@embedded /] reload --admin-only=false
10:13:57,873 INFO  [org.jboss.as] (MSC service thread 1-8) WFLYSRV0050:
JBoss EAP 7.0.0.GA (WildFly Core 2.1.2.Final-redhat-1) stopped in 30ms
10:13:57,876 INFO  [org.jboss.as] (MSC service thread 1-5) WFLYSRV0049:
JBoss EAP 7.0.0.GA (WildFly Core 2.1.2.Final-redhat-1) starting
10:13:58,158 INFO  [org.jboss.as.server] (Controller Boot Thread)
WFLYSRV0039: Creating http management service using socket-binding
(management-http)
10:13:58,184 INFO  [org.xnio] (MSC service thread 1-2) XNIO version
3.3.6.Final-redhat-1
10:13:58,194 INFO  [org.xnio.nio] (MSC service thread 1-2) XNIO NIO
Implementation Version 3.3.6.Final-redhat-1
10:13:58,272 INFO  [org.jboss.as.clustering.infinispan] (ServerService
Thread Pool -- 38) WFLYCLINF0001: Activating Infinispan subsystem.
10:13:58,279 WARN  [org.jboss.as.txn] (ServerService Thread Pool -- 54)
WFLYTX0013: Node identifier property is set to the default value. Please
make sure it is unique.
10:13:58,302 INFO  [org.jboss.as.naming] (ServerService Thread Pool -- 46)
WFLYNAM0001: Activating Naming Subsystem
10:13:58,315 INFO  [org.jboss.as.security] (ServerService Thread Pool --
53) WFLYSEC0002: Activating Security Subsystem
10:13:58,334 INFO  [org.wildfly.extension.io] (ServerService Thread Pool --
37) WFLYIO001: Worker 'default' has auto-configured to 8 core threads with
64 task threads based on your 4 available processors
10:13:58,350 INFO  [org.jboss.remoting] (MSC service thread 1-2) JBoss
Remoting version 4.0.18.Final-redhat-1
10:13:58,351 INFO  [org.jboss.as.webservices] (ServerService Thread Pool --
56) WFLYWS0002: Activating WebServices Extension
10:13:58,350 INFO  [org.jboss.as.jsf] (ServerService Thread Pool -- 44)
WFLYJSF0007: Activated the following JSF Implementations: [main]
10:13:58,394 INFO  [org.jboss.as.security] (MSC service thread 1-4)
WFLYSEC0001: Current PicketBox version=4.9.6.Final-redhat-1
10:13:58,430 INFO  [org.wildfly.extension.undertow] (MSC service thread
1-7) WFLYUT0003: Undertow 1.3.21.Final-redhat-1 starting
10:13:58,436 INFO  [org.jboss.as.mail.extension] (MSC service thread 1-3)
WFLYMAIL0001: Bound mail session [java:jboss/mail/Default]
10:13:58,437 INFO  [org.wildfly.extension.undertow] (ServerService Thread
Pool -- 55) WFLYUT0003: Undertow 1.3.21.Final-redhat-1 starting
10:13:58,434 INFO  [org.jboss.as.naming] (MSC service thread 1-6)
WFLYNAM0003: Starting Naming Service
10:13:58,472 INFO  [org.jboss.as.connector] (MSC service thread 1-6)
WFLYJCA0009: Starting JCA Subsystem (WildFly/IronJacamar 1.3.3.Final-
redhat-1)
10:13:58,481 INFO  [org.jboss.as.connector.subsystems.datasources]
(ServerService Thread Pool -- 33) WFLYJCA0004: Deploying JDBC-compliant
driver class org.h2.Driver (version 1.3)
```

```
10:13:58,502 INFO  [org.jboss.as.connector.deployers.jdbc] (MSC service
thread 1-8) WFLYJCA0018: Started Driver service with driver-name = h2
10:13:58,810 INFO  [org.wildfly.extension.undertow] (ServerService Thread
Pool -- 55) WFLYUT0014: Creating file handler for path
'/opt/rh/eap7/welcome-content' with options [directory-listing: 'false',
follow-symlink: 'false', case-sensitive: 'true', safe-symlink-paths: '[]']
10:13:58,834 INFO  [org.jboss.as.ejb3] (MSC service thread 1-6)
WFLYEJB0482: Strict pool mdb-strict-max-pool is using a max instance size
of 16 (per class), which is derived from the number of CPUs on this host.
10:13:58,834 INFO  [org.jboss.as.ejb3] (MSC service thread 1-5)
WFLYEJB0481: Strict pool slsb-strict-max-pool is using a max instance size
of 64 (per class), which is derived from thread worker pool sizing.
10:13:58,860 INFO  [org.wildfly.extension.undertow] (MSC service thread
1-3) WFLYUT0012: Started server default-server.
10:13:58,861 INFO  [org.wildfly.extension.undertow] (MSC service thread
1-3) WFLYUT0018: Host default-host starting
10:13:58,950 INFO  [org.wildfly.extension.undertow] (MSC service thread
1-4) WFLYUT0006: Undertow HTTP listener default listening on 127.0.0.1:8080
10:13:59,135 INFO  [org.jboss.as.server.deployment.scanner] (MSC service
thread 1-5) WFLYDS0013: Started FileSystemDeploymentService for directory
/opt/rh/eap7/standalone/deployments
10:13:59,441 INFO  [org.jboss.ws.common.management] (MSC service thread
1-4) JBWS022052: Starting JBossWS 5.1.3.SP1-redhat-1 (Apache CXF
3.1.4.redhat-1)
10:13:59,443 INFO  [org.infinispan.factories.GlobalComponentRegistry] (MSC
service thread 1-5) ISPN000128: Infinispan version: Infinispan 'Mahou'
8.1.2.Final-redhat-1
10:13:59,754 INFO  [org.jboss.as.connector.subsystems.datasources] (MSC
service thread 1-3) WFLYJCA0001: Bound data source
[java:jboss/datasources/ExampleDS]
10:13:59,816 INFO  [org.jboss.as] (Controller Boot Thread) WFLYSRV0060:
Http management interface listening on http://127.0.0.1:9990/management
10:13:59,816 INFO  [org.jboss.as] (Controller Boot Thread) WFLYSRV0051:
Admin console listening on http://127.0.0.1:9990
10:13:59,817 INFO  [org.jboss.as] (Controller Boot Thread) WFLYSRV0025:
JBoss EAP 7.0.0.GA (WildFly Core 2.1.2.Final-redhat-1) started in 1938ms -
Started 267 of 553 services (371 services are lazy, passive or on-demand)
[standalone@embedded /]
```

Using the CLI in graphical mode

If you really don't feel comfortable with the CLI shell, but still don't want to use the Web console, Red Hat engineers thought that you may like thick clients instead. There is a GUI client for the CLI, and it's available by issuing the following command:

```
$JBOSS_HOME/bin/jboss-cli.sh --gui
```

And it shows the CLI within a GUI, as depicted here:

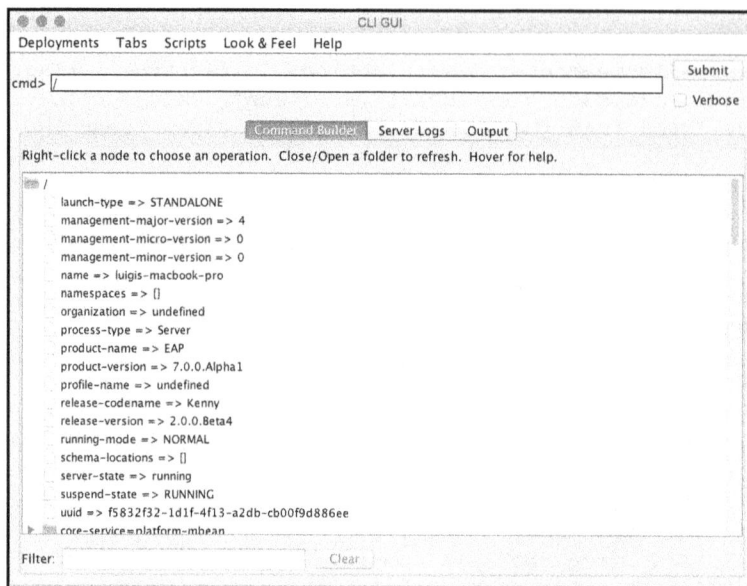

At the bottom of the interface there is a useful textbox, which lets you easily find resources, as shown here using `data` as the filter:

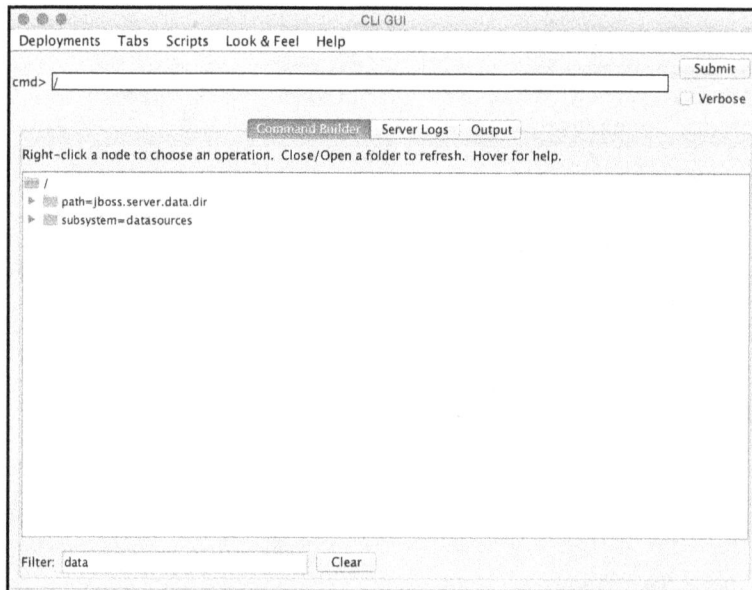

Summary

In this chapter, you learned what the CLI is and its powerful features. You saw how to connect to it both locally and remotely, where its configuration file is located, and how you can interact with it. You also learned about the use of the *Tab* key, which helps you out in traversing the whole tree of resources and their operations and attributes.

The CLI needs a little extra time to get acquainted with, but as long as you get used to it, you will become a master of configuring and managing your JBoss platform.

You saw the different approaches to working with the CLI, such as the **batch** mode, and recalling the batch procedure using the **holdback-batch** feature. You also saw that by generally using the batch mode along with external .cli files, you can accomplish complex tasks for the operative, standalone, and domain modes.

Additionally, you saw how we can back up our application server configuration by taking snapshots, and how you can use the CLI via its GUI version, which might get you used to it a little faster.

From now on in the book, we will use the CLI as our main tool to manage and configure the JBoss Enterprise Application Platform 7.

In the next chapter, we will see how we can take advantage of the domain mode, and how to configure and create homogeneous servers across different servers, both local and remote.

3
Managing EAP in Domain Mode

At this point you already have some basic concepts about the domain mode. This chapter dives deep into application server management using the domain mode and its main components, and discusses how to shift to advanced configurations that resemble real-world projects. Here are the main topics covered:

- Domain mode breakdown
- Creating a domain configuration using the CLI
- Managing disaster and recovery scenarios in domain mode
- Additional features introduced in EAP 7

Domain mode breakdown

Managing the application server in the domain mode means, in a nutshell, controlling multiple servers from a centralized single point of control. The servers that are part of the domain can span across multiple machines (or even across the cloud) and they can be grouped with similar servers of the domain to share a common configuration. To make some rationale, we will break down the domain components into two main categories:

- **Physical components**: These are the domain elements that can be identified with a Java process running on the operating system
- **Logical components**: These are the domain elements that can span across several physical components

Domain physical components

When you start the application server through the `domain.sh` script, you will be able to identify the following processes:

- **Host controller**: Each domain installation contains a host controller. This is a Java process that is in charge of starting and stopping the servers that are defined within the `host.xml` file. The host controller is only aware of the items that are specific to the local physical installation such as the domain controller host and port and the JVM settings of the servers or their system properties.

- **Domain controller**: One host controller of the domain (and only one) is configured to act as a domain controller. This means basically two things: keeping the domain configuration (in the `domain.xml` file) and assisting the host controller with managing the servers of the domain.

- **Servers**: Each host controller can contain any number of servers which are the actual server instances. These server instances cannot be started autonomously. The host controller is in charge of starting and stopping single servers when the domain controller commands them.

If you start the default domain configuration on a Linux machine, you will see that the following processes will show in your operating system:

```
[francesco@localhost bin]$ ps -ef | grep java
frances+  5090  5004  1 08:34 pts/1    00:00:01 java -D[Process Controller] -server -Xms64m
 -Xmx512m -Djava.net.preferIPv4Stack=true -Djboss.modules.system.pkgs=org.jboss.byteman -Dj
ava.awt.headless=true -Dorg.jboss.boot.log.file=/home/francesco/jboss/jboss-eap-7.0/domain/
log/process-controller.log -Dlogging.configuration=file:/home/francesco/jboss/jboss-eap-7.0
/domain/configuration/logging.properties -jar /home/francesco/jboss/jboss-eap-7.0/jboss-mod
ules.jar -mp /home/francesco/jboss/jboss-eap-7.0/modules org.jboss.as.process-controller -j
boss-home /home/francesco/jboss/jboss-eap-7.0 -jvm java -mp /home/francesco/jboss/jboss-eap
-7.0/modules -- -Dorg.jboss.boot.log.file=/home/francesco/jboss/jboss-eap-7.0/domain/log/ho
st-controller.log -Dlogging.configuration=file:/home/francesco/jboss/jboss-eap-7.0/domain/c
onfiguration/logging.properties -server -Xms64m -Xmx512m -Djava.net.preferIPv4Stack=true -D
jboss.modules.system.pkgs=org.jboss.byteman -Djava.awt.headless=true -- -default.jvm java
frances+  5107  5090 16 08:34 pts/1    00:00:10 java -D[Host Controller] -Dorg.jboss.boot.l
og.file=/home/francesco/jboss/jboss-eap-7.0/domain/log/host-controller.log -Dlogging.config
uration=file:/home/francesco/jboss/jboss-eap-7.0/domain/configuration/logging.properties -s
erver -Xms64m -Xmx512m -Djava.net.preferIPv4Stack=true -Djboss.modules.system.pkgs=org.jbos
s.byteman -Djava.awt.headless=true -jar /home/francesco/jboss/jboss-eap-7.0/jboss-modules.j
ar -mp /home/francesco/jboss/jboss-eap-7.0/modules org.jboss.as.host-controller -mp /home/f
rancesco/jboss/jboss-eap-7.0/modules --pc-address 127.0.0.1 --pc-port 49127 -default-jvm ja
va -Djboss.home.dir=/home/francesco/jboss/jboss-eap-7.0
frances+  5176  5090 28 08:34 pts/1    00:00:17 /home/francesco/jdk1.8.0_60/jre/bin/java -D
[Server:server-one] -Xms64m -Xmx512m -server -Djava.awt.headless=true -Djava.net.preferIPv4
Stack=true -Djboss.home.dir=/home/francesco/jboss/jboss-eap-7.0 -Djboss.modules.system.pkgs
=org.jboss.byteman -Djboss.server.log.dir=/home/francesco/jboss/jboss-eap-7.0/domain/server
s/server-one/log -Djboss.server.temp.dir=/home/francesco/jboss/jboss-eap-7.0/domain/servers
/server-one/tmp -Djboss.server.data.dir=/home/francesco/jboss/jboss-eap-7.0/domain/servers/
server-one/data -Dlogging.configuration=file:/home/francesco/jboss/jboss-eap-7.0/domain/ser
vers/server-one/data/logging.properties -jar /home/francesco/jboss/jboss-eap-7.0/jboss-modu
les.jar -mp /home/francesco/jboss/jboss-eap-7.0/modules org.jboss.as.server
frances+  5220  5090 27 08:34 pts/1    00:00:16 /home/francesco/jdk1.8.0_60/jre/bin/java -D
[Server:server-two] -Xms64m -Xmx512m -server -Djava.awt.headless=true -Djava.net.preferIPv4
Stack=true -Djboss.home.dir=/home/francesco/jboss/jboss-eap-7.0 -Djboss.modules.system.pkgs
=org.jboss.byteman -Djboss.server.log.dir=/home/francesco/jboss/jboss-eap-7.0/domain/server
s/server-two/log -Djboss.server.temp.dir=/home/francesco/jboss/jboss-eap-7.0/domain/servers
/server-two/tmp -Djboss.server.data.dir=/home/francesco/jboss/jboss-eap-7.0/domain/servers/
server-two/data -Dlogging.configuration=file:/home/francesco/jboss/jboss-eap-7.0/domain/ser
vers/server-two/data/logging.properties -jar /home/francesco/jboss/jboss-eap-7.0/jboss-modu
les.jar -mp /home/francesco/jboss/jboss-eap-7.0/modules org.jboss.as.server
```

As you can see, the process controller is identified by the **[Process Controller]** label, while the domain controller corresponds to the **[Host Controller]** label. Each server shows in the process table with the name defined in the `host.xml` file. You can use common operating system commands such as `grep` to further restrict the search to a specific process.

Domain logical components

A domain configuration with only physical elements in it would not add much to a line of standalone servers. The following components can abstract the domain definition, making it dynamic and flexible:

- **Server Group**: A server group is a collection of servers. They are defined in the `domain.xml` file, hence they don't have any reference to an actual host controller installation. You can use a server group to share configurations and deployments across a group of servers.
- **Profile**: A profile is an EAP configuration. A domain can hold as many profiles as you need. Out of the box the following configurations are provided:

  * **default**: This configuration matches with the standalone.xml configuration (in standalone mode), hence it does not include JMS, IIOP, or HA

  * **full**: This configuration matches with the standalone-full.xml configuration (in standalone mode), hence it includes JMS and OpenJDK IIOP to the default server

  * **ha**: This configuration matches with the standalone-ha.xml configuration (in standalone mode), so it enhances the default configuration with clustering (HA)

  * **full-ha**: This configuration matches with the standalone-full-ha.xml configuration (in standalone mode), hence it includes JMS, IIOP, and HA

Handy domain properties

So far we have learnt the default configuration files used by JBoss EAP and the location where they are placed. These settings can, however, be varied by means of system properties. The following table shows how to customize the domain configuration file names:

Option	Description
`--domain-config`	The domain configuration file (default `domain.xml`)
`--host-config`	The host configuration file (default `host.xml`)

On the other hand, this table summarizes the available options to adjust the domain directory structure:

Property	Description
`jboss.domain.base.dir`	The base directory for domain content
`jboss.domain.config.dir`	The base configuration directory
`jboss.domain.data.dir`	The directory used for persistent data file storage
`jboss.domain.log.dir`	The directory containing the `host-controller.log` and `process-controller.log` files
`jboss.domain.temp.dir`	The directory used for temporary file storage
`jboss.domain.deployment.dir`	The directory used to store deployed content
`jboss.domain.servers.dir`	The directory containing the managed server instances

For example, you can start EAP 7 in domain mode using the domain configuration file `mydomain.xml` and the host file named `myhost.xml` based on the base directory `/home/jboss/eap7domain` using the following command:

```
$ ./domain.sh -domain-config=mydomain.xml -host-
config=myhost.xml -Djboss.domain.base.dir=/home/jboss/eap7domain
```

Electing the domain controller

Before creating your first domain, we will learn more in detail the process which connects one or more host controllers to one domain controllers and how to elect a host controller to be a domain controller.

The physical topology of the domain is stored in the `host.xml` file. Within this file, you will find as the first line the **host controller** name, which makes each host controller unique:

```
<host xmlns="urn:jboss:domain:4.0" name="master">
```

One of the host controllers will be configured to act as a **domain controller**. This is done in the `domain-controller` section with the following block, which states that the domain controller is the host controller itself (hence, `local`):

```
<domain-controller>
    <local/>
</domain-controller>
```

All other host controllers will connect to the domain controller, using the following example configuration which uses the `jboss.domain.master.address` and `jboss.domain.master.port` properties to specify the domain controller address and port:

```
<domain-controller>
    <remote protocol="remote"
        host="${jboss.domain.master.address}"
        port="${jboss.domain.master.port:9999}"
        security-realm="ManagementRealm"/>
</domain-controller>
```

The host controller-domain controller communication happens behind the scenes through a `jboss.management.native.port attribute` that is defined as well in the `host.xml` file:

```
<management-interfaces>
    <native-interface security-realm="ManagementRealm">
        <socket interface="management"
        port="${jboss.management.native.port:9999}"/>
    </native-interface>
    <http-interface security-realm="ManagementRealm" http-upgrade-
    enabled="true">
        <socket interface="management"
        port="${jboss.management.http.port:9990}"/>
    </http-interface>
</management-interfaces>
```

The other highlighted attribute is the `management.http.port` that can be used by the administrator to reach the domain controller. This port is especially relevant if the host controller is the domain controller. Both sockets use the *management* interface, which is defined in the interfaces section of the `host.xml` file, and exposes the domain controller on a network available address:

```
<interfaces>
        <interface name="management">
         <inet-address
          value="${jboss.bind.address.management:127.0.0.1}"/>
```

```
    </interface>
    <interface name="public">
        <inet-address value="${jboss.bind.address:127.0.0.1}"/>
    </interface>
</interfaces>
```

> **TIP**
>
> If you want to run *multiple* host controllers on the same machine, you need to provide a unique **jboss.management.native.port** for each host controller or a different **jboss.bind.address.management**.

Creating an advanced domain

The basic domain configuration is a good exercise for learning the domain's main actors and their responsibilities. In real-world scenarios you will need to create domain configurations that span multiple hosts, providing redundancy of the services across different hosts. Also, it would be recommended to use the domain controller just as the management platform of your domain, thus removing the application server from its installation.

Based on these assumptions we will arrange the following domain, which consists of three EAP 7 host controllers, one of them elected as domain controller:

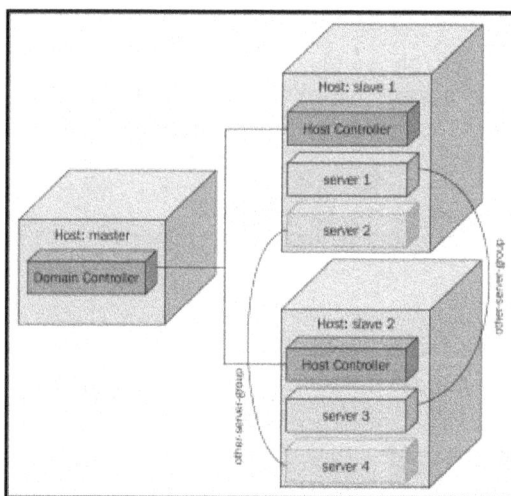

The Command Line Interface will be used to create the domain, starting from a vanilla server installation. As proof of concept, we will include also the generated XML configuration.

Building up your domain

For the purpose of this example, we will install our domain on a single machine. Later on in this book, we will discuss a more complex configuration where each host controller will be on a separate docker container.

So, first of all, we will perform three server installations for the host controllers. Let's create three folders to contain the installations:

```
$ mkdir -p /home/jboss/dc
$ mkdir -p /home/jboss/slave1
$ mkdir -p /home/jboss/slave2
```

Next unzip the application server on each host:

```
$ unzip jboss-eap-7.0.0.zip -d /home/jboss/dc
$ unzip jboss-eap-7.0.0.zip -d /home/jboss/slave1
$ unzip jboss-eap-7.0.0.zip -d /home/jboss/slave2
```

Good, now let's create an admin user on the domain controller, say named `eap7admin`:

```
$ cd /home/jboss/dc/jboss-eap-7.0/bin
$ ./add-user.sh
What type of user do you wish to add?
a) Management User (mgmt-users.properties)
b) Application User (application-users.properties)
(a): a
Enter the details of the new user to add.
Using realm 'ManagementRealm' as discovered from the existing
property files.
Username : eap7admin
Password :
Re-enter Password :
. . . .
To represent the user add the following to the server-
identities definition <secret
value="RXJpY3Nzb24xIQ==" />
```

We have created a management user that will be used by the domain controller to accept host controller connections. Now start the application server in domain mode:

```
$ ./domain.sh
```

A default domain installation will start. Our first job will be removing the unnecessary EAP servers from the domain controller. Hence, start the CLI and connect to it:

```
$ ./jboss-cli.sh -c
```

Once connected, make sure that the servers are stopped:

```
/host=master/server-config=server-one:stop
/host=master/server-config=server-two:stop
/host=master/server-config=server-three:stop
```

Now remove all the servers from the configuration:

```
/host=master/server-config=server-one:remove
/host=master/server-config=server-two:remove
/host=master/server-config=server-three:remove
```

Finally, as we are going to use the `full` profile configuration, we will set the profile and socket-binding-group attribute accordingly (out of the box, the `main-server-group` is already using the `full` profile configuration; we are, however, setting it in case you have varied the default configuration):

```
/server-group=main-server-group:write-
attribute(name=profile,value=full)
/server-group=main-server-group:write-attribute(name=socket-
binding-group,value=full-sockets)
/server-group=other-server-group:write-
attribute(name=profile,value=full)
/server-group=other-server-group:write-attribute(name=socket-
binding-group,value=full-sockets)
```

Within the `host.xml` configuration, you can verify that the servers have been removed.

Configuring host controllers

The domain controller needed only some cleanup. On the other hand, the host controller configurations need to be shaped up by including servers and specifying the domain controller location. Let's configure first the host controller installed in the `slave1` folder of your home directory:

```
$ cd /home/jboss/slave1/jboss-eap-7.0/bin
```

We will start another host controller. Since there is already a running host on our machine using the management ports, we will need to specify a custom management port for this host controller:

```
./domain.sh -Djboss.management.native.port=19999 -
Djboss.management.http.port=19990
```

Check that the server started correctly as indicated by the following picture:

Now we will connect to the host controller using the CLI:

```
$./jboss-cli.sh -c controller=127.0.0.1:19990
```

Some settings need to be changed. The first one will be renaming the host controller, otherwise there will be a conflict when joining the domain controller named master:

```
/host=master:write-attribute(name=name, value=slave1)
```

A reload is needed for changes to take effect:

```
/host=master:reload
```

Now you can manage the host controller as slave1 instead of master. As for the domain controller, we will stop and remove the existing server definitions first:

```
/host=slave1 /server-config=server-one:stop
/host=slave1 /server-config=server-two:stop
/host=slave1 /server-config=server-three:stop
/host=slave1 /server-config=server-one:remove
/host=slave1 /server-config=server-two:remove
/host=slave1 /server-config=server-three:remove
```

We will now create two servers named server1 and server2 which will be respectively bound to the port offsets 0 and 100 and to the server groups main-server-group and other-server-group:

```
/host=slave1/server-config=server1:add(group=main-server-
group,socket-binding-port-offset=0)
/host=slave1/server-config=server2:add(group=other-server-
```

```
group,socket-binding-port-offset=100)
```

Good. The host controller slave1, as it is configured, runs as the domain controller. We will need to switch it to be a host controller, linking it to our running domain controller. The `write-remote-domain-controller` command can be used to configure the domain controller settings as follows:

```
/host=slave1:write-remote-domain-controller
(username=eap7admin,host=127.0.0.1,port=9999,
security-realm=ManagementRealm)
```

Although not required for a local domain controller, we will include the `secret` information that we have acquired, when the user `eap7admin` has been created:

```
/host=slave1/core-service=management/security-realm
=ManagementRealm/server-identity=secret:add
(value="RXJpY3Nzb24xIQ==")
```

Our host controller configuration is now complete. We can reload the host in order to propagate changes:

```
/host=slave1:reload
```

When the reload command completes, you will be able to see on the domain controller a notice that a host controller has joined our domain:

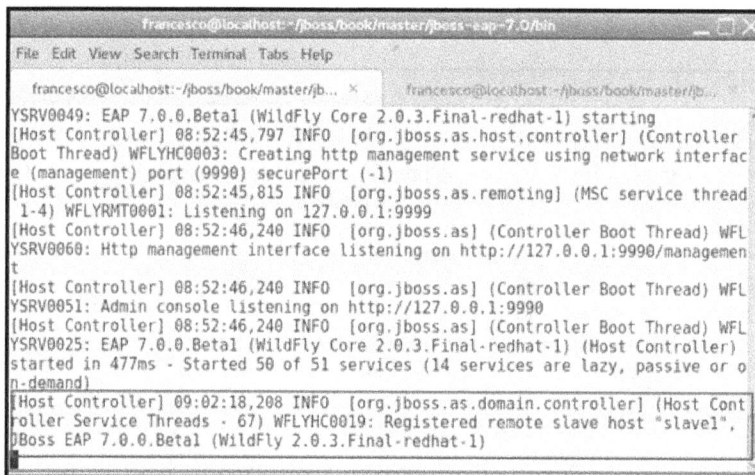

You can check as well that, by switching to the domain controller CLI, that now the list of hosts controlled includes both the `master` and the `slave1` host:

```
[domain@localhost:9990 /] :read-children-names(child-type=host)
{
    "outcome" => "success",
    "result" => [
        "master",
        "slave1"
    ]
}
```

Connecting other host controllers

With the scripts we have created so far, we can create as many host controllers as we want. The only tweak is that the host controller `slave1` runs a server (indeed, `server1`) on the default offset (0). We can easily solve this problem by using the `--admin-only` option.

> When starting the application server with the `--admin-only` option, only the administrative interfaces will be activated, hence it's a lifesaver option if you have trouble with the single servers and possibly the applications deployed on them.

Here is how we can start additional host controllers on the same machine to avoid any port conflict:

```
$ cd /home/jboss/slave2/jboss-eap-7.0/bin
$ ./domain.sh -Djboss.management.native.port=29999 -
Djboss.management.http.port=29990 --admin-only
```

We have also increased the management port offset to avoid conflicts with other host controllers as well. Now connect to the Command Line of the new host controller to operate changes:

```
$ ./jboss-cli.sh -c controller=127.0.0.1:29990
```

Here follows the script we will use to configure the `slave2` host controller. If you have gone through the former section, an inline comment on each command will be sufficiently clear:

```
#Rename Host
/host=master:write-attribute(name=name, value=slave2)
/host=master:reload
# Stop and Remove Servers
/host=slave2/server-config=server-one:stop
```

```
/host=slave2/server-config=server-two:stop
/host=slave2/server-config=server-three:stop
/host=slave2/server-config=server-one:remove
/host=slave2/server-config=server-two:remove
/host=slave2/server-config=server-three:remove
# Connect to Remote Domain Controller
/host=slave2:write-remote-domain-controller
(username=eap7admin,host=127.0.0.1,port=9999,security-
realm=ManagementRealm)
# Write Security Info
/host=slave2/core-service=management/security-realm
=ManagementRealm/server-identity=secret:add
(value="RXJpY3Nzb24xIQ==")
#Create Server three and four
/host=slave2/server-config=server3:add
(group=main-server-group,socket-binding-port-offset=300)
/host=slave2/server-config=server4:add
(group=other-server-group,socket-binding-port-offset=450)
#Reload
/host=slave2:reload(admin-only=false)
```

Notice that we are reloading the host `slave2` setting the `admin-only` parameter to `false`. This way, the servers that are included in the host definition will start as well. The new host controller will join the domain as indicated by the following picture of the domain controller console:

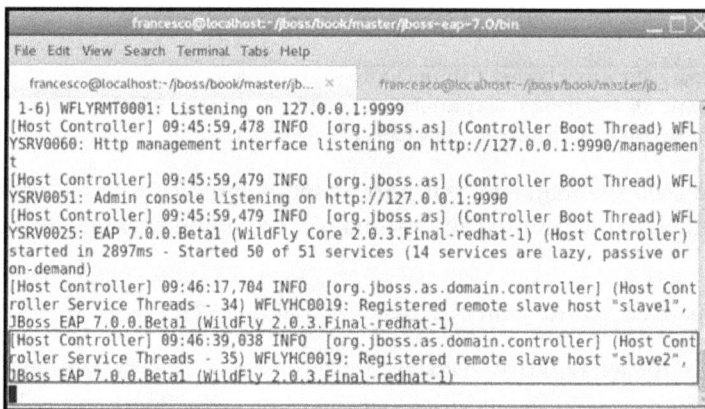

As a proof of concept, issue again the `read-children-names` query over the host element:

```
[domain@localhost:9990 /] :read-children-names(child-type=host)
{
    "outcome" => "success",
    "result" => [
```

```
            "master",
            "slave1",
            "slave2"
        ]
    }
```

Tweaking the domain settings

So far we have created a custom domain topology; most of the configuration is, however, the *vanilla* configuration that ships with the application server. Throughout this book we will learn how to vary the single profile settings; right now we will learn how to tune the JVM settings, which is a bit more of a complex affair when running in domain mode.

The JVM settings, such as the system properties, are a kind of attribute which can be defined at multiple settings:

- At host level: In this case the settings will be propagated to all servers configured on that host, provided that no server group or server configuration has been defined for them
- At server group level: In this case the settings will be propagated to all servers configured on that host, provided that no server configuration has been defined for them
- At server level: In this case the settings will be propagated to all servers with no exceptions.

With the default server configuration, some JVM settings are defined both at the server group level and at the host level. Here are the default JVM settings for the server groups (domain-xml):

```xml
<server-groups>
   <server-group name="main-server-group" profile="full">
      <jvm name="default">
         <heap size="64m" max-size="512m"/>
      </jvm>
      <socket-binding-group ref="full-sockets"/>
   </server-group>
   <server-group name="other-server-group" profile="full">
      <jvm name="default">
         <heap size="64m" max-size="512m"/>
      </jvm>
      <socket-binding-group ref="full-sockets"/>
   </server-group>
</server-groups>
```

And here are the settings which are, by default, included in the `host.xml` file of each host:

```
<jvms>
    <jvm name="default">
        <heap size="64m" max-size="256m"/>
        <permgen size="256m" max-size="256m"/>
            <jvm-options>
                <option value="-server"/>
            </jvm-options>
    </jvm>
</jvms>
```

A proof of concept of this configuration can be done through a simple process lookup of a node, say `server1`:

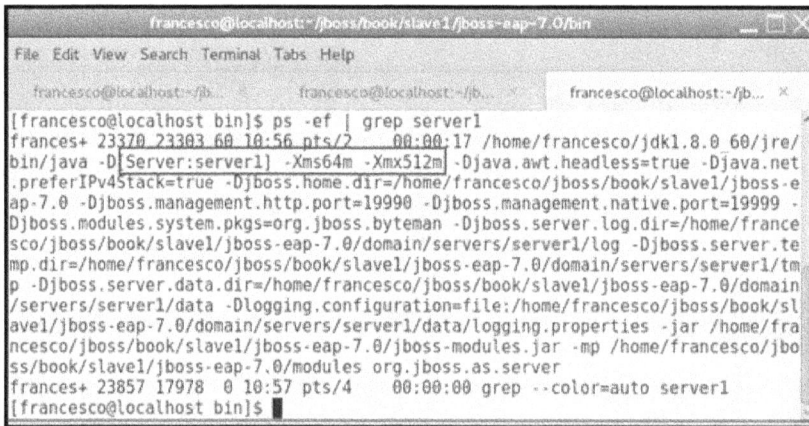

So as you can see, the server group JVM settings, being the most specific ones, prevail. What if we want to apply **Host specific JVM settings**? We will need basically to undefine the server group settings and apply our specific host settings. From the CLI we will execute the following commands:

```
/server-group=main-server-group/jvm=default/:undefine-attribute(name=max-heap-size)
/server-group=main-server-group/jvm=default/:undefine-attribute(name=heap-size)
/host=slave1/jvm=default/:write-attribute(name=heap-size,value=128m)
/host=slave1/jvm=default/:write-attribute(name=max-heap-size,value=756m)
```

The host slave1 needs to be restarted. Then, by checking again the JVM settings we can verify that the host settings will be used, being the only JVM settings defined:

Now let's restore the server group JVM settings. This time, however, we will include also some specific settings for the `server1`:

```
/server-group=main-server-group/jvm=default/:write-attribute(name=heap-
size,value=64m)
/server-group=main-server-group/jvm=default/:write-attribute(name=max-heap-
size,value=512m)
/host=slave1/server-config=server1/jvm=custom-jvm/:add(debug-
enabled=false,env-classpath-ignored=false,heap-size=512m,max-heap-
size=512m)
```

As you can see from the following process table, the `server1` has been configured to use its own settings:

Conversely, the `server3` (configured on the same server group) will inherit the server group settings:

```
francesco@localhost:~/jboss/book/slave2/jboss-eap-7.0/bin
File  Edit  View  Search  Terminal  Tabs  Help
 francesco@localhost:~/jboss/book/slave2/jbo...          francesco@localhost:~/jboss/book/slave2/jbo...  ×
[francesco@localhost bin]$ ps -ef | grep server3
frances+  24331 24264 99 11:18 pts/5    00:00:17 /home/francesco/jdk1.8.0_60/jre/
bin/java -D[Server:server3] -Xms64m -Xmx512m -server -Djava.awt.headless=true -D
java.net.preferIPv4Stack=true -Djboss.home.dir=/home/francesco/jboss/book/slave2
/jboss-eap-7.0 -Djboss.management.http.port=29990 -Djboss.management.native.port
=29999 -Djboss.modules.system.pkgs=org.jboss.byteman -Djboss.server.log.dir=/hom
e/francesco/jboss/book/slave2/jboss-eap-7.0/domain/servers/server3/log -Djboss.s
erver.temp.dir=/home/francesco/jboss/book/slave2/jboss-eap-7.0/domain/servers/se
rver3/tmp -Djboss.server.data.dir=/home/francesco/jboss/book/slave2/jboss-eap-7.
0/domain/servers/server3/data -Dlogging.configuration=file:/home/francesco/jboss
/book/slave2/jboss-eap-7.0/domain/servers/server3/data/logging.properties -jar /
home/francesco/jboss/book/slave2/jboss-eap-7.0/jboss-modules.jar -mp /home/franc
esco/jboss/book/slave2/jboss-eap-7.0/modules org.jboss.as.server
frances+  24662 24601  0 11:18 pts/6    00:00:00 grep --color=auto server3
[francesco@localhost bin]$
```

Domain controller failover

As we have indicated, within a domain there can be a single management point. This can be seen as a limit for your environment or not, depending on your standards. In this section we will provide some possible solutions with different degrees of complexity; all these solutions, however, are based on detective measures: this means that there is no automatic strategy to guarantee the continuity of the domain controller, but rather you need to perform some manual steps to achieve it (or obviously automate the steps with some scripts).

Basic solution – building a watchdog procedure

The most basic solution consists of creating a watchdog procedure that monitors the status of the domain controller. Depending on the complexity of the environment, you can also opt for an automatic restart of the domain controller process.

There are many possible ways to develop such a solution: for example, on a Linux box you could include in your system's cron, a script based on the `netstat` command, which checks the status of services connected to your machine. For example, here is how to check for port `9999` being open:

```
$ netstat -an | grep -wF 9999
tcp   0   0 127.0.0.1:9999   0.0.0.0:*   LISTEN
```

Notice the -wF option, which checks for the exact 9999 pattern to be used by the grep command.

With a little effort you can turn the previous command in a script to be included in your cron:

```
#!/bin/bash
  AVAILABLE=$(netstat -an | grep -wF 9999 | wc -l)
    while [ $AVAILABLE -gt 0 ]
    do
    sleep 20
  AVAILABLE=$(netstat -an | grep -wF 9999 | wc -l)
  done
echo "Lost Domain Controller. Perform actions here!"
```

Similar solutions can be adopted using the CLI, which as we have seen, can be configured to run in a non-interactive way. So for example, we could create a heart-beat script by executing read-attribute of some domain's controller's attribute:

```
$ ./jboss-cli.sh -c controller=127.0.0.1:9999 --command=":read-
attribute(name=product-version)
```

Using domain start up options to allow host controller restart

In some other scenarios, the major issue is that the host controller process terminated as well. This scenario can be even more critical as services and applications will not be available any more so it is, in fact, possible that you will need an immediate host controller restart, without the cooperation of the domain controller. In such a case, you could use two domain startup options:

- --backup: This option keeps a copy of the persistent domain configuration even if this host is not the domain controller
- --cached-dc: If this host is not the domain controller and cannot contact the domain controller at boot, it will boot using the local backup copy of the domain configuration

Let's see a practical scenario. Start up the domain controller as usual:

```
$ ./domain.sh
```

Next, start up also the host controller using the `--backup` option:

```
./domain.sh --backup -Djboss.management.native.port=19999 -
Djboss.management.http.port=19990
```

> You will see that on the host controller, a backup copy of the Domain's configuration will be maintained in the file `domain.cached-remote.xml`.

Now terminate both processes in any way to simulate the system failure (for example, *Ctrl +* *C*). When all processes are terminated, if you try to restart the host controller, it will eventually fail as it cannot contact the domain controller. By using the `--cached-dc` option, on the other hand, the restart will work, using the `cached domain.cached-remote.xml` file:

```
./domain.sh -cached-dc -Djboss.management.native.port=19999 -
Djboss.management.http.port=19990
```

The major limitation of this approach is that when the domain controller returns available, you need to perform a restart of each host controller (with no `--cached-dc` option) since, when you are using the cached configuration, no attempt to reconnect to the domain controller will be performed.

Using domain discovery to elect a new domain controller

This scenario can be taken into account if you are planning to elect a new domain controller that will replace the failed one. This is possible thanks to a special section in the `host.xml` file named `discovery-options` that allows one or more additional domain controllers, should the remote host fail.

Let's make a practical use case. We will assume that in case of failure of the domain controller (named `master` in our examples), the available host controllers will try to reach the host controller `slave2` and eventually elect a new domain controller.

Connect first to the host controller:

```
$ cd /home/jboss/dc/jboss-eap-7.0/bin
$ ./jboss-cli.sh -c
```

Next, from the CLI, issue the following commands:

```
/host=slave1/core-service=discovery-options/static-
discovery=backupdc/:add(host=127.0.0.1,port=29999,protocol=remote)
/host=slave1:reload
```

The following configuration will be created on the slave1's `host.xml` file:

```
<domain-controller>
    <remote host="127.0.0.1" port="9999" security-
    realm="ManagementRealm" username="eap7admin">
    <discovery-options>
      <static-discovery name="backupdc" protocol="remote"
      host="127.0.0.1" port="29999"/>
    </discovery-options>
    </remote>
</domain-controller>
```

In order to test our failover scenario, shut down first the domain controller (use *Ctrl + C* or issue the shutdown command from the CLI). Next, connect to the slave2 host controller and use **write-local-domain-controller** to let it reclaim the role of domain controller:

```
$ ./jboss-cli.sh –c controller=127.0.0.1:29990
```

Execute the following command from the CLI:

```
/host=slave2:write-local-domain-controller
```

A reload of the host configuration will be required to propagate changes:

```
/host=slave2:reload
```

You should expect, on the other host controllers (in our case slave1), a successful connection to the new domain controller:

As proof, you can check that the domain is fully manageable through the new endpoint, as depicted by the following image of the web admin console:

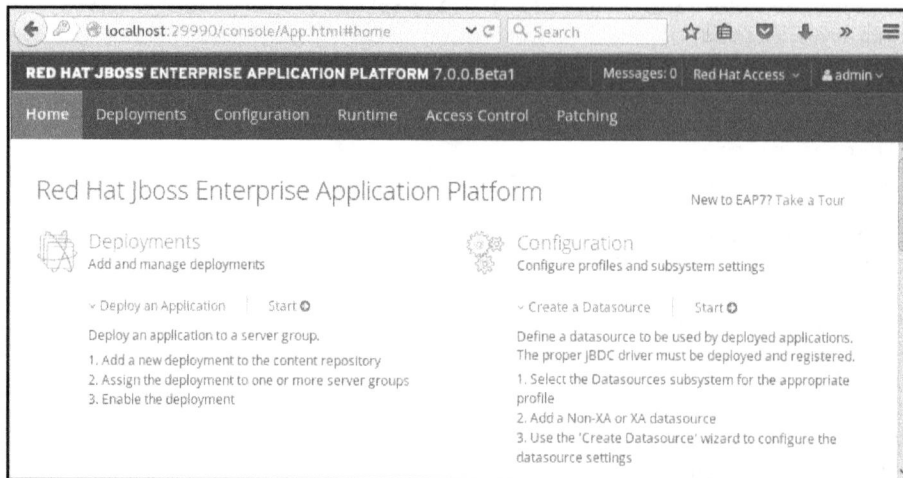

The major limitation of this approach is that, in case you want to handle the returning of the former domain controller, you need to reset the domain-controller policy, in our case on the `slave2`:

```
/host=slave2/core-service=discovery-options/static-
  discovery=backupdc/:add(host=127.0.0.1,port=29999,protocol=remote)
  /host=slave2:reload
```

Besides this, there is a major concern regarding the `domain.xml` configuration which needs to be re-synchronized from `slave2` to the `master` Host. In the following section we will add some ideas that can be used to make your domain failover process more robust.

Using a centralized store for your server configurations

All the solutions discussed so far involve some actions to recover the domain capabilities or synchronize the configuration, which is maybe the most delicate topic. One way you can solve this issue is by means of infrastructure tools available on your Enterprise. For example, when using **Red Hat Enterprise Linux**, `rsync` can be used as a daemon so that multiple clients can directly communicate with it as a central server, in order to house centralized files and keep them synchronized.

This kind of approach can be particularly interesting when using virtual machines or containers that can be quickly restarted to provide continuity in the domain services and management. For example, you could house the domain configuration in a central server to be used by a domain controller. This way, when your watchdog procedure detects a failure in the domain controller, you can seamlessly start a new virtual machine or container using the centralized configuration.

You can find more information and examples about `rsync` via the following link: `https://access.redhat.com/documentation/en-US/Red_Hat_Enterprise_Linux/6/html/Managing_Confined_Services/sect-Managing_Confined_Services-rsync-Configuration_Examples.html`.

Additional EAP 7 features

Some new features related to the domain mode are currently being developed at the time of writing. We would like to mention connectivity with EAP 6 legacy host controllers, hierarchical profiles, and profile cloning, which are already available in the current release of EAP 7.

Connecting EAP 6 host controllers to an EAP 7 domain controller

The migration process from EAP 6 to EAP 7 might now be so immediate for large enterprises. As a matter of fact, a cohabitation of legacy EAP 6 host controllers in an EAP 7 domain would be needed in many cases. The main challenges for this hybrid approach are the following ones:

- EAP 6 host controllers are not aware of subsystems introduced in EAP 7 (such as the batch subsystem, for example).
- Some subsystems have been deprecated (such as the web subsystem, replaced by Undertow). Others simply have been removed from the default configuration (such as the threads subsystem).

For the previous reasons, connecting EAP 6 host controllers to an EAP 7 domain is therefore not available out of the box, simply by starting your host controllers. You can, however, achieve it with some steps which will let you categorize some server groups as legacy EAP 6 host controllers.

Take as an example the following excerpt from an EAP 7 `domain.xml`:

```
<host-exclude name="EAP64" active-server-groups="640main-server-group">
            <host-release id="EAP6.4"/>
            <excluded-extensions>
                <extension module="org.wildfly.extension.batch.jberet"/>
                <extension module="org.wildfly.extension.bean-validation"/>
                <extension
module="org.wildfly.extension.clustering.singleton"/>
                <extension module="org.wildfly.extension.io"/>
                <extension module="org.wildfly.extension.messaging-
activemq"/>
                <extension module="org.wildfly.extension.request-
controller"/>
                <extension
module="org.wildfly.extension.security.manager"/>
                <extension module="org.wildfly.extension.undertow"/>
                <extension module="org.wildfly.iiop-openjdk"/>
            </excluded-extensions>
        </host-exclude>
```

The directive `host-exclude` specifies that a server group of your domain will be using a different version of EAP, in our case the EAP 6.4 version that includes as the server group the **640main-server-group**.

In order to set up the EAP 7-EAP 6 connectivity, you will need to complete the following steps:

1. Include the EAP 6 **deprecated subsystems** in your EAP 7 `domain.xml` configuration:

   ```
   <extension module="org.jboss.as.configadmin"/>
   <extension module="org.jboss.as.threads"/>
   <extension module="org.jboss.as.web"/>
   ```

2. Include the EAP 6 profile(s) in your EAP 7 `domain.xml` configuration. For example, we will be adding the profile named `640default`:

   ```
   <domain xmlns="urn:jboss:domain:4.1">
   . . .
       <profiles>
         <profile name="640default">
           . . . .
         </profile>
       </profiles>
   . . .
   </domain>
   ```

3. Include the socket-binding configuration related to EAP 6 server groups in the EAP 7 `domain.xml` configuration:

```
<socket-binding-groups>
<socket-binding-group name="640standard-sockets"
 default-interface="public">
<socket-binding name="ajp" port="${jboss.ajp.port:18009}"/>
<socket-binding name="http" port="${jboss.http.port:18080}"/>
<socket-binding name="https" port="${jboss.https.port:18443}"/>
<socket-binding name="txn-recovery-environment" port="14712"/>
<socket-binding name="txn-status-manager" port="14713"/>
<outbound-socket-binding name="mail-smtp">
    <remote-destination host="localhost" port="125"/>
</outbound-socket-binding>
</socket-binding-group>
```

4. Include your EAP 6 server groups (and their related socket binding) in the EAP 7 `domain.xml` configuration:

```
<server-groups>
    <server-group name="640main-server-group" profile="640default">
        <jvm name="default">
            <heap size="64m" max-size="1000m"/>
        </jvm>
    <socket-binding-group ref="640standard-sockets"/>
    </server-group>
    <server-group name="other-server-group" profile="full">
        <jvm name="default">
            <heap size="64m" max-size="1000m"/>
        </jvm>
        <socket-binding-group ref="full-sockets"/>
    </server-group>
</server-groups>
```

5. Now start the EAP 7 domain controller as usual:

   ./domain.sh

6. We will need to execute some commands through the CLI, so execute the `jboss-cli` script:

   ./jbosscli.sh

7. First, to make portable EAP 6 profiles, we will need to remove some features such as **CDI Bean validation** from the Weld subsystem. Execute from the CLI the following commands:

```
/profile=640default/subsystem=bean-validation:remove()
/profile=640default/subsystem=weld:write-attribute
 (name=require-bean-descriptor,value=true)
/profile=640default/subsystem=weld:write-attribute
 (name=non-portable-mode,value=true)
```

8. Finally, we need to bind the `host-exclude` component (which we met at the beginning of this section) to the EAP 6 server groups. Still in the CLI, execute the following command:

```
/host-exclude=EAP64:list-add
(name=active-server-groups,value=640main-server-group)
```

9. Now you can start the EAP 6 host controller and it will eventually connect to the EAP domain controller:

```
./domain.sh -Djboss.management.native.port=19999 -
Djboss.management.http.port=19990
As a result, the EAP 7 Domain controller will register the
remote slave using a different EAP version:
```

```
LYUT0012: Started server default-server.
[Server:server-700] 12:19:38,565 INFO  [org.wildfly.extension.undertow] (MSC service thread 1-4) WF
LYUT0018: Host default-host starting
[Server:server-700] 12:19:38,719 INFO  [org.wildfly.extension.undertow] (MSC service thread 1-6) WF
LYUT0006: Undertow HTTP listener default listening on 127.0.0.1:8230
[Server:server-700] 12:19:38,726 INFO  [org.jboss.as.ejb3] (MSC service thread 1-1) WFLYEJB0481: St
rict pool slsb-strict-max-pool is using a max instance size of 64 (per class), which is derived fro
m thread worker pool sizing.
[Server:server-700] 12:19:38,726 INFO  [org.jboss.as.ejb3] (MSC service thread 1-3) WFLYEJB0482: St
rict pool mdb-strict-max-pool is using a max instance size of 16 (per class), which is derived from
 the number of CPUs on this host.
[Server:server-700] 12:19:38,963 INFO  [org.jboss.as.connector.subsystems.datasources] (MSC service
 thread 1-2) WFLYJCA0001: Bound data source [java:jboss/datasources/ExampleDS]
[Server:server-700] 12:19:39,474 INFO  [org.jboss.ws.common.management] (MSC service thread 1-8) JB
WS022052: Starting JBossWS 5.1.3.SP1-redhat-1 (Apache CXF 3.1.4.redhat-1)
[Server:server-700] 12:19:39,566 INFO  [org.infinispan.factories.GlobalComponentRegistry] (MSC serv
ice thread 1-3) ISPN000128: Infinispan version: Infinispan 'Mahou' 8.1.2.Final-redhat-1
[Server:server-700] 12:19:39,742 INFO  [org.jboss.as] (Controller Boot Thread) WFLYSRV0025: JBoss E
AP 7.0.0.GA (WildFly Core 2.1.0.Final-redhat-1) started in 4527ms - Started 257 of 545 services (36
9 services are lazy, passive or on-demand)
[Host Controller] 12:23:16,414 INFO  [org.jboss.as.domain.controller] (Host Controller Service Thre
ads - 43) WFLYHC0019: Registered remote slave host "slave", JBoss EAP 6.4.0.GA (WildFly 7.5.0.Final
-redhat-21)
```

Although several steps are required to configure the EAP 6-EAP 7 connectivity, in the end, all changes are centralized in the EAP 7 configuration, without any variation in the legacy EAP 6 host controllers.

Hierarchical profiles

In order to promote configuration reuse, a domain's profile can now inherit configuration from other domain profiles. Take as example the following excerpt:

```
<profile name="base">
    <subsystem xmlns="urn:jboss:domain:logging:3.0">
    . . . .
    </subsystem>
</profile>
<profile name="child" includes="base">
    <subsystem xmlns="urn:jboss:domain:batch-jberet:1.0">
    . . . .
</profile>
```

In the previous example, the profile named `base` configures the logging subsystem. The profile named `child` includes the base profile. This means that the logging configuration will be inherited from the base profile.

> At the time of writing, overriding base profiles is not supported, hence you cannot include a subsystem which has been inherited with the `includes` directive.

Profile cloning

Until EAP 7 there was no officially supported way to clone an existing profile using the management instruments. The command clone is now available and it can be used directly on a profile to specify a target profile which will contain a copy of it. See the following example:

```
[domain@localhost:9990 /] /profile=full:clone(to-profile=full-cloned)
{
  "outcome" => "success",
  "result" => undefined,
  "server-groups" => undefined
}
```

For the sake of completeness, we will mention a utility script developed by T. Fonteyn which allows you to create a cloned version of a profile as a set of CLI commands. You can check it out at `https://github.com/tfonteyn/profilecloner`.

Summary

In this chapter we have some essentials of domain management along with some advanced tactics to provide continuity in domain administration and to configure a non-trivial domain topology via scripting. In the next chapter we will cover the deployment of applications, exploring the options available both in the domain mode and in the standalone mode.

4
Deploying Applications

In this chapter, we will see how we can take advantage of the CLI to deploy applications. We will first overview deployments and discuss what kind of deployments JBoss EAP 7 supports.

Next, we will see how to deploy applications in both standalone and domain mode. We will also discuss the differences between those two operative modes in terms of CLI commands – they are very similar, but there are some differences that are worth mentioning. Also, we will have a quick look at how to deploy applications using the web console.

We will then end our chapter with an advanced deployment strategy, which is called deployment overlay. We will see what this deployment strategy can provide, how to do it, and most importantly, when to use or not to use it.

Overview of deployments

When talking about Java applications, we can categorize at least three types of application: Java Archive, Web Archive, and Enterprise Archive.

Each of the previously mentioned application types have their own specific extensions that are just for a readable purpose:

- .jar – Java Archive
- .war – Web Archive
- .ear – Enterprise Archive

As a matter of fact, all of them are essentially ZIP archive files.

When it comes to JBoss, there actually are two more types of application you can deploy. One is called Service Archive (.sar extension), and the other is an XML file which declares, essentially, a piece of EAP configuration, such as data sources, JMS queues, and so on.

> Keep in mind that using *-ds.xml and *-jms.xml files might be a good idea in a development environment to configure those resources, but there are many drawbacks you should consider:
>
> Management tools, such as CLI and Web Console, cannot be used to manage resources deployed in such a way.
>
> Any security concerns related to those resources cannot be used. This includes password vaults and security domains. Deployment is not available in domain mode.

The Service Archive is a service component application with no dependencies at all, meant for monitoring, much like JMX MBean.

Deployment in standalone mode

We will begin by deploying an application in a standalone EAP. First we will see how the application server takes care of your bundles automatically just by dropping them into the deployments folder. We will then see how you can manage the life cycle of your application by using marker files.

Automatic deployment

To deploy an application, JBoss provides a deployment folder named deployment, where a service called DeploymentScanner waits for changes.

Let's start an EAP instance by issuing the following command:

```
$JBOSS_HOME/bin/standalone.sh
```

Once an EAP is started, copy the helloworld application into the standalone/deployments folder of JBOSS_HOME. After a few seconds you should see similar entries in your log file:

```
10:56:14,771 INFO  [org.jboss.as.repository] (DeploymentScanner-threads -
1) WFLYDR0001: Content added at location /opt/rh/jboss-
eap-7.0/ch04/data/content/fe/044dec09339f4837635b266fd7e5344a4f6b75/content
10:56:14,795 INFO  [org.jboss.as.server.deployment] (MSC service thread
1-6) WFLYSRV0027: Starting deployment of "jboss-helloworld.war" (runtime-
```

```
name: "jboss-helloworld.war")
10:56:15,237 INFO  [org.jboss.weld.deployer] (MSC service thread 1-5)
WFLYWELD0003: Processing weld deployment jboss-helloworld.war
10:56:15,321 INFO  [org.hibernate.validator.internal.util.Version] (MSC
service thread 1-5) HV000001: Hibernate Validator 5.2.2.Final-redhat-2
10:56:15,523 INFO  [org.jboss.weld.deployer] (MSC service thread 1-4)
WFLYWELD0006: Starting Services for CDI deployment: jboss-helloworld.war
10:56:15,577 INFO  [org.jboss.weld.Version] (MSC service thread 1-4)
WELD-000900: 2.3.1 (redhat)
10:56:15,632 INFO  [org.jboss.weld.deployer] (MSC service thread 1-6)
WFLYWELD0009: Starting weld service for deployment jboss-helloworld.war
10:56:16,806 INFO  [org.wildfly.extension.undertow] (ServerService Thread
Pool -- 63) WFLYUT0021: Registered web context: /jboss-helloworld
10:56:16,855 INFO  [org.jboss.as.server] (DeploymentScanner-threads - 1)
WFLYSRV0010: Deployed "jboss-helloworld.war" (runtime-name : "jboss-
helloworld.war")
```

Once the deployment scanner has terminated its task, it marks your application as
deployed.

By default, the deployment scanner has the following configuration:

```
<subsystem xmlns="urn:jboss:domain:deployment-scanner:2.0">
    <deployment-scanner path="deployments" relative-to=
    "jboss.server.base.dir" scan-interval="5000" runtime-failure-
    causes-rollback="${jboss.deployment.scanner.rollback.
    on.failure:false}"/>
</subsystem>
```

As you can see, you can easily configure the path to find application bundles. The path is
treated as an absolute path unless you specify the relative-to condition. Also, you can
change the scan interval, which is an interval in which the deployment scanner should
check for changes (deploy or undeploy operations). The last parameter is a flag that, if set to
true, forces all the deployments to roll back in case of failure, even if there are deployments
not related to each other. Obviously its default is false.

There are other attributes that you can use, and they are all summarized in the following table for you as a reference:

Attribute name	Default value	Req. Opt.	Description
name	default	optional	The name of the deployment scanner. That is, you can have more than one, as long as their names are different and their paths are not overlaying each other.
path		required	It represents the absolute path of the repository of your applications. In case the relative-to attribute is specified, the path value will be considered as relative.
relative-to	jboss.server.base.dir	optional	It specifies the starting path for the path attribute.
scan-enabled	true	optional	It specifies if the deployment scanner should be active or not.

`scan-interval`	0	optional	It specifies the number of milliseconds for which the deployment scanner should check the repository location for changes. A zero value means that the deployment scanner only checks for changes at initial startup.
`auto-deploy-zipped`	`true`	optional	It specifies if the .zip bundle should be automatically deployed without the need for the `.dodeploy` marker file.
`auto-deploy-exploded`	`false`	optional	It specifies the content of the exploded bundle should be automatically deployed without the need for the `.dodeploy` marker file.
`auto-deploy-xml`	`true`	optional	It specifies if the .xml bundle should be automatically deployed without the need for the `.dodeploy` marker file.
`deployment-timeout`	`600`	optional	It specifies if the number of seconds in which a deployment should be cancelled and marked as a `.failed` file.

runtime-failure-causes-rollback	false	optional	If it is set to true and a deployment failure exists, all deployments within that scan operation will be cancelled and rolled back.

One more thing you should be aware of is that you can have multiple deployment scanners running, each one with its own name and path. Just to give you an example, having two deployment scanners handling different repositories will result in having two distinct deployment scanner instances running in your JBoss, as shown in the following log entries:

```
11:26:18,926 INFO  [org.jboss.as.server.deployment.scanner] (MSC service
thread 1-8) WFLYDS0013: Started FileSystemDeploymentService for directory
/opt/rh/jboss-eap-7.0/ch04/deployments
11:26:18,921 INFO  [org.jboss.as.server.deployment.scanner] (MSC service
thread 1-1) WFLYDS0013: Started FileSystemDeploymentService for directory
/opt/rh/jboss-eap-7.0/ch04/bundles
11:26:18,944 INFO  [org.jboss.as.server.deployment] (MSC service thread
1-8) WFLYSRV0027: Starting deployment of "jboss-helloworld.war" (runtime-
name: "jboss-helloworld.war")
11:26:18,944 INFO  [org.jboss.as.server.deployment] (MSC service thread
1-1) WFLYSRV0027: Starting deployment of "jboss-helloworld-rs.war"
(runtime-name: "jboss-helloworld-rs.war")
```

Once the deployment scanner has finished deploying your application, the latter gets marked by creating a new file with the same name as your application, appending to it the .deployed suffix. You can find the file within the deployments folder itself. In case of failure, the deployment scanner creates a different file, marking the file as .failed.

This mechanism enables the system administrator to manage the deployment life cycle of each bundle present in the deployments folder.

Deployment triggered by the user

The following is a table that summarizes all available marker file extensions to manage application deployment phases:

Name	Owner	Description
`.dodeploy`	User generated	This indicates that the content should be deployed or redeployed into the runtime.
`.skipdeploy`	User generated	This disables auto-deployment of an application while present. It is useful as a method of temporarily blocking the auto-deployment of exploded content, preventing the risk of incomplete content edits pushing live. It can be used with zipped content, although the scanner detects in-progress changes to zipped content and waits until completion.
`.undeploy`	User generated	This indicates that the content should be undeployed from the runtime.
`.isdeploying`	System generated	Indicates the initiation of deployment. The marker file will be deleted when the deployment process completes.
`.deployed`	System generated	Indicates that the content has been deployed. The content will be undeployed if this file is deleted.
`.failed`	System generated	Indicates deployment failure. The marker file contains information about the cause of failure. If the marker file is deleted, the content will be visible to the auto-deployment again.
`.isundeploying`	System generated	This indicates a response to a .deployed file deletion. The content will be undeployed and the marker will be automatically deleted upon completion.
`.undeployed`	System generated	This indicates that the content has been undeployed. Deletion of the marker file has no impact on content redeployment.
`.pending`	System generated	This indicates that deployment instructions will be sent to the server pending resolution of a detected issue. This marker serves as a global deployment road-block. The scanner will not instruct the server to deploy or undeploy any other content while this condition exists.

Alternatively, you can deploy your application by relying on the CLI.

Deploying using the CLI

As previously mentioned in `Chapter 2`, *The CLI Management Tool* (Deploy and undeploy an application), we can rely on the CLI to manage our deployment.

To deploy your application using the CLI, do as follows:

```
[root@dev jboss-eap-7.0]# ./bin/jboss-cli.sh
You are disconnected at the moment. Type 'connect' to connect to the server
or 'help' for the list of supported commands.
[disconnected /] connect 192.168.59.103:9990
[standalone@192.168.59.103:9990 /] deploy /opt/rh/jboss-helloworld.war
[standalone@192.168.59.103:9990 /]
```

The previous command triggers a few entries in your logs, as follows:

```
12:33:35,881 INFO  [org.jboss.as.repository] (management-handler-thread -
8) WFLYDR0001: Content added at location /opt/rh/jboss-
eap-7.0/ch04/data/content/fe/044dec09339f4837635b266fd7e5344a4f6b75/content
12:33:35,883 INFO  [org.jboss.as.server.deployment] (MSC service thread
1-5) WFLYSRV0027: Starting deployment of "jboss-helloworld.war" (runtime-
name: "jboss-helloworld.war")
12:33:35,912 INFO  [org.jboss.weld.deployer] (MSC service thread 1-1)
WFLYWELD0003: Processing weld deployment jboss-helloworld.war
12:33:35,940 INFO  [org.jboss.weld.deployer] (MSC service thread 1-8)
WFLYWELD0006: Starting Services for CDI deployment: jboss-helloworld.war
12:33:35,953 INFO  [org.jboss.weld.deployer] (MSC service thread 1-6)
WFLYWELD0009: Starting weld service for deployment jboss-helloworld.war
12:33:36,120 INFO  [org.wildfly.extension.undertow] (ServerService Thread
Pool -- 78) WFLYUT0021: Registered web context: /jboss-helloworld
12:33:36,132 INFO  [org.jboss.as.server] (management-handler-thread - 8)
WFLYSRV0010: Deployed "jboss-helloworld.war" (runtime-name : "jboss-
helloworld.war")
```

The most important log entry from the previous ones is the first one, which specifies where JBoss stores your deployment. Despite the `data/content/` folder, which is quite self-explanatory, `fe` and `044dec09339f4837635b266fd7e5344a4f6b75`, are not! These two folders are calculated by hashing the content of the bundle using the SHA1 algorithm.

Using a tool that generates hashes based on file content and by specifying the SHA1 algorithm will output `fe044dec09339f4837635b266fd7e5344a4f6b75`.

Unix, like systems have the `shasum` command available, as follows:

```
sha1sum jboss-helloworld.war
fe044dec09339f4837635b266fd7e5344a4f6b75  jboss-helloworld.war
```

Now, if you look a bit closer at the hash, you can see that the first two bytes of the hash compose the first folder, `fe`, and the rest of the hash composes the name of the second folder. Lastly, the file named `content` is essentially your application bundle you deployed using the CLI.

Now that you know how this works, you can easily and manually back up your deployments... or maybe not. If you lose the log file where the deployment has been traced, you cannot reference your deployment to a hash. Right? Well, actually, there is a way. Just open your `standalone.xml` configuration file, and at the end you should find your deployment definition, as follows:

```
<deployments>
    <deployment name="jboss-helloworld.war" runtime-name="jboss-
    helloworld.war">
        <content sha1="fe044dec09339f4837635b266fd7e5344a4f6b75"/>
    </deployment>
</deployments>
```

By the way, once you're done, you can check the deployment:

```
[standalone@192.168.59.103:9990 /] deployment-info --name=jboss-
helloworld.war
NAME                    RUNTIME-NAME          PERSISTENT ENABLED STATUS
jboss-helloworld.war jboss-helloworld.war true          true    OK
[standalone@192.168.59.103:9990 /]
```

To undeploy your application, you can use the `undeploy` command, as follows:

```
[standalone@192.168.59.103:9990 /] undeploy jboss-
helloworld.war
[standalone@192.168.59.103:9990 /]
```

If you don't know the exact name of your application, you can list the applications available to undeploy, as follows:

```
[standalone@192.168.59.103:9990 /] undeploy -l
NAME                    RUNTIME-NAME          ENABLED STATUS
jboss-helloworld.war jboss-helloworld.war true    OK
[standalone@192.168.59.103:9990 /]
```

In case you just want to disable an application, for example, due to maintenance, you can do as follows:

```
[standalone@192.168.59.103:9990 /] undeploy jboss-helloworld.war --keep-
content
[standalone@192.168.59.103:9990 /]
```

Check the deployment status by invoking the `deployment-info` command:

```
[standalone@192.168.59.103:9990 /] deployment-info --name=jboss-
helloworld.war
     NAME                     RUNTIME-NAME            PERSISTENT ENABLED STATUS
     jboss-helloworld.war jboss-helloworld.war true         false   STOPPED
     [standalone@192.168.59.103:9990 /]
```

You can effectively enable your application using the `deploy` command followed by the name of the deployment, as follows:

```
[standalone@192.168.59.103:9990 /] deploy --name=jboss-
helloworld.war
[standalone@192.168.59.103:9990 /]
```

In case you prefer the web console, deployment is very easy, and the logic of it is in line with what has been explained so far.

Deploying using the web console

Once you log in into the web console (`http://localhost:8080/console`), click on the **Deployments** tab and you should see a page similar to the following:

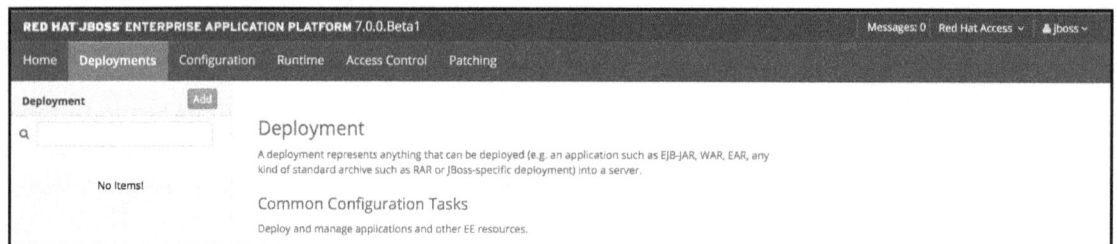

Standalone – Deployment page

Just press the blue **Add** button to add a new application as deployment. The page should pop up the following interface:

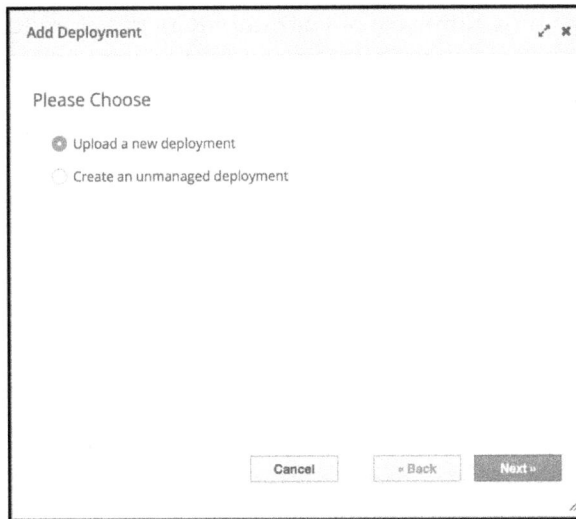

Standalone – Uploading a new deployment

By choosing **Upload a new deployment** and clicking the **Next** button, the deployment wizard should prompt you to select the file you want to upload, from the local filesystem, by pressing the **Browse** button.

Once you have selected the bundle, click the **Next** button, as follows:

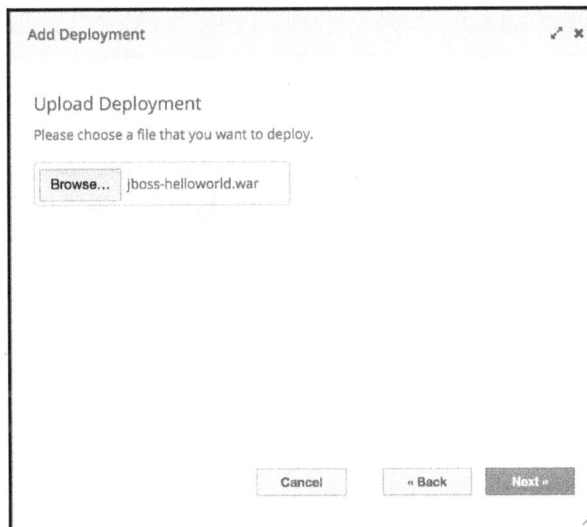

Standalone – Browsing for the bundle to upload

Next, the wizard shows you a summary of your deployment before confirmation, as depicted in the screenshot that follows:

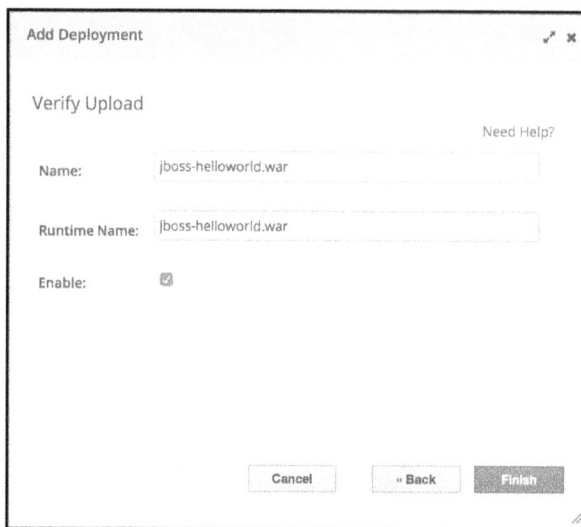

Standalone – Completing the deployment upload wizard

As you can see, you can make your deployment available or not by checking and unchecking the **Enable** flag.

You can confirm and terminate the deployment task by clicking the **Finish** button.

Once done, your deployment appears in the list of deployments. Click on it to see its details, as follows:

Standalone – Deployment overview

By clicking on your deployment, you should have noticed a drop-down menu which lets you **View**, **Disable**, **Replace**, and **Remove** your applications, as shown in the screenshot as follows:

Standalone – List of commands for deployments

Now that we know exactly how to manage our deployments in standalone mode, let's see how we can handle them in domain mode.

Deployment in domain mode

We will start this section by saying that there is no `deployments` folder.

Having said that, we will rely on the default configuration so that we can get up and running quickly.

By default, the domain mode starts the domain controller and two server instances named `server-one` and `server-two`. There is also an instance named `server-three`, but it's not started during the boot phase.

Those server instances belong to two different server groups, named `main-server-group` and `other-server-group`.

Deployment using the CLI

As already described in `Chapter 3`, *Managing EAP in Domain Mode,* there is a different startup script to launch the domain mode, which is `domain.sh` (`domain.bat` if you are running Windows), available under the `$JBOSS_HOME/bin` folder.

Without going any further, let's start the domain mode, as follows:

```
cd $JBOSS_HOME
./bin/domain.sh
```

Within your shell, you should have noticed the startup entries in the log, as follows:

```
...
[Server:server-one] 16:25:38,641 INFO  [org.jboss.as] (Controller Boot
Thread) WFLYSRV0025: EAP 7.0.0.Beta1 (WildFly Core 2.0.3.Final-redhat-1)
started in 5843ms - Started 290 of 537 services (343 services are lazy,
passive or on-demand)
...
[Server:server-two] 16:25:41,803 INFO  [org.jboss.as] (Controller Boot
Thread) WFLYSRV0025: EAP 7.0.0.Beta1 (WildFly Core 2.0.3.Final-redhat-1)
started in 7041ms - Started 290 of 537 services (343 services are lazy,
passive or on-demand)
```

So `server-one` and `server-two` are both up and running. Now we can jump into the CLI and deploy our best application ever, `jboss-helloworld.war`, to all servers.

But first, let's start the lazy `server-three` instance, as follows:

```
./bin/jboss-cli.sh
You are disconnected at the moment. Type 'connect' to connect to the server
or 'help' for the list of supported commands.
[disconnected /] connect 192.168.59.103:9990
[domain@192.168.59.103:9990 /] [domain@192.168.59.103:9990 /]
/host=master/server-config=server-three:start()
    {
        "outcome" => "success",
        "result" => "STARTED
    }
[domain@192.168.59.103:9990 /]
```

Once server-three has started, let's deploy the application, as follows:

```
[domain@192.168.59.103:9990 /] deploy /opt/rh/jboss-helloworld.war --all-
server-groups
[domain@192.168.59.103:9990 /]
```

The preceding `deploy` command will issue the following entries in the log file:

```
[Host Controller] 16:50:41,154 INFO  [org.jboss.as.repository] (management-
handler-thread - 17) WFLYDR0001: Content added at location /opt/rh/jboss-
eap-7.0/ch04d/data/content/fe/044dec09339f4837635b266fd7e5344a4f6b75/conten
t
[Server:server-two] 16:50:41,187 INFO  [org.jboss.as.server.deployment]
```

```
(MSC service thread 1-2) WFLYSRV0027: Starting deployment of "jboss-
helloworld.war" (runtime-name: "jboss-helloworld.war")
[Server:server-one] 16:50:41,210 INFO  [org.jboss.as.server.deployment]
(MSC service thread 1-5) WFLYSRV0027: Starting deployment of "jboss-
helloworld.war" (runtime-name: "jboss-helloworld.war")
[Server:server-one] 16:50:41,310 INFO  [org.jboss.weld.deployer] (MSC
service thread 1-1) WFLYWELD0003: Processing weld deployment jboss-
helloworld.war
[Server:server-two] 16:50:41,318 INFO  [org.jboss.weld.deployer] (MSC
service thread 1-7) WFLYWELD0003: Processing weld deployment jboss-
helloworld.war
[Server:server-one] 16:50:41,360 INFO  [org.jboss.weld.deployer] (MSC
service thread 1-3) WFLYWELD0006: Starting Services for CDI deployment:
jboss-helloworld.war
[Server:server-one] 16:50:41,379 INFO  [org.jboss.weld.deployer] (MSC
service thread 1-8) WFLYWELD0009: Starting weld service for deployment
jboss-helloworld.war
[Server:server-two] 16:50:41,409 INFO  [org.jboss.weld.deployer] (MSC
service thread 1-5) WFLYWELD0006: Starting Services for CDI deployment:
jboss-helloworld.war
[Server:server-two] 16:50:41,429 INFO  [org.jboss.weld.deployer] (MSC
service thread 1-3) WFLYWELD0009: Starting weld service for deployment
jboss-helloworld.war
[Server:server-three] 16:50:41,515 INFO  [org.jboss.as.server.deployment]
(MSC service thread 1-4) WFLYSRV0027: Starting deployment of "jboss-
helloworld.war" (runtime-name: "jboss-helloworld.war")
[Server:server-two] 16:50:41,854 INFO  [org.wildfly.extension.undertow]
(ServerService Thread Pool -- 94) WFLYUT0021: Registered web context:
/jboss-helloworld
[Server:server-one] 16:50:41,926 INFO  [org.wildfly.extension.undertow]
(ServerService Thread Pool -- 91) WFLYUT0021: Registered web context:
/jboss-helloworld
[Server:server-three] 16:50:42,065 INFO  [org.jboss.weld.deployer] (MSC
service thread 1-4) WFLYWELD0003: Processing weld deployment jboss-
helloworld.war
[Server:server-three] 16:50:42,117 INFO
[org.hibernate.validator.internal.util.Version] (MSC service thread 1-4)
HV000001: Hibernate Validator 5.2.2.Final-redhat-2
[Server:server-three] 16:50:42,338 INFO  [org.jboss.weld.deployer] (MSC
service thread 1-5) WFLYWELD0006: Starting Services for CDI deployment:
jboss-helloworld.war
[Server:server-three] 16:50:42,371 INFO  [org.jboss.weld.Version] (MSC
service thread 1-5) WELD-000900: 2.3.1 (redhat)
[Server:server-three] 16:50:42,430 INFO  [org.jboss.weld.deployer] (MSC
service thread 1-1) WFLYWELD0009: Starting weld service for deployment
jboss-helloworld.war
[Server:server-three] 16:50:43,369 INFO  [org.wildfly.extension.undertow]
(ServerService Thread Pool -- 80) WFLYUT0021: Registered web context:
```

```
/jboss-helloworld
[Server:server-two] 16:50:43,422 INFO  [org.jboss.as.server] (ServerService
Thread Pool -- 89) WFLYSRV0010: Deployed "jboss-helloworld.war" (runtime-
name : "jboss-helloworld.war")
[Server:server-one] 16:50:43,423 INFO  [org.jboss.as.server] (ServerService
Thread Pool -- 86) WFLYSRV0010: Deployed "jboss-helloworld.war" (runtime-
name : "jboss-helloworld.war")
[Server:server-three] 16:50:43,424 INFO  [org.jboss.as.server]
(ServerService Thread Pool -- 75) WFLYSRV0010: Deployed "jboss-
helloworld.war" (runtime-name : "jboss-helloworld.war")
```

All servers now have their own `jboss-helloworld` application deployed and available.

In case we want our application to be deployed into a specific `server-group`, we need to use the `--server-groups` directive, instead of the `--all-server-groups` one.

Here is an example:

```
[domain@192.168.59.103:9990 /] deploy /opt/rh/jboss-helloworld.war --
server-groups=main-server-group
[domain@192.168.59.103:9990 /]
```

As per the previous deploy command invocation, we have log entries tracing the deployment for all servers belonging to the `main-server-group`, as follows:

```
[Host Controller] 16:52:42,640 INFO  [org.jboss.as.repository] (management-
handler-thread - 21) WFLYDR0001: Content added at location /opt/rh/jboss-
eap-7.0/ch04d/data/content/fe/044dec09339f4837635b266fd7e5344a4f6b75/conten
t
[Server:server-two] 16:52:42,664 INFO  [org.jboss.as.server.deployment]
(MSC service thread 1-2) WFLYSRV0027: Starting deployment of "jboss-
helloworld.war" (runtime-name: "jboss-helloworld.war")
[Server:server-one] 16:52:42,665 INFO  [org.jboss.as.server.deployment]
(MSC service thread 1-6) WFLYSRV0027: Starting deployment of "jboss-
helloworld.war" (runtime-name: "jboss-helloworld.war")
[Server:server-one] 16:52:42,716 INFO  [org.jboss.weld.deployer] (MSC
service thread 1-3) WFLYWELD0003: Processing weld deployment jboss-
helloworld.war
[Server:server-two] 16:52:42,720 INFO  [org.jboss.weld.deployer] (MSC
service thread 1-4) WFLYWELD0003: Processing weld deployment jboss-
helloworld.war
[Server:server-one] 16:52:42,734 INFO  [org.jboss.weld.deployer] (MSC
service thread 1-4) WFLYWELD0006: Starting Services for CDI deployment:
jboss-helloworld.war
[Server:server-one] 16:52:42,740 INFO  [org.jboss.weld.deployer] (MSC
service thread 1-2) WFLYWELD0009: Starting weld service for deployment
jboss-helloworld.war
[Server:server-two] 16:52:42,761 INFO  [org.jboss.weld.deployer] (MSC
```

```
service thread 1-3) WFLYWELD0006: Starting Services for CDI deployment:
jboss-helloworld.war
[Server:server-two] 16:52:42,789 INFO  [org.jboss.weld.deployer] (MSC
service thread 1-4) WFLYWELD0009: Starting weld service for deployment
jboss-helloworld.war
[Server:server-one] 16:52:43,083 INFO  [org.wildfly.extension.undertow]
(ServerService Thread Pool -- 97) WFLYUT0021: Registered web context:
/jboss-helloworld
[Server:server-two] 16:52:43,131 INFO  [org.wildfly.extension.undertow]
(ServerService Thread Pool -- 97) WFLYUT0021: Registered web context:
/jboss-helloworld
[Server:server-two] 16:52:43,155 INFO  [org.jboss.as.server] (ServerService
Thread Pool -- 95) WFLYSRV0010: Deployed "jboss-helloworld.war" (runtime-
name : "jboss-helloworld.war")
[Server:server-one] 16:52:43,155 INFO  [org.jboss.as.server] (ServerService
Thread Pool -- 93) WFLYSRV0010: Deployed "jboss-helloworld.war" (runtime-
name : "jboss-helloworld.war")
```

Before getting into the `undeploy` command, let's see what information we can get for our deployment.

For the domain mode as well, we can rely on the `deployment-info` command, as follows:

```
[domain@192.168.59.103:9990 /] deployment-info --name=jboss-helloworld.war
  NAME                     RUNTIME-NAME
  jboss-helloworld.war jboss-helloworld.war

  SERVER-GROUP       STATE
  main-server-group  enabled
  other-server-group enabled
  [domain@192.168.59.103:9990 /]
```

This time, the `deployment-info` command gives the state and the `server-group` where your application is deployed.

There is an alternative view, which consists of listing the deployment belonging to a particular `server-group`, as follows:

```
[domain@192.168.59.103:9990 /] deployment-info --server-group=main-server-
group
  NAME                     RUNTIME-NAME              STATE
  jboss-helloworld.war jboss-helloworld.war enabled
  [domain@192.168.59.103:9990 /]
```

The `--server-groups` directive accepts a comma-separated list of server-group names. This means that relying on the default domain configuration and specifying the `--server-groups=main-server-group,other-server-group` is the same as specifying the `--all-server-groups` directive.

Now it's time to undeploy our application. As per the `deploy` command, the same logic applies to the `undeploy` command. To undeploy all server groups, do as follows:

```
[domain@192.168.59.103:9990 /] undeploy /opt/rh/jboss-helloworld.war --all-
server-groups
[domain@192.168.59.103:9990 /]
```

If you want to undeploy your application just from a specific server-group, you can use the directive `--server-groups`, as follows:

```
[domain@192.168.59.103:9990 /] undeploy jboss-helloworld.war --server-
groups=main-server-group
Undeploy failed: {"WFLYCTL0062: Composite operation failed and was rolled
back. Steps that failed:" => {"Operation step-3" => "WFLYDC0043: Cannot
remove deployment jboss-helloworld.war from the domain as it is still used
by server groups [other-server-group]"}}
[domain@192.168.59.103:9990 /]
```

Ouch!

As the error description points out, we cannot undeploy the `jboss-helloworld.war` application from `main-server-group`. This is because the `undeploy` command also removes deployment content from the domain and servers data folders. And because the application, and therefore its content, is used by the `other-server-group`, we get the error.

So, the correct command should be invoked by adding the `--keep-content` flag, as follows:

```
[domain@192.168.59.103:9990 /] undeploy jboss-helloworld.war --server-
groups=main-server-group --keep-content
[domain@192.168.59.103:9990 /]
```

Now, the deployment content is removed from the servers belonging to `main-server-group` and kept on the domain controller, and the servers belonging to `other-server-group` are kept on `server-three`.

Just for reference, in domain mode the `undeploy` command can be invoked to list all available deployments, but there is no indication as which servers and `server-groups` they belong to:

```
[domain@192.168.59.103:9990 /] undeploy -l
NAME                      RUNTIME-NAME
jboss-helloworld.war jboss-helloworld.war
[domain@192.168.59.103:9990 /]
```

As pointed out previously in this section, the `deployment-info` command gives you more information regarding your deployments.

By the way, you can always count on the `domain.xml` file, where all deployments are defined and referenced to their `server-groups`, as shown here:

```
<deployments>
    <deployment name="jboss-helloworld.war" runtime-name="jboss-
    helloworld.war">
        <content sha1="fe044dec09339f4837635b266fd7e5344a4f6b75"/>
    </deployment>
</deployments>

<server-groups>
    <server-group name="main-server-group" profile="full">
        <jvm name="default">
            <heap size="64m" max-size="512m"/>
        </jvm>
        <socket-binding-group ref="full-sockets"/>
        <deployments>
            <deployment name="jboss-helloworld.war"
             runtime-name="jboss-helloworld.war"/>
        </deployments>
    </server-group>
    <server-group name="other-server-group" profile="full-ha">
        <jvm name="default">
            <heap size="64m" max-size="512m"/>
        </jvm>
        <socket-binding-group ref="full-ha-sockets"/>
        <deployments>
            <deployment name="jboss-helloworld.war"
             runtime-name="jboss-helloworld.war"/>
        </deployments>
    </server-group>
</server-groups>
```

In case you prefer the web console, the deployment process is very easy, and the logic of it is in line with what has been explained so far.

Deployment using the web console

Once you log in into the Web console (`http://localhost:8080/console`), click on the
Deployments tab and you should see a page similar to the following:

Domain – Deployment page

By selecting the **Content Repository** label on the left and by clicking on the blue
Add button, you will start the wizard to upload and deploy your applications, as depicted
in the following screenshot:

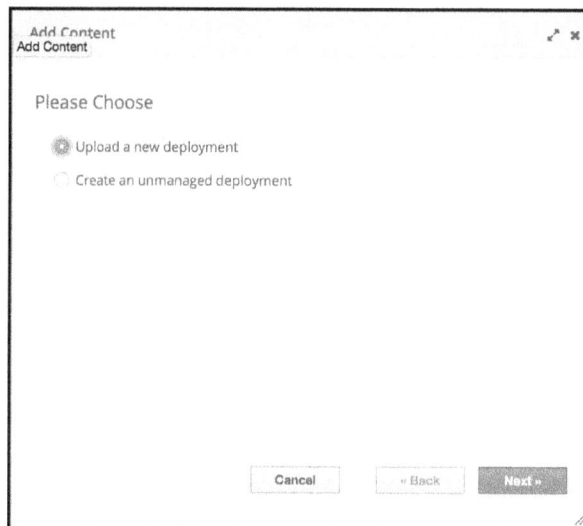

By choosing **Upload a new deployment** and clicking the **Next >>** button, the deployment
wizard should prompt you to select the file you want to upload from the local filesystem,
by pressing the **Browse** button.

Once you have selected the bundle, click the **Next** button, as shown here:

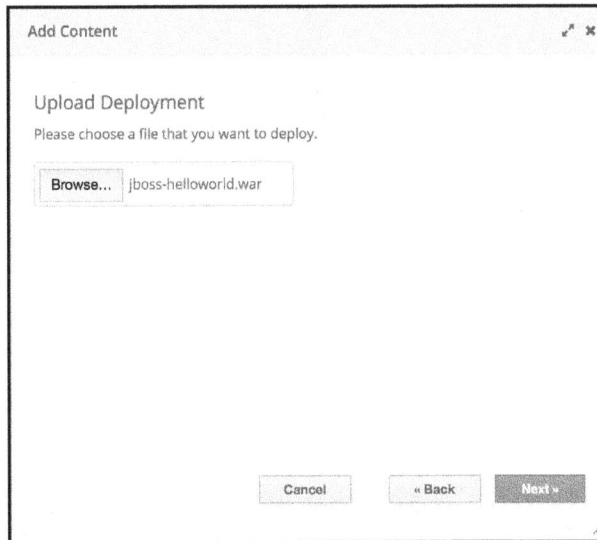

Next, the wizard shows you a summary from where you can eventually change the name and the runtime-name associated with your deployment. To end the deployment upload phase just press the **Finish** button, as follows:

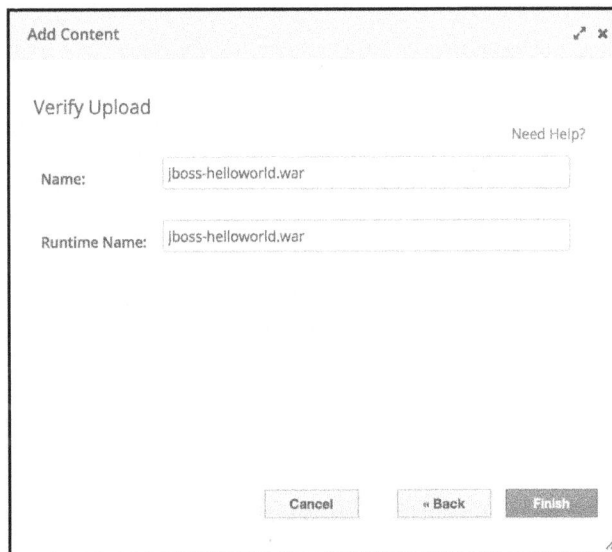

Once you're done, the **Content Repository** page gets updated, showing the newly uploaded content. Nonetheless, the application you have provided is not associated with any server-groups, as depicted here:

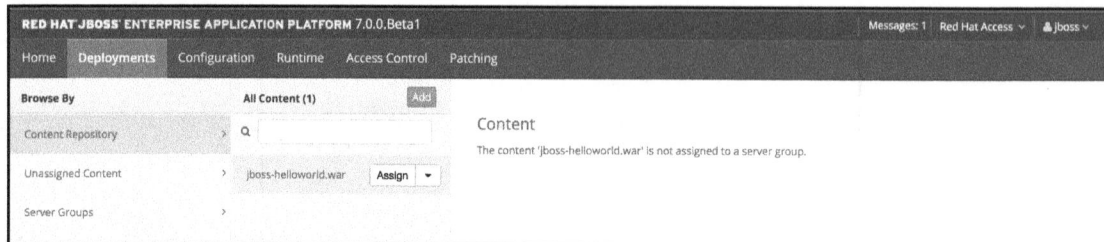

Right next to our application there is a little drop-down menu, which contains all the actions, **View**, **Unassign**, **Replace**, and **Remove,** that we can take on our deployment, as shown here:

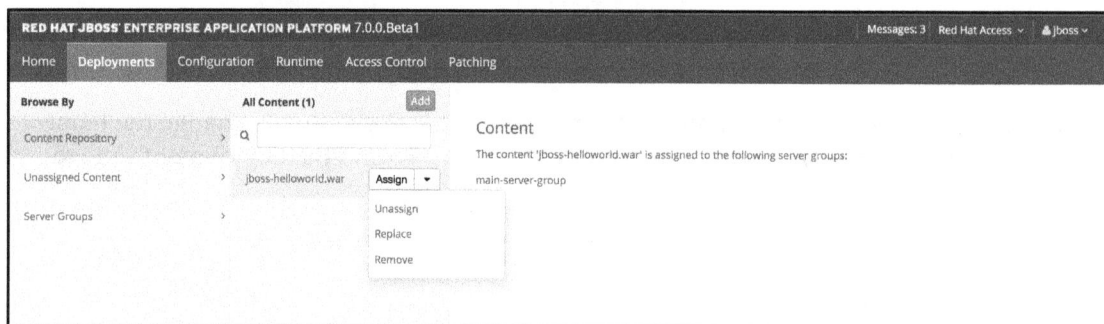

By clicking on the **Assign** drop-down menu, you can set which server-group your application should belong to. Because we relied on the domain's default configuration, we will be able to assign our application to the `main-server-group` and/or the `other-server-group`.

Just check the `main-server-group` and press the **Assign** button, as shown here:

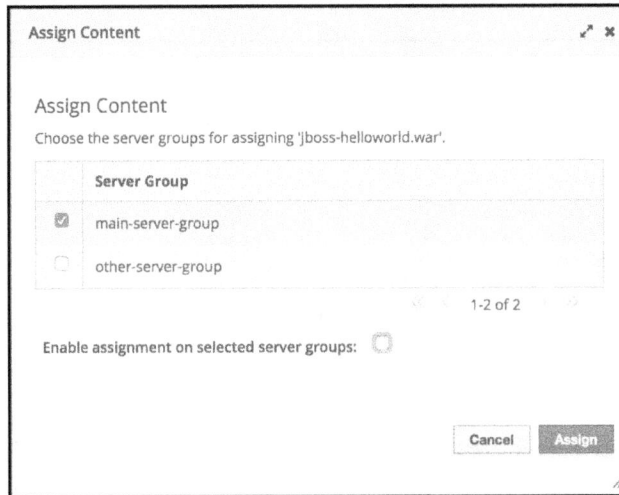

Again, the **Content Repository** page for our deployment gets updates, now showing the server-groups our application belongs to, as depicted here:

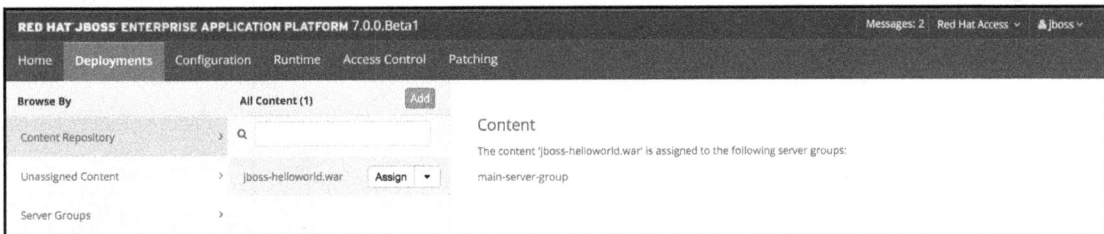

If we also want to assign the application to the other-server-group, we can just press the **Assign** label from the drop-down-menu and check the other-server-group, as follows:

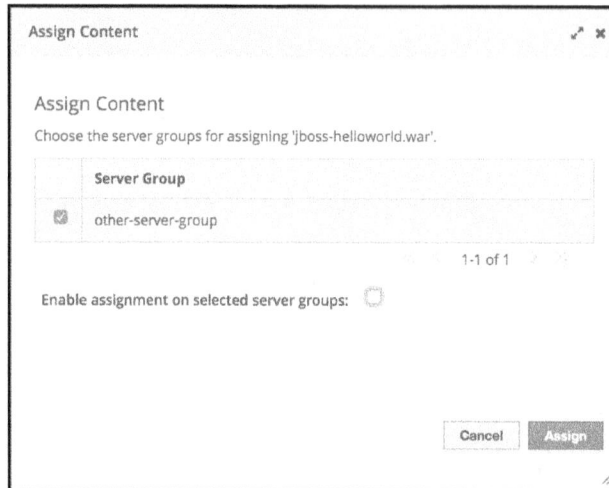

By the way, we can unassign our application from a server-group just by selecting the **Unassign** label from the drop-down menu, unchecking the server-group, and clicking the **Assign** button, as shown here:

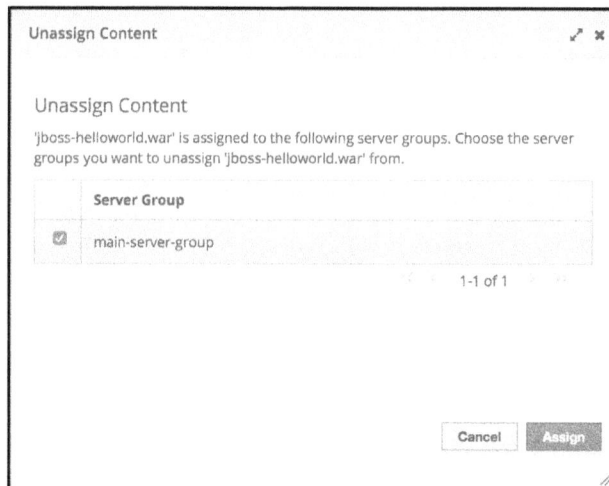

The Web Console also provides a different view to gather information between applications and server-groups. On the left, by selecting the **Server Groups** label, you can choose a server-group to see all the deployments belonging to it. The following screenshot is showing such a view:

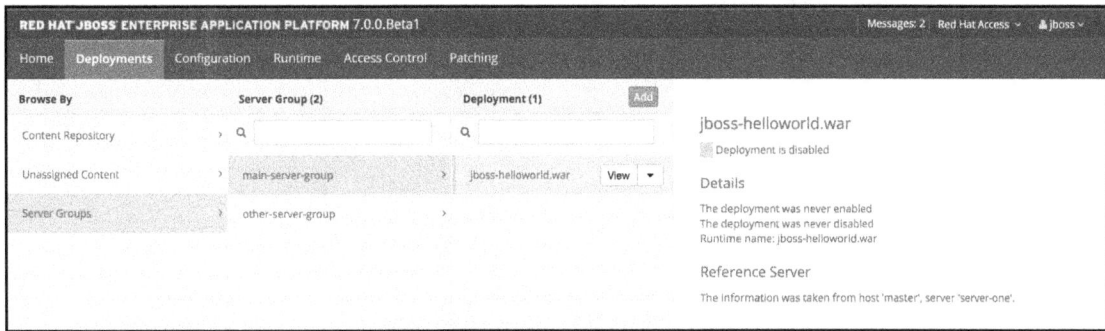

Furthermore, as per the standalone mode, an application can be deployed and enabled at a later time. In this case, too, we can enable the application by clicking on its relative drop-down-menu and selecting the label **Enable**, as depicted in the following screenshot:

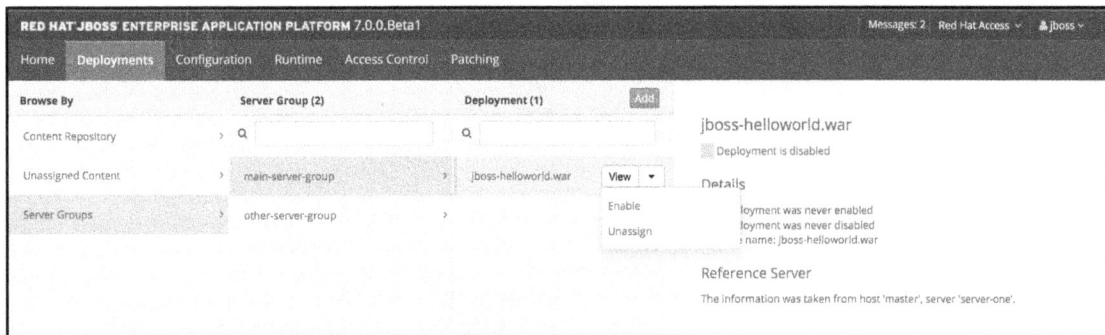

Because enabling an application effectively deploys it, a confirmation dialog will appear, as follows:

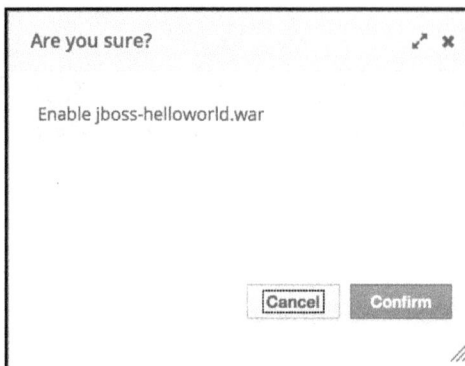

Just click on the **Confirm** blue button. Once done, the page of details of our application gets an update, now showing a green status saying **Deployment is enabled**, along with additional information. The following is a screenshot of the page showing what was just described:

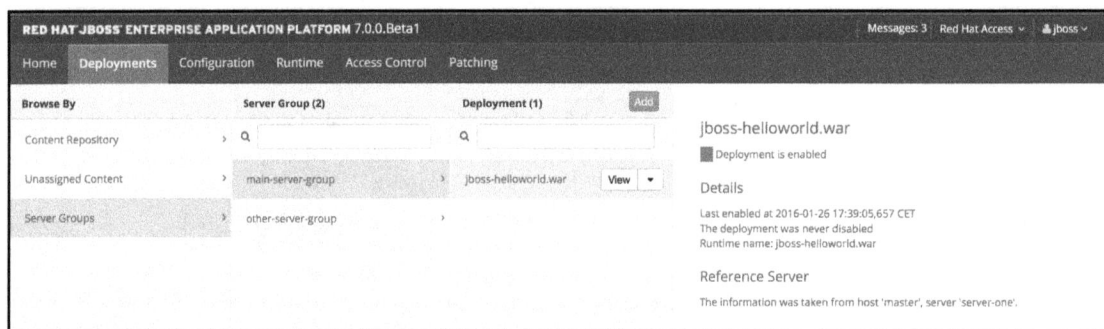

That's all you can do with the web console. In the next section, we will discuss advanced deployment strategies.

Advanced deployment strategies

So far, we have seen how you can effectively deploy an application, and despite it being a web application or an enterprise application, the deployment process is the same.

Furthermore, sometimes there is a need to just update a portion of an application due to environment settings, and despite all best practices in software life cycle management and enterprise DevOps patterns, you still have to deal with scenarios in which such practices are just not practicable.

Fortunately, JBoss provides a neat feature named deployment overlays.

Deployment overlays

Deployment overlays are ways to overlay, to cover, and to replace the content of a deployment without altering the application itself. Let's say it's a way to gently hack current modules.

First, let me explain how it works, and then we will look at an example.

Despite its name, a deployment overlay has a different life cycle. We first need to create the overlay and then we apply the overlay to an existing deployment. The application needs to be redeployed so that the overlay can take effect.

So, suppose we have already deployed our web application `jboss-helloworld.war` and we want to replace our `Hello World` welcome page with a different one. First, we need to create the new page, name it `index.html`, and add the following content to it:

```html
<html>
    <head>
      <title>Deployment overlay example</title>
    </head>
    <body>
      <h1>Hello World, we now have overlays!</h1>
    </body>
</html>
```

Once done, we can create our overlay via CLI, as follows:

```
[standalone@192.168.59.103:9990 /] deployment-overlay add --name=myOverlay
--content=/index.html=/opt/rh/index.html
[standalone@192.168.59.103:9990 /]
```

The previous command effectively says: add an overlay, call it myOverlay, and replace the file /index.html with the file /opt/rh/index.html.

As you confirm the CLI command, in your log you should see the following entry:

```
17:58:10,287 INFO  [org.jboss.as.repository] (management-handler-thread -
8) WFLYDR0001: Content added at location /opt/rh/jboss-
eap-7.0/ch04/data/content/c9/
86bb79e0b3997003fbd757977cc7c77cfa261d/content
```

Now we need to link the overlay to the deployment, as follows:

```
[standalone@192.168.59.103:9990 /] deployment-overlay link --name=myOverlay
--deployments=jboss-helloworld.war --redeploy-affected
[standalone@192.168.59.103:9990 /]
```

The previous command issues the redeployment of the application jboss-hellowolrd.war, and you can check this in your log, where you should find similar entries:

```
17:59:39,280 INFO  [org.wildfly.extension.undertow] (ServerService Thread
Pool -- 72) WFLYUT0022: Unregistered web context: /jboss-helloworld
17:59:39,294 INFO  [org.jboss.weld.deployer] (MSC service thread 1-3)
WFLYWELD0010: Stopping weld service for deployment jboss-helloworld.war
17:59:39,336 INFO  [org.jboss.as.server.deployment] (MSC service thread
1-1) WFLYSRV0028: Stopped deployment jboss-helloworld.war (runtime-name:
jboss-helloworld.war) in 70ms
17:59:39,338 INFO  [org.jboss.as.server.deployment] (MSC service thread
1-1) WFLYSRV0027: Starting deployment of "jboss-helloworld.war" (runtime-
name: "jboss-helloworld.war")
17:59:39,385 INFO  [org.jboss.weld.deployer] (MSC service thread 1-1)
WFLYWELD0003: Processing weld deployment jboss-helloworld.war
17:59:39,413 INFO  [org.jboss.weld.deployer] (MSC service thread 1-1)
WFLYWELD0006: Starting Services for CDI deployment: jboss-helloworld.war
17:59:39,421 INFO  [org.jboss.weld.deployer] (MSC service thread 1-3)
WFLYWELD0009: Starting weld service for deployment jboss-helloworld.war
17:59:39,638 INFO  [org.wildfly.extension.undertow] (ServerService Thread
Pool -- 75) WFLYUT0021: Registered web context: /jboss-helloworld
17:59:39,660 INFO  [org.jboss.as.server] (management-handler-thread - 13)
WFLYSRV0013: Redeployed "jboss-helloworld.war"
```

Now open the browser and point it to this URL http://localhost:8080/jboss-helloworld/index.html.You should see a page as depicted here:

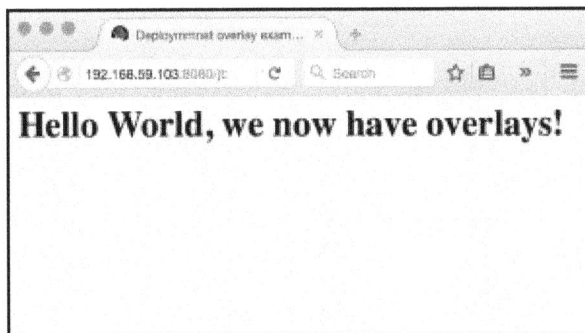

Deployment overlay

The previous commands can be expressed as a single command, as follows:

```
deployment-overlay add \
--name=myOverlay \
--content=/index.html=/opt/rh/index.html \
--deployments=jboss-helloworld.war \
--redeploy-affected
```

The slash (\) symbol is just used for readable purposes.

For the domain mode, you can also use overlays, and the command would be as follows:

```
deployment-overlay add \
--name=myOverlay \
--content=/index.html=/opt/rh/index.html \
--deployments=jboss-helloworld.war \
--server-groups=main-server-group \
--redeploy-affected
```

This was an easy example, just to give you an idea of what you can do with overlays. Deployment overlays can be applied to .class files, .xml files, and .jar files, but be aware that before using overlays, you should consider and use different approaches such as Continuous Build, Continuous Integration, and Continuous Delivery. For such topics, have a look at the following titles:

For Continuous Build and Integration: https://www.packtpub.com/books/content/jenkins-continuous-integration.

For Continuous Delivery: https://www.packtpub.com/application-development/continuous-delivery-and-devops-%E2%8%93-quickstart-guide-second-edition.

Summary

In this chapter, you learned how to deploy an application in both standalone and domain modes. You first learned how to deploy with the CLI and then saw how to achieve the same goal using the Web console.

By now, you should understand how powerful the CLI is and how you can leverage that power to suit your programming needs!

In the next chapter, we will see how we can use load balancing techniques to acquire high availability for your system. We will rely on more pieces of software such as Apache HTTPD, Nginx, mod-jk, and mod-cluster.

5
Load Balancing

In this chapter, you will learn how to load balance requests to EAP 7 servers from a web frontend layer. We can achieve load balancing using a variety of tools; we will however focus on the EAP HTTP balancing solution named `mod_cluster`. Overall in this chapter we will cover the following topics:

- At first, we will introduce and discuss `mod_cluster` communication, which can be carried out natively by Undertow or with the mediation of the Apache web server
- Next we will cover some other legacy solutions that can be installed on Apache or on third-party products (nginx)

The need for balancing

Placing a web server as a front door to your application server is a common practice that can provide the following benefits:

- **Load balancing and clustering**: By using a web server as a frontend you can handle traffic in multiple backend server instances. If one of your backend servers fails, the communication transparently continues to another node in the cluster.
- **Speed**: You can improve the performance by serving static content from your web server, which generally uses the native API.
- **Security**: The application server, where sensitive data is stored, can be placed in a protected area while exposing the frontend to an untrusted network. Essentially, you need to secure only the frontend, which normally does not contain business code.

The list of available software solutions for balancing JBoss EAP has grown in the last few years as new tools or software have been released whilst new balancing functionalities have been added into the application server. We can broadly divide these solutions into two main groups:

- mod_cluster **based solutions**: This solution is recommended in most cases because of its dynamicity and of course because it is part of the EAP support
- **Legacy solutions**: We can balance using Apache-based modules (such as mod_jk, or mod_proxy) or third-party products (for example, nginx), which are however widely adopted in many enterprise contexts

Load balancing with mod_cluster

mod_cluster is an HTTP-based load balancer that can be used to forward a request to a set of application server instances. Compared to legacy balancing solutions balancing solutions such as mod_jk or mod_proxy, mod_cluster provides the following benefits:

- Dynamic balancing configuration
- Pluggable server-side balancing metrics

As far as the first point is concerned, a load balancer is commonly based on a static list of servers where requests are directed. In many cases this can be a limiting factor especially when server nodes can be varied at runtime; besides this, maintaining a static list of servers is error-prone and needs to reshaped every time there is a change in your network.

About the next point, mod_cluster (in contrast to other frontend based balancers) uses load balance factors calculated and provided by the backend application servers, rather than computing these in the proxy. Consequently, mod_cluster offers a more robust and accurate set of load metrics than is available from the proxy.

Since EAP 7, the application server is *natively* able to proxy-request to a group of EAP servers. This means that you can run a full EAP solution both as a frontend and as a backend, without installing any other software. We will at first discuss this solution and later quickly recap the mod_cluster installation on an Apache web server frontend, which is unchanged since EAP 6.

Configuring EAP 7 as load balancer

In order to discuss this scenario we will need to install the following components:

- A standalone EAP distribution that will serve as a frontend load balancer
- A set of EAP servers as a backend where applications are available

The following screenshot depicts this scenario:

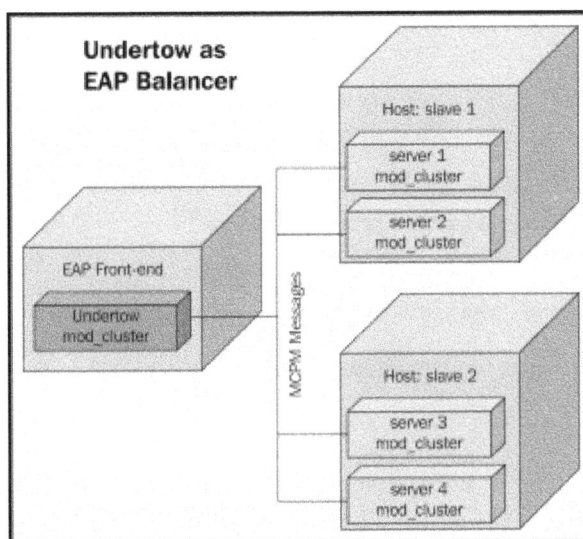

For this purpose, we will install another EAP server to work in front of our domain servers created in Chapter 3, *Managing EAP in Domain Mode*.

Let's start with folder creation:

```
$ mkdir -p /home/jboss/balancer-fe
```

As usual unzip the application server on the destination folder:

```
$ unzip jboss-eap-7.0.0.zip -d /home/jboss/balancer-fe
```

Now start the domain as discussed in Chapter 3, *Managing EAP in Domain Mode*:

```
$ cd /home/jboss/dc/jboss-eap-7.0/bin
$ ./domain.sh
```

Next, start the host controllers:

```
$ cd /home/jboss/slave1/jboss-eap-7.0/bin
./domain.sh -Djboss.management.native.port=19999 -
Djboss.management.http.port=19990
$ cd /home/jboss/slave2/jboss-eap-7.0/bin
$ ./domain.sh -Djboss.management.native.port=29999 -
Djboss.management.http.port=29990
```

The domain should be ready shortly. Now connect to the domain controller using the CLI:

```
$ ./jboss-cli.sh -c
```

The first change we need to apply is turning a server-group into a ha (or full-ha) profile since mod_cluster is included in high availability profiles. Execute the following commands from the CLI:

```
/server-group=main-server-group:write-
attribute(name=profile,value=ha)
/server-group=main-server-group:write-attribute(name=socket-
binding-group,value=ha-sockets)
```

Now reload the configuration for the changes to take effect:

```
/host=master:reload
```

You can verify from the bash prompt that mod_cluster multicast messages (using UDP as transport) are active on your network, on the ports defined by the mod_cluster socket bindings:

```
$ netstat -an | grep 224.0.1.105
udp 0 0 224.0.1.105:23364 0.0.0.0:*
```

Our backend needs to expose an application so deploy the application balancer.war (available within the book's code). Assuming that the application is available on the path /home/jboss/code/chapter5, issue this command from the CLI:

```
deploy /home/jboss/code/chapter5/balancer.war --server-
groups=main-server-group
```

Configuring the frontend server

Now it's time to start the standalone server that will be the frontend layer:

```
$ cd /home/jboss/balancer-fe/jboss-eap-7.0/bin
$ ./standalone.sh -c standalone-ha.xml -
```

```
Djboss.socket.binding.port-offset=10
```

As you can see, we have used a port offset to avoid conflicts with the domain ports. Also we need a ha profile to activate mod_cluster.

In order to redirect the communication to the backend, we will need to create an **Undertow filter** that proxies the incoming HTTP requests to mod_cluster nodes using mod_cluster's advertise ports (port=23364, multicastaddress=224.0.1.105).

Launch the CLI from the bin folder of the standalone distribution:

```
$ cd /home/jboss/balancer-fe/jboss-eap-7.0/bin
./jboss-cli.sh -c controller=127.0.0.1:10000
```

You can execute a batch script to perform both the filter creation and the socket binding it refers to:

```
batch
/subsystem=undertow/configuration=filter/mod-
cluster=modcluster:add(management-socket-binding=http,advertise-socket-
binding=modcluster)
/subsystem=undertow/server=default-server/host=default-host/filter-
ref=modcluster:add

run-batch
```

Now reload your configuration for the changes to take effect:

```
reload
```

As a result, the modcluster filter will be added to the default-host server:

```
<subsystem xmlns="urn:jboss:domain:undertow:3.0">
    <buffer-cache name="default"/>
    <server name="default-server">
        <http-listener name="default" redirect-socket="https" socket-
        binding="http"/>
        <host name="default-host" alias="localhost">
            <location name="/" handler="welcome-content"/>
            <filter-ref name="server-header"/>
            <filter-ref name="x-powered-by-header"/>
            <filter-ref name="modcluster"/>
        </host>
    </server>
    . . . .
    <filters>
        <response-header name="server-header" header-value="JBoss-
        EAP/7" header-name="Server"/>
```

```
        <response-header name="x-powered-by-header" header-
        value="Undertow/1" header-name="X-Powered-By"/>
        <mod-cluster name="modcluster" advertise-socket-
        binding="modcluster" management-socket-binding="http"/>
    </filters>
</subsystem>
```

Now let's try to reach the `balancer.war` application which, is available on the backend, but pointing to the frontend server: `http://localhost:8090/balancer`

As you can see, the application is available through the frontend web server running on the port `8090`.When you are done with this example, you can shut down the frontend server as we are going to use the Apache web server to front our domain.

Advantages of an all-in-one solution

The Undertow based solution for load balancing is an elegant and simple pattern to provide a single point of access to a form of backend servers. This avoids some possible misalignments between Apache and your balancer module; also it keeps your environment in a supported perimeter. On the other hand, you might still need a wider set of web server/proxy options which are well consolidated on the Apache web server. Also, at the time of writing, the only management console for `mod_cluster` is available on `mod_cluster` bundles for Apache, although, you can query `mod_cluster` from the CLI to gather the balancer statistics.

Configuring mod_cluster with Apache

Before EAP 7, the only available option for using `mod_cluster` was fronting the application server with Apache web server, loaded with `mod_cluster` native libraries. `mod_cluster` native libraries need to be installed on the HTTPD side. These libraries will use an advertising channel to publish its address, and the advertising channel is actually an IP multicast group.

Which version of Apache can be used?

It is likely that you already have an Apache web server installation available; however, please note that, to be supported as an enterprise customer, you should use Apache version 2.2.14 or later. You can check your Apache version with `httpd -v`.

Installing mod_cluster on the Apache web server

Start by downloading `mod_cluster` from `http://mod-cluster.jboss.org/downloads`, `mod_cluster` binaries are distributed in three different formats:

- `mod_cluster` **modules for HTTPD**: This package includes the native modules to be installed on your own Apache web server
- `mod_cluster` **native bundles with HTTPD**: This package includes an Apache web server with an already bundled and configured `mod_cluster`
- `mod_cluster` **native bundles with HTTPD and openssl**: This package includes an Apache web server with an already bundled and configured `mod_cluster` and support for SSL

All formats are available for most operating systems: we will assume that you already have a running Apache web server instance so download the `mod_cluster` modules for HTTPD.

We also assume that your Apache installation is available on `/opt/httpd`. You can vary the following scripts accordingly.

Once you have downloaded the `mod_cluster` modules, uncompress them into an Apache modules directory:

```
tar zxvf mod_cluster-1.2.6.Final-linux2-x64-so.tar.gz -C
/opt/httpd/modules
```

Now, edit the `/opt/httpd/conf/httpd.conf` file and disable `mod_proxy_balancer` (which conflicts with `mod_cluster`) by commenting out the `LoadModule` directive for `mod_proxy_balancer.so`

```
#LoadModule proxy_balancer_module modules/mod_proxy_balancer.so
```

To keep your `mod_cluster` configuration in a separate file, create a new file named
`mod_cluster.conf` and place it into the `/opt/httpd/conf/extra` folder. Within this file,
include the following configuration:

```
LoadModule slotmem_module modules/mod_slotmem.so
LoadModule manager_module modules/mod_manager.so
LoadModule proxy_cluster_module modules/mod_proxy_cluster.so
LoadModule advertise_module modules/mod_advertise.so

Listen 127.0.0.1:6666

<VirtualHost 127.0.0.1:6666>
  <Directory "/">
    Order deny,allow
    Deny from all
    Allow from 127.0.0.1
  </Directory>

KeepAliveTimeout 60
MaxKeepAliveRequests 0
ManagerBalancerName mycluster
EnableMCPMReceive
AdvertiseFrequency 5
</VirtualHost>

<Location /manager>
    SetHandler mod_cluster-manager
    Order deny,allow
    Deny from all
    Allow from 127.0.0.1
</Location>
```

At first we have loaded the modules needed for `mod_cluster` communication and one
module (`mod_cluster-manager`) for basic balancer administration.

Within the **Virtual Host** section, we are allowing access only from the loop-back interface
address. In real-world scenarios, you would need to state an IP address or hostname. A
flexible policy is however used so, for example, by stating the IP address as `123.155` you
are going to allow all IP addresses starting with `123.155`:

```
<Directory "/">
   Order deny,allow
   Deny from all
   Allow from 123.155.
</Directory>
```

If you want to gain some more flexibility, you can also use hostnames and allow for reverse-DNS mapping for their IP addresses. As for IP addresses, you can also include part of the full qualified hostname.

A core directive included in the configuration is EnableMCPMReceive which allows the VirtualHost to receive MCPM traffic from the nodes. This is essential for the advertising mechanism to work.

> For security reasons EnableMCPMReceive should only be enabled on VirtualHosts with a port that is not publicly accessible; it should only be accessible to the JBoss backend servers that you want to use with the mod_cluster balancer.

Next, the context mapped with /manager is the mod_manager, which is a native module that reads information from EAP 7 and returns a minimal administration interface with the list of nodes which have been discovered by mod_cluster.

Now, edit the httpd.conf file to include the following directive, which will load the external mod_cluster configuration:

```
Include conf/extra/mod_cluster.conf
```

Restart Apache with the following command:

```
service httpd restart
```

Testing mod_cluster

Now if your domain is still running, point your browser to the following URL: http://127:0.0.1:6666/manager.

Since only the main-server-group is a ha profile, you should be able to see its nodes on the Apache web server:

---

mod_cluster/1.2.6.Final

Auto Refresh show DUMP output show INFO output

Node slave2:server3 (ajp://127.0.0.1:8309):

Enable Contexts Disable Contexts
Balancer: mycluster,LBGroup: ,Flushpackets: Off,Flushwait: 10000,Ping: 10000000,Smax: 26,Ttl: 60000000,Status: OK

Virtual Host 1:

Contexts:

/balancer, Status: ENABLED Request: 0 Disable

Aliases:

localhost
default-host

Node slave1:server1 (ajp://127.0.0.1:8009):

Enable Contexts Disable Contexts
Balancer: mycluster,LBGroup: ,Flushpackets: Off,Flushwait: 10000,Ping: 10000000,Smax: 26,Ttl: 60000000,Status: OK

Virtual Host 1:

Contexts:

/balancer, Status: ENABLED Request: 0 Disable

You should also be able to reach the `balancer` web application through the Apache default port (`80`):

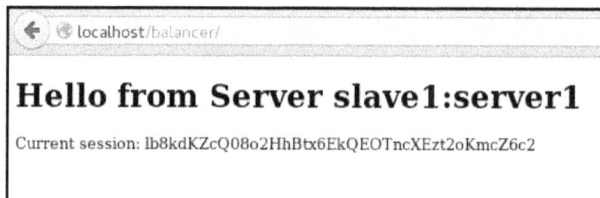

← ⊛ localhost/balancer/

Hello from Server slave1:server1

Current session: lb8kdKZcQ08o2HhBtx6EkQEOTncXEzt2oKmcZ6c2

In the next sections, we will cover some more advanced scenarios using `mod_cluster`. Before that, we will solve some common troubleshooting issues you might find.

Troubleshooting mod_cluster

Although this troubleshooting section might look lengthy, don't get overwhelmed by it. As with all network services, chances are that you will need to perform some network or security tweaks to your environment to allow communication between the server nodes and Apache.

Security checks

First of all, *if* you are running a Linux/Unix box the usual culprits are SELinux and iptables which might be blocking your messages. We will temporarily make your communication permissive to quickly identify if firewalls are blocking your communication. You can disable iptables, with root permission by issuing the following command:

```
# /etc/init.d/iptables stop
```

Making the SELinux security module permissive requires changing as root a configuration file. In RHEL or Fedora distributions you have to edit /etc/selinux/config. Search for the following line:

```
SELINUX=enforcing
```

Just change SELINUX=enforcing to SELINUX=permissive, and you're done. Reboot your machine for the changes to take effect.

If mod_cluster advertising now works correctly, then you should fine-tune your security policies to allow only multicast traffic. As an example, you can use the following iptables command to allow mod_cluster UDP traffic:

```
sudo iptables -I INPUT 1 -p udp -d 224.0.1.0/24 -j ACCEPT -m
comment --comment "allow mod_cluster udp multicast traffic"
```

Finally make your iptables rule persistent with the following command:

```
sudo /etc/init.d/iptables save
```

Network checking

The next block of checks is about multicast communication since by default mod_cluster relies on UDP multicast to transfer its packets. Checking if your network is running multicast can be done on a Linux machine with the ifconfig command as follows:

```
[root@localhost ~]# ifconfig
eth0: flags=4163<UP,BROADCAST,RUNNING> mtu 1500
inet 192.168.1.67 netmask 255.255.255.0 broadcast 192.168.1.255
inet6 fe80::6af7:28ff:fef3:b97d prefixlen 64 scopeid 0x20<link>
ether 68:f7:28:f3:b9:7d txqueuelen 1000 (Ethernet)
RX packets 26615 bytes 34887639 (33.2 MiB)
RX errors 0 dropped 0 overruns 0 frame 0
TX packets 18205 bytes 1842719 (1.7 MiB)
TX errors 0 dropped 0 overruns 0 carrier 0 collisions 0
device interrupt 20 memory 0xe1200000-e1220000
```

If the `multicast` attribute in the first line of your network card (`eth0` in our case) is not included, it's possible that your kernel has not been compiled with multicast support. This is however an unlikely circumstance. Before doing that, you can try enabling multicast on your network interface using `ifconfig`:

```
$ /sbin/ifconfig etho multicast
```

Next, check that multicast routing is configured, by running the `route` command:

```
$ /sbin/route -n
[root@localhost ~]# route -n
Kernel IP routing table
Destination  Gateway      Genmask      Flags Metric Ref  Use Iface
0.0.0.0      192.168.1.254 0.0.0.0       G    100    0    0   eth0
192.168.1.0  0.0.0.0      255.255.255.0 U    100    0    0   eth0
```

If the destination `224.0.0.0` entry is not present, you need to enable multicast routing by running the `route` command as `root`:

```
# /sbin/route -n add -net 224.0.0.0 netmask 240.0.0.0 dev eth0
```

Great. Now you should expect to find multicast available in your network card:

```
[root@localhost ~]# ifconfig
eth0: flags=4163<UP,BROADCAST,MULTICAST RUNNING> mtu 1500
inet 192.168.1.67 netmask 255.255.255.0 broadcast 192.168.1.255
inet6 fe80::6af7:28ff:fef3:b97d prefixlen 64 scopeid 0x20<link>
ether 68:f7:28:f3:b9:7d txqueuelen 1000 (Ethernet)
RX packets 26615 bytes 34887639 (33.2 MiB)
RX errors 0 dropped 0 overruns 0 frame 0
TX packets 18205 bytes 1842719 (1.7 MiB)
TX errors 0 dropped 0 overruns 0 carrier 0 collisions 0
device interrupt 20 memory 0xe1200000-e122000
```

If communication is working correctly, you should be able to scan for multicast packets using the network utility `tcpdump`, available on most Linux distributions:

```
tcpdump -i eth0 ip multicast
listening on eth0, link-type EN10MB (Ethernet), capture size
262144 bytes
22:11:29.036962 IP localhost.localdomain.23364 >
ntds1r.mcast.net.23364: UDP, length 312
22:11:32.571652 IP localhost.localdomain.55200 >
230.0.0.4.45688: UDP, length 105
22:11:32.885444 IP localhost.localdomain.55200 >
230.0.0.4.45688: UDP, length 83
```

Network checks for non-Linux machines

A Linux machine already includes clear-cut utilities for setting up your network. If you are not using a Linux distribution or you need to use a common approach, then you can turn to the `jgroups` test utilities bundled in the application server. Change your directory to the location where the `jgroups` core libraries are located:

```
cd modules/system/layers/base/org/jgroups/main
```

Now execute the `McastReceiverTest` class, a utility that can receive multicast packets. We will be passing as an argument the multicast address and port:

```
java -classpath jgroups-3.6.8.Final-redhat-2.jar
org.jgroups.tests.McastReceiverTest -mcast_addr 224.0.1.105 -
port 23364
```

Next, in another shell, also start the sender using the following shell:

```
java -classpath jgroups-3.6.8.Final-redhat-2.jar
org.jgroups.tests.McastSenderTest -mcast_addr 224.0.1.105
-port
23364
```

Type in some messages in the sender's shell.

You should be able to read the messages on the receiver application:

Configuring mod_cluster to use TCP transport

As we have already discussed, the `mod_cluster` subsystem uses UDP multicast as the default network transport. We have checked some options to verify if multicast is available or not. However, if for some reason multicast is not available in your network, you can switch to **TCP Unicast**, which provides a static list of servers for node discovery and communication instead.

TCP Unicast configuration is discussed in the next chapter, which covers extensively the `jgroups` configuration. Once you have configured TCP Unicast, your to-do-list on the `mod_cluster` side is pretty short. First disable advertising in your Apache `mod_cluster.conf` (or `httpd.conf`) file with the following directive:

```
ServerAdvertise Off
```

Next, disable advertising also within the `mod_cluster` subsystem of your EAP 7 configuration and provide a static list of Apache web servers. For example, in our domain configuration we could issue the following CLI command to disable advertising on the `ha` profile and specify the IP address as the HTTPD proxy :
`10.10.110.3`:

```
/profile=ha/subsystem=modcluster/mod-cluster-
config=configuration/:write-
attribute(name=advertise,value=false)
/profile=ha/subsystem=modcluster/mod-cluster-
config=configuration/:write-attribute(name=proxy-
list,value="10.10.110.3:6666")
```

Determining the optimal load configuration between Apache and JBoss

Choosing the optimal load balancing settings can require some time and is generally dependent on the applications you are delivering. Nevertheless, the load balancer tool, which is a web application available at `https://access.redhat.com/labs/lbconfig`, is considerably helpful. This tool can help you set up an optimal balance between Apache-based load balancers and JBoss EAP.

As you can see from the following picture, once you input the relevant settings about Apache/JBoss and network configuration, you will get some quick advice on the suggested environment settings:

Besides the suggested settings, the load balancer application also provides relevant code you can include in your `httpd.conf` configuration both for `mod_cluster` and older options such as `mod_jk` and `mod_proxy`.

Configuring balancing groups

Load balancing groups are an advanced feature of `mod_cluster` that can be used in conjunction with a distributed clustering mode (see `Chapter 6`, *Clustering EAP 7* for more on clustering). By using load balancer groups, you can divide your cluster into logical groups in order to minimize the bandwidth cost of data sent across the cluster. In the case of failover of a node, the `mod_cluster` balancer will failover to a node in the same balancing group.

> If you are migrating from a `mod_jk` configuration, this parameter is equivalent to `mod_jk`'s domain directive .

Let's see a practical example based (on our domain) servers that will be split into two balancing groups named **group1** and **group2** as depicted by this picture:

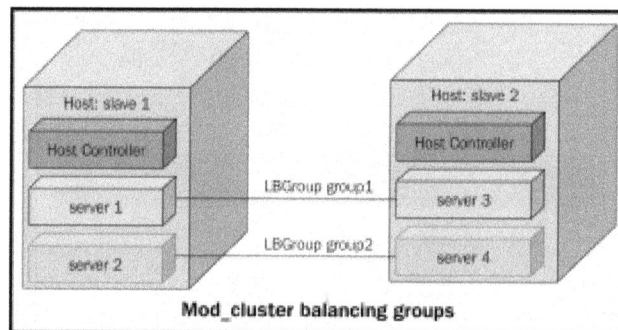

Mod_cluster balancing groups

For this purpose we will also setup the `other-server group` with an `ha` profile and `ha-sockets` so that its nodes will join the cluster as well:

```
/server-group=other-server-group:write-
  attribute(name=profile,value=ha)
/server-group=other-server-group:write-attribute(name=socket-
  binding-group,value=ha-sockets)
```

Also, we will need to deploy our balancing application on the other-server-group, too:

```
deploy /home/jboss/code/chapter5/balancer.war --server-
groups=other-server-group
```

Finally, we will start the other server group servers:

```
/server-group=other-server-group:start-servers
```

As a consequence, all server nodes in our domain will join the cluster. In order to determine the ownership of a group, we will store a system property on each server as follows:

```
/host=slave1/server-config=server1/system-
 property=modcluster.group/:add(value=group1)
/host=slave1/server-config=server2/system-
 property=modcluster.group/:add(value=group2)
/host=slave2/server-config=server3/system-
 property=modcluster.group/:add(value=group1)
/host=slave2/server-config=server4/system-
 property=modcluster.group/:add(value=group2)
```

Now issue the following command on the ha profile so that the load-balancing-group property is based on the modcluster.group property that we have set at the server level:

```
/profile=ha/subsystem=modcluster/mod-cluster-
config=configuration/:write-attribute(name=load-balancing-
group,value=${modcluster.group})
```

As a consequence, our cluster topology is still made up of four nodes, but it's partitioned into two groups. You can check from the mod-cluster manager that now each server is advertising its LBGroup:

LBGroup group1: <u>Enable Nodes</u> <u>Disable Nodes</u>

Node slave1: server1 (ajp://127.0.0.1:8009):

<u>Enable Contexts</u> <u>Disable Contexts</u>

Virtual Host 1:

Contexts:

/balancer, Status: ENABLED Requests: 0 <u>Disable</u>

Node slave2: server3 (ajp://127.0.0.1:8309):

<u>Enable Contexts</u> <u>Disable Contexts</u>

Virtual Host 1:

Contexts:

/balancer, Status: ENABLED Requests: 0 <u>Disable</u>

LBGroup group2: <u>Enable Nodes</u> <u>Disable Nodes</u>

Node slave2: server4 (ajp://127.0.0.1:8459):

<u>Enable Contexts</u> <u>Disable Contexts</u>

Virtual Host 1:

Contexts:

/balancer, Status: ENABLED Requests: 0 <u>Disable</u>

Node slave1: server2 (ajp://127.0.0.1:8109):

<u>Enable Contexts</u> <u>Disable Contexts</u>

Virtual Host 1:

Contexts:

/balancer, Status: ENABLED Requests: 0 <u>Disable</u>

You can test the balancing group feature by first requesting the application to `mod_cluster`:

`localhost`/balancer/

Hello from Server slave2:server3

Current session: _saX8DnRc8t6a5RvyubFTXIQAgQ_NNxOsA4q6o57

In this case, the request was a server by the `server3` node, part of the LBGroup **group1**. Since sticky sessions are turned on by default on `mod_cluster`, subsequent requests of the same session will be maintained on the same server. However, in the case of `server3` failing, you can check that the request will be handled by `server1`, the other member of LBGroup **group1**:

> localhost/balancer/
>
> # Hello from Server slave1:server1
>
> Current session: _saX8DnRc8t6a5RvyubFTXIQAgQ_NNxOsA4q6o57

In the case of the failure of all nodes in the balancing group, the request will be handled by other cluster members, if any, and the session will be transferred onto the survivor nodes.

Why use balancing groups?

The practical advantage of using load balancer groups in a cluster is that you can partition the balancing of data in your cluster in a deterministic way, assuming that you are not using full replication (where data is replicated across all server nodes in the cluster). After setting the load balancing group info (LBGroup) in your EAP 7 configuration, this information will then be sent to the Apache web server through the mod_cluster management protocol (MCMP), as part of the request. This allows for a proper balancing and partitioning of the cluster data, so that in the case of a node failing, subsequent requests will be sent to another node in the same group.

Configuring mod_cluster balancing factors

A core feature of `mod_cluster` is the ability to use backend load metrics to determine how best to balance requests. The built-in configuration of `mod_cluster` distributes requests using the CPU by default:

```
<subsystem xmlns="urn:jboss:domain:modcluster:2.0">
  <mod-cluster-config advertise-socket="modcluster"
   connector="ajp">
    <dynamic-load-provider>
      <load-metric type="cpu"/>
    </dynamic-load-provider>
  </mod-cluster-config>
</subsystem>
```

A set of different metrics is available so that you can balance the load based on other variables. The following metric types are supported:

Metric	Description
cpu	Balances on the CPU usage
mem	Balances on the system memory usage
heap	Balances on the heap percentage usage
sessions	Balances on active sessions
busyness	Balances on the percentage of connector threads from the thread pool that are busy servicing requests
connection-pool	Balances on the percentage of connections from a connection pool that are in use
receive-traffic	Balances on the incoming request traffic in KB/sec
send-traffic	Balances on the outgoing request traffic in KB/sec

Each metric can be computed using two variables: weight and capacity. The **weight** (by default 1) indicates the impact of a metric with respect to the other metrics. The **capacity**, on the other hand, can be used for fine-grained control over the load metrics. By setting a different capacity for each metric, you can actually favor one node instead of another while preserving the metric weights.

Here is, for example, how to vary the load-metric for your ha profile to include heap memory usage as a factor with weight = 2:

```
/profile=ha/subsystem=modcluster/mod-cluster-
config=configuration:add-metric(type=heap, weight=2,
capacity=1)
```

Adding custom mod_cluster metrics

The list of metrics can be expanded by your own developed metrics, which need to extend the org.jboss.modcluster.container.Engine.AbstractLoadMetric that serves as a superclass for all mod_cluster metrics. As a template, consider the HeapMemoryUsageLoadMetric class that overrides the getLoad method of the org.jboss.modcluster.load.metric.impl.AbstractLoadMetric to provide a load-metric based on the **heap memory usage** of the node:

```
public class HeapMemoryUsageLoadMetric extends AbstractLoadMetric {
 private final MemoryMXBean bean;

public HeapMemoryUsageLoadMetric() {

this(ManagementFactory.getMemoryMXBean());
}

 public HeapMemoryUsageLoadMetric(MemoryMXBean bean) {
  this.bean = bean;
 }

 @Override
 public double getLoad(Engine engine) throws Exception {
  MemoryUsage usage = this.bean.getHeapMemoryUsage();
  long max = usage.getMax();
  double used = usage.getUsed();
  // Max may be undefined, so fall back to committed
  return used / ((max >= 0) ? max : usage.getCommitted());
 }
}
```

The load range is returned by the `getLoad` method with a range of 0 to 1 (1 being the max load, 0 being no load).

Once you have crafted your custom metric class, pack it in a JAR file, say `custom-metric.jar`, and include it in the `mod_cluster`'s `module.xml` file located in the `modules\system\layers\base\org\jboss\mod_cluster\container\spi\main` folder:

```
<module xmlns="urn:jboss:module:1.3" name="org.jboss.mod_cluster.core">
    <properties>
        <property name="jboss.api" value="private"/>
    </properties>

    <resources>
        <resource-root path="mod_cluster-core-1.3.2.Final-redhat-1.jar"/>
        <resource-root path="custom-metric.jar"/>

    </resources>
    . . .
</module>
```

Your metric is now ready to be used by your configuration. For example, if your custom metric class is named `com.acme.CustomMetric`, you can use the class attribute of the `custom-load-metric` element as follows:

```
<subsystem xmlns="urn:jboss:domain:modcluster:2.0">
  <mod-cluster-config advertise-socket="modcluster"
   connector="ajp">
    <dynamic-load-provider>
      <custom-load-metric class="com.acme.CustomMetric"/>
    </dynamic-load-provider>
  </mod-cluster-config>
</subsystem>
```

Using other balancing solutions

mod_cluster is Red Hat's only supported balancing solution. A minor exception to this rule is Apache's mod_jk, which is supported on the **Enterprise Web Server** (https://www.redhat.com/en/resources/jboss-enterprise-web-server) configured with EAP on a RHEL server. Chances are however that some different balancing solutions are dictated by your company's standards so we will shortly include their configuration with our domain of servers.

Configuring mod_jk

Apache mod_jk is a single native module, the mod_jk.so module, which needs to be installed on Apache to forward requests to JBoss EAP using the AJP protocol. Here is a quick list of the steps needed to install mod_jk:

1. Copy the mod_jk module (downloadable from https://tomcat.apache.org/download-connectors.cgi) on Apache:

   ```
   $ cp mod_jk.so $APACHE_HOME/modules
   ```

2. Create a configuration file in the conf folder of Apache named, for example, mod_jk.conf, with the following content:

   ```
   LoadModule jk_module modules/mod_jk.so
   # Where to find workers.properties
   JkWorkersFile conf/workers.properties
   # Where to put jk logs
   JkLogFile logs/mod_jk.log
   # Set the jk log level [debug/error/info]
   JkLogLevel info
   # Mount your applications
   JkMount /balancer/* loadbalancer
   JkShmFile logs/jk.shm
   ```

3. Within this file we are passing requests to the `balancer` web application to `mod_jk`'s load-balancer. Include a reference to this file in `httpd.conf`:

```
Include conf/mod-jk.conf
```

4. Finally, the `workers.properties`, where you specify a list of available nodes, follows here; settings are compatible with our domain:

```
worker.list=loadbalancer,status
# Define server1
worker.server1.port=8009
worker.server1.host=localhost
worker.server1.type=ajp13
worker.server1.lbfactor=1
# Define server2
worker.server2.port=8159
worker.server2.host=localhost
worker.server2.type=ajp13
worker.server2.lbfactor=1
# Define server3
worker.server3.port=8309
worker.server3.host=localhost
worker.server3.type=ajp13
worker.server3.lbfactor=1
# Define server4
worker.server4.port=8459
worker.server4.host=localhost
worker.server4.type=ajp13
worker.server4.lbfactor=1
# Load-balancing behavior
worker.loadbalancer.type=lb
worker.loadbalancer.balance_workers=server1,
server2,server3,server4
worker.loadbalancer.sticky_session=1
worker.status.type=status
```

5. Restart the Apache web server to allow the changes.

By default the `ajp` listener is active on ha profiles; however, you can activate AJP communication on other profiles, such as `full`, for example, with the following CLI:

```
/profile=full/subsystem=undertow/server=default-server/ajp-
listener=default-ajp:add(socket-binding=ajp)
```

Configuring mod_proxy

Apache `mod_proxy` is natively included in the Apache web server so its advantage is that you don't need to download any library and that its configuration is pretty simple and concise. The following directive needs to be included in your Apache `httpd.conf` file in order to enable it:

```
LoadModule proxy_module modules/mod_proxy.so
```

Then, include the following directives in your `httpd.conf` file for any web application that you wish to forward to JBoss EAP. For example, in our case:

```
ProxyPass /balancer http://localhost:8080/balancer
ProxyPassReverse /balancer http://localhost:8080/balancer
ProxyPass /balancer http://localhost:8230/balancer
ProxyPassReverse /balancer http://localhost:8230/balancer
ProxyPass /balancer http://localhost:8380/balancer
ProxyPassReverse /balancer http://localhost:8380/balancer
ProxyPass /balancer http://localhost:8530/balancer
ProxyPassReverse /balancer http://localhost:8530/balancer
```

The preceding configuration will proxy requests from Apache using the HTTP protocol. For the sake of completeness, we will also mention that an Apache native module is also available for AJP communication. The module is called `mod_proxy_ajp` and can be configured in much the same way on `httpd.conf` as follows:

```
LoadModule proxy_module_ajp modules/mod_proxy_ajp.so

ProxyPass /balancer ajp://localhost:8009/balancer
ProxyPassReverse /balancer http://localhost:8009/balancer
ProxyPass /balancer ajp://localhost:8159/balancer
ProxyPassReverse /balancer http://localhost:8159/balancer
ProxyPass /balancer ajp://localhost:8309/balancer
ProxyPassReverse /balancer http://localhost:8309/balancer
ProxyPass /balancer ajp://localhost:8309/balancer
ProxyPassReverse /balancer http://localhost:8459/balancer
```

Configuring Nginx load balancer

Nginx is an open-source, high-performance web server capable of handling a huge number of concurrent connections easily thanks to its non-blocking I/O, event-driven model. Configuring nginx with JBoss EAP just requires few a directives to be included in your nginx configuration. Here is a sample configuration file (located by default in `/etc/nginx/nginx.conf`) that is able to connect to our domain of servers:

```
server {
listen 80;
server_name localhost;

    location /balancer {
        proxy_set_header Host $host;
        proxy_set_header X-Real-IP $remote_addr;
        proxy_set_header X-Forwarded-For $proxy_add_x_forwarded_for;
        proxy_pass http://mycluster;
    }

    upstream mycluster {
    # Use IP Hash for session persistence
        ip_hash;

        server localhost:8080;
        server localhost:8230;
        server localhost:8380;
        server localhost:8530;
    }

}
```

As you can see, to configure load balancing we have created an `upstream group` named `mycluster` that lists the backend servers available. With the `ip_hash` directive, nginx calculates for every request a hash based on the client's IP address, and associates the hash with one of the listed upstream servers. This is used to send all requests with that hash to the same server, thus establishing a sticky session.

Summary

In this chapter, we have extensively covered all the options available to balance requests to a set of backend servers with special focus on `mod_cluster`, which is the most advanced (and supported) solution in the scope of Red Hat products. We have learnt how to install it, configure it, and troubleshoot most common issues both as a standalone load balancer and when embedded in the Apache web server. Besides this, you had some exposure to balancing solutions such as `mod_proxy`, `mod_jk`, and `nginx`. In the next chapter we will delve into clustering, covering the JGroups and infinispan subsystems.

6
Clustering EAP 7

In the previous chapter, we learned how to provide high availability to our system infrastructure based on JBoss EAP 7.

In this chapter, we will learn the following topics:

- Clustering overview and misconceptions
- Clustering in standalone mode
- Clustering from a network point of view
- Clustering in domain mode
- Clustering using TCP
- EJBs in a clustered environment

We will also see how to troubleshoot network and application issues.

Clustering overview and misconceptions

Clustering is the ability to mitigate and take care of server failures, such as JVM crashes, physical server crashes, network unavailability, and everything that can take down your system.

Clustering means that when your application is running on a server, it can continue its task on another server exactly at the same point it was at, without any manual failover. This means that the application's state is replicated across cluster members.

The term clustering is meant at the application level; it's not a system cluster, thus at OS level. Hence, your applications, at least your web application, needs to be cluster aware, which means that it needs to be declared as distributable in its deployment descriptor, as follows:

```
<web-app>
   <distributable/>
</web-app>
```

Pretty easy, right?

> One more thing that you should keep in mind is that clustering a stateless application does not make sense, so your RESTful Web services do **not** need clustering, but they do need high availability, which is achieved by a load balancing technique, as explained in `Chapter 5`, *Load Balancing*.

The following is a diagram that depicts the failover capability:

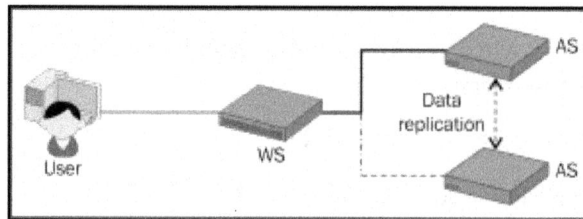

Clustering schema

Essentially, when the user first accesses your application, the web server (the load balancer **WS**) forwards the user's request to an application server (the red **AS** one), which creates the user's session and it stores the user's data.

The user keeps working on their tasks, regardless of the underlying environment (one server or several servers could compose the latter). At a certain time, the server that was serving the user's application, becomes unavailable, for some reason. At this point, the web server would forward the user's requests to a new application server (the green AS one).

At this point, the user would lose all of their work, but because the good system administrator cares about their users, they enabled failover, so all the user's data got replicated across the other servers. This means that all data needs to be `java.io.Serializable`.

The user without even knowing about server unavailability, can finish their task successfully.

To get the clustering feature, JBoss provides two profiles:

- ha
- full-ha

The first one is meant to be used by web applications and EJB modules; the second one is meant to be used by JMS, or more generally, messaging applications.

In this book, we have a dedicated chapter about messaging, so for a deep-dive into it refer to Chapter 10, *Messaging Administration*.

So clustering is about failover, and the automatic failover is handled in JBoss by two components: Infinispan and JGroups.

Infinispan is an open source project and it's one of the major projects in the JBoss community.

> Infinispan is a high-performing caching system, also used to store in-memory objects such as HTTP sessions, database entities, and EJBs. If you want to know a lot more about Infinispan, you may want to take a look at two titles available on Packt Publishing's site:
> https://www.packtpub.com/big-data-and-business-intelligence/infinispan-data-grid-platform
> https://www.packtpub.com/big-data-and-business-intelligence/infinispan-data-grid-platform-definitive-guide

Infinispan is configured in JBoss via its subsystem and the default configuration looks as follows:

```
<subsystem xmlns="urn:jboss:domain:infinispan:4.0">
   <cache-container name="server" aliases="singleton cluster"
    default-cache="default" module=
    "org.wildfly.clustering.server">
      <transport lock-timeout="60000"/>
      <replicated-cache name="default" mode="SYNC">
         <transaction mode="BATCH"/>
      </replicated-cache>
   </cache-container>
   <cache-container name="web" default-cache="dist"
    module="org.wildfly.clustering.web.infinispan">
      <transport lock-timeout="60000"/>
      <distributed-cache name="dist" mode="ASYNC"
       l1-lifespan="0" owners="2">
         <locking isolation="REPEATABLE_READ"/>
         <transaction mode="BATCH"/>
         <file-store/>
      </distributed-cache>
   </cache-container>
   <cache-container name="ejb" aliases="sfsb" default-
    cache="dist" module="org.wildfly.clustering.ejb.infinispan">
      <transport lock-timeout="60000"/>
      <distributed-cache name="dist" mode="ASYNC"
```

```
                l1-lifespan="0" owners="2">
                    <locking isolation="REPEATABLE_READ"/>
                    <transaction mode="BATCH"/>
                    <file-store/>
                </distributed-cache>
        </cache-container>
        <cache-container name="hibernate" default-cache="local-query"
         module="org.hibernate.infinispan">
                <transport lock-timeout="60000"/>
                <invalidation-cache name="entity" mode="SYNC">
                    <transaction mode="NON_XA"/>
                    <eviction strategy="LRU" max-entries="10000"/>
                    <expiration max-idle="100000"/>
                </invalidation-cache>
                <local-cache name="local-query">
                    <eviction strategy="LRU" max-entries="10000"/>
                    <expiration max-idle="100000"/>
                </local-cache>
                <replicated-cache name="timestamps" mode="ASYNC"/>
        </cache-container>
    </subsystem>
```

As you can see, Infinispan provides by default four different cache containers, which in turn contain the caches and their configuration. We will come back to Infinispan configuration and its details later on in this chapter.

To achieve automatic failover, JBoss uses another component called JGroups.

JGroups is another open source project from the JBoss community, and it has a tiny memory footprint of just 2 megabytes. It's a pluggable protocol stack framework used for network communication between systems. JBoss uses it to provide its clustering capabilities.

JGroups is configured in JBoss via its subsystem and the default configuration looks as follows:

```
<subsystem xmlns="urn:jboss:domain:jgroups:4.0">
    <channels default="ee">
        <channel name="ee" stack="udp"/>
    </channels>
    <stacks>
        <stack name="udp">
            <transport type="UDP" socket-binding="jgroups-udp"/>
            <protocol type="PING"/>
            <protocol type="MERGE3"/>
            <protocol type="FD_SOCK" socket-binding="jgroups-
             udp-fd"/>
            <protocol type="FD_ALL"/>
```

```
        <protocol type="VERIFY_SUSPECT"/>
        <protocol type="pbcast.NAKACK2"/>
        <protocol type="UNICAST3"/>
        <protocol type="pbcast.STABLE"/>
        <protocol type="pbcast.GMS"/>
        <protocol type="UFC"/>
        <protocol type="MFC"/>
        <protocol type="FRAG2"/>
    </stack>
    <stack name="tcp">
        <transport type="TCP" socket-binding="jgroups-tcp"/>
        <protocol type="MPING" socket-binding=
         "jgroups-mping"/>
        <protocol type="MERGE3"/>
        <protocol type="FD_SOCK" socket-binding=
         "jgroups-tcp-fd"/>
        <protocol type="FD"/>
        <protocol type="VERIFY_SUSPECT"/>
        <protocol type="pbcast.NAKACK2"/>
        <protocol type="UNICAST3"/>
        <protocol type="pbcast.STABLE"/>
        <protocol type="pbcast.GMS"/>
        <protocol type="MFC"/>
        <protocol type="FRAG2"/>
    </stack>
  </stacks>
</subsystem>
```

As you can see, JGroups provides by default two different stacks, named udp and tcp, each one with its own particular protocol stack. We will come back to JGroups configuration and its details later in this chapter.

Clustering in standalone mode

As previously mentioned, to get clustering capabilities you need to use either the ha profile or the full-ha profile. We will stick with the ha profile for now. In standalone mode, this means that your configuration file is meant to be the one named standalone-ha.xml.

Let's give a first run to the default configuration and let's see what happens.

Do as follows:

```
cd $JBOSS_HOME
cp -a standalone cluster-1
$JBOSS_HOME/bin/standalone.sh -Djboss.server.base.dir=cluster-1 --
server-config=standalone-ha.xml
```

We first cloned the standalone folder to the `cluster-1` folder. Then we used the `cluster-1` folder as the server base directory, and then used the `standalone-ha.xml` file as the server configuration file.

That's because, by default, `standalone.sh` uses `standalone` as the base directory and `standalone.xml` as the configuration file.

Once your `cluster-1` instance started, did you see any cluster topology information? I guess you didn't. Is this because we are just running one instance instead of two or more? Nope. It's not that.

Because all JBoss's services are activated on demand, clustering capabilities do not make an exception. So, we need a cluster-aware application to have our clustering services turned on in JBoss.

For this chapter, we've arranged a Git repository for you, which you will find at the following site: `https://github.com/mjbeap7`.

The repository for this chapter is called `ch06`, so you need to clone it locally in your computer, into a folder of your choice that we will refer to as `$GIT_MJBEAP7`. To do this, just run the following command:

```
git clone https://github.com/mjbeap7/ch06
Cloning into 'ch06'...
remote: Counting objects: 4, done.
remote: Total 4 (delta 0), reused 0 (delta 0), pack-reused 4
Unpacking objects: 100% (4/4), done.
Checking connectivity... done.
```

And to build our cluster-aware application, issue the following Maven command:

```
cd $GIT_MJBEAP7/ch06
mvn -e clean package -f cluster-test/pom.xml
```

Once done, you should find your WAR bundle ready to be deployed, into the `cluster-test/target` folder.

With our EAP instance up and running, drop the WAR into the `deployment` folder of our `cluster-1` instance, and have a look at the log. You should find similar entries:

```
01:41:47,354 INFO  [org.jboss.as.repository] (management-handler-thread - 7) WFLYDR0001: Content added at location /opt/rh/jboss-eap-7.0/cluster-1/data/co
ntent/a6/c18d6f5382b3ab9faf290b9111f97235f59a18/content
01:41:47,378 INFO  [org.jboss.as.server.deployment] (MSC service thread 1-8) WFLYSRV0027: Starting deployment of "cluster-test.war" (runtime-name: "cluste
r-test.war")
01:41:48,031 WARN  [org.jgroups.protocols.UDP] (MSC service thread 1-2) JGRP000015: the send buffer of socket ManagedDatagramSocketBinding was set to 1MB,
 but the OS only allocated 212.99KB. This might lead to performance problems. Please set your max send buffer in the OS correctly (e.g. net.core.wmem_max
 on Linux)
01:41:48,032 WARN  [org.jgroups.protocols.UDP] (MSC service thread 1-2) JGRP000015: the receive buffer of socket ManagedDatagramSocketBinding was set to 2
0MB, but the OS only allocated 212.99KB. This might lead to performance problems. Please set your max receive buffer in the OS correctly (e.g. net.core.rm
em_max on Linux)
01:41:48,032 WARN  [org.jgroups.protocols.UDP] (MSC service thread 1-2) JGRP000015: the send buffer of socket ManagedMulticastSocketBinding was set to 1MB
, but the OS only allocated 212.99KB. This might lead to performance problems. Please set your max send buffer in the OS correctly (e.g. net.core.wmem_max
 on Linux)
01:41:48,033 WARN  [org.jgroups.protocols.UDP] (MSC service thread 1-2) JGRP000015: the receive buffer of socket ManagedMulticastSocketBinding was set to
25MB, but the OS only allocated 212.99KB. This might lead to performance problems. Please set your max receive buffer in the OS correctly (e.g. net.core.r
mem_max on Linux)
01:41:51,658 INFO  [org.infinispan.remoting.transport.jgroups.JGroupsTransport] (MSC service thread 1-5) ISPN000078: Starting JGroups channel ejb
01:41:51,659 INFO  [org.infinispan.remoting.transport.jgroups.JGroupsTransport] (MSC service thread 1-8) ISPN000078: Starting JGroups channel web
01:41:51,659 INFO  [org.infinispan.remoting.transport.jgroups.JGroupsTransport] (MSC service thread 1-4) ISPN000078: Starting JGroups channel server
01:41:51,658 INFO  [org.infinispan.remoting.transport.jgroups.JGroupsTransport] (MSC service thread 1-2) ISPN000078: Starting JGroups channel hibernate
01:41:51,675 INFO  [org.infinispan.remoting.transport.jgroups.JGroupsTransport] (MSC service thread 1-2) ISPN000094: Received new cluster view for channel
hibernate: [dev|0] (1) [dev]
01:41:51,676 INFO  [org.infinispan.remoting.transport.jgroups.JGroupsTransport] (MSC service thread 1-8) ISPN000094: Received new cluster view for channel
web: [dev|0] (1) [dev]
01:41:51,675 INFO  [org.infinispan.remoting.transport.jgroups.JGroupsTransport] (MSC service thread 1-4) ISPN000094: Received new cluster view for channel
server: [dev|0] (1) [dev]
01:41:51,680 INFO  [org.infinispan.remoting.transport.jgroups.JGroupsTransport] (MSC service thread 1-5) ISPN000094: Received new cluster view for channel
ejb: [dev|0] (1) [dev]
01:41:51,683 INFO  [org.infinispan.remoting.transport.jgroups.JGroupsTransport] (MSC service thread 1-4) ISPN000079: Channel server local address is dev,
physical addresses are [192.168.59.103:55200]
01:41:51,684 INFO  [org.infinispan.remoting.transport.jgroups.JGroupsTransport] (MSC service thread 1-2) ISPN000079: Channel hibernate local address is de
v, physical addresses are [192.168.59.103:55200]
01:41:51,683 INFO  [org.infinispan.remoting.transport.jgroups.JGroupsTransport] (MSC service thread 1-8) ISPN000079: Channel web local address is dev, phy
sical addresses are [192.168.59.103:55200]
01:41:51,688 INFO  [org.infinispan.factories.GlobalComponentRegistry] (MSC service thread 1-2) ISPN000128: Infinispan version: Infinispan 'Infinite Darkne
ss' 8.0.1.Final-redhat-1
01:41:51,697 INFO  [org.infinispan.configuration.cache.EvictionConfigurationBuilder] (ServerService Thread Pool -- 68) ISPN000152: Passivation configured
without an eviction policy being selected. Only manually evicted entities will be passivated.
01:41:51,700 INFO  [org.infinispan.configuration.cache.EvictionConfigurationBuilder] (ServerService Thread Pool -- 68) ISPN000152: Passivation configured
without an eviction policy being selected. Only manually evicted entities will be passivated.
01:41:51,702 INFO  [org.infinispan.configuration.cache.EvictionConfigurationBuilder] (ServerService Thread Pool -- 71) ISPN000152: Passivation configured
without an eviction policy being selected. Only manually evicted entities will be passivated.
01:41:51,704 INFO  [org.infinispan.configuration.cache.EvictionConfigurationBuilder] (ServerService Thread Pool -- 71) ISPN000152: Passivation configured
without an eviction policy being selected. Only manually evicted entities will be passivated.
01:41:51,705 INFO  [org.infinispan.remoting.transport.jgroups.JGroupsTransport] (MSC service thread 1-5) ISPN000079: Channel ejb local address is dev, phy
sical addresses are [192.168.59.103:55200]
01:41:51,705 INFO  [org.infinispan.configuration.cache.EvictionConfigurationBuilder] (ServerService Thread Pool -- 68) ISPN000152: Passivation configured
without an eviction policy being selected. Only manually evicted entities will be passivated.
01:41:51,709 INFO  [org.infinispan.configuration.cache.EvictionConfigurationBuilder] (ServerService Thread Pool -- 68) ISPN000152: Passivation configured
without an eviction policy being selected. Only manually evicted entities will be passivated.
01:41:51,986 INFO  [org.jboss.as.clustering.infinispan] (ServerService Thread Pool -- 68) WFLYCLINF0002: Started routing cache from web container
01:41:51,986 INFO  [org.jboss.as.clustering.infinispan] (ServerService Thread Pool -- 71) WFLYCLINF0002: Started cluster-test.war cache from web container
01:41:52,228 INFO  [org.wildfly.extension.undertow] (ServerService Thread Pool -- 71) WFLYUT0021: Registered web context: /cluster-test
01:41:52,285 INFO  [org.jboss.as.server] (management-handler-thread - 7) WFLYSRV0010: Deployed "cluster-test.war" (runtime-name : "cluster-test.war")
```

Clustering – Logging information

Despite the WARN entries, those that I've highlighted in the preceding screenshot are the ones we want. They say that the cluster has received a new view, with 1 member named dev (that is actually my physical server name).

Now let's add another member to the cluster by issuing the following commands:

```
cd $JBOSS_HOME
cp -a standalone cluster-2
cp cluster-1/deployments/cluster-test.war cluster-2/deployments
$JBOSS_HOME/bin/standalone.sh
-Djboss.server.base.dir=cluster-2 --server-config=standalone-
```

```
ha.xml -Djboss.socket.binding.port-offset=100
```

Once done, have a look at the `cluster-1` log entries. Here is what you should find:

```
01:47:18,778 INFO [org.infinispan.remoting.transport.jgroups.JGroupsTransport] (Incoming-2,ee,dev) ISPN000094: Received new cluster view for channel serv
er: [dev|1] (2) [dev, dev]
01:47:18,780 INFO [org.infinispan.remoting.transport.jgroups.JGroupsTransport] (Incoming-2,ee,dev) ISPN000094: Received new cluster view for channel web:
[dev|1] (2) [dev, dev]
01:47:18,783 INFO [org.infinispan.remoting.transport.jgroups.JGroupsTransport] (Incoming-2,ee,dev) ISPN000094: Received new cluster view for channel ejb:
[dev|1] (2) [dev, dev]
01:47:18,785 INFO [org.infinispan.remoting.transport.jgroups.JGroupsTransport] (Incoming-2,ee,dev) ISPN000094: Received new cluster view for channel hibe
rnate: [dev|1] (2) [dev, dev]
01:47:19,827 INFO [org.infinispan.CLUSTER] (remote-thread--p5-t1) ISPN000310: Starting cluster-wide rebalance for cache routing, topology CacheTopology{i
d=1, rebalanceId=1, currentCH=DefaultConsistentHash{ns=80, owners = (1)[dev: 80+0]}, pendingCH=DefaultConsistentHash{ns=80, owners = (2)[dev: 40+40, dev:
40+40]}, unionCH=null, actualMembers=[dev, dev]}
01:47:19,849 INFO [org.infinispan.CLUSTER] (remote-thread--p5-t2) ISPN000310: Starting cluster-wide rebalance for cache cluster-test.war, topology CacheT
opology{id=1, rebalanceId=1, currentCH=DefaultConsistentHash{ns=80, owners = (1)[dev: 80+0]}, pendingCH=DefaultConsistentHash{ns=80, owners = (2)[dev: 40+
40, dev: 40+40]}, unionCH=null, actualMembers=[dev, dev]}
01:47:20,039 INFO [org.infinispan.CLUSTER] (remote-thread--p5-t2) ISPN000336: Finished cluster-wide rebalance for cache cluster-test.war, topology id = 1
01:47:20,085 INFO [org.infinispan.CLUSTER] (remote-thread--p5-t2) ISPN000336: Finished cluster-wide rebalance for cache routing, topology id = 1
```

Clustering – Two members

The cluster has received a new view, now with 2 members named `dev` and `dev`.

Yes, I know even if it's right, it's not nice, and we should use different names. Let's do it. What we need is to just add the `jboss.node.name` property and specify its value when we launch the instance. For the instance named `cluster-1`, do as follows:

```
$JBOSS_HOME/bin/standalone.sh
-Djboss.server.base.dir=cluster-1 --server-config=standalone-
ha.xml -Djboss.node.name=cluster-1
...
03:34:15,149 INFO
[org.infinispan.remoting.transport.jgroups.JGroupsTransport]
(MSC service thread 1-7) ISPN000094: Received new cluster
view for channel web: [cluster-1|0] (1) [cluster-1]
...
```

For the instance named `cluster-2`, do as follows:

```
$JBOSS_HOME/bin/standalone.sh
-Djboss.server.base.dir=cluster-2 --server-config=standalone-
ha.xml -Djboss.socket.binding.port-offset=100
-Djboss.node.name=cluster-2
...
03:35:13,251 INFO
[org.infinispan.remoting.transport.jgroups.JGroupsTransport]
(MSC service thread 1-6) ISPN000094: Received new cluster view
for channel web: [cluster-1|1] (2) [cluster-1, cluster-2]
...
```

As you can see from the previous log entries, you can discern which member has joined the cluster. Furthermore, there is some hermetic information in log entries that the wise JGroups lead developer (Mr. Bela Ban) has traced for us.

Let's investigate the previous logs by just keeping the content we need:

```
LOG1... [cluster-1|0]  (1)  [cluster-1]
LOG2... [cluster-1|1]  (2)  [cluster-1, cluster-2]
```

From the preceding code, we can say:

- LOG1
    - The instance named cluster-1 is the coordinator; it owns cluster topology
    - Cluster topology has never changed (zero 0)
    - The cluster was composed by one member
    - The list of the member of the cluster is composed of cluster-1

- LOG2
    - The instance named cluster-1 is the coordinator; it owns cluster topology
    - Cluster topology has changed 1 time
    - The cluster was composed by two members
    - The list of the member of the cluster is composed of cluster-1 and cluster-2

So here is the pattern to gather the cluster view information provided by JGroups into the log:

```
[cluster-topology-coordinator|view_changes]
(number_of_members) [comma_separated_cluster_members_list]
```

Try yourself to stop and start instances, and check whether everything works correctly. Bear in mind that if you stop all cluster members, all cluster information will be reset.

Testing in standalone mode

So far we have just looked at the log, now it's time to look at the application we deployed, in our cluster-1 and cluster-2 instances, still up and running. Open your browser and point to the following URL:
http://localhost:8080/cluster-test/

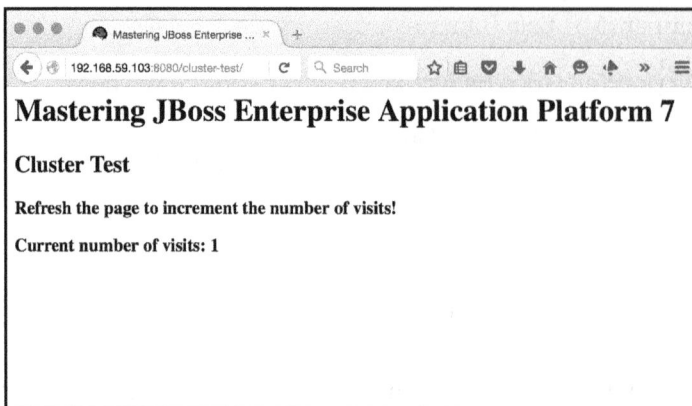

Cluster application running on a cluster-1 instance

In your `cluster-1` instance's log, you should find the following entries:

```
21:45:38,075 INFO  [stdout] (default task-1)
*******************************+
21:45:38,076 INFO  [stdout] (default task-1) Number of visits: 1
21:45:38,076 INFO  [stdout] (default task-1)
*******************************+
```

If you refresh the page a few times, the number of visits should increase accordingly – I refreshed the page three times, getting four as the total number of visits.

Now, let's point the browser to the `cluster-2` instance's URL, by changing the port number to `8180` as follows: `http://localhost:8180/cluster-test/`.

What we should see is the same page as the preceding screenshot, with the number of visits incremented by one, as follows:

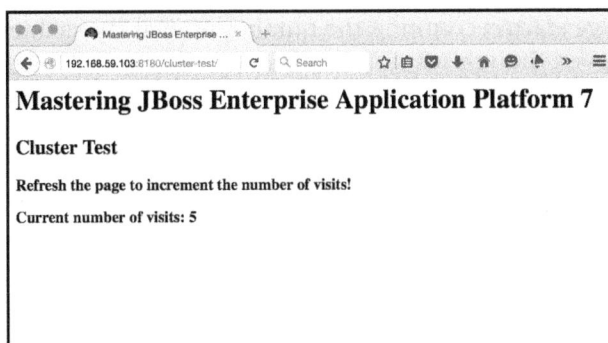

Cluster application running on a cluster-2 instance

And in the `cluster-2` instance's log, you should find the following entries:

```
21:54:15,331 INFO  [stdout] (default task-1)
********************************+
21:54:15,331 INFO  [stdout] (default task-1) Number of visits: 5
21:54:15,332 INFO  [stdout] (default task-1)
********************************+
```

To be very sure, let's refresh the page until the number of visits hits 10, and then let's stop the `cluster-2` instance.

Now that the `cluster-2` instance is down, we cannot access the application from it, as we will get an `Unable to connect` error from the browser. We then need to point the browser back to the `cluster-1` instance's URL and load the page. The page from the `cluster-1` instance looks as follows:

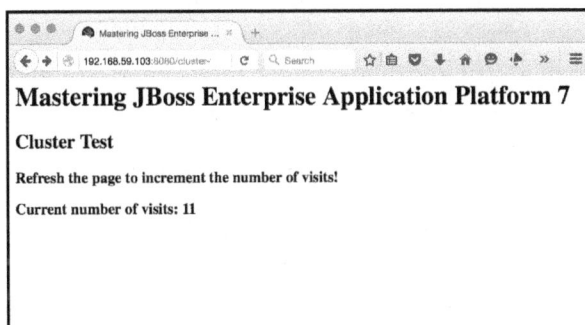

Cluster application running back on a cluster-1 instance

As you can see, the page started counting the number of visits we achieved on the `cluster-2` instance, even though we first stopped the `cluster-2` instance and then switched the `cluster-1` instance back on. That's an automatic failover!

Clustering from a network point of view

For a cluster to work properly, it needs a network where all members can advertise themselves and receive notifications. Despite TCP or UDP network configurations, cluster members need to find each other to be able to exchange information and states.

In JBoss EAP, a cluster is composed of an IP and a port number. These two types of information uniquely identify a cluster on a network.

By default, EAP uses the following configurations:

```
<socket-binding-group name="standard-sockets" default-interface="public"
port-offset="${jboss.socket.binding.port-offset:0}">
    <socket-binding name="management-http" interface="management"
    port="${jboss.management.http.port:9990}"/>
    <socket-binding name="management-https" interface="management"
    port="${jboss.management.https.port:9993}"/>
    <socket-binding name="ajp" port="${jboss.ajp.port:8009}"/>
    <socket-binding name="http" port="${jboss.http.port:8080}"/>
    <socket-binding name="https" port="${jboss.https.port:8443}"/>
    <socket-binding name="jgroups-mping" port="0" multicast-
    address="${jboss.default.multicast.address:230.0.0.4}"
    multicast-port="45700"/>
    <socket-binding name="jgroups-tcp" port="7600"/>
    <socket-binding name="jgroups-tcp-fd" port="57600"/>
    <socket-binding name="jgroups-udp" port="55200" multicast-
    address="${jboss.default.multicast.address:230.0.0.4}"
    multicast-port="45688"/>
    <socket-binding name="jgroups-udp-fd" port="54200"/>
    <socket-binding name="modcluster" port="0" multicast-
    address="224.0.1.105" multicast-port="23364"/>
    <socket-binding name="txn-recovery-environment" port="4712"/>
    <socket-binding name="txn-status-manager" port="4713"/>
    <outbound-socket-binding name="mail-smtp">
        <remote-destination host="localhost" port="25"/>
    </outbound-socket-binding>
</socket-binding-group>
```

And because JGroups, by default, uses the `udp` stack, we need to look at the socket binding named `jgroups-udp`.

The following is the description of the attributes for the socket binding named jgroups-udp:

Attribute's name	Description
port	The number of the port to which the socket should be bound.
multicast-address	The multicast address on which the socket should receive multicast traffic (used by cluster members).
multicast-port	The number of the port on which the socket should receive multicast traffic.

Just for reference, the jgroups-udp-fd is used by the FD_SOCK protocol type, as specified in the udp stack – FD stands for Failure Detection.

So multicast-address and multicast-port form the cluster.

To have a separated cluster, thus not sharing views between members, you need to specify a different multicast-address or a different multicast-port.

Let's try with our cluster-1 and cluster-2 instances. For cluster-1, do as follows:

```
$JBOSS_HOME/bin/standalone.sh -Djboss.server.base.dir=cluster-1 --
server-config=standalone-ha.xml -Djboss.node.name=cluster-1 -
Djboss.default.multicast.address=230.0.0.1
...
05:17:21,354 INFO
[org.infinispan.remoting.transport.jgroups.JGroupsTransport] (MSC service
thread 1-2) ISPN000094: Received new cluster view for channel web:
[cluster-1|0] (1) [cluster-1]
...
```

For the instance named cluster-2, do as follows:

```
$JBOSS_HOME/bin/standalone.sh -Djboss.server.base.dir=cluster-2 --
server-config=standalone-ha.xml -Djboss.socket.binding.port-offset=100 -
Djboss.node.name=cluster-2 -Djboss.default.multicast.address=230.0.0.2
...
05:17:38,360 INFO
[org.infinispan.remoting.transport.jgroups.JGroupsTransport] (MSC service
thread 1-3) ISPN000094: Received new cluster view for channel web:
[cluster-2|0] (1) [cluster-2]
...
```

As you can see from the previous log entries, each view has its own coordinator, and it never changes, so the list of the members is different!

If you want to play around further, first try the application on both port-offsets, and then try adding a third instance and associate it to one of the clusters, by specifying the same `jboss.default.multicast.address` property at startup.

> From a technical point of view, you can mix both standalone and domain mode while clustering. What counts is the cluster network topology.

Ok, that's enough for standalone mode; let's try clustering in domain mode.

Clustering in domain mode

Continuing from the previous sections, we will see how to configure a cluster using domain mode. The same concepts apply to the domain mode, which means that to get clustering capabilities, we need to choose between the `ha` or `full-ha` profile.

As you already know, in domain mode, all the available and configured profiles reside in a single file, `domain.xml`. Each profile is then referenced by one or more server-groups.

To make it simple and clear, we belong to the default configuration and we will use the `ha` profile.

Server-group configuration

Before we begin, as usual, we will create a custom folder to run our JBoss in domain mode and we will define the necessry server-group.

We will first launch the application server with the `--admin-only` flag, so we can configure it without any running instances. We will then set all the configurations and restart the whole EAP with the `--admin-only=false` flag, which is `normal-running`.

Do as follows:

```
cd $JBOSS_HOME
cp -a domain master
./bin/domain.sh -Djboss.domain.base.dir=master --admin-only
```

Once started, let's log in to the CLI and execute the following commands:

```
/host=master/server-config=server-one:remove()
/host=master/server-config=server-two:remove()
/host=master/server-config=server-three:remove()
/server-group=main-server-group:remove()
/server-group=other-server-group:remove()
/server-group=clustering-server-group:add
(profile=ha,socket-binding-group=ha-sockets)
/host=master/server-config=cluster-1:add(group=clustering-
  server-group,auto-start=true,socket-binding-port-offset=100)
/host=master/server-config=cluster-2:add
  (group=clustering-server-group,auto-start=true,
  socket-binding-port-offset=200)
/profile=ha/subsystem=undertow:write-attribute
  (name=instance-id,value=${jboss.node.name})
/profile=ha/subsystem=transactions:write-attribute
  (name=node-identifier,value=${jboss.tx.id})
/host=master/server-config=cluster-1/system-property
  =jboss.node.name:add(value=cluster-1)
/host=master/server-config=cluster-1/
  system-property=jboss.tx.id:add(value=cluster_1)
/host=master/server-config=cluster-2/system-property
  =jboss.node.name:add(value=cluster-2)
/host=master/server-config=cluster-2/system-property
  =jboss.tx.id:add(value=cluster_2)
deploy /opt/rh/cluster-test.war --server-groups=clustering-
server-group
reload --admin-only=false --host=master
```

So, here is what we have done:

1. We cloned the domain folder into one named master.
2. We started EAP in domain mode with master as the base folder, setting the admin-only flag.
3. We removed all default servers and server-groups.
4. We added our own server-group named clustering-ha.
5. We referenced the ha profile to the clustering-ha server-group.
6. We added the server named cluster-1 and associated it to clustering-ha, also setting port-offset to 100.
7. We added the server named cluster-2 and associated it to clustering-ha, also setting port-offset to 200.
8. We set the instance-id attribute to the Undertow subsystem, setting a dynamic value.

9. We set the `node-identifier` attribute to the Transactions subsystem, setting a dynamic value.

10. We added two system properties to each server, as per the dynamic properties – see steps **8** and **9**.

11. We deployed our `cluster-test.war` web application to the `clustering-ha` server-group.

12. We restarted the whole system, setting the `--admin-only` flag to `false`.

Now let's check that everything is correct by looking at our application.

Testing in domain mode

Open your browser and point it to the following URL: `http://localhost:8180/cluster-test/`.

Then refresh the page a couple of times. The page should look like the following:

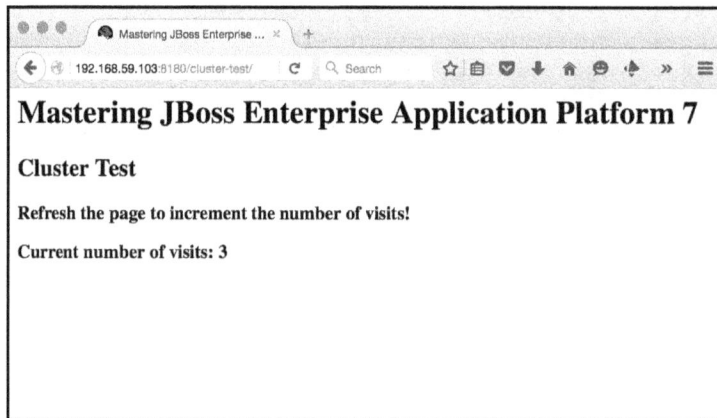

Clustering in domain mode viewing a cluster-1 instance

When looking at the log, you should find the following entries:

```
    [Server:cluster-1] 02:17:38,351 INFO  [stdout] (default task-1)
********************************+
    [Server:cluster-1] 02:17:38,351 INFO  [stdout] (default task-1) Number
of visits: 1
    [Server:cluster-1] 02:17:38,351 INFO  [stdout] (default task-1)
********************************+
```

```
    [Server:cluster-1] 02:19:27,590 INFO    [stdout] (default task-2)
*******************************+
    [Server:cluster-1] 02:19:27,591 INFO    [stdout] (default task-2) Number
of visits: 2
    [Server:cluster-1] 02:19:27,591 INFO    [stdout] (default task-2)
*******************************+
    [Server:cluster-1] 02:19:28,445 INFO    [stdout] (default task-3)
*******************************+
    [Server:cluster-1] 02:19:28,445 INFO    [stdout] (default task-3) Number
of visits: 3
    [Server:cluster-1] 02:19:28,446 INFO    [stdout] (default task-3)
*******************************+
```

Now, switching to the cluster-2 instance, we should see our number of visits incremented by one, starting from three. Point the browser to the following URL: http://localhost:8280/cluster-test/.

The page should look like the following:

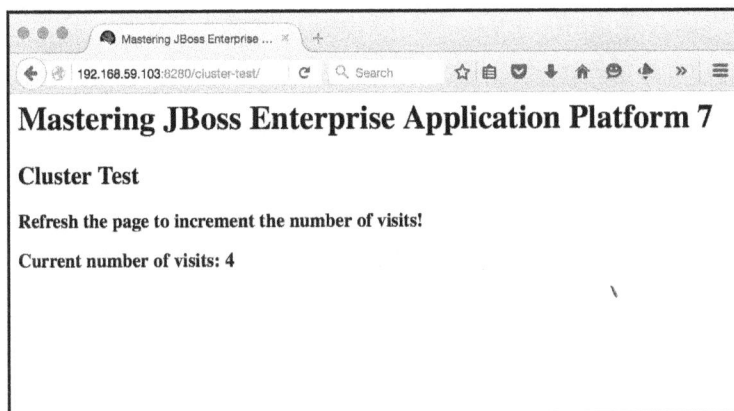

Clustering in domain mode viewing a cluster-2 instance

When looking at the log, you should find the following entries:

```
    [Server:cluster-1] 02:19:28,445 INFO    [stdout] (default task-3)
*******************************+
    [Server:cluster-1] 02:19:28,445 INFO    [stdout] (default task-3) Number
of visits: 3
    [Server:cluster-1] 02:19:28,446 INFO    [stdout] (default task-3)
*******************************+
    [Server:cluster-2] 02:24:48,344 INFO    [stdout] (default task-1)
*******************************+
    [Server:cluster-2] 02:24:48,345 INFO    [stdout] (default task-1) Number
of visits: 4
```

```
[Server:cluster-2] 02:24:48,345 INFO  [stdout] (default task-1)
*******************************+
```

As you can see from the previous log entries, we successfully switched from three visits on the `cluster-1` instance to four visits on the `cluster-2` instance.

Clustering is pretty easy, and it doesn't take much. Nonetheless, often the IT department, for security or any kind of network reason, will not let you rely on UDP as a communication protocol, so you will probably need to switch to a TCP configuration.

That's what we will see in the next sections of this chapter.

Advanced topics

In the following sections, we will discuss some advanced topics in regards to clustering. We will especially see how you can rely on a TCP stack to create your cluster configuration, to use the TCP protocol for communication and transfer purposes, that is, the cluster member's advertising and state replication. Additionally, we will see what clustering means for applications bundling Enterprise Java Beans and how clients are affected.

For simplicity, we will stack with standalone mode, using the `standalone-ha.xml` configuration file.

Clustering using TCP

As we have seen at the beginning of the chapter, to achieve cluster capabilities, JBoss relies on two components: JGroups and Infinispan.

The first one is used for communication purposes; the second one is used for persistence purposes. To switch from a UDP cluster to a TCP cluster, we need to modify the JGroups configuration.

Let's first create a standalone clone folder, named `tcp-cluster-1`, as follows:

```
cd $JBOSS_HOME
cp -a standalone tcp-cluster-1
```

Then run the newly created server configuration with the `--admin-only` flag, so we can manage the whole instance without reloading the server when requested. Do as follows:

```
./bin/standalone.sh -Djboss.server.base.dir=tcp-cluster-1
--server-config=standalone-ha.xml -Djboss.node.name=tcp-
cluster-1 --admin-only
```

Now, in a different terminal, connect to the CLI and execute the following commands:

```
/subsystem=jgroups/stack=mytcp:add(transport={type=TCP,socket-
binding=jgroups-tcp,diagnostics-socket-binding=jgroups-
diagnostics})
/subsystem=jgroups/stack=mytcp/transport=TCP:write-
attribute(name=socket-binding,value=jgroups-tcp)
/subsystem=jgroups/stack=mytcp
/protocol=TCPPING:add(type=TCPPING)
/subsystem=jgroups/stack=mytcp/protocol=TCPPING
/property=initial_hosts:add(value="192.168.59.103[7600],
 192.168.59.103[7700]")
/subsystem=jgroups/stack=mytcp/protocol=TCPPING
/property=port_range:add(value="0")
/subsystem=jgroups/stack=mytcp/protocol=MERGE3:add(type=MERGE3)
/subsystem=jgroups/stack=mytcp
/protocol=FD_SOCK:add(type=FD_SOCK,socket-binding=jgroups
 -tcp-fd)
/subsystem=jgroups/stack=mytcp/protocol=FD:add(type=FD)
/subsystem=jgroups/stack=mytcp
/protocol=VERIFY_SUSPECT:add(type=VERIFY_SUSPECT)
/subsystem=jgroups/stack=mytcp
/protocol=BARRIER:add(type=BARRIER)
/subsystem=jgroups/stack=mytcp
/protocol=pbcast.NAKACK2:add(type=pbcast.NAKACK2)
/subsystem=jgroups/stack=mytcp
/protocol=UNICAST3:add(type=UNICAST3)
/subsystem=jgroups/stack=mytcp
/protocol=pbcast.STABLE:add(type=pbcast.STABLE)
/subsystem=jgroups/stack=mytcp
/protocol=pbcast.GMS:add(type=pbcast.GMS)
/subsystem=jgroups/stack=mytcp/protocol=pbcast.GMS
/property=join_timeout:add(value=3000)
/subsystem=jgroups/stack=mytcp/protocol=MFC:add(type=MFC)
/subsystem=jgroups/stack=mytcp/protocol=FRAG2:add(type=FRAG2)
/subsystem=jgroups/stack=mytcp/protocol=RSVP:add(type=RSVP)
/subsystem=jgroups/channel=ee:write-
 attribute(name=stack,value=mytcp)
 deploy /opt/rh/cluster-test.war
 reload --admin-only=false
```

We have created a new JGroups stack configuration named `mytcp`, and referenced it to the JGroups channel named `ee`, which is the default one. Then we deployed our `cluster-test` application and finally reloaded the server, setting the `--admin-only` flag to false.

To fully proof our cluster configuration, we need at least one more member to join the cluster. Do exactly what we have done for `tcp-cluster-1`, except for its name. In a new terminal, do as follows:

```
cd $JBOSS_HOME
cp -a standalone tcp-cluster-2
./bin/standalone.sh -Djboss.server.base.dir=tcp-cluster-2
--server-config=standalone-ha.xml -Djboss.node.name=tcp-
cluster-2 -Djboss.socket.binding.port-offset=100 --admin-only
```

Now open a new terminal and connect to the CLI, then execute the following commands (they are just the same as what we have done for the `tcp-cluster-1` instance):

```
/subsystem=jgroups/stack=mytcp:add(transport={type=TCP,
 socket-binding=jgroups-tcp,diagnostics-socket-binding=
 jgroups-diagnostics})
/subsystem=jgroups/stack=mytcp/transport=TCP:write-attribute
 (name=socket-binding,value=jgroups-tcp)
/subsystem=jgroups/stack=mytcp/protocol=
 TCPPING:add(type=TCPPING)
/subsystem=jgroups/stack=mytcp/protocol=TCPPING
/property=initial_hosts:add(value="192.168.59.103[7600],
 192.168.59.103[7700]")
/subsystem=jgroups/stack=mytcp/protocol=TCPPING
/property=port_range:add(value="0")
/subsystem=jgroups/stack=mytcp/protocol=MERGE3:add(type=MERGE3)
/subsystem=jgroups/stack=mytcp
/protocol=FD_SOCK:add(type=FD_SOCK,socket-binding=
 jgroups-tcp-fd)
/subsystem=jgroups/stack=mytcp/protocol=FD:add(type=FD)
/subsystem=jgroups/stack=mytcp
/protocol=VERIFY_SUSPECT:add(type=VERIFY_SUSPECT)
/subsystem=jgroups/stack=mytcp
/protocol=BARRIER:add(type=BARRIER)
/subsystem=jgroups/stack=mytcp
/protocol=pbcast.NAKACK2:add(type=pbcast.NAKACK2)
/subsystem=jgroups/stack=mytcp
/protocol=UNICAST3:add(type=UNICAST3)
/subsystem=jgroups/stack=mytcp
/protocol=pbcast.STABLE:add(type=pbcast.STABLE)
/subsystem=jgroups/stack=mytcp
/protocol=pbcast.GMS:add(type=pbcast.GMS)
/subsystem=jgroups/stack=mytcp/protocol=pbcast.GMS
/property=join_timeout:add(value=3000)
/subsystem=jgroups/stack=mytcp/protocol=MFC:add(type=MFC)
/subsystem=jgroups/stack=mytcp/protocol=FRAG2:add(type=FRAG2)
/subsystem=jgroups/stack=mytcp/protocol=RSVP:add(type=RSVP)
/subsystem=jgroups/channel=ee:write-attribute
```

```
(name=stack,value=mytcp)
deploy /opt/rh/cluster-test.war
reload --admin-only=false
```

Now if you look at both servers' log entries, you should find that the instances joined the same cluster, exchanging their view state.

In my test, I first started `tcp-cluster-1`, getting the following relevant information:

```
    . . .
    06:14:21,014 INFO  [org.jboss.as] (Controller Boot Thread) WFLYSRV0025:
EAP 7.0.0.Beta1 (WildFly Core 2.0.3.Final-redhat-1) started in 6253ms –
Started 408 of 649 services (406 services are lazy, passive or on-demand)
    06:15:36,134 INFO
[org.infinispan.remoting.transport.jgroups.JGroupsTransport]
(Incoming-2,ee,tcp-cluster-1) ISPN000094: Received new cluster view for
channel server: [tcp-cluster-1|1] (2) [tcp-cluster-1, tcp-cluster-2]
    06:15:36,136 INFO
[org.infinispan.remoting.transport.jgroups.JGroupsTransport]
(Incoming-2,ee,tcp-cluster-1) ISPN000094: Received new cluster view for
channel web: [tcp-cluster-1|1] (2) [tcp-cluster-1, tcp-cluster-2]
    06:15:36,139 INFO
[org.infinispan.remoting.transport.jgroups.JGroupsTransport]
(Incoming-2,ee,tcp-cluster-1) ISPN000094: Received new cluster view for
channel hibernate: [tcp-cluster-1|1] (2) [tcp-cluster-1, tcp-cluster-2]
    06:15:36,141 INFO
[org.infinispan.remoting.transport.jgroups.JGroupsTransport]
(Incoming-2,ee,tcp-cluster-1) ISPN000094: Received new cluster view for
channel ejb: [tcp-cluster-1|1] (2) [tcp-cluster-1, tcp-cluster-2]
    06:15:36,955 INFO  [org.infinispan.CLUSTER] (remote-thread--p5-t1)
ISPN000310: Starting cluster-wide rebalance for cache routing, topology
CacheTopology{id=1, rebalanceId=1, currentCH=DefaultConsistentHash{ns=80,
owners = (1)[tcp-cluster-1: 80+0]}, pendingCH=DefaultConsistentHash{ns=80,
owners = (2)[tcp-cluster-1: 40+40, tcp-cluster-2: 40+40]}, unionCH=null,
actualMembers=[tcp-cluster-1, tcp-cluster-2]}
    06:15:36,955 INFO  [org.infinispan.CLUSTER] (remote-thread--p5-t2)
ISPN000310: Starting cluster-wide rebalance for cache cluster-test.war,
topology CacheTopology{id=1, rebalanceId=1,
currentCH=DefaultConsistentHash{ns=80, owners = (1)[tcp-cluster-1: 80+0]},
pendingCH=DefaultConsistentHash{ns=80, owners = (2)[tcp-cluster-1: 40+40,
tcp-cluster-2: 40+40]}, unionCH=null, actualMembers=[tcp-cluster-1, tcp-
cluster-2]}
    06:15:37,153 INFO  [org.infinispan.CLUSTER] (remote-thread--p5-t1)
ISPN000336: Finished cluster-wide rebalance for cache routing, topology id
= 1
    06:15:37,161 INFO  [org.infinispan.CLUSTER] (remote-thread--p5-t1)
ISPN000336: Finished cluster-wide rebalance for cache cluster-test.war,
topology id = 1
```

And in `tcp-cluster-2`, I found the following relevant information:

```
    06:15:36,555 INFO
[org.infinispan.remoting.transport.jgroups.JGroupsTransport] (MSC service
thread 1-8) ISPN000078: Starting JGroups channel ejb
    06:15:36,555 INFO
[org.infinispan.remoting.transport.jgroups.JGroupsTransport] (MSC service
thread 1-7) ISPN000078: Starting JGroups channel hibernate
    06:15:36,555 INFO
[org.infinispan.remoting.transport.jgroups.JGroupsTransport] (MSC service
thread 1-1) ISPN000078: Starting JGroups channel web
    06:15:36,555 INFO
[org.infinispan.remoting.transport.jgroups.JGroupsTransport] (MSC service
thread 1-3) ISPN000078: Starting JGroups channel server
    06:15:36,575 INFO
[org.infinispan.remoting.transport.jgroups.JGroupsTransport] (MSC service
thread 1-3) ISPN000094: Received new cluster view for channel server: [tcp-
cluster-1|1] (2) [tcp-cluster-1, tcp-cluster-2]
    06:15:36,577 INFO
[org.infinispan.remoting.transport.jgroups.JGroupsTransport] (MSC service
thread 1-7) ISPN000094: Received new cluster view for channel hibernate:
[tcp-cluster-1|1] (2) [tcp-cluster-1, tcp-cluster-2]
    06:15:36,578 INFO
[org.infinispan.remoting.transport.jgroups.JGroupsTransport] (MSC service
thread 1-1) ISPN000094: Received new cluster view for channel web: [tcp-
cluster-1|1] (2) [tcp-cluster-1, tcp-cluster-2]
    06:15:36,588 INFO
[org.infinispan.remoting.transport.jgroups.JGroupsTransport] (MSC service
thread 1-8) ISPN000094: Received new cluster view for channel ejb: [tcp-
cluster-1|1] (2) [tcp-cluster-1, tcp-cluster-2]
    06:15:36,591 INFO
[org.infinispan.remoting.transport.jgroups.JGroupsTransport] (MSC service
thread 1-8) ISPN000079: Channel ejb local address is tcp-cluster-2,
physical addresses are [192.168.59.103:7700]
    06:15:36,591 INFO
[org.infinispan.remoting.transport.jgroups.JGroupsTransport] (MSC service
thread 1-3) ISPN000079: Channel server local address is tcp-cluster-2,
physical addresses are [192.168.59.103:7700]
    06:15:36,591 INFO
[org.infinispan.remoting.transport.jgroups.JGroupsTransport] (MSC service
thread 1-7) ISPN000079: Channel hibernate local address is tcp-cluster-2,
physical addresses are [192.168.59.103:7700]
    06:15:36,591 INFO
[org.infinispan.remoting.transport.jgroups.JGroupsTransport] (MSC service
thread 1-1) ISPN000079: Channel web local address is tcp-cluster-2,
physical addresses are [192.168.59.103:7700]
    ...
    06:15:37,480 INFO  [org.jboss.as] (Controller Boot Thread) WFLYSRV0025:
```

```
EAP 7.0.0.Beta1 (WildFly Core 2.0.3.Final-redhat-1) started in 3554ms -
Started 408 of 649 services (406 services are lazy, passive or on-demand)
```

You can now test the application yourself and see its behavior.

> All the settings made for the JGroups subsystem reflect Infinispan behavior. This means that if you set the stack to `mytcp`, even the state across cluster members is replicated with the same transportation protocol.

EJBs in a clustered environment

So far we have seen how to configure JBoss EAP 7 to support clustering capabilities, but what happens to one of the most-used Java components, the EJBs?

As you have seen at the beginning of the chapter, Infinispan comes with a pre-configured cache container, where the `ejb` cache container is used to cache EJBs.

For reference, here is the `ejb` cache container configuration:

```
<cache-container name="ejb" aliases="sfsb"
module="org.wildfly.clustering.ejb.infinispan" default-cache="dist">
    <transport lock-timeout="60000"/>
    <distributed-cache name="dist" mode="ASYNC" l1-lifespan="0" owners="2">
        <locking isolation="REPEATABLE_READ"/>
        <transaction mode="BATCH"/>
        <file-store/>
    </distributed-cache>
</cache-container>
```

In a Java EE 7 environment, we have three different kinds of EJB:

- **Stateless Session Beans (SLSBs)**
- **Stateful Session Beans (SFSBs)**
- **Singleton Session Beans**

Stateless session beans by definition do not maintain states between invocations, so the only reason to mark them as `@Clustered` is to specify the load balancing policy, which you can achieve with the following Java annotation:

```
@Clustered(loadBalancePolicy="FirstAvailable")
```

You can choose from the following load balancing policies:

- FirstAvailable – A random selection of the node, but subsequent invocations will be made against the same node, until it fails; the next node will be randomly picked.
- RoundRobin – It's the default. The EJB's client proxy iterates to all available nodes.
- RandomRobin – Each request is redirected to a random node by the proxy.
- FirstAvailableIdenticalAllProxies – It's just like FirstAvailable, except that the node selection will be shared across all proxies.

> Since JBoss EAP 7 and EJBs are clustered automatically if the JBoss profile has this capability, choosing ha or full-ha automatically clusters EJBs.

Testing clustered EJB

Let's try a simple EJB application with a client and see what happens.

First we need to create our environment. For convenience, we will use domain mode, running two servers, both configured with the ha profile.

Just do as follows:

```
cd $JBOSS_HOME
cp -a domain ejb-cluster
```

Now add a user to access the EJB using the add-user.sh script, as depicted in the following screenshot:

```
./bin/add-user.sh -dc ejb-cluster/configuration

What type of user do you wish to add?
 a) Management User (mgmt-users.properties)
 b) Application User (application-users.properties)
(a): b

Enter the details of the new user to add.
Using realm 'ApplicationRealm' as discovered from the existing property files.
Username : ejb
Password recommendations are listed below. To modify these restrictions edit the add-user.properties configuration file.
 - The password should be different from the username
 - The password should not be one of the following restricted values {root, admin, administrator}
 - The password should contain at least 8 characters, 1 alphabetic character(s), 1 digit(s), 1 non-alphanumeric symbol(s)
Password :
Re-enter Password :
What groups do you want this user to belong to? (Please enter a comma separated list, or leave blank for none)[ ]:
About to add user 'ejb' for realm 'ApplicationRealm'
Is this correct yes/no? yes
Added user 'ejb' to file '/opt/rh/jboss-eap-7.0/ejb-cluster/configuration/application-users.properties'
Added user 'ejb' with groups  to file '/opt/rh/jboss-eap-7.0/ejb-cluster/configuration/application-roles.properties'
Is this new user going to be used for one AS process to connect to another AS process?
e.g. for a slave host controller connecting to the master or for a Remoting connection for server to server EJB calls.
yes/no? yes
To represent the user add the following to the server-identities definition <secret value="ZWpiLjIwMTU=" />
```

Adding a user to invoke the EJB

Now we are ready to launch our JBoss EAP in domain mode to configure it via CLI, as follows:

```
./bin/domain.sh -Djboss.server.base.dir=ejb-cluster
--admin-only
```

Now in a different terminal window, connect to the CLI and invoke the following commands:

```
/host=master/core-service=management/security-realm
 =ApplicationRealm/server-identity=secret:add
 (value="ZWpiLjIwMTU=")
 reload --host=master --admin-only=true
/host=master/server-config=server-one:remove()
/host=master/server-config=server-two:remove()
/host=master/server-config=server-three:remove()
/server-group=main-server-group:remove()
/server-group=other-server-group:remove()
/server-group=ejb-clustering-server-group:add
  (profile=ha,socket-binding-group=ha-sockets)
/host=master/server-config=ejb-cluster-1:add
  (group=ejb-clustering-server-group,auto-start=true,
  socket-binding-port-offset=100)
/host=master/server-config=ejb-cluster-2:add
  (group=ejb-clustering-server-group,auto-start=true,
```

```
   socket-binding-port-offset=200)
/profile=ha/subsystem=undertow:write-attribute
  (name=instance-id,value=${jboss.node.name})
/profile=ha/subsystem=transactions:write-attribute
  (name=node-identifier,value=${jboss.tx.id})
/host=master/server-config=ejb-cluster-1/system-property=
  jboss.node.name:add(value=ejb-cluster-1)
/host=master/server-config=ejb-cluster-1/system-property=
  jboss.tx.id:add(value=ejb_cluster_1)
/host=master/server-config=ejb-cluster-2/system-property=
  jboss.node.name:add(value=ejb-cluster-2)
/host=master/server-config=ejb-cluster-2/system-property=
  jboss.tx.id:add(value=ejb_cluster_2)
reload --admin-only=false --host=master
```

As already mentioned in the `Clustering in standalone mode` section, we arranged a Git repository for this chapter, which you will find at the following site: `https://github.com/mjbeap7`.

The repo for this chapter is called `ch06`, so you need to clone it locally in your computer, into a folder of your choice that we will refer to as `$GIT_MJBEAP7`. Just do as follows:

```
git clone https://github.com/mjbeap7/ch06
Cloning into 'ch06'...
remote: Counting objects: 4, done.
remote: Total 4 (delta 0), reused 0 (delta 0), pack-reused 4
Unpacking objects: 100% (4/4), done.
Checking connectivity... done.
```

And to build our EJB example application, issue the following `Maven` command:

```
cd $GIT_MJBEAP7/ch06
mvn -e clean package -f ejb-example/pom.xml
```

Once done, you should find an EAR bundle containing the EJB module, in the `ejb-example/era/target` folder.

Deploy the EAR via CLI, as follows:

```
deploy /opt/rh/ear.ear --server-groups=ejb-clustering-server-
group
```

The EJB is now deployed and available for invocations on both server instances.

You can use the client we provided with the maven project, by issuing the following commands:

```
cd $GIT_MJBEAP7/ch06/ejb-example/ejb-client
mvn -e exec:java -Dexec.mainClass=
"com.packtpub.mjbeap7.ejb.client.Client"
```

Now, if you stop the instance that logged the EJB's invocation and re-execute the client, you can see that the invocation is made against the other instance.

Summary

In this chapter, you learned what a cluster is and what it is useful for. You also saw how it differs from plain high availability.

You also learned how to make an application cluster aware and how to configure a cluster running in standalone mode.

You saw the differences between standalone and domain mode. Additionally, you learned how to configure a cluster using the CLI, so that every setup can be replicable at any time on any server.

You then learned that clusters could be configured using two different network protocols, TCP and UDP.

In the next chapter, we will see how we can use and customize the logging subsystem to gain the best out of it in terms of log readability and overall performance using an appropriate log level and asynchronous handlers.

7
Logging

This chapter provides a comprehensive description of the logging services available in EAP 7. Logging is a core element of server configuration: when done correctly, it allows us to monitor code behavior and find issues or bugs. A poorly configured logging system makes it more difficult to trace problems; on the other hand, overly verbose logging activity can take up a lot of your system resources. Hence, we need to focus on the resources we want a closer look at. Within this chapter, we will learn the default paths used by the server for logging events along with their configuration; next, we will discuss tools that you can use in the enterprise to manage all the information contained in the log files. We will cover the following topics:

- Basic logging concepts
- How to configure server logging
- How to configure application logging
- Building an advanced and scalable logging system

The basics of logging

JBoss EAP provides a highly configurable logging system that can be used both by the application server and the applications running on top of it. The logging subsystem is based on the `JBoss LogManager` project, which internally uses the `java.util.logging` API. The core components of the `LogManager` project are the following:

- **Categories**: They define which messages need to be captured
- **Handlers**: They define how to deal with these messages (for example, log to file, console, and so on)
- **Formatters**: They define how log messages appear in log files and so on

Before digging into the details of logging components, we will point out the default log file locations for quick reference.

Default log file locations

By default, the log files for a standalone server can be found in the `log` directory of the `jboss.server.base.dir` with the name `server.log`. Hence, by default, you will find the latest `server.log` in the folder `$JBOSS_HOME/standalone/log`. As you will see in a minute, this server log file gets rotated on a daily basis.

In a managed domain, there are two types of log files: the host controller logs and the logs emitted by single servers. The host controller emits the `log` file `host-controller.log` in the `domain/log` folder. Here you can find information about the relevant services inherent to the host controller. The process controller log, named `process-controller.log`, contains information about inter-process communication between server nodes. Most of the time, the amount of information contained in it is negligible.

Most important for us are the logs emitted by single servers, where the subsystems contained in the servers trace their activity. To sum up, here is a table containing the logs emitted by the domain we created in Chapter 3, *Managing EAP in Domain mode*:

JVM process	Log file
host controller	/home/jboss/dc/jboss-eap-7.0/domain/log/host-controller.log
process controller	/home/jboss/dc/jboss-eap-7.0/domain/log/process-controller.log
Server1	/home/jboss/slave1/jboss-eap-7.0/domain/servers/server1/log/server.log
Server2	/home/jboss/slave1/jboss-eap-7.0/domain/servers/server2/log/server.log
Server3	/home/jboss/slave2/jboss-eap-7.0/domain/servers/server3/log/server.log
Server4	/home/jboss/slave2/jboss-eap-7.0/domain/servers/server4/log/server.log

As you can see from the following excerpt, a log file, by default, exhibits the timestamp when the log was issued, the severity of the log event, the class package that emitted the log, its thread, and the log message:

```
2016-01-27 23:10:02,841 INFO [org.jboss.as.naming] (MSC service thread
1-2) WFLYNAM0003: Starting Naming Service
2016-01-27 23:10:02,842 INFO [org.jboss.as.mail.extension] (MSC service
thread 1-5) WFLYMAIL0001: Bound mail session [java:jboss/mail/Default]
```

```
2016-01-27 23:10:03,038 INFO [org.wildfly.extension.undertow]
(ServerService Thread Pool -- 55) WFLYUT0014: Creating file handler for
path '/home/francesco/jboss/jboss-eap-7.0/welcome-content' with options
[directory-listing: 'false', follow-symlink: 'false', case-sensitive:
'true', safe-symlink-paths: '[]']
```

Log levels are enumerated sets that indicates the nature and severity of a log event. The level of a particular log message is specified by a piece of code using the appropriate methods of the logging framework.

JBoss EAP supports a wide list of log levels; in practice, the following ones are used to emit logs by application server classes (in order of lowest to highest):

- **TRACE**: This log level allows for deep probing of the JBoss EAP behavior when necessary. When the TRACE level priority is enabled, you can expect the number of messages in the application server log to grow by at least a x N, where N is the number of requests received by the server and is a constant. Consider also that these log messages are often temporary, and might be turned off eventually, in future releases.
- **DEBUG**: This log level is used for log messages that convey extra information regarding life cycle events. Most of the information generated by this log level is developers' stuff; however, the important point is that, when the DEBUG level priority is enabled, the server log should not grow proportionally with the number of server requests.
- **INFO**: This is the default logging level for the application server root logger and should be used to capture logging events related to business processes. By using this level, you should capture changes in the state of the application or external resources (such as a change in the user's settings or a database update).
- **WARN**: This log level is used for events that may indicate a non-critical service error. Recoverable errors or minor issues in request expectations fall into this category. The distinction between WARN and ERROR is a narrow one and sometimes up to the developer to judge.
- **ERROR**: This log level is used to indicate a disruption in a request or the inability to complete a request. A service should have some capacity to continue to service requests in the presence of ERRORs.
- **FATAL**: This log level is used for events that indicate a critical service failure. If a service issues a FATAL error, it is completely unable to service requests of any kind.

Loggers and handlers are assigned to a particular log level and they only process log messages of that level or higher. For example, if your handler is set to an INFO level, it will process all log messages of type INFO, WARN, ERROR, and FATAL.

Loggers are more specific than handlers; therefore, if you specify a logger for a particular package, its log level will prevail over the handler log level.

Configuring handlers

Handlers are the core components that deal with logging events. We will go through the handlers that are available on the EAP and how to create new loggers to keep the server logs separate from the application logs.

In the following section, we will first cover the handlers, starting with the default ones provided in the configuration, and then look at how to create custom handler configurations.

Console handler

This handler writes log messages to your operating system's standard output (std out) or to the standard error (std err). Console messages are displayed when the application server is executed from the command line. Note that, unless you redirect the console logs on a file, they will not be saved. You can query the console handler as follows:

```
/subsystem=logging/console-handler=CONSOLE/:read-resource()
{
 "outcome" => "success",
 "result" => {
 "autoflush" => true,
 "enabled" => true,
 "encoding" => undefined,
 "filter" => undefined,
 "filter-spec" => undefined,
 "formatter" => "%d{HH:mm:ss,SSS} %-5p [%c] (%t) %s%e%n",
 "level" => "INFO",
 "name" => "CONSOLE",
 "named-formatter" => "COLOR-PATTERN",
 "target" => "System.out"
 }
}
```

As you can see from the properties, the console handler is configured to automatically flush each `Log` event (hence no buffering of messages); the handler is also enabled by default. There is no encoding specified in the handler, so it will use the JVM default encoding. In standalone mode, you can vary this parameter, for example, to use `UTF-8` x, as follows:

```
/subsystem=logging/console-handler=CONSOLE:write-
attribute(name=encoding,value="UTF-8")
```

The corresponding command in domain mode, for the full profile, would be:

```
/profile=full/subsystem=logging/console-handler=CONSOLE:write-
attribute(name=encoding,value="UTF-8")
```

Another aspect of interest, common to all handlers, is filters. By using filters, you can effectively restrict the amount of information that goes through the logger with some restriction on the content. See the *Filtering logs* section for more information about this.

Periodic log handlers

Periodic log handlers write log messages to a named file until its time period elapses. After that, the old log file is renamed by prepending a timestamp to the log file name and a new log file is created with the original name. Here is the default configuration for the periodic file handler on a standalone server:

```
/subsystem=logging/periodic-rotating-file-handler=FILE/:read-
resource(recursive=false)
    {
     "outcome" => "success",
     "result" => {
     "append" => true,
     "autoflush" => true,
     "enabled" => true,
     "encoding" => undefined,
     "file" => {
      "path" => "server.log",
      "relative-to" => "jboss.server.log.dir"
     },
     "filter" => undefined,
     "filter-spec" => undefined,
     "formatter" => "%d{HH:mm:ss,SSS} %-5p [%c] (%t) %s%e%n",
     "level" => "ALL",
     "name" => "FILE",
     "named-formatter" => "PATTERN",
     "suffix" => ".yyyy-MM-dd"
     }
```

```
}
```

The periodic file handler is, by default, used by the root logger; hence, if you modify its configuration, you will alter the application server logging. The `suffix` attribute comes into play to determine when the log file is rolled. The `java.text` expression `.yyyy-MM-dd` causes the file to be rolled daily; on the other hand, if you want to roll the log file every hour, you can apply the following pattern `.yyyy-MM-dd-HH`:

```
/subsystem=logging/periodic-rotating-file-handler=FILE:write-
attribute(name=suffix,value=".yyyy-MM-dd-HH")
```

As usual, for domain mode, prepend the profile name to the logging subsystem:

```
/profile=full/subsystem=logging/periodic-rotating-file-handler=FILE:write-
attribute(name=suffix,value=".yyyy-MM-dd-HH")
```

Size handlers

Size handlers can be configured to write log messages to a file until the file reaches a certain size. At that point, the file is renamed with a numeric suffix as well and the logging will continue with the new file. This handler contains a built-in cleanup policy, so you can specify the maximum number of log files to be maintained.

The following command can be used to create a size handler that rotates log files when they reach 2 MB in size, keeping the last 10 log files as backup:

```
/subsystem=logging/size-rotating-file-handler=size:add(append=true,rotate-
on-boot=true, rotate-size="2m", named-formatter=PATTERN, max-backup-
index=10, file={relative-to=jboss.server.log.dir, path=new-server.log})
```

Here is a description of the attributes available for the size handler:

- `autoflush`: When set to true, it automatically flushes after each write.
- `append`: When set to true, it specifies whether to append the log to the target file.
- `encoding`: The character encoding used by this Handler.
- `filter`: Defines a simple filter type (see the *Filtering logs* section later in this chapter).
- `file`: This element contains two sub-properties: an absolute file path and an optional. relative-to path expression.
- `level`: The log level specifying which message levels will be logged by this.
- `max-backup-index`: This is the maximum number of backups to keep.

- `named-formatter`: The name of the defined printing formatter to be used on the handler.
- `rotate-size`: This is the size at which to rotate the log file.
- `rotate-on-boot`: Indicates the file should be rotated each time the file attribute is changed. This always happens at initialization time.

Combining size and periodic log files

One of the limitations of the periodic handler is that you cannot specify a cleanup policy for your older logs. You can, however, combine the features of the periodic handler and size handler by using the **Periodic Size Handler**. The following command line interface (CLI) command shows how to specify a backup strategy to a handler which rotates its log on a daily basis:

```
/subsystem=logging/periodic-size-rotating-file-handler=size-
time:add(append=false,autoflush=true,rotate-on-boot=true,suffix=".yyyy-MM-
dd", named-formatter=PATTERN, max-backup-index=10, file={relative-
to=jboss.server.log.dir, path=new-server.log})
```

You can further include a `rotate-size` policy to the preceding handler, though it can be misleading to have a logging policy which traces log events with both a time-based and a size-based policy.

Adding asynchronous behavior

All log handlers, by default, use a synchronous mechanism to handle logs. For applications which are CPU-bound, this approach could reduce the stress on your machine, as no additional threads will be created for log elaboration. On the other hand, applications experiencing input/output issues (for example, writing to a remote file system) can improve their performance by using **async log handlers,** which are wrapper log handlers that provide asynchronous behavior.

As an example, here is how you can configure the `FILE` handler to be an `asynchronous handler`:

```
/subsystem=logging/async-handler=asynchandler/:add(queue-
length=1024,level=INFO,overflow-action=BLOCK,subhandlers=["size"])
```

Note that aysnc handlers use a queue of logging events and a policy to be used when the queue of events is full. In the preceding example, we are allowing `1024` logging events to be queued, using a `BLOCK` policy when the log events overflow the queue size.

Custom handlers

A custom handler lets you extend the `java.util.logging.Handler` class to use it for customizing your log events. In order to be visible to the application server, the custom logger needs to be packaged in a module in the application server.

As an example, you can take a look at the **Log Manager extensions**, which contain some extended support for JBoss log manager, such as the TCP socket handler. We will show how to install it on the application server as follows:

1. Download the socket handler API from the `Maven` repository: `http://mvnreposi tory.com/artifact/org.jboss.logmanager/jboss-logmanager-ext`.

2. Next, install it as a module and assign it to a handler. For example, you can assign it to the root handler so that you will see log messages as the application server boots.

3. The following CLI script will install the `log manager`:

```
batch
module add --name=org.jboss.logmanager.ext
--dependencies=org.jboss.logmanager,javax.json.api,
javax.xml.stream.api --resources=jboss-logmanager-
ext-1.0.0.Alpha3.jar
/subsystem=logging/custom-handler=socket-
handler:add(class=org.jboss.logmanager.ext.handlers.
SocketHandler,module=org.jboss.logmanager.ext,named-
formatter=PATTERN,properties={hostname=localhost,
port=7080})

/subsystem=logging/root-logger=ROOT:add-handler
(name=socket-handler)
:reload
run-batch
```

The script works in the following way:

- The first instruction will install the `logmanager` extension on the application server
- The next one creates a custom handler using the `socket handler` API
- The third one adds the custom handler to the root logger

All you need is a TCP Server that listens on port `7080` and captures the incoming messages. As an example, if you use camel routes in your projects, then you can route log messages to any of the camel components, as in the following example, where log messages are redirected to a mock component to be part of a route test:

```
RouteBuilder builder = new RouteBuilder() {
    public void configure() {
        from("tcp://localhost:7080?textline=true&sync=false")
            .to("mock:result");
    }
};
```

JBoss SyslogHandler

In many organizations, it is required that the system log manager stores the logs emitted by services or applications. This is possible as well in EAP 7 thanks to the SYSLOG handler. You can install it on the application server with the following CLI:

```
/subsystem=logging/syslog-handler=SYSLOG/:add(app-
name=JBoss,facility=local-use-6,
hostname=localhost,level=ALL,port=514,server-address=localhost,syslog-
format=RFC3164)
/subsystem=logging/root-logger=ROOT:add-handler(name=SYSLOG)
```

And here is a list of configurable attributes for the syslog-handler:

- server-address: The address of the syslog server
- port: The port of the syslog server
- app-name: The name of the application that is logging
- facility: The facility used to calculate the priority of the log message
- hostname: The name of the host the messages are being sent from
- syslog-format: Choose either RFC5424 or RFC3164

Since we have bound the root logger to the SYSLOG Handler using the JBoss application name, then you should expect to find logs in the standard /var/log path as follows:

```
tail -f /var/log/JBoss/jboss.log
    Jan 28 15:27:41 localhost JBOSS[3589]: WFLYDS0013: Started
FileSystemDeploymentService for directory /home/francesco/jboss/jboss-
eap-7.0/standalone/deployments
    Jan 28 15:27:41 localhost JBOSS[3589]: ISPN000128: Infinispan version:
Infinispan 'Infinite Darkness' 8.0.1.Final-redhat-1
    Jan 28 15:27:41 localhost JBOSS[3589]: WFLYUT0006: Undertow HTTPS
listener default-https listening on 127.0.0.1:8443
    Jan 28 15:27:41 localhost JBOSS[3589]: JBWS022052: Starting JBoss Web
Services - Stack CXF Server 5.1.0.Final-redhat-1
    Jan 28 15:27:41 localhost JBOSS[3589]: WFLYSRV0060: Http management
interface listening on http://127.0.0.1:9990/management
```

```
        Jan 28 15:27:41 localhost JBOSS[3589]: WFLYSRV0051: Admin console
    listening on http://127.0.0.1:9990
        Jan 28 15:27:41 localhost JBOSS[3589]: WFLYSRV0025: EAP 7.0.0.Beta1
    (WildFly Core 2.0.3.Final-redhat-1) started in 3798ms - Started 269 of 517
    services (337 services are lazy, passive or on-demand).
```

Filtering logs

Filters can be applied on handlers to restrict or even replace the information that is generated by loggers. The following predicates can be used to apply filters and substitutions to the handlers:

Predicate	Description
`accept`	Accepts all log messages.
`deny`	Denies all log messages.
`not(filterExpression)`	Accepts a filter as an argument and inverts the returned value.
`all(filterExpressions)`	A filter consisting of several filters in a chain. If any filter finds the log message to be unloggable, the message will not be logged and subsequent filters will not be checked.
`any(filterExpressions)`	A filter consisting of several filters in a chain. If any filter finds the log message to be loggable, the message will be logged and the subsequent filters will not be checked.
`levelChange(level)`	A filter that modifies the log record with a new level.
`levels(levels)`	A filter that includes log messages with a level that is listed in the list of levels.
`levelRange([minLevel,maxLevel])`	A filter that logs records that are within the level range.
`match("pattern")`	A regular-expression-based filter. The raw, unformatted message is used against the pattern.
`substitute("pattern", "replacement value")`	A filter that replaces the first match to the pattern with the replacement value.

`substituteAll("pattern", "replacement value")`	A filter that replaces all matches of the pattern with the replacement value.

For example, the following expression can be used to remove from the logs the expressions WFLYJCA0001 and WFLYJCA0002 on the full profile of your domain:

```
/profile=full/subsystem=logging/console-handler=CONSOLE:write-
attribute(name=filter-spec,value=not(match("WFLYJCA0001|WFLYJCA0002")))
```

On the other hand, the following filter expression performs a replacement of the string WFLYJCA with JACAMAR:

```
/subsystem=logging/console-handler=CONSOLE:write-attribute(name=filter-
spec, value="substituteAll("WFLYJCA"\,"JACAMAR")")
```

> Please note that, in the second example, we needed to escape the comma and quotation marks in the value and wrap the entire expression in quotation marks, so that the value is correctly interpreted to be a string. Otherwise, it would be parsed as a list.

Configuring loggers

Each time a log event is emitted, it contains information about the log level and the fully qualified class name bound to that event. In order to associate this information with a specific handler, you can use loggers.

Loggers are associated with a specific namespace, hence they have a hierarchy that contains, at the root, the root logger that is the ancestor of all loggers. All classes that don't have a configured logger will therefore be captured by the root logger. The root logger by default is associated with the CONSOLE and FILE handlers. You can vary it by specifying the list of Handlers as follows:

```
/subsystem=logging/root-logger=ROOT/:write-
attribute(name=handlers,value=["CONSOLE","FILE","SYSLOG"])
```

By default, the root logger traces logs with the INFO (or higher) level. You can change at any time the root logger level through the `change-root-log-level` operation. For example:

```
/subsystem=logging/root-logger=ROOT/:change-root-log-level(level=WARN)
```

Defining new loggers

Changing the root logger level is not a granular approach, as you will vary the log levels of all Loggers which don't have their own logger. Instead, it is recommended you create specific loggers to trace specific packages or branches of packages. For example, if you want to look in depth into the security subsystem (for example, you want to trace authentication issues), then you can add a logger at TRACE level on the `org.jboss.security` namespace:

```
/subsystem=logging/logger=org.jboss.security/:add(handlers=["FILE"],level=T
RACE,use-parent-handlers=false)
```

As a result, the configuration will now contain the following logger:

```
<logger category="org.jboss.security" use-parent- handlers="false">
    <level name="TRACE"/>
    <handlers>
        <handler name="FILE"/>
    </handlers>
</logger>
```

Please note that each logger has the `use-parent-handlers` attribute, which, when set to true, will use the handlers of its ancestors (if no handler has been associated, the log messages will still be intercepted by the root logger).

Managing your application logging

In the first part of this chapter, you learnt that the application server uses the JBoss LogManager to trace server activities. As far as applications are concerned, you have a wider set of options. For example, you can use the following:

- Package any Java logging framework with your application (such as log4j), also known as *per-deployment logging*.
- Define a logging profile in your EAP configuration, which is dedicated to your applications.

- Define a specific logger (and associate it with a handler) to keep your application logs separate from your server logs. You can check the *Defining new loggers* section for an example of creating a new logger.

Per-deployment logging

As we said, per-deployment logging allows you to package a logging framework to your application, which includes its configuration file and (if not bundled into the application server) its libraries. If you are packaging an EAR, the configuration should be added in the META-INF directory. On the other hand, for a WAR or JAR deployment, the configuration file must be added respectively in the WEB-INF/classes or META-INF folders.

In the following example, we will show how to use log4j in your applications. Log4j libraries are bundled as a module in the org.apache.log4j folder of the JBOSS_MODULEPATH. It is, however, not an automatic dependency so you have to activate it with the jboss-deployment-structure.xml file as follows:

```
<jboss-deployment-structure>
    <deployment>
        <dependencies>
            <module name="org.apache.log4j" />
        </dependencies>
    </deployment>
</jboss-deployment-structure>
```

Now place the log4j.xml configuration file in the correct folder (for example, in the src folder of your Maven project). Here is an example of it which configures a file handler emitting logs on the file /var/log/jboss/application/app.log:

```
<!DOCTYPE log4j:configuration SYSTEM "log4j.dtd">
<log4j:configuration xmlns:log4j=
 "http://jakarta.apache.org/log4j/"debug="false">
    <appender name="FILE" class=
    "org.apache.log4j.RollingFileAppender">
    <param name="File" value="/var/log/jboss/application/app.log"
     />
    <param name="MaxFileSize" value="1MB" />
    <param name="MaxBackupIndex" value="100" />
    <layout class="org.apache.log4j.PatternLayout">
      <param name="ConversionPattern" value="[%d{dd/MM/yy
      hh:mm:ss:sss z}] %5p %c{2}: %m%n" />
    </layout>
    </appender>
    <root>
```

```
        <priority value="info" />
            <appender-ref ref="FILE" />
    </root>
</log4j:configuration>
```

Per-deployment logging is enabled by default; you can, however, disable it with the following action to be performed on the logging subsystem:

```
/subsystem=logging:write-attribute(name=use-deployment-logging-
config,value=false)
```

Logging profiles

A logging profile is another viable option for keeping your application logs separated from your server logs. Unlike per-application logging, the logging profile configuration is still governed by the logging subsystem. So you need to add it to the logging subsystem. In the following CLI command, we are adding the `custom-log-profile` to the logging subsystem:

```
/subsystem=logging/logging-profile=custom-log-profile:add
```

Next, create a file handler related to this logging profile:

```
/subsystem=logging/logging-profile=custom-log-profile/file-
handler=application-handler:add(file={path=>"app.log", "relative-
to"=>"jboss.server.log.dir"})
/subsystem=logging/logging-profile=custom-log-profile/file-
handler=application-handler:write-attribute(name="level", value="INFO")
```

Let's say you want to apply the logging profile to the com.acme package. Hence, we will create a specific logger to handle log events from that namespace:

```
/subsystem=logging/logging-profile=custom-log-
profile/logger=com.acme:add(level=INFO)
```

Finally, assign a file handler to the previous logger:

```
/subsystem=logging/logging-profile=custom-log-profile/logger=com.acme:add-
handler(name="application-handler")
```

Your logging configuration is complete and should result in the following:

```
    <logging-profiles>
        <logging-profile name="custom-log-profile">
            <file-handler name="application-handler">
                <level name="INFO"/>
```

```
        <file relative-to="jboss.server.log.dir"
         path="app.log"/>
      </file-handler>
      <logger category="com.acme">
         <level name="INFO"/>
      </logger>
   </logging-profile>
 </logging-profiles>
```

In order to use the logging profile, you can assign the `custom-log-profile` to a deployment via the deployments manifest. Add a `Logging-Profile` entry to the `MANIFEST.MF` file with the logging profile value:

```
Manifest-Version: 1.0
Logging-Profile:  custom-log-profile
```

A logging profile can be assigned to any number of deployments. Using a logging profile also allows for runtime changes to the configuration. This is an advantage over per-deployment logging configuration as a redeployment is not required for logging changes to take effect.

Reading logs with management interfaces

Log files can also be read or downloaded with the management interfaces of the application server. This is quite useful if you don't have an operating system account for inspecting your log files.

You have multiple options for reading logs with management interfaces. We will show at first how to do it with the CLI; next, we will use the REST services of the administration console to read it from a common browser.

Reading logs from the CLI

The logging subsystem includes a log-file resource that can be used to read the list of log files that have been created:

```
/subsystem=logging:read-children-names(child-type=log-file)
{
    "outcome" => "success",
    "result" => [
        "server.log",
        "server.log.2015-02-12",
        "server.log.2015-02-13"
```

```
                    ]
             }
```

If you want to inspect a single log file, then you can use the `read-log-file` operation which is available on each `log-file` resource:

```
/subsystem=logging/log-file=server.log:read-log-file
{
"outcome" => "success",
"result" => [
"2016-02-08 12:09:50,386 INFO
[org.infinispan.configuration.cache.EvictionConfigurationBuilder]
(ServerService Thread Pool -- 58) ISPN000152: Passivation configured
without an eviction policy being selected. Only manually evicted entities
will be passivated.",
"2016-02-08 12:09:51,004 INFO [org.jboss.as.clustering.infinispan]
(ServerService Thread Pool -- 62) WFLYCLINF0002: Started routing cache from
web container",
"2016-02-08 12:09:51,398 INFO [org.wildfly.extension.undertow]
(ServerService Thread Pool -- 58) WFLYUT0021: Registered web context:
/web",
"2016-02-08 12:09:51,453 INFO [org.jboss.as.server] (Controller Boot
Thread) WFLYSRV0010: Deployed "web.war" (runtime-name : "web.war")",
"2016-02-08 12:09:51,585 INFO [org.jboss.as] (Controller Boot Thread)
WFLYSRV0060: Http management interface listening on
http://127.0.0.1:9990/management",
"2016-02-08 12:09:51,586 INFO [org.jboss.as] (Controller Boot Thread)
WFLYSRV0051: Admin console listening on http://127.0.0.1:9990",
"2016-02-08 12:09:51,587 INFO [org.jboss.as] (Controller Boot Thread)
WFLYSRV0025: EAP 7.0.0.Beta1 (WildFly Core 2.0.3.Final-redhat-1) started in
6393ms - Started 373 of 601 services (354 services are lazy, passive or on-
demand)"
]
}
```

The `read-log-file` operation accepts the following parameters:

- `encoding`: The encoding the file should be read in.
- `lines`: The number of lines from the file. A value of -1 indicates all lines should be read.
- `skip`: The number of lines to skip before reading.
- `tail`: True to read from the end of the file up or false to read from the top down.

Besides the CLI, the web console also can be used to download remote log files. You can do that by choosing Runtime | Server | [Selected Server] | Log Files | View.

Streaming logging through HTTP

JBoss EAP allows you to use the HTTP channel to stream server logs from a remote
location. This can be useful if you want to perform some filtering/operations on the content
of log files remotely. You can test it by opening the browser and issuing the following:
`http://localhost:9990/management/subsystem/logging/log-file/server.log?`
`operation=attribute&name=stream&useStreamAsResponse&user=admin&password`
`=mYpassword1!.`

Replace the user and password attribute in the previous URL with a management user and
password

You should expect your browser to request whether you are going to open the log file or
save it locally:

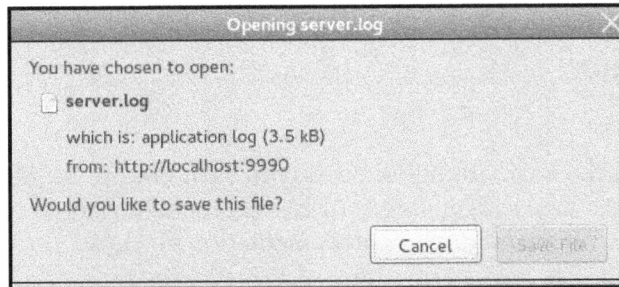

A more programmatic approach consists in using a utility such as curl to request the log file
and save it locally. This offers the benefit that you can choose the log format (in our
example, JSON):

```
curl --digest -L -D - http://127.0.0.1:9990
/management?useStreamAsResponse \
--header "Content-Type: application/json" -u
admin:mYpassword1! \
-d '{"operation":"read-attribute","address":
[{"subsystem":"logging"},{"log-
file":"server.log"}],"name":"stream"}'
```

Building a centralized logging system

In the enterprise, managing log files from a large set of domains can soon become a complex task. For this reason, many enterprises turn to centralized logging. As a matter of fact, centralized logging proves to be quite useful when attempting to identify problems, as it allows you to search through all of your logs in a single place. It is also useful because it allows you to spot issues that span multiple application server nodes by correlating their logs during a specific time frame.

In this chapter we have gone through the `SocketHandler`, which is a generic approach that lends itself to multiple options, such as collecting logs from a central TCP server. If you need to rely on a more robust solution, then you can consider using the **Elasticsearch Logstash Kibana (ELK) Stack**, which is an environment that lets you collect and visualize your logs with the following:

- Logstash for centralized logging, log enrichment and parsing
- Elasticsearch for searching and data analytics
- Kibana for visualizing the data

Using the ELK approach can guarantee scalability to your enterprise, thanks to the Elasticsearch search and analytics engine, which is designed for horizontal scalability, reliability, and easy management (see the documentation at `https://www.elastic.co/guide/en/elasticsearch/guide/current/distributed-cluster.html` for more information about clustering Elasticsearch).

Here is the log pipeline that we are going to set up using these instruments:

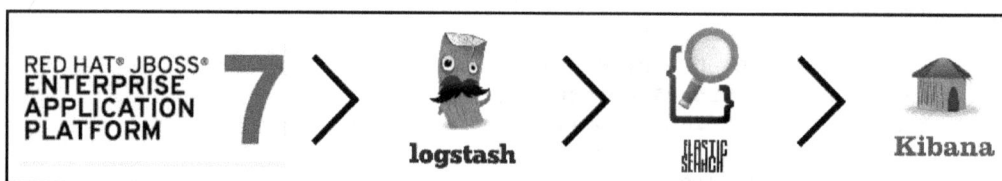

Instructions for installing and configuring the ELK stack can be found on Elastic's site at `https://www.elastic.co/downloads`. As an example, we will create a custom Logstash configuration file.

A basic configuration file for Logstash has three sections:

- `input`: Inputs are the mechanism for passing log data to Logstash.
- `filter`: Filters are workhorses for processing inputs in the Logstash chain.
- `output`: Outputs are the final phase of the Logstash pipeline. An event may pass through multiple outputs during processing, but once all outputs are complete the event has finished its execution.

In the following `logstash.conf` configuration file, we are listening for input messages on port 7080 and outputting them on the default Elasticsearch port 9200:

```
input {
  tcp {
    port => 7080
  }
}

filter {
  json {
    source => "message"
  }
}

output {

  elasticsearch {
  }
}
```

> The previous example assumes `logstash` and `elasticsearch` to be running on the same instance.

You can start `logstash` as follows:

```
$ ./bin/logstash-f logstash.conf
```

Now start the `elasticsearch` engine:

```
$ ./bin/elasticsearch
```

You can verify that `elasticsearch` is running by pointing the browser to the default port `9200`:

On the EAP side, configure the `SocketHandler` as described in the *Custom handlers* section. The application server will start sending log messages through the TCP socket port `7080`.

Finally, launch the Kibana data visualizer:

$ ./bin/kibana

If you have correctly configured the pipeline of messages, you should be able to visualize your log message through the browser on the address `http://localhost:5601`:

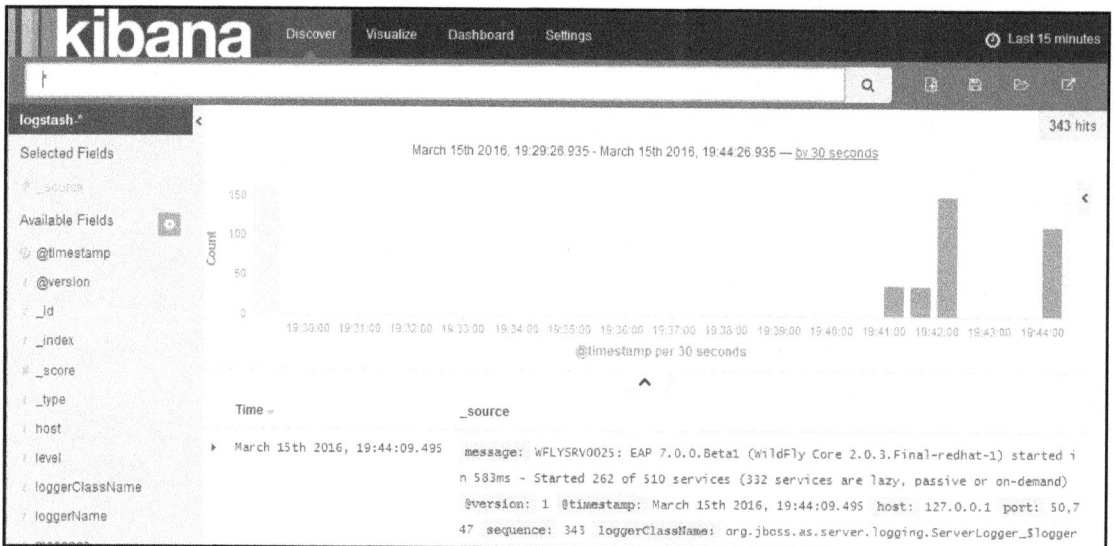

From the **Discover** tab, you should be able to browse through the log messages and visualize the specific fields that have been derived from the log message.

As you can see, Kibana completes the ELK stack pipeline and helps give you a powerful all-in-one solution for log parsing, analysis, and graphical visualization.

Summary

In this chapter, we have extensively covered how to configure log events produced by the application server and the application installed on it. We have provided some initial background on the default configuration, then we have covered advanced features such as custom loggers and producing log data to a centralized system.

The next chapter will cover another key subsystem: the configuration of database connectivity.

8
Configuring Database Connectivity

In this chapter, you will learn what a datasource is and how to configure it via CLI. To configure datasources, JBoss EAP 7 provides a specific subsystem named `urn:jboss:domain:datasources`.

The following are the topics you will learn about as we progress through this chapter on datasources:

- Datasource overview
- Adding a JDBC 4 Driver
- Defining a new datasource
- Using connection pools
- Defining an XA-datasource
- The difference between XA e non-XA datasources
- Hardening datasource configuration

To keep things simple and easy to understand, we will rely on a MySQL 5 database to explain the configuration settings throughout this chapter.

Also, because the datasource configuration is independent of the JBoss EAP running mode, we will use the standalone mode to test our configuration; we will, however, provide scripts for both modes.

Introduction to datasources

One of the most important features an application ever has, is the ability to save its state to a database.

JBoss EAP 7 supports this ability with the concept of a `datasource`, which is the place you configure connectivity settings. Furthermore, JBoss supports your environment even more, by providing an in- memory database for development purposes, named `H2 database`.

JBoss EAP 7 has a dedicated subsystem to configure `datasources`. By default, the `ExampleDS` is configured and bound to the `H2 database` by its driver, as follows:

```
<subsystem xmlns="urn:jboss:domain:datasources:4.0">
    <datasources>
        <datasource jndi-name="java:jboss/datasources/ExampleDS"
         pool-name="ExampleDS" enabled="true"
         use-java-context="true">
            <connection-url>jdbc:h2:mem:test;DB_CLOSE_DELAY=
             -1;DB_CLOSE_ON_EXIT=FALSE</connection-url>
            <driver>h2</driver>
            <security>
                <user-name>sa</user-name>
                <password>sa</password>
            </security>
        </datasource>
        <drivers>
            <driver name="h2" module="com.h2database.h2">
                <xa-datasource-class>org.h2.jdbcx.JdbcDataSource
                </xa-datasource-class>
            </driver>
        </drivers>
    </datasources>
</subsystem>
```

Later in the chapter, we will configure the `datasource` subsystem within the CLI.

Datasource overview

A datasource is a component used to connect to a database. Through the datasource, an application can persist its state (generally speaking) to reuse it later on.

A datasource can connect to any database, as long as the application server provides a connector for it, which is the driver.

JBoss EAP 7 requires that all drivers must be compliant with the JDBC 4 specification. We will see this in detail in the following sections.

Prerequisites

Before we begin, we should have MySQL 5 installed on the system. In case you don't have it set up, it's time to take a dive into the operational world and install what is needed, and it's not just MySQL.

Let's now give a warm welcome to Docker, as our enabling technology to better understand the book. We have a chapter dedicated to Docker and will learn more about it in detail in Chapter 13, *Using EAP 7 with Docker*.

Regardless of your operating system, whether, Windows, Linux, or OS X, you should be able to install Docker in a few steps. I am using a Fedora 23 server as my working environment, and I'll explain how to install Docker and run a MySQL 5 server in a container. For a deeper understanding of the background working, please refer to Chapter 13, *Using EAP 7 with Docker*.

Ok, let's stop starting and start finishing.

Open a terminal window and type in the following command:

```
dnf -y install docker
```

Once installed, you need to activate the Docker daemon, as follows:

```
sudo service docker start
```

Now we can run a MySQL 5 server containerized. Just issue the following command in a new terminal window:

```
docker run -it --rm=true -p 3306:3306 -e MYSQL_ROOT_PASSWORD=root --name=mjbeap7_mysql mysql
```

The preceding command should trigger a pull from Docker's public registry for the MySQL version labeled latest, downloading all the layers it needs to run the container on, as depicted in the following screenshot:

```
docker run -it --rm=true -p 3306:3306 -e MYSQL_ROOT_PASSWORD=root --name=mjbeap7_mysql mysql
Unable to find image 'mysql:latest' locally
Trying to pull repository docker.io/library/mysql ... latest: Pulling from library/mysql
f32095d4ba8a: Pull complete
9b607719a62a: Pull complete
077420be376c: Pull complete
4ccc44ce8a54: Pull complete
2b650acda9c9: Pull complete
4bf729879498: Pull complete
74ed6f421f3f: Pull complete
be67940d8706: Pull complete
7020fa944237: Pull complete
d18d6899b7ef: Pull complete
5d07762772f4: Pull complete
755dbdf60599: Pull complete
4102ac5c18f9: Pull complete
4e0aacde4bdd: Pull complete
87c87999729e: Pull complete
9ece564cf894: Pull complete
Digest: sha256:7665507aea0785e89e51c193381ec33ec8662d02cd5c995b9f31e432fcaaa541
Status: Downloaded newer image for docker.io/mysql:latest
```

Docker downloading MySQL, official image from Docker's public registry

After MySQL has been downloaded and loaded on the local (your PC) Docker repository, the image will be launched as a container.

Sometimes you might encounter an error, as follows:

```
Error response from daemon: Cannot start container
d6bccc42a7e3ba761666c80b33de8c6aa3d2df8f6901644dca39c98acbb0e245: failed to
create endpoint mjbeap7_mysql on network bridge: iptables failed: iptables
--wait -t nat -A DOCKER -p tcp -d 0/0 --dport 3306 -j DNAT --to-destination
172.17.0.2:3306 ! -i docker0: iptables: No chain/target/match by that name.
    (exit status 1)
```

In that event, apply the `first IT principle`, as follows:

```
service docker restart
docker run -it --rm=true -p 3306:3306 -e MYSQL_ROOT_PASSWORD=root --
name=mjbeap7_mysql mysql
```

You should now be able to see the last log line from Docker's output console, as follows:

```
...
Version: '5.7.9'  socket: '/var/run/mysqld/mysqld.sock'  port: 3306
MySQL Community Server (GPL)
```

That means everything worked as expected. For simplicity, we will stop the container and run it back, by putting it in the background, as shown in the following screenshot:

```
# docker ps -a
CONTAINER ID        IMAGE           COMMAND                 CREATED         STATUS          PORTS                   NAMES
888b9e38599b        mysql           "/entrypoint.sh mysql"  4 seconds ago   Up 35 seconds   0.0.0.0:3306->3306/tcp  mjbeap7_mysql
# docker stop 888b9e38599b
888b9e38599b
# docker run -d -p 3306:3306 -e MYSQL_ROOT_PASSWORD=root --name=mjbeap7_mysql mysql
621b065a0faf9d3c8093a21282602a698af2089211e8f008f28f757d0af0bb12
# docker ps -a
CONTAINER ID        IMAGE           COMMAND                 CREATED         STATUS          PORTS                   NAMES
621b065a0faf        mysql           "/entrypoint.sh mysql"  4 seconds ago   Up 2 seconds    0.0.0.0:3306->3306/tcp  mjbeap7_mysql
```

Running MySQL 5 container in the background

The command docker ps -a gives you the list of the created containers, either running or not running. From the output, we get the container ID and use it within the docker stop command, to stop such containers.

Then, we run the container again, but removing the -it and --rm=true flags, and adding instead the -d flag, which means in the background.

Ok, that's enough Docker for the moment, we will come back to it in detail later in the book.

Now we can take care of our JBoss EAP 7 and its datasource configuration, and all that comes along with it.

Adding a JDBC 4 driver module

First of all, we need to download the JDBC 4-compliant driver from the database vendor site. In our case, as previously mentioned, our database is a MySQL 5 server, so we will download the MySQL 5 connector from the following site: https://dev.mysql.com/downloads/connector/j/.

In case you need the direct link to the bundle, visit the following link: https://dev.mysql.com/get/Downloads/Connector-J/mysql-connector-java-5.1.38.zip.

Now extract the archive and open the JBoss EAP 7 CLI, as follows:

```
unzip /opt/rh/mysql-connector-java-5.1.38.zip -d /tmp
cd $JBOSS_HOME
./bin/jboss-cli.sh
module add --name=com.mysql --slot=main --resources=/tmp/mysql- connector-
java-5.1.38/mysql-connector-java-5.1.38-bin.jar --
dependencies=javax.api,javax.transaction.api
```

This will automatically create the path folder `com/mysql` under the `modules` folder of `$JBOSS_HOME`, and it will also copy the resource `mysql-connector-java-5.1.38-bin.jar` into it.

Additionally, a `module.xml` file descriptor will be generated according to paths, resources, and dependencies.

For reference, it follows the `module.xml` generated:

```xml
<?xml version="1.0" ?>
<module xmlns="urn:jboss:module:1.1" name="com.mysql" slot="main">
    <resources>
        <resource-root path="mysql-connector-java-5.1.38-bin.jar"/>
    </resources>
    <dependencies>
        <module name="javax.api"/>
        <module name="javax.transaction.api"/>
    </dependencies>
</module>
```

Once the JDBC 4-compliant driver module has been installed, we can proceed by adding the driver into the JBoss EAP 7 configuration, so it can be used, and thus referenced, by datasources.

Configuring a JDBC 4-compliant driver

Before configuring the driver, we need to create a custom base directory to store our configuration, and run the instance with the flag `--admin-only`, as follows:

```
cp -a standalone mysql
./bin/standalone.sh -Djboss.server.base.dir=mysql --admin-only
```

Now, in a new terminal window, connect to CLI, and issue the following command:

```
/subsystem=datasources/jdbc-driver=mysql:add(driver-name=mysql,driver-
module-name=com.mysql,driver-xa-datasource-class-
name=com.mysql.jdbc.jdbc2.optional.MysqlXADataSource,driver-class-
name=com.mysql.jdbc.Driver)
```

The previous command will add the specified driver to the list of available drivers in the datasource subsystem. Here it is for reference:

```xml
<subsystem xmlns="urn:jboss:domain:datasources:4.0">
    <datasources>
        <datasource jndi-name="java:jboss/datasources/ExampleDS"
```

```
            pool-name="ExampleDS" enabled="true"
            use-java-context="true">
                <connection-url>jdbc:h2:mem:test;
                 DB_CLOSE_DELAY=-1;DB_CLOSE_ON_EXIT=FALSE
                </connection-url>
                <driver>h2</driver>
                <security>
                    <user-name>sa</user-name>
                    <password>sa</password>
                </security>
            </datasource>
            <drivers>
                <driver name="h2" module="com.h2database.h2">
                    <xa-datasource-class>
                     org.h2.jdbcx.JdbcDataSource</xa-datasource-class>
                </driver>
                <driver name="mysql" module="com.mysql">
                    <driver-class>com.mysql.jdbc.Driver</driver-class>
                    <xa-datasource-class>
                     com.mysql.jdbc.jdbc2.optional.MysqlXADataSource
                    </xa-datasource-class>
                </driver>
            </drivers>
        </datasources>
    </subsystem>
```

If running in domain mode, it follows this command:

```
/profile=default/subsystem=datasources/jdbc-driver=mysql:add(driver-
name=mysql,driver-module-name=com.mysql,driver-xa-datasource-class-
name=com.mysql.jdbc.jdbc2.optional.MysqlXADataSource,driver-class-
name=com.mysql.jdbc.Driver)
```

There are a lot of options you can use to configure a datasource. The following is a table that summarizes them all:

Name	Description
driver-name	Specifies the symbolic name of the driver, used to reference this driver.
driver-minor-version	Specifies the minor version of this driver. If the major and minor versions are omitted, the first available driver in the module will be used.
driver-major-version	Specifies the major version of this driver. If the major and minor versions are omitted the first available driver in the module will be used.

`jdbc-compliant`	Specifies whether the driver is compliant or not.
`profile`	Deprecated – specifies the profile to belong to; only available in domain mode.
`driver-module-name`	Specifies the name of the EAP module providing this driver.
`module-slot`	Specifies the slot from where the module was loaded.
`deployment-name`	Specifies the runtime name of the deployment from which the driver was loaded.
`driver-class-name`	Specifies the fully qualified name of the JDBC driver class.
`driver-datasource-class-name`	Specifies the fully qualified name of the `javax.sql.DataSource` implementation class.
`driver-xa-datasource-class-name`	Specifies the fully qualified name of the `javax.sql.XADataSource` implementation class.

We can now create our first datasource to connect to our MySQL, running in a Docker container.

Defining a new datasource

Let's start this step by creating a datasource, providing basic configuration settings such as:

- Its name
- The JNDI name – used by the application to reference it
- The connection URL to the database we want to connect to
- The credentials to access the database (username and password)
- The driver to use

Connect to the CLI and do as follows:

```
data-source add --name=MySQLDS --driver-name=mysql --user-name=root --password=root --connection-url="jdbc:mysql://192.168.59.104:3306/mysql?autoReconnect=true&useSSL=false" --jndi-name=java:jboss/MySQLDS
```

The preceding command should have added the datasource definition inside the `standalone.xml` file. Here it is for reference:

```
<datasource jndi-name="java:jboss/MySQLDS" pool-name="MySQLDS">
    <connection-
url>jdbc:mysql://192.168.59.104:3306/mysql?autoReconnect=true&amp;useSSL=fa
lse</connection-url>
    <driver>mysql</driver>
    <security>
        <user-name>root</user-name>
        <password>root</password>
    </security>
</datasource>
```

In my case, Docker's container IP is `192.168.59.104`; you should replace that with the one assigned to your environment.

If running in domain mode, it follows this command:

```
data-source --profile=default add --name=MySQLDS --driver-name=mysql --
user-name=root --password=root --connection-
url="jdbc:mysql://192.168.59.104:3306/mysql?autoReconnect=true&useSSL=false
" --jndi-name=java:jboss/MySQLDS
```

There is no need to enable the `data-source`, as it is enabled by default. In fact, by looking at the logs, right after the `data-source add` command, we can see the following entry:

```
21:16:14,488 INFO  [org.jboss.as.connector.subsystems.datasources] (MSC
service thread 1-4) WFLYJCA0001: Bound data source [java:jboss/MySQLDS]
```

What we want next is to test our datasource and see if it can correctly connect to the database. To do this, we use a nice command to apply to the `data-source`, as follows:

```
[standalone@localhost:9990 /] data-source test-connection-in-pool --
name=MySQLDS
    true
```

If running in domain mode, it follows this command:

```
/host=master/server=YOUR-SERVER-NAME/subsystem=datasources/data-
source=MySQLDS:test-connection-in-pool
```

That was a basic configuration, but we can extend it by adding more interesting settings.

Connection pool for a datasource

Briefly, a connection pool is a bucket where the application server stores connections ready to be used as needed. Each time we need a connection, one is taken from the pool, obviously from the appropriate datasource.

If there are no more connections in the pool, we need to wait for one to be released so we can use it. This behavior should suggest that we can dimension our pool capacity based on the concurrent queries our application can handle, along with database settings (if the database cannot open more than 10 connections simultaneously, it's quite obvious we should not dimension our pool greater than that value).

There are two properties for the connection pool we can provide:

* `min-pool-size` – the minimum number of connections the pool should hold
* `max-pool-size` – the maximum number of connections the pool can hold

To set the minimum and maximum number of connections a pool should hold, you need to connect to the CLI and invoke the following two commands:

```
[standalone@localhost:9990 /] /subsystem=datasources/data-
source=MySQLDS:write-attribute(name=min-pool-size,value=5)
    {"outcome" => "success"}
[standalone@localhost:9990 /] /subsystem=datasources/data-
source=MySQLDS:write-attribute(name=max-pool-size,value=20)
    {"outcome" => "success"}
```

The preceding command added the following settings to our XML configuration file:

```
<pool>
    <min-pool-size>5</min-pool-size>
    <max-pool-size>20</max-pool-size>
</pool>
```

If running in domain mode, it follows this command:

```
/profile=default/subsystem=datasources/data-source=MySQLDS:write-
attribute(name=min-pool-size,value=5)
/profile=default/subsystem=datasources/data-source=MySQLDS:write-
attribute(name=max-pool-size,value=20)
```

So now, every time an application using our MySQLDS datasource asks for a connection, first the EAP looks for a connection in the pool, if it exists, it grabs it and gives it to the application. On the other hand, if there is no connection available, it creates a new one and gives it to the application.

Once the application is done using it, the connection is not thrown away, it is just placed in the pool, ready to be used again later on. So if the application needs another connection, the pool will not generate a new one, but it gives back the one it already holds.

This will maintain the actual number of available connections in the pool equal to 1, as long as the application asks for another connection when the first one is already in use. That would increase the number of available connections in the pool to 2, and so on, until it reaches the max-pool-size; then the application will wait for a connection (until time out).

In case you want the pool to have the exact minimum number of connections at start-up, we need to instruct the pool to pre-fill itself with that minimum number of connections.

To do it, connect to the CLI, and invoke the following commands:

```
/subsystem=datasources/data-source=MySQLDS:write-attribute(name=pool-
prefill,value=true)
    {
        "outcome" => "success",
        "response-headers" => {
            "operation-requires-reload" => true,
            "process-state" => "reload-required"
        }
    }
```

If running in domain mode, it follows this command:

```
/profile=default/subsystem=datasources/data-source=MySQLDS:write-
attribute(name=pool-prefill,value=true)
```

So, to make the change take effect, reload the application server with the reload command directly from the CLI.

Ok, now what?

Should I just trust my new settings? How can I see if effectively there are five available connections in the pool?

Each datasource can be monitored, as long as you enable its statistics usage. We can do this by issuing the following from the CLI:

```
/subsystem=datasources/data-source=MySQLDS:write-
attribute(name=statistics-enabled,value=true)
    {
        "outcome" => "success",
        "response-headers" => {
            "operation-requires-reload" => true,
            "process-state" => "reload-required"
        }
    }
```

If running in domain mode, it follows this command:

```
/profile=default/subsystem=datasources/data-source=MySQLDS:write-
attribute(name=statistics-enabled,value=true)
```

Once you have reloaded JBoss EAP 7, you can obtain the pool statistics with the following command:

```
/subsystem=datasources/data-source=MySQLDS/statistics=pool:read-
resource(include-defaults=true,include-runtime=true)
```

The previous command produces the following output:

```
{
    "outcome" => "success",
    "result" => {
        "ActiveCount" => 5,
        "AvailableCount" => 20,
        "AverageBlockingTime" => 0L,
        "AverageCreationTime" => 69L,
        "AverageGetTime" => 0L,
        "AveragePoolTime" => 0L,
        "AverageUsageTime" => 0L,
        "BlockingFailureCount" => 0,
        "CreatedCount" => 5,
        "DestroyedCount" => 0,
        "IdleCount" => 5,
        "InUseCount" => 0,
        "MaxCreationTime" => 330L,
        "MaxGetTime" => 0L,
        "MaxPoolTime" => 0L,
        "MaxUsageTime" => 0L,
        "MaxUsedCount" => 1,
        "MaxWaitCount" => 0,
        "MaxWaitTime" => 0L,
        "TimedOut" => 0,
        "TotalBlockingTime" => 0L,
        "TotalCreationTime" => 346L,
        "TotalGetTime" => 0L,
        "TotalPoolTime" => 0L,
        "TotalUsageTime" => 0L,
        "WaitCount" => 0,
        "XACommitAverageTime" => 0L,
        "XACommitCount" => 0L,
        "XACommitMaxTime" => 0L,
        "XACommitTotalTime" => 0L,
        "XAEndAverageTime" => 0L,
        "XAEndCount" => 0L,
        "XAEndMaxTime" => 0L,
        "XAEndTotalTime" => 0L,
        "XAForgetAverageTime" => 0L,
        "XAForgetCount" => 0L,
        "XAForgetMaxTime" => 0L,
        "XAForgetTotalTime" => 0L,
        "XAPrepareAverageTime" => 0L,
        "XAPrepareCount" => 0L,
        "XAPrepareMaxTime" => 0L,
        "XAPrepareTotalTime" => 0L,
        "XARecoverAverageTime" => 0L,
        "XARecoverCount" => 0L,
        "XARecoverMaxTime" => 0L,
        "XARecoverTotalTime" => 0L,
        "XARollbackAverageTime" => 0L,
        "XARollbackCount" => 0L,
        "XARollbackMaxTime" => 0L,
        "XARollbackTotalTime" => 0L,
        "XAStartAverageTime" => 0L,
        "XAStartCount" => 0L,
        "XAStartMaxTime" => 0L,
        "XAStartTotalTime" => 0L,
        "statistics-enabled" => true
    }
}
```

Displaying datasource's pool statistics

If running in domain mode, it follows this command:

```
/host=master/server=YOUR-SERVER-NAME/subsystem=datasources/data-
source=MySQLDS/statistics=pool:read-resource(include-runtime=true)
```

Ok, setting the minimum and maximum was quite easy and reasonable, but I think there is something we should focus on, and it is what happens to the connections in the pool if the database becomes unavailable?

The connections are not valid anymore, they have a socket reference to something that does not exist anymore, or at least it has changed its socket!

So what do I do with my now invalid connections? How can I throw them away so I can make room for new and valid ones?

Flushing a pool's connections

There are quite a few actions you can take to solve the problem. The most immediate is a manual action that consists of instructing the pool to flush its connections via the CLI. This approach consists of connecting to the CLI and issuing a flush strategy. We have the following strategies:

- `flush-all-connection-in-pool`: This flushes all connections in the pool from the given datasource
- `flush-gracefully-connection-in-pool`: This flushes connections once they come back to the pool from the application
- `flush-idle-connection-in-pool`: This flushes all idle connections in the pool from the given datasource
- `flush-invalid-connection-in-pool`: This flushes all connections that result as invalid

The command to invoke in the CLI is the following:

```
data-source FLUSH-STRATEGY --name=MySQLDS
```

Whereas `FLUSH-STRATEGY` can be any of the previously-mentioned flush strategies, using the `flush-all-connection-in-pool` strategy can lead to problems if the application code does not consider connection problems when using it, not just when retrieving a connection.

If running in domain mode, here is the the command:

```
/host=master/server=YOUS-SERVER-NAME/subsystem=datasources/data-
source=MySQLDS:flush-idle-connection-in-pool()
```

> **TIP**
>
> A manual approach surely gives you more confidence, but an automatic mechanism could guarantee your service functionality and availability.

Validating pool's connection

JBoss EAP 7 provides features by which a connection can be validated when it is obtained from the pool.

You can specify a `validation-on-match` (true or false) setting that if set to true will validate the connection against the database. You can also choose a `background-validation` setting (true or false) that if set to true will validate the connection against the database, based on intervals. As a matter of fact, you will also have to specify `background-validation-millis`, which defines how often, in milliseconds, connections must be validated.

To add a validation method, connect to the CLI and do as follows:

```
batch
/subsystem=datasources/data-source=MySQLDS:write-attribute
  (name=validate-on-match,value=true)
/subsystem=datasources/data-source=MySQLDS:write-attribute
  (name=background-validation,value=false)
run-batch
The batch executed successfully
process-state: reload-required
```

The preceding command will create the following definition in the `datasource` section of EAP's configuration file (`domain.xml` or `standalone.xml`):

```
<validation>
    <validate-on-match>true</validate-on-match>
    <background-validation>false</background-validation>
</validation>
```

In the case of `background-validation`, it follows this CLI command:

```
batch
/subsystem=datasources/data-source=MySQLDS:write-
```

```
attribute(name=validate-on-match,value=false)
    /subsystem=datasources/data-source=MySQLDS:write-
attribute(name=background-validation,value=true)
    /subsystem=datasources/data-source=MySQLDS:write-
attribute(name=background-validation-millis,value=5000)
    run-batch
```

And here it comes, the XML definition in the `datasource` section:

```
<validation>
    <validate-on-match>false</validate-on-match>
    <background-validation>true</background-validation>
    <background-validation-millis>5000</background-validation-millis>
</validation>
```

By the way, an invalid connection is found, the next connection in the pool will be checked, until the entire pool is cycled. Otherwise, you can rely on the `use-fast-fail` flag.

Now, we need to define a validation mechanism that determines when a connection is to be considered not valid. JBoss EAP 7 provides a series of `Connection Checker` Java classes that you can use in relation to the underlying database to validate a connection.

Here are the available classes:

```
org.jboss.jca.adapters.jdbc.extensions.db2.DB2ValidConnectionChecker
org.jboss.jca.adapters.jdbc.extensions.mssql.MSSQLValidConnectionChecker
org.jboss.jca.adapters.jdbc.extensions.mysql.MySQLReplicationValidConnectio
nChecker
org.jboss.jca.adapters.jdbc.extensions.mysql.MySQLValidConnectionChecker
org.jboss.jca.adapters.jdbc.extensions.oracle.OracleValidConnectionChecker
org.jboss.jca.adapters.jdbc.extensions.postgres.PostgreSQLValidConnectionCh
ecker
org.jboss.jca.adapters.jdbc.extensions.sybase.SybaseValidConnectionChecker
org.jboss.jca.adapters.jdbc.extensions.novendor.JDBC4ValidConnectionChecker
```

You can specify the `Connection Checker` via the CLI using the following command:

```
/subsystem=datasources/data-source=MySQLDS:write-attribute(name=valid-
connection-checker-class-
name,value=org.jboss.jca.adapters.jdbc.extensions.mysql.MySQLValidConnectio
nChecker)
```

Alternatively, you can provide an `always` working query that will be issued against the database to check a connection's validity, by adding the `check-valid-connection-sql` element, as follows:

```
/subsystem=datasources/data-source=MySQLDS:write-attribute(name=check-
valid-connection-sql,value="select 1")
```

Keep in mind that when a fatal exception appears, the connection gets closed immediately even in the case of a transaction. Thus, we need a component to clean up resources. JBoss provides the following:

```
org.jboss.jca.adapters.jdbc.extensions.db2.DB2ExceptionSorter
org.jboss.jca.adapters.jdbc.extensions.informix.InformixExceptionSorter
org.jboss.jca.adapters.jdbc.extensions.mssql.MSSQLExceptionSorter
org.jboss.jca.adapters.jdbc.extensions.mysql.MySQLExceptionSorter
org.jboss.jca.adapters.jdbc.extensions.oracle.OracleExceptionSorter
org.jboss.jca.adapters.jdbc.extensions.postgres.PostgreSQLExceptionSorter
org.jboss.jca.adapters.jdbc.extensions.sybase.SybaseExceptionSorter
org.jboss.jca.adapters.jdbc.extensions.novendor.AlwaysExceptionSorter
org.jboss.jca.adapters.jdbc.extensions.novendor.NullExceptionSorter
```

To provide such a feature via CLI, do as follows:

```
/subsystem=datasources/data-source=MySQLDS:write-attribute(name=stale-
connection-checker-class-
name,value=org.jboss.jca.adapters.jdbc.extensions.mysql.MySQLExceptionSorte
r)
```

The preceding command adds the following XML definition:

```
<stale-connection-checker class-
name="org.jboss.jca.adapters.jdbc.extensions.mysql.MySQLExceptionSorter"/>
```

By providing all the previously mentioned settings, you can mitigate issues due to network problems, database maintenance, or other events that may cause JBoss to lose the connection to the database.

Defining an XA-datasource

There is not much difference between creating a datasource and an XA-datasource. The main differences between these two kinds of data source are linked to subsystem configuration and transactions.

The same concepts explained for the Data-source also apply to the XA-datasource, so we will just see how to define and configure an XA-datasource.

To create an XA-Datasource, you can start with a basic configuration, as follows:

- Its name
- The JNDI name – used by the application to reference it

- The connection properties – connection information to the database are provided as properties, instead of a URL
- The credentials to access the database (username and password)
- The driver to use

Connect to the CLI and do as follows:

```
xa-data-source add --name=MySQLXADS --jndi-name=java:jboss/MySQLXADS --
driver-name=mysql --user-name=root --password=root --xa-datasource-
properties={"ServerName"=>"192.168.59.104","DatabaseName"=>"mysql"}
```

The preceding command should have added the `xa-data-source` definition inside the `standalone.xml` file. Here it is for reference:

```
<xa-datasource jndi-name="java:jboss/MySQLXADS" pool-name="MySQLXADS">
    <xa-datasource-property name="ServerName">
        192.168.59.104
    </xa-datasource-property>
    <xa-datasource-property name="DatabaseName">
        mysql
    </xa-datasource-property>
    <driver>mysql</driver>
    <security>
        <user-name>root</user-name>
        <password>root</password>
    </security>
</xa-datasource>
```

There is no need to enable the datasource, as it is enabled by default. In fact, by looking at the logs, right after the `xa-data-source add` command, we can see the following entry:

```
10:36:22,774 INFO  [org.jboss.as.connector.subsystems.datasources] (MSC
service thread 1-2) WFLYJCA0001: Bound data source [java:jboss/MySQLXADS]
```

What we want next is to test our `xa-data-source` and see if it can correctly connect to the database. To do this, we will use a nice command to apply to the `xa-data-source`, as follows:

```
xa-data-source test-connection-in-pool --name=MySQLXADS
true
```

If running in domain mode, it follows this command:

```
/host=master/server=YOUR-SERVER-NAME/subsystem=datasources/xa-data-
source=MySQLXADS:test-connection-in-pool
```

That was a basic configuration, but we can extend it by adding more interesting settings.

Connection pool for an XA-datasource

The connection pool concepts are the same for the non-XA datasource, so we will just see how we can define the connection pool for the XA-datasource.

Here again there are two properties for the connection pool we can provide:

- min-pool-size – The minimum number of connections the pool should hold
- max-pool-size – The maximum number of connections the pool can hold

To set the minimum and maximum number of connections a pool should hold, you need to connect to the CLI and invoke the following two commands:

```
xa-data-source --name=MySQLXADS --min-pool-size=5
xa-data-source --name=MySQLXADS --max-pool-size=20
```

The preceding command added the following settings to our XML configuration file:

```
<xa-pool>
    <min-pool-size>5</min-pool-size>
    <max-pool-size>20</max-pool-size>
</xa-pool>
```

If running in domain mode, it follows this command:

```
/profile=default/subsystem=datasources/xa-data-source=MySQLXADS:write-
attribute(name=min-pool-size,value=5)
/profile=default/subsystem=datasources/xa-data-source=MySQLXADS:write-
attribute(name=max-pool-size,value=20)
```

To use the `prefill` options, just do as follows:

```
[standalone@192.168.59.104:9990 /] xa-data-source --name=MySQLXADS --
pool-prefill=true
operation-requires-reload: true
process-state: reload-required
```

An `xa-data-source` can also be monitored, as long as you enable its statistics usage. We can do this by issuing the following from the CLI:

```
xa-data-source --name=MySQLXADS --statistics-enabled=true
operation-requires-reload: true
process-state: reload-required
```

If running in domain mode, it follows this command:

```
/profile=default/subsystem=datasources/xa-data-source=MySQLXADS:write-
attribute(name=statistics-enabled,value=true)
```

Once you have reloaded JBoss EAP 7, you can obtain the pool statistics with the following command:

```
/subsystem=datasources/xa-data-source=MySQLXADS/statistics=pool:read-
resource(include-defaults=true,include-runtime=true)
```

As the output is the same for both an XA-datasource and a datasource, please refer to the screenshot `Displaying Data-source's pool statistics`.

If running in domain mode, it follows this command:

```
/host=master/server=YOUR-SERVER-NAME/subsystem=datasources/xa-data-
source=MySQLXADS/statistics=pool:read-resource(include-runtime=true)
```

The concepts and techniques described for a non-XA datasource in regards to `Flushing pool's connections` and `Validating pool's connection` are just the same for an XA-datasource, so please feel free to refer to them for more details.

What we should concentrate on is when to use an XA-datasource and when to use a non-XA datasource. To make the right decision, we must know the difference between XA and non-XA, which is about transactions.

Difference between XA and non-XA datasource

Generally speaking, an XA transaction is a `global transaction` that can be distributed across multiple resources. Instead, a non-XA transaction always implies only one resource.

To coordinate such global transactions across one or more databases, or other resources such as JMS, a transaction manager is required.

For non-XA transactions, there is no need for a transaction manager, because it only involves one resource which coordinates its transaction itself (local transaction).

Most software components are non-XA, because they integrate with a single database.

So XA transactions get involved when integrating with multiple resources; in this scenario, you will have an application server such as JBoss EAP or WildFly acting as the transaction manager, and your heterogeneous resources (MySQL, PostgreSQL, HornetQ JMS, ActiveMQ, whatever) acting as transaction resources.

When your software alters the state of a resource, and you apply a `commit`, all resulting states get committed across all resources. Vice versa is also true: when you apply with a `rollback`, all resulting states get rolled back to their previous state across all resources. These kinds of operations are called `Two Phase Commit` (2PC), which are fully supported and implemented by the transaction manager.

Hardening datasource configuration

As you have seen by reading this chapter, configuring a datasource, either XA or non-XA, includes providing passwords. As long as you keep the configuration to yourself, there is no issue with that. But what happens if you are working with different people, or a different team, who are not related directly to your company? Would you mind giving passwords out? I guess you would, or at least you should.

Fortunately, JBoss EAP 7 (actually, since JBoss EAP 5) provides two ways to *hide* your password.

One way is to encrypt your password by using hashing. The other way is to use a vault to protect one or more password in one place. We will look at both procedures in detail.

Password encryption

First of all, let's talk about hashing. Hashing is about integrity. This means that it is used to check whether a message (a text, a password, a file, and so on) that has arrived at its destination has been changed during its journey or not. A hash is not reversible. Given an input value, you will always get the same hash output. If you make a tiny change to your source, you will get a totally different hash output. There are several hash function algorithms, such as MD5, SHA-3, and so on.

One of the most used (but you should use a better one) is MD5, which is used to generate a checksum of your file. In Unix-like OS (there are also available utilities on Windows as well), you can try to generate a hash of a text, as follows:

```
md5sum <<< JbossEAP7
17a53e651a44332976fafb4ad935be0e  -
```

Now, if you change the b from lower case to an upper case B, you will get the following output:

```
md5sum <<< JBossEAP7
fdeadd8dc1b0c212bac0c7dd1e342853  -
```

As you can see, a little tiny change will generate a totally different value.

Going back to JBoss EAP 7, there is a class called `org.picketbox.datasource.security.SecureIdentityLoginModule`, which can be used to hash a password, and it is also used as a login module within a security domain. That is exactly what we need and will use.

Let's encrypt our MySQL password, as follows:

```
cd $JBOSS_HOME
java -cp
modules/system/layers/base/org/picketbox/main/picketbox-4.9.4.Final-
redhat-1.jar org.picketbox.datasource.security.SecureIdentityLoginModule
root
    Encoded password:  6f8e652f571678f2
```

Now that we have the secret password, we can define a security domain and use it.

Connect to the CLI and do as follows:

```
batch
/subsystem=security/security-domain=datasource-secret-
password:add(cache-type=default)
/subsystem=security/security-domain=datasource-secret-
password/authentication=classic:add
/subsystem=security/security-domain=datasource-secret-
password/authentication=classic/login-
module=SecureIdentityLoginModule:add(code=org.picketbox.datasource.security
.SecureIdentityLoginModule,flag=required,module-
options=[("username"=>"root"),("password"=>"6f8e652f571678f2")])
run-batch
```

Once done and the CLI says *The batch executed successfully*, then you can invoke the `reload` CLI command to have your changes take effect.

Now if you open your `standalone.xml` configuration file, you should find the following configuration:

```
<security-domain name="datasource-secret-password" cache-type="default">
    <authentication>
        <login-module name="SecureIdentityLoginModule"
         code="org.picketbox.datasource.security.SecureIdentityLoginModule"
         flag="required">
            <module-option name="username" value="root"/>
            <module-option name="password" value="6f8e652f571678f2"/>
        </login-module>
    </authentication>
```

```
</security-domain>
```

Now, we can use our security domain within our `MySQLDS data-source`, by issuing the following CLI command:

```
batch
data-source --name=MySQLDS --password=undefined
data-source --name=MySQLDS --user-name=undefined
data-source --name=MySQLDS --security-domain=datasource-secret-password
run-batch
```

Once done and the CLI says *The batch executed successfully*, then you can invoke the `reload` CLI command to have your changes take effect.

Now if you open your `standalone.xml` configuration file, you should find the following configuration:

```
<datasource jndi-name="java:jboss/MySQLDS" pool-name="MySQLDS"
  statistics- enabled="true">
    <connection-url>jdbc:mysql://192.168.59.104:3306/mysql?autoReconnect=
    true&amp;useSSL=false</connection-url>
    <driver>mysql</driver>
    <new-connection-sql>select 1</new-connection-sql>
    <pool>
        <min-pool-size>5</min-pool-size>
        <max-pool-size>20</max-pool-size>
        <prefill>true</prefill>
    </pool>
    <security>
        <security-domain>datasource-secret-password</security-domain>
    </security>
    <validation>
     <valid-connection-checker class-name=
"org.jboss.jca.adapters.jdbc.extensions.mysql.MySQLValidConnectionChecker"/
>
        <check-valid-connection-sql>select 1</check-valid-connection-sql>
        <validate-on-match>false</validate-on-match>
        <background-validation>true</background-validation>
        <background-validation-millis>5000</background-validation-millis>
        <stale-connection-checker class-name=
"org.jboss.jca.adapters.jdbc.extensions.mysql.MySQLExceptionSorter"/>
    </validation>
</datasource>
```

As you can see, now the datasource delegates its security to the specified `security-domain`. Let's test the datasource connection by invoking the `test-connection-in-pool` method on it, as follows:

```
data-source test-connection-in-pool --name=MySQLDS
true
```

By encrypting your password, you can share your configuration without any security or privacy issues.

There is a stronger and better password encryption, which can be used to further protect your overall configuration, using the `VAULT`.

Password protection using the vault

The vault is a place where you can store and protect your passwords. You can store as many passwords as you want, which means that you can encrypt any password for any reason, such as datasource connection credentials and LDAP credentials; everything that needs a password can be encrypted and stored in the vault.

Before we can begin, we need to create a `keystore`, which is used to encrypt our password that will be stored in the vault. We will rely on the JDK `keytool` application.

Open a terminal window and do as follows:

```
cd $JBOSS_HOME
   keytool -genseckey -alias vault -keystore vault.keystore -storetype
jceks -keyalg AES -keysize 128 -storepass jbosseap7 -keypass jbosseap7 -
dname "CN=Mastering JBoss EAP 7,OU=picketbox,O=JBoss,L=chicago,ST=il,C=us"
```

If you list your directory files, you should find the one named `vault.keystore`. We can now proceed with the creation of the vault, as follows:

```
Cd $JBOSS_HOME
./bin/vault.sh
```

You will be prompted to fill in a few interactive steps and provide some information, as depicted in the following screenshot:

```
./bin/vault.sh
WARNING JBOSS_HOME may be pointing to a different installation - unpredictable results may occur.


=============================================================================

  JBoss Vault

  JBOSS_HOME: /opt/rh/eap7

  JAVA: /opt/rh/jdk8/bin/java


=============================================================================

**********************************
****  JBoss Vault  ***************
**********************************
Please enter a Digit::   0: Start Interactive Session  1: Remove Interactive Session  2: Exit
0
Starting an interactive session
Enter directory to store encrypted files: /opt/rh/eap7
Enter Keystore URL: /opt/rh/eap7/vault.keystore
Enter Keystore password: jbosseap7
Enter Keystore password again: jbosseap7
Values match
Enter 8 character salt: 24681357
Enter iteration count as a number (e.g.: 44): 31
Enter Keystore Alias: vault
WFLYSEC0056: Initializing Vault
Mar 05, 2016 1:38:48 PM org.picketbox.plugins.vault.PicketBoxSecurityVault init
INFO: PBOX00361: Default Security Vault Implementation Initialized and Ready
WFLYSEC0048: Vault Configuration in WildFly configuration file:
********************************************
...
</extensions>
<vault>
  <vault-option name="KEYSTORE_URL" value="/opt/rh/eap7/vault.keystore"/>
  <vault-option name="KEYSTORE_PASSWORD" value="MASK-3sdaLJuMR0uYdai7eoCdyJ"/>
  <vault-option name="KEYSTORE_ALIAS" value="vault"/>
  <vault-option name="SALT" value="24681357"/>
  <vault-option name="ITERATION_COUNT" value="31"/>
  <vault-option name="ENC_FILE_DIR" value="/opt/rh/eap7/"/>
</vault><management> ...
********************************************
WFLYSEC0057: Vault is initialized and ready for use
WFLYSEC0058: Handshake with Vault complete
Please enter a Digit::  0: Store a secured attribute  1: Check whether a secured attribute exists  2: Remove secured attribute  3: Exit
0
Task: Store a secured attribute
Please enter secured attribute value (such as password) root
Please enter secured attribute value again root
Values match
Enter Vault Block:MySQLDS
Enter Attribute Name:password
WFLYSEC0047: Secured attribute value has been stored in Vault.
Please make note of the following:
********************************************
Vault Block:MySQLDS
Attribute Name:password
Configuration should be done as follows:
VAULT::MySQLDS::password::1
********************************************
Please enter a Digit::  0: Store a secured attribute  1: Check whether a secured attribute exists  2: Remove secured attribute  3: Exit
3
```

Creating a vault

From the `vault.sh` script output, we need to copy and paste the vault's definition into our `standalone.xml` configuration file. So edit the file and insert the following XML snippet:

```
<vault>
  <vault-option name="KEYSTORE_URL" value="/opt/rh/eap7
  /vault.keystore"/>
  <vault-option name="KEYSTORE_PASSWORD" value=
  "MASK-3sdaLJuMR0uYdai7eoCdyJ"/>
  <vault-option name="KEYSTORE_ALIAS" value="vault"/>
  <vault-option name="SALT" value="24681357"/>
  <vault-option name="ITERATION_COUNT" value="31"/>
  <vault-option name="ENC_FILE_DIR" value="/opt/rh/eap7/"/>
</vault>
```

Beware of placing the preceding vault's definition between the `</extensions>` and `<management>` elements.

As we modified the `standalone.xml` configuration file, we need to stop and start JBoss EAP for the changes to take effect.

Once it's up and running again, we need to reference our password stored in the vault, by using the CLI as follows:

```
batch
data-source --name=MySQLDS --security-domain=undefined
data-source --name=MySQLDS --user-name=root
data-source --name=MySQLDS --password=
                           "${VAULT::MySQLDS::password::1}"
run-batch
```

Once done and the CLI says `The batch executed successfully`, then you can invoke the `reload` CLI command to have your changes take effect.

Now if you open your `standalone.xml` configuration file, you should find the following configuration:

```
<datasource jndi-name="java:jboss/MySQLDS" pool-name="MySQLDS" statistics-
enabled="true">
    <connection-url>jdbc:mysql://192.168.59.104:3306
    /mysql?autoReconnect=true&amp;useSSL=false</connection-url>
    <driver>mysql</driver>
    <new-connection-sql>select 1</new-connection-sql>
    <pool>
        <min-pool-size>5</min-pool-size>
        <max-pool-size>20</max-pool-size>
        <prefill>true</prefill>
    </pool>
```

```
<security>
    <user-name>root</user-name>
    <password>${VAULT::MySQLDS::password::1}</password>
</security>
<validation>
    <valid-connection-checker class-name=
     "org.jboss.jca.adapters.jdbc.extensions.mysql.
     MySQLValidConnectionChecker"/>
    <check-valid-connection-sql>select 1
    </check-valid-connection-sql>
    <validate-on-match>false</validate-on-match>
    <background-validation>true</background-validation>
    <background-validation-millis>5000
    </background-validation-millis>
    <stale-connection-checker class-name=
     "org.jboss.jca.adapters.jdbc.extensions.mysql.
     MySQLExceptionSorter"/>
</validation>
</datasource>
```

As you can see, now the datasource delegates its security to the specified vault, providing the password with that special pattern. Let's test the datasource connection by invoking the `test-connection-in-pool` method on it, as follows:

```
data-source test-connection-in-pool --name=MySQLDS
true
```

Now you can have your entire password secured and protected in a safe place.

Summary

In this chapter, you learned how to define a datasource to connect to a database. You also learned how to improve your connection settings by using connection pools.

You also learned that connections could be invalidated by network issues, and how to mitigate issues by using validation methods and mechanisms.

You learned a little bit of Docker, and its powerful features to deliver a clean environment.

Last, but not least, you learned how to secure your configuration by providing password encryption using a `security-domain` and a `VAULT`.

In the next chapter, we will see how we can configure and manage messaging systems. We will see the messaging broker that JBoss EAP 7 provides, Artemis MQ, which is the combination of two great open source messaging systems: HornetQ and Active MQ.

Configuring EAP 7 for Java EE Applications

9

This chapter describes how to configure the services needed for server-side applications. We will cover a mix of different subsystems but we will also show how to monitor and collect statistics from the application server both using graphical tools and developer tools. Here is our topic list:

- First, we will discuss the **Enterprise Java Beans(EJB)** container
- Next, we will cover Undertow, the new web server
- Finally, we will show how to monitor key attributes from the subsystems involved in application development

Configuring the EJB container

An EJB container serves as the runtime environment for EJB deployed on the application server. An EJB container provides some core services such as the following:

- Transactions
- Instance life cycle management
- Instance pooling
- Security
- Thread safety

There are basically three types of EJB:

- **Stateless Session Beans(SLSBs):** SLSBs are components which don't have a conversational state. Hence, when they are not servicing a client, they are all equivalent.
- **Stateful Session Beans (SFSBs):** SFSBs are conversational components that are tightly coupled with clients. An SFSB accomplishes a task for a particular client and maintains the state for the duration of a client session. After that, the state is not retained.
- **Message-driven beans(MDBs):** MDBs are also components that don't hold a conversational state; however, they are able to asynchronously process messages sent by any JMS producer.

The first type of EJB we will dive deep into is the SLSB, which is typically used to provide stateless business logic to its clients. Since, as we said, they are not bound to a specific client, they are held in a pool of instances that can be used by their clients. Each time a bean is requested, a check is made in the pool to see whether any instance is available. If the instance is available, then it executes the business methods, otherwise the EJB container attempts to create another instance in the pool.

Configuring the stateless EJB pool

The default pool for SLSBs is named `slsb-strict-max-pool` and it can be set via the `default-instance-pool` attribute:

```
/subsystem=ejb3/:read-attribute(name=default-slsb-instance-pool)
{
    "outcome" => "success",
    "result" => "slsb-strict-max-pool"
}
```

The configuration of the pool can be retrieved with the read-resource command as follows:

```
/subsystem=ejb3/strict-max-bean-instance-pool=slsb-strict-max-pool/:read-
resource(recursive=false)
{
    "outcome" => "success",
    "result" => {
        "derive-size" => "from-worker-pools",
        "max-pool-size" => 20,
        "timeout" => 5L,
        "timeout-unit" => "MINUTES"
    }
}
```

```
}
```

The EJB pool has a **maximum size** that determines how many concurrent requests can be made for that EJB. The factor that calculates the pool size is `derive-size`, which can be set to the following attributes:

- `from-worker-pools`: This is the default setting for the `slsb-strict-max-pool` and equals the maximum pool size defined from the IO worker pool. (Please note that, by default, the IO worker pool size is calculated based on the CPU count; see the *Configuring the pool of threads used by Undertow* section.)
- `from-cpu-count`: Indicates that the `max-pool-size` should be derived from the total number of processors available on the system. Note that the computation isn't a 1:1 mapping; the values may or may not be augmented by other factors.
- `none`: The EJB pool is derived from the `max-pool-size`, which will be the upper limit for the pool.

For example, with the following command, you can set the `slsb-strict-max-pool` `derive-size` to none, in case you want to rely on the `max-pool-size` dimension:

```
/subsystem=ejb3/strict-max-bean-instance-pool=slsb-strict-max-pool:write-
attribute(name=derive-size,value=none)
```

Whatever the policy is, you must be aware that if the EJB container cannot fulfill a request within the `timeout` specified (default 5 minutes), an exception will be returned to the client. The following error message will be returned in the event that the EJB container cannot provide an instance to a client:

16:20:43,903 ERROR [io.undertow.request] (myworker task-13) UT005023: Exception handling request to /web/Test: javax.ejb.EJBException: WFLYEJB0378: Failed to acquire a permit within 30 SECONDS
at org.jboss.as.ejb3.pool.strictmax.StrictMaxPool.get(StrictMaxPool.java:110)

Checking for the current size of the EJB pool is therefore a critical metric when you are rolling out your applications in production. In order to gather useful metrics for your EJB, you have at first to enable statistics on the EJB subsystem as follows:

```
/subsystem=ejb3:write-attribute(name=enable-statistics,value=true)
{"outcome" => "success"}
```

Next, you can dig into the `/deployment` subsystem and query for the metrics of your application. For example, if your EJB named `DemoSLSB` is packed in an archive `ejb.jar`, you can query statistics as follows:

/deployment=ejb.jar/subsystem=ejb3/stateless-session-bean=DemoSLSB/:read-resource(recursive=false,include-runtime=true)

```
{
    "outcome" => "success",
    "result" => {
        "component-class-name" => "DemoEJB",
        "declared-roles" => [],
        "execution-time" => 2000L,
        "invocations" => 10L,
        "methods" => {"doSomething" => {
         "execution-time" => 2000L,
         "invocations" => 10L,
        "wait-time" => 0L            }},
        "peak-concurrent-invocations" => 2L,
        "pool-available-count" => 64,
        "pool-create-count" => 2,
        "pool-current-size" => 2,
        "pool-max-size" => 64,
        "pool-name" => "slsb-strict-max-pool",
        "pool-remove-count" => 0,
        "run-as-role" => undefined,
        "security-domain" => "other",
        "timers" => [],
        "wait-time" => 0L,
        "service" => undefined
    }
}
```

In the preceding example, the DemoSLSB has created two SLSBs and the current size of the pool is 2 units.

Configuring the message driven bean pool

The other pool of beans available in the container is related to MDBs. Just like SLSBs, MDBs are also stateless components since they don't store any conversational state. MDBs, however, are activated upon receipt of a JMS message.

Configurations featuring a messaging subsystem (such as full or full-ha) have a default message-driven bean pool definition:

```
/subsystem=ejb3/:read-attribute(name=default-mdb-instance-pool)
{
    "outcome" => "success",
    "result" => "mdb-strict-max-pool"
}
```

The main difference with the SLSB counterpart is that the default MDB pool has a CPU-based derived size:

```
/subsystem=ejb3/strict-max-bean-instance-pool=mdb-strict-max-
pool/:read-resource(recursive=false)
    {
        "outcome" => "success",
        "result" => {
            "derive-size" => "from-cpu-count",
            "max-pool-size" => 20,
            "timeout" => 5L,
            "timeout-unit" => "MINUTES"
        }
    }
```

Configuring the stateful EJB cache

Stateful session beans are conversational components that preserve their state contained in instance variables. Each stateful bean that is instantiated is stored in a **cache,** which is a memory area of the EJB container. You can verify how many stateful beans are being stored in the cache by querying the specific deployment, as in this example:

```
/deployment=ejb.jar/subsystem=ejb3/stateful-session-
bean=DemoSFSB/:read-resource(include-runtime=true)
    {
        "outcome" => "success",
        "result" => {
            "cache-size" => 1,
            "component-class-name" => "DemoEJB",
            "declared-roles" => [],
            "execution-time" => 0L,
            "invocations" => 0L,
            "methods" => {},
            "passivated-count" => 0,
            "peak-concurrent-invocations" => 0L,
            "run-as-role" => undefined,
            "security-domain" => "other",
            "total-size" => 1,
            "wait-time" => 0L,
            "service" => undefined
        }
    }
```

Here, the EJB container has created a cache for the DemoSFSB which contains one element. The passivated-count accounts for the number of passivated EJB.

> **Passivation** is a process that can be used by the EJB container to avoid excessive usage of heap memory, by serializing EJBs from the memory into storage.

By default, the application server is not configured to passivate SSB:

```
/subsystem=ejb3:read-attribute(name=default-sfsb-cache)
{
    "outcome" => "success",
    "result" => "simple"
}
```

The `simple` cache strategy implementation uses an `in-memory` storage and eager expiration of data. As you don't have much control over this process, it is recommended in an Enterprise context to configure the `default-sfsb-cache` as a `distributable` cache which uses, under the hood, the `infinispan` subsystem to manage the passivation of the cache. You can enable the distributable cache through the CLI as follows:

```
/subsystem=ejb3/:write-attribute(name=default-sfsb-
cache,value=distributable)
```

Controlling the amount of stateful beans in the cache

If you are using infinispan's distributable cache, you have greater control over the number of EJBs in the cache. On each EJB container, an **eviction thread** will run to analyze the contents of the cache and decide what to evict. This process does not take into account the amount of free memory in the JVM to remove the beans from the cache. You have to set the `max-entries` attribute of the eviction component to be greater than zero in order for eviction to be turned on:

```
/subsystem=infinispan/cache-container=ejb/local-
cache=passivation/component=eviction/:read-resource(recursive=false)
{
    "outcome" => "success",
    "result" => {
        "max-entries" => -1L,
        "strategy" => "NONE"
    }
}
```

As you can see, `out-of-the-box` eviction is not configured to remove any entry from the cache. You have to set it with a reasonable value, as in the following CLI statement:

```
/subsystem=infinispan/cache-container=ejb/local-
cache=passivation/component=eviction/:write-attribute(name=max-
entries,value=5000)
```

> Please take into account that `max-entries` is relative to each stateful bean deployed on a server. So consider a multiplying factor if you are deploying multiple SFSBs.

When eviction takes places, however, the SFSBs are not lost forever but are passivated to a file store. The location of the file store is, by default, `jboss.server.data.dir`:

```
/subsystem=infinispan/cache-container=ejb/local-
cache=passivation/store=file/:read-attribute(name=relative-to)
{
    "outcome" => "success",
    "result" => "jboss.server.data.dir"
}
```

Unlike eviction, expiration allows you to attach a lifespan and/or a maximum idle time to your stateful EJBs. Entries that exceed these times are *permanently removed* from the cache. This is different from eviction as no passivation takes place.

By default, expiration is not enabled on the passivation cache; however, you can set the lifespan of SFSBs in the cache by means of the `lifespan` attribute, which accepts values in ms (in this example, 120 seconds):

```
/subsystem=infinispan/cache-container=ejb/local-
cache=passivation/component=expiration/:write-
attribute(name=lifespan,value=120000)
```

In much the same way, you can set the `max-idle` time through the max-idle attribute:

```
/subsystem=infinispan/cache-container=ejb/local-
cache=passivation/component=expiration/:write-attribute(name=max-
idle,value=60000)
```

Configuring the web server

In the new version of the application server, the JBoss Web Server engine has been replaced by a high-performance web server named **Undertow,** featuring the following:

- A lightweight HTTP server supporting both blocking and non-blocking IO APIs
- A Servlet 3.1-compliant implementation
- A web socket-compliant implementation
- A reverse proxy server

The Undertow configuration can be broadly split into two main topics: the core server configuration and the servlet container. We will first cover the server infrastructure and then see some important aspects of the Servlet container.

Undertow core server configuration

In terms of architecture, the Undertow web server uses the following core blocks:

- **Connectors**: These components are invoked when a connection is first received. They will do any work required to set up the connection and translate the incoming request into an `io.undertow.server.HttpServerExchange` object, setting up any protocol-specific information and delegating to the first Handler in the Handler chain.
- **Handlers**: These are classes implementing `io.undertow.server.HttpHandler`. They are in charge of providing the core Undertow functionalities. Each Handler, when it has completed its job, can call another Handler in the chain and eventually end the exchange, returning the response to the client.
- **XNIO workers**: This component is in charge of driving the execution of the incoming request. A worker includes two thread pools: an XNIO and IO thread pool which uses *non-blocking* XNIO channels. These channels typically dispatch the execution to worker threads which, on the other hand, allow for *blocking* operations (think, for example, of a standard, non-blocking servlet).

> XNIO is an I/O framework which can be used to provide simplified access to low-level network elements with the introduction of callbacks, thread management, and advanced resource management capabilities. See this link for more information about XNIO: `https://docs.jboss.org/author/display/XNIO/About+XNIO`.

Configuring Undertow connectors

Each Undertow server ships a set of `connectors` (ajp, http, https), which are named listeners in terms of configuration. The default and full configurations include only an http and https listener, whilst the `ha` configuration also includes an ajp listener. Within each listener, you will configure a set of attributes that are common to its protocol. For example, here is the list of attributes that are pertinent to the `http-listener`:

```
/subsystem=undertow/server=default-server/http-listener=default/:read-
resource()
{
    "outcome" => "success",
    "result" => {
        "allow-encoded-slash" => false,
        "allow-equals-in-cookie-value" => false,
        "always-set-keep-alive" => true,
        "buffer-pipelined-data" => true,
        "buffer-pool" => "default",
        "certificate-forwarding" => false,
        "decode-url" => true,
        "disallowed-methods" => ["TRACE"],
        "enable-http2" => false,
        "enabled" => true,
        "max-buffered-request-size" => 16384,
        "max-connections" => undefined,
        "max-cookies" => 200,
        "max-header-size" => 1048576,
        "max-headers" => 200,
        "max-parameters" => 1000,
        "max-post-size" => 10485760L,
        "no-request-timeout" => undefined,
        "proxy-address-forwarding" => false,
        "read-timeout" => undefined,
        "receive-buffer" => undefined,
        "record-request-start-time" => false,
        "redirect-socket" => "https",
        "request-parse-timeout" => undefined,
        "resolve-peer-address" => false,
        "send-buffer" => undefined,
        "socket-binding" => "http",
        "tcp-backlog" => undefined,
        "tcp-keep-alive" => undefined,
        "url-charset" => "UTF-8",
        "worker" => "default",
        "write-timeout" => undefined
    }
}
```

Describing each attribute in the listeners would overly inflate this chapter; however, you can retrieve a description of all attributes via the `read-resource-description` command, as in the following example:

```
/subsystem=undertow/server=default-server/http-listener=default:read-
resource-description
    {
        "outcome" => "success",
        "result" => {
                "allow-encoded-slash" => {
                    "type" => BOOLEAN,
                    "description" => "If a request comes in with encoded /
characters (i.e. %2F), will these be decoded.",
                    "expressions-allowed" => true,
                    "nillable" => true,
                    "default" => false,
                    "access-type" => "read-write",
                    "storage" => "configuration",
                    "restart-required" => "no-services"
                },
    . . . .
```

Configuring the pool of threads used by Undertow

One key attribute of each listener is the `worker` attribute (its default value is *default*) which refers to the pool of threads of the `io` subsystem, which serves as the thread pool for Undertow. Hence, you can manage this thread pool through the `io` subsystem. The default io worker, which is indeed named default, has the following configuration:

```
/subsystem=io/worker=default/:read-resource(recursive=false)
{
    "outcome" => "success",
    "result" => {
       "io-threads" => undefined,
       "stack-size" => 0L,
       "task-keepalive" => 60,
       "task-max-threads" => undefined
    }
}
```

`io-threads` refers to the non-blocking XNIO channels created during the initial part of the exchange process. The execution is then moved to worker threads, whose upper limit is controlled by `task-max-threads`.

As you can see, by default these attributes are undefined, which merely means that some defaults will be used. In practice, if the number of `io-threads` is undefined, a default will be calculated using the following formula:

*Default IO Threads = CPU count * 2*

The same goes for `task-max-threads` which, by default, is calculated with this formula:

*Default Max Threads = CPU count * 16*

Setting a value for this attribute will override the default formulas, for example:

```
/subsystem=io/worker=default/:write-attribute(name=io-threads,value=5)
/subsystem=io/worker=default/:write-attribute(name=task-max-
threads,value=30)
```

In most cases, however, it is recommended to create a custom `io` worker thread for your listeners. This is mostly helpful for monitoring the activities of your threads. Here is how to create a new worker thread named `customworker`:

```
/subsystem=io/worker=customworker:add(io-threads=5, task-max-
threads=25)
```

Next, assign it to `http-listener` as follows:

```
/subsystem=undertow/server=default-server/http-listener=default:write-
attribute(name=worker,value=customworker)
{
    "outcome" => "success",
    "response-headers" => {
        "operation-requires-reload" => true,
        "process-state" => "reload-required"
    }
}
```

Migrating from web configurations

In order to assist the process of migration from EAP 6 / JBoss AS 7 configurations, an automatic migration command has been included in the command line to transform the legacy subsystems into the new EAP 7 subsystems. In our case, we will show how to transform an existing EAP 6 configuration (using the web subsystem) into an Undertow configuration automatically.

> **TIP**
>
> Before starting the migration procedure, make sure no web applications are deployed, otherwise their deployment will remain pinned to the Undertow subsystem!

As the first step, start the server in `--admin-only` mode, which allows us to execute the migration procedure:

```
$ ./standalone.sh --admin-only
```

Now connect with the CLI to your server:

```
$ ./jboss-cli.sh -c
```

The first set of commands we will execute will `remove` the undertow subsystem and extension and restore the legacy web subsystem:

```
/subsystem=undertow:remove
/extension=org.wildfly.extension.undertow:remove
/extension=org.jboss.as.web:add
```

Now you can enter via CLI the configuration of your web subsystem:

```
/subsystem="web":add(default-virtual-server=
  "default-host",native="false")
/subsystem="web"/configuration="container":add()
/subsystem="web"/configuration="static-resources":add()
/subsystem="web"/configuration="jsp-configuration":add()
/subsystem="web"/virtual-server="default-host":add
  (alias=["localhost","example.com"],
  enable-welcome-root="true",name="default-host")
```

Now you can issue the `migrate` command, which will convert the web configuration into an equivalent Undertow configuration:

```
/subsystem=web:migrate
```

> **i**
>
> At the end of the procedure, the legacy `web` subsystem will be automatically removed.

The previous procedure can also be completed by manually including the former web subsystem into the server configuration and commenting out the existing undertow subsystem. Performing these steps manually is, however, error-prone and cannot be automated. If you find reverse engineering your CLI configuration complex, you can have a

look at the profilecloner open source tool, which is available at:
`https://github.com/tfonteyn/profilecloner`.

Migrating Valve components

Migrating the web configuration is a necessary step of the infrastructure migration; it is, however, possible that your existing applications make use of features such as the **Apache Tomcat Valve**, which is declared in the `web.xml` of your applications. Most of the former Valve components can be directly migrated 1:1 to Undertow Handlers. The following table depicts the matches between Valves and Handlers:

Tomcat Valve	Undertow Handler
`org.apache.catalina.valves` `AccessLogValve`	`io.undertow.server.handlers.RequestDumpingHandler`
`org.apache.catalina.valves` `RequestDumperValve`	`io.undertow.server.handlers.` `RequestDumpingHandler`
`org.apache.catalina.valves` `RewriteValve`	`io.undertow.server.handlers.SetAttributeHandler`
`org.apache.catalina.valves` `RemoteHostValve`	`io.undertow.server.handlers.` `AccessControlListHandler`
`org.apache.catalina.valves` `RemoteAddrValve`	`io.undertow.server.handlers.` `IPAddressAccessControlHandler`
`org.apache.catalina.valves` `RemoteIpValve`	`io.undertow.server.handlers.` `ProxyPeerAddressHandler`

As an example, take the following excerpt from the `web.xml` of an application running on EAP 6:

```
<valve>
  <class-name>
    org.apache.catalina.valves.RequestDumperValve
  </class-name>
</valve>
```

As the first step, remove the Valve declaration from `web.xml`. Next, include in the Undertow configuration the corresponding Handler, which is `io.undertow.server.handlers.RequestDumpingHandler`. You can activate it via the CLI as follows:

```
/subsystem=undertow/configuration=filter/custom-filter=request-
dumper:add(class-name=io.undertow.server.handlers.RequestDumpingHandler,
module=io.undertow.core)
    /subsystem=undertow/server=default-server/host=default-host/filter-
ref=request-dumper:add
```

Configuring Undertow to serve static content

Undertow can be also configured to serve static content just like an Apache web server would do. Static content can be provided by means of a file handler. By default, there is a file handler that serves the root web application, as you can see from this excerpt of the configuration file:

```
<handlers>
   <file name="welcome-content" path="${jboss.home.dir}/
   welcome- content"/>
</handlers>
```

You can, of course, create additional file handlers pointing to path resources. Here is the CLI command to create a new file handler pointing its document root to a location on your file system:

```
/subsystem=undertow/configuration=handler/file=static-
content:add(path="/path/to/docroot")
```

In order to improve the performance of static resources, a cache engine **named the Buffer cache** is used. Buffers are allocated in-memory areas called regions and are a fixed size. The values for the default Buffer cache are the following:

```
/subsystem=undertow/buffer-cache=default/:read-resource()
{
    "outcome" => "success",
    "result" => {
        "buffer-size" => 1024,
        "buffers-per-region" => 1024,
        "max-regions" => 10
    },
}
```

As you can see, by multiplying buffer size * buffers-per-region * max-regions, a default value of 10 MB is used for the Buffer cache. You can reserve more space for this area by increasing, for example, the buffer-size attribute:

```
/subsystem=undertow/buffer-cache=default/:write-attribute(name=buffer-
size,value=2048)
```

Undertow servlet container

The other core block of Undertow is the **servlet container**, which is a Servlet 3.1 and web socket-compliant engine. Its functionalities are managed through the `servlet-container` element, which corresponds to an instance of an Undertow servlet container. For most configurations, only a single servlet container would be required; however, there may be cases where it makes sense to create multiple containers. Here is the default servlet Container configuration:

```
/subsystem=undertow/servlet-container=default/:read-
resource(recursive=false)
    {
        "outcome" => "success",
        "result" => {
            "allow-non-standard-wrappers" => false,
            "default-buffer-cache" => "default",
            "default-encoding" => undefined,
            "default-session-timeout" => 30,
            "directory-listing" => undefined,
            "disable-caching-for-secured-pages" => true,
            "eager-filter-initialization" => false,
            "ignore-flush" => false,
            "max-sessions" => undefined,
            "proactive-authentication" => true,
            "session-id-length" => 30,
            "stack-trace-on-error" => "local-only",
            "use-listener-encoding" => false,
            "mime-mapping" => undefined,
            "setting" => {
                "jsp" => undefined,
                "websockets" => undefined
            },
            "welcome-file" => undefined
        }
    }
```

Just like we did for the connectors, we can retrieve a description of each attribute through the `read-resource-description` command:

```
/subsystem=undertow/servlet-container=default/:read-resource-
description
```

Some interesting attributes deserve particular attention. For example, you can specify the default **HTTP Session Timeout** through the `default-session-timeout` property. The value of this attribute is specified in minutes and defaults to 30.

To configure the `default-session-timeout` to a different value, you can use the following CLI (in this example, `60` minutes):

```
/subsystem=undertow/servlet-container=default:write-
attribute(name=default-session-timeout, value=60)
```

> The configuration provided in the servlet container can be overridden by the `session-timeout` attribute of the `web.xml` configuration file.

The servlet container is also capable of defining the **maximum number of sessions** that can be active at the same time. This attribute is undefined by default; you can, however, set it through the `max-sessions` attribute. In the following example, we are setting it to 100 units:

```
/subsystem=undertow/servlet-container=default/:write-
attribute(name=max-sessions,value=100)
```

Finally, another attribute worth noting is the **development mode**. Basically, the idea with this parameter is that when the development mode is set to true, the server behaves in a developer-friendly mode, allowing hot redeploy of JSP files. The default for this attribute is `false`; you can turn it to true with the following CLI:

```
/subsystem=undertow/servlet-container=default/setting=jsp/:write-
attribute(name=development,value=true)
```

Monitoring your applications

So far, we have learnt how to gather basic statistics from the CLI about some key attributes. The values extracted from the CLI can be easily extended into a scripting system, which includes some more advanced functionalities such as alerts or triggers. In an Enterprise context, however, it is often required to gather information that is not directly exposed by the CLI or to create graphical views or even business intelligence from this data. We will show which tools are commonly used for this purpose.

Using JConsole to display graphical attributes

A common and widely used tool for visualizing insights about your server's key attributes is **JConsole,** which ships as part of the JDK. A detailed description of this tool is available on the Oracle site at:

`http://docs.oracle.com/javase/8/docs/technotes/guides/management/jconsole.html`.

You can start JConsole using a patched script included in your `JBOSS_HOME`/`bin`, named `jconsole.sh`. This script includes in the classpath some EAP 7 libraries such as the `jboss-cli-client.jar` to make it EAP 7 friendly:

```
$ ./jconsole.sh
```

By executing JConsole, you can get information about server memory usage, active threads, class loading, and the MBeans that are running on your platform. Here is the startup window of JConsole once you are connected to the application server:

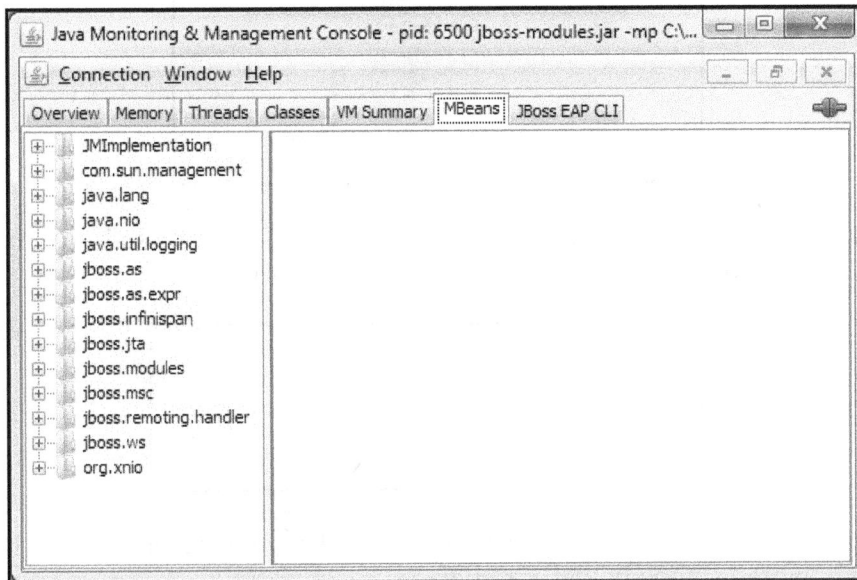

We want to focus in more detail here on gathering information about a specific subsystem. For this purpose, click on the **MBeans** tab. The tree displayed on the left shows all the MBeans that are currently running. When you select an MBean in the left-hand tree, its `MBeanInfo` and `MBean Descriptor` will be displayed on the right, and any attributes, operations, or notifications appear in the tree below it.

For example, here is the MBean tree for the `org.xnio.default` pool:

By selecting a specific attribute, you can read the corresponding `Info` and `Descriptor` in the right-hand panel of JConsole:

By clicking on the selected attribute, you can switch to the graphical view of it, which is an XY time-based representation of that attribute:

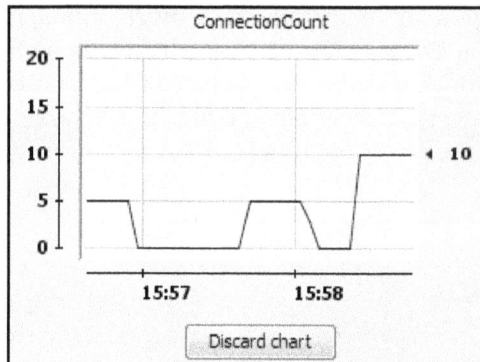

As you can see, JConsole is a pretty simple-to-use tool, which can be used for a generic overview of the server's internals. Besides its simplicity, however, you will be limited for an in-depth analysis as it does not provide a way to compare multiple attributes at runtime, nor a way to store the charts.

Data mining using the ELK stack

In `Chapter 7`, *Logging*, we introduced the ELK stack as an effective and emerging technology stack to acquire input, process it and display it in various formats. In the case of logging, we have seen how to use it with a Push strategy, which sends the log event to the ELK chain through a TCP socket. The Logstash input can, however, be configured to also Poll for data periodically and send this information to the ELK chain. Our source of information will be the **HTTP Management API,** which can mimic the behavior of the CLI using the HTTP protocol.

For example, supposing we want to gather information about the SLSB named `DemoEJB` deployed in the `web.war` application, then the following CLI was used formerly to acquire information about it:

```
/deployment=web.war/subsystem=ejb3/stateless-session-
bean=DemoEJB/:read-resource(include-runtime=true)
```

In terms of the HTTP Management API, the equivalent command follows:

```
http://localhost:9990/management/deployment/web.war/subsystem/ejb3/stat
eless-session-bean/DemoEJB?include-
runtime=true&user=admin&password=mYpassword1!
```

We can now instruct Logstash to poll for metrics using the HTTP Management API application server, using a plugin named `http_poller`. This plugin does not ship out of the box with Logstash, but it is easy to install by running the plugin command contained in the `bin` folder of Logstash:

```
$ plugin install logstash-input-http_poller
```

Now create the following `logstatsh.conf` file:

```
input {
  http_poller {
  urls => {
  http_listener_metrics => {
        method => "get"
        url => "http://localhost:9990/management/deployment
        /web.war/subsystem/ejb3/stateless-session-bean
```

```
        /DemoEJB?include-runtime=true"
        headers => {
                "Content-Type" => "application/json"
        }
        auth => {
                user => "admin"
                password => "mYpassword1!"
                }
        }
    }
    request_timeout => 30
    interval => 5
    codec => "json"
    type => "eap_default_listener_metrics"
    }
}
filter { }
output {
 elasticsearch {
 }
}
```

Besides the `http_poller` plugin, we also had to include the credentials of a management user to execute the Management API. The output is sent, as usual, to the Elasticsearch engine.

> **TIP**
> In order to avoid connection faults in your logs, we suggest you start the ELK chain in the following order: Kibana, Elasticsearch, and finally LogStash.

With the ELK stack available, connect to the the Kibana console at `http://localhost:5601`

From the **Discover** tab, add to the list of selected fields the ones you want to monitor, for example the `pool-available-count` and `pool-current-size`. You should be able to see a tabular view of the attributes based on a timestamp of 30 seconds:

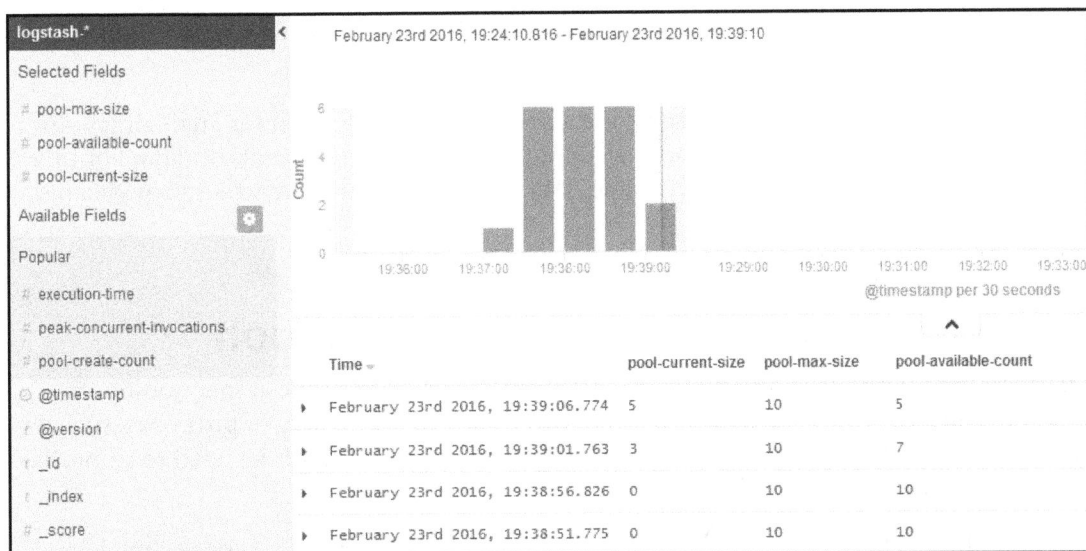

Data can be aggregated through the **Visualize** tab. For example, if you want an *XY* aggregated graph, assign to the *X* axis a **Date Histogram** element and include on the *Y* axis one or more fields that can be aggregated using common statistical functions, such as in the following view, where the Average function has been used:

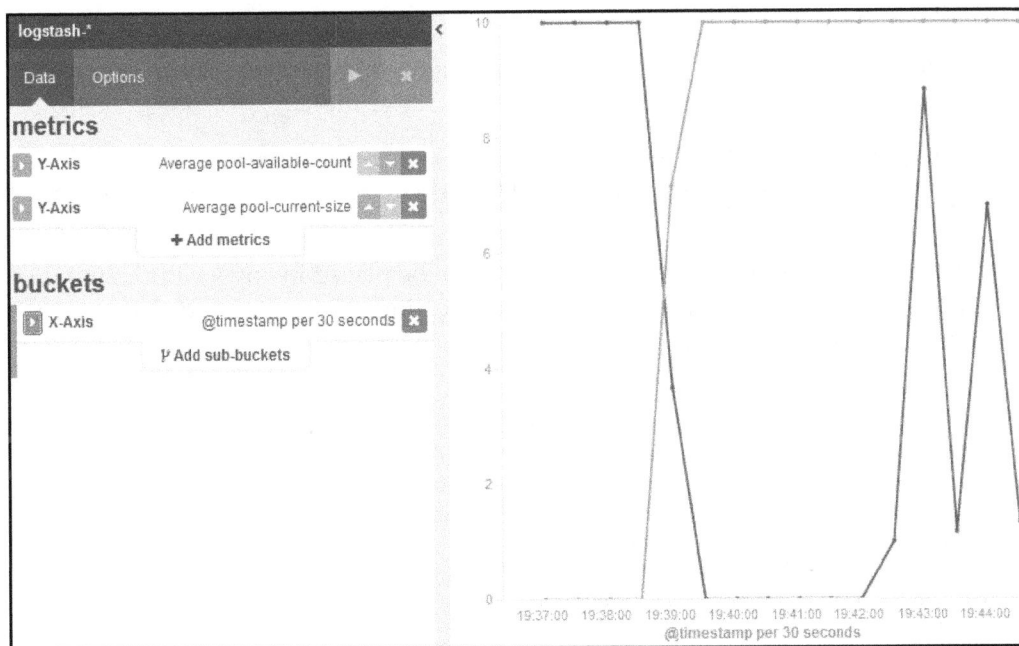

Data can be refreshed at any time by clicking on the right icon available on the right-hand side.

ELK is a versatile platform that can provide a scalable search solution for analyzing your applications. It provides an aggregated view of data, even huge amounts of data. For this reason, it is not intended to pinpoint single data points in a chart, but rather provide an analytical view of data.

Using Byteman to trace your application

A digression about tracing and monitoring cannot be complete without mentioning the Byteman project. Byteman is a Java tool that can be used for a variety of purposes, such as monitoring the JVM, injecting data, and testing it at runtime without the need to recompile or redeploy your application.

In a nutshell, you need to provide Byteman with one or more rules that specify the Java code you want to be executed and the class and method location where you want it to be injected. Behind the scenes, Byteman works out how to rewrite the bytecode of your classes so that it includes the source-level changes you have requested.

In order to install Byteman, download it from the site page at:

```
http://byteman.jboss.org/downloads.html.
```

The byteman.jar file needs to be passed as javaagent to the server startup options of the server. Replace it with the actual path to the byteman.jar file:

```
JAVA_OPTS="$JAVA_OPTS -Dorg.jboss.byteman.transform.all -
javaagent:/home/byteman/lib/byteman.jar=script:stats.btm,boot:/home/byteman
/lib/byteman.jar"
```

The Byteman example script, named stats.btm, can be placed in any location; in our case, we have added it in the same folder where the application server is started. The stats.btm script contains the following rule:

```
RULE Count Active Threads
CLASS java.util.concurrent.ThreadPoolExecutor
METHOD  beforeExecute(Thread, Runnable)
BIND size:int = $0.getActiveCount();
name:String = Thread.currentThread().getName();
IF name.matches(".*customworker.*")
DO traceln(name +"  active size: " + size);

ENDRULE
```

The first line states the **rule name**. This rule is going to intercept calls to the
`java.util.concurrent.ThreadPoolExecutor` that is used by the server pool of web
threads. In detail, we want to intercept invocations of the `beforeExecute` method, which is
invoked prior to executing the given `Runnable` in the thread.

The `BIND` instruction, as its name suggests, binds some `Class` attributes to `Rule` variables
(`$0` is a positional parameter that refers to the Class that has been invoked).

In our case, we want to match the current thread name to the worker IO thread we have
formerly created (see the *Configuring the pool of threads used by Undertow* section). If the name
matches, we will print on the Console the current number of active Threads for this worker.

When we launched the application server and hit some requests to web applications, the
following lines were printed on the console, to account for the number of active threads in
our worker:

```
[stdout] (myworker task-7) customworker active size 2
[stdout] (myworker task-2) customworker active size 3
[stdout] (myworker task-4) customworker active size 4
```

That's a very basic example; however, it shows how you can gather in-depth insights from
Byteman. By default, the set of operations that are available for use in Byteman rules are
defined by the `org.jboss.byteman.rule.helper.Helper` class. You can alter this
behavior by providing an alternative helper class. For example, you can provide a class that
registers some critical information over JMX, such as the following `SimpleHelper` class:

```
public class SimpleHelper extends Helper {

    Data user = new Data("activeCount", 1);
    private static boolean DEBUG;

    // Lifecycle method: Rule has been activated
    public static void activated() {
      DEBUG = Boolean.getBoolean
      ("org.jboss.byteman.sample.helper.debug");
      if (DEBUG) {
     System.err.println("ThreadHistoryMonitorHelper.activated, ");
      }
    }

    // Lifecycle method: Rule has been installed
    public static void installed(Rule rule) {
        if (DEBUG) {
            System.err.println
            ("ThreadHistoryMonitorHelper.installed, " + rule);
        }
```

```
        }

        protected SimpleHelper(Rule rule) {
            super(rule);

        }
// This method registers an instance of the DataMBean class
// which contains the activeCount field variable
        public void registerHelperMBean(String name) {
        MBeanServer mbs =
        ManagementFactory.getPlatformMBeanServer();
        synchronized (this) {

            try {
                ObjectName oname = new ObjectName(name);

                if (mbs.isRegistered(oname) == false) {

                    StandardMBean mbean = new StandardMBean
                    (user, DataMBean.class);

                    mbs.registerMBean(mbean, oname);
                }
            } catch (Exception e) {
                e.printStackTrace();
            }
        }
    }
// Method called by the ByteMan rule when condition evaluates to true
    public void updateMBean(int active) {

        user.setValue(active);
    }

    }
```

The `activated` and `installed` methods provide life cycle debug information if the variable DEBUG is set to `true`. The core job done by this class is in the `registerHelperMBean` method which registers the MBean `DataMBean` that is used to store information about the `ActiveCount` attribute so far printed on the console.

Finally, the `updateMBean` method is used to update the instance of the MBean with the current value of the active count.

We will update our rule script with the custom `SimpleHelper` class that will be triggered when the `main` method of the application server is executed:

```
RULE Register JMXHelper mbean
CLASS org.jboss.modules.Main
METHOD main
HELPER org.jboss.byteman.sample.helper.SimpleHelper
AT EXIT
IF TRUE
DO registerHelperMBean("org.jboss.byteman:helper=SimpleHelper")
ENDRULE
RULE Count Active Threads
CLASS java.util.concurrent.ThreadPoolExecutor
METHOD  beforeExecute(Thread, Runnable)

HELPER org.jboss.byteman.sample.helper.SimpleHelper

BIND size:int = $0.getActiveCount();
name:String = Thread.currentThread().getName();
IF name.matches(".*worker.*")
DO updateMBean(size);

ENDRULE
```

The second rule (*Count Active Theads*) has been slightly modified so that instead of printing on the console the `activeCount` attribute, it updates the MBean attribute through the `SimpleHelper` class.

Before starting the application server, some minor changes are required so that the JMX classes will be able to access the application server's `LogManager`. Also, the helper class needs to be passed to the `javaagent` block so that it can be found at runtime:

```
JAVA_OPTS="$JAVA_OPTS -
Djava.util.logging.manager=org.jboss.logmanager.LogManager -
Xbootclasspath/p:/home/francesco/jboss/jboss-
eap-7.0/modules/system/layers/base/org/jboss/logmanager/main/jboss-
logmanager-2.0.3.Final-redhat-1.jar"

JAVA_OPTS="$JAVA_OPTS -Dorg.jboss.byteman.transform.all -
javaagent:/home/byteman/lib/byteman.jar=script:/home/byteman
/scripts/stats.btm,boot:/home/byteman/helper/helper.jar,boot:/home/byteman/
lib/byteman.jar"
```

Now start the application server and send some load to the http connector. You can switch back to JConsole and check our registered MBean, `org.jboss.byteman:helper=SimpleHelper`, which gets updated each time the `activeCount` of the thread varies:

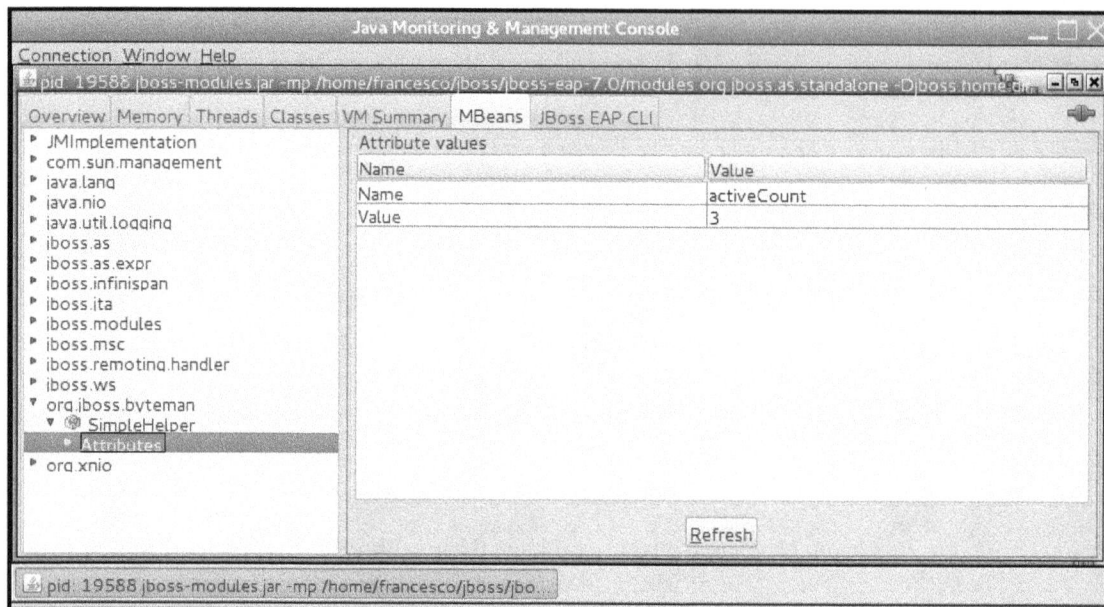

Summary

In this chapter, we have covered the EJB and web subsystems, which represent the backbone and the frontend of Java Enterprise applications. We have gone through the key attributes of each subsystem and how to configure the application server for collecting these attributes and visualizing them. The next chapter will be devoted to the messaging system, which is the way applications can communicate in a loosely coupled style.

10
Messaging Administration

In this chapter, you will learn how to configure and run Apache ActiveMQ Artemis, which is the broker embedded into JBoss EAP 7. To configure the messaging system, JBoss EAP 7 provides a specific subsystem named `urn:jboss:domain:messaging-activemq:1.0`.

The following are the topics that we will cover in this chapter:

- Introduction to Artemis MQ
- Configuring broker transport
- Configuring persistence
- Configuring the ridge
- Clustering configuration

Introduction to Artemis MQ

Previously, JBoss EAP, JBoss AS, and WildFly (until version 9) had their messaging system based on HornetQ, a well known project from the JBoss community.

The latter decided to donate its messaging system to the Apache Software Foundation community, and the HornetQ project has been renamed Apache ActiveMQ Artemis.

Artemis implements the JMS 1.x and 2.0 specifications, and as stated before, it provides support for many protocols such as AMQP, OpenWire, MQTT, STOMP, and HornetQ core protocols.

Apache Artemis is a **Message Oriented Middleware** (**MOM**) used to exchange messages between heterogeneous systems in an asynchronous way, by using the Java EE Connector Architecture – JCA. Because of that, JBoss EAP also provides out-of-the-box support for connection pooling, JTA transactions, and container-managed security.

To be able to use the messaging subsystem, we need to choose the `full` or the `full-ha` profile, within our EAP configuration.

If we are running the standalone mode, we can find the messaging configuration in the files `standalone-full.xml` and `standalone-full-ha.xml`. On the other hand, if we are running in domain mode, we can find the proper configuration in EAP supplied profiles such as `full` and `full-ha`. The `full` configuration enables the messaging systems, while the `full-ha` also adds clustering and load-balancing capabilities.

> For this chapter, it is assumed that you are familiar with JMS concepts such as Queue, Topic, DLQ, point-to-point, and publish/subscribe.

As Artemis is essentially HornetQ, this means that your code does not need to change at all.

> Artemis is designed by a set of POJOs, allowing Apache ActiveMQ Artemis to be easily embedded in your own project or container (as JBoss does), or instantiated in any framework.

Each Apache ActiveMQ Artemis server has its own ultra high performance persistent journal. This journal is used for message and other persistence, and allows outrageous persistence message performance. This is a real advantage over other databases as this is something that cannot be achieved by using a relational database for persistence.

Apache ActiveMQ Artemis clients on different physical machines interact with the Apache ActiveMQ Artemis server. For messaging at the client side, Apache ActiveMQ Artemis currently provides two APIs:

- Core client API – This is a simple, in-built Java API that allows the full set of messaging functionality without some of the complexities of JMS
- JMS client API – The standard JMS API that is available at the client side

Apache ActiveMQ Artemis also provides different protocol implementations on the server so you can use them as well. As the Apache ActiveMQ Artemis server supports many protocols, it's main interaction is based on its wire format protocol. This means that, even if you use the JMS API, they are translated and converted to Artemis core client API. This has the advantage of being protocol-agnostic and therefore the broker can be used with multiple different protocols.

The following is a diagram taken from the Apache ActiveMQ Artemis site
(`https://activemq.apache.org/artemis`), which explains the overall architecture:

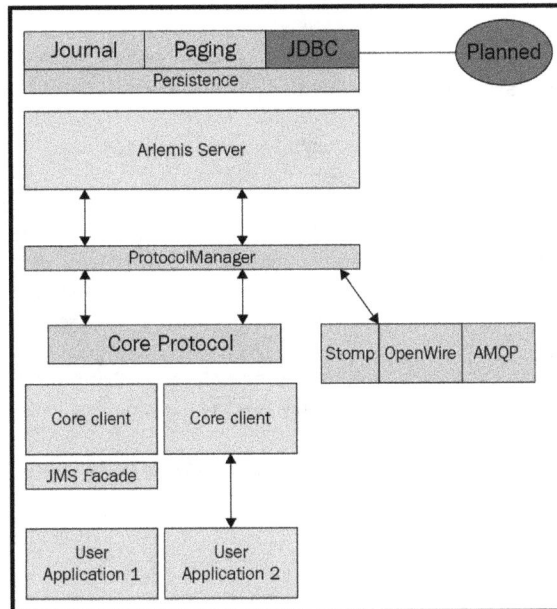

Artemis Architecture

From a configuration point of view, JBoss EAP 7 provides support for messaging using the
`full` or `full-ha` profiles. The following is the default configuration within the `full`
profile:

```
<subsystem xmlns="urn:jboss:domain:messaging-activemq:1.0">
    <server name="default">
        <security-setting name="#">
            <role name="guest" send="true" consume="true"
            create-non-durable-queue="true" delete-non-durable-
queue="true"/>
        </security-setting>
        <address-setting name="#" dead-letter-address="jms.queue.DLQ"
         expiry-address="jms.queue.ExpiryQueue"
         max-size-bytes="10485760" page-size-bytes="2097152"
         message-counter-history-day-limit="10"/>
        <http-connector name="http-connector" socket-binding=
         "http" endpoint="http-acceptor"/>
        <http-connector name="http-connector-throughput" socket-binding=
         "http" endpoint="http-acceptor-throughput">
            <param name="batch-delay" value="50"/>
```

```
        </http-connector>
        <in-vm-connector name="in-vm" server-id="0"/>
        <http-acceptor name="http-acceptor" http-listener="default"/>
        <http-acceptor name="http-acceptor-throughput" http-
listener="default">
            <param name="batch-delay" value="50"/>
            <param name="direct-deliver" value="false"/>
        </http-acceptor>
        <in-vm-acceptor name="in-vm" server-id="0"/>
        <jms-queue name="ExpiryQueue"
entries="java:/jms/queue/ExpiryQueue"/>
        <jms-queue name="DLQ" entries="java:/jms/queue/DLQ"/>
        <connection-factory name="InVmConnectionFactory" connectors=
         "in-vm" entries="java:/ConnectionFactory"/>
        <connection-factory name="RemoteConnectionFactory" connectors=
         "http-connector"
         entries="java:jboss/exported/jms/RemoteConnectionFactory"/>
        <pooled-connection-factory name="activemq-ra" transaction=
         "xa" connectors="in-vm"
         entries="java:/JmsXA java:jboss/DefaultJMSConnectionFactory"/>
    </server>
</subsystem>
```

Configuring broker transport

Artemis uses two fundamental concepts: acceptors and connectors. Acceptors determine how the broker accepts incoming connections, while connectors determine how to connect to other Artemis brokers or servers that support its protocols (as described in the introduction).

Two types of acceptor and connector exist:

- invm – The connections are within the same JVM (more performance, obviously)
- http – The connections are over HTTP to/from remote clients; they use Undertow to upgrade from an HTTP connection

Each configured connector is used just to reach a server if there is the same type of acceptor configured on the other server. In other words, if we are making a connection with an invm connector, the other server must have an invm acceptor configured. On the other hand, if we are making a connection with an http-connector, the other server must have an http-acceptor configured.

To read the connector and acceptor configuration you can invoke the following CLI commands:

```
[standalone@192.168.59.104:9990 /] /subsystem=messaging-
activemq/server=default:read-children-resources(include-
runtime=true,include-defaults=true,recursive=true,child-type=http-
connector)
{
    "outcome" => "success",
    "result" => {
        "http-connector" => {
            "endpoint" => "http-acceptor",
            "params" => undefined,
            "socket-binding" => "http"
        },
        "http-connector-throughput" => {
            "endpoint" => "http-acceptor-throughput",
            "params" => {"batch-delay" => "50"},
            "socket-binding" => "http"
        }
    }
}
[standalone@192.168.59.104:9990 /] /subsystem=messaging-
activemq/server=default:read-children-resources(include-
runtime=true,include-defaults=true,recursive=true,child-type=http-acceptor)
{
    "outcome" => "success",
    "result" => {
        "http-acceptor" => {
            "http-listener" => "default",
            "params" => undefined,
            "upgrade-legacy" => true
        },
        "http-acceptor-throughput" => {
            "http-listener" => "default",
            "params" => {
                "batch-delay" => "50",
                "direct-deliver" => "false"
            },
            "upgrade-legacy" => true
        }
    }
}
[standalone@192.168.59.104:9990 /]
```

As you can see, the httpconnectors, which use Undertow to reach the ActiveMQ Artemis server, contain two kinds of connector:

- Standard `httpconnector`: Provides a configuration completely based on defaults
- Throughput `httpconnector`: Contains a specialized configuration in order to guarantee a higher level of messaging throughput

Here is a description of the included parameters:

- `batch-delay` – allows the broker to fill up an internal buffer for a maximum of `batch-delay` milliseconds before sending messages. Writing more messages at once will increase performance, if globally the message size is small.
- `direct-deliver` – when set to true, the broker delivers the message to the client within the same thread the message arrived on.

The list of properties which can be set on your connectors and acceptors are the following:

- `use-nio`: When set to true, the Java non-blocking NIO will be used. On the other hand, when set to false, the old blocking Java IO will be used.
- `host`: This specifies the host name to connect to (when configuring a connector) or to listen on (when configuring an acceptor). The default value is `localhost`.
- `port`: This specifies the port to connect to (when configuring a connector) or to listen on (when configuring an acceptor). The default value is `5445`.
- `tcp-nodelay`: When set to true, Nagle's algorithm will be enabled. The default value is `true`.
- `tcpsendbuffer-size`: This parameter specifies the size of the TCP send buffer in bytes. The default value is `32768 bytes` (32KB).
- `tcpreceivebuffersize`: This parameter specifies the size of the TCP receive buffer in bytes. The default value is `32768 bytes` (32KB).
- `nioremotingthreads`: When configured to use NIO, ActiveMQ Artemis will, by default, use a number of available processors as per the `Runtime.getRuntime().availableProcessors()` for processing incoming packets.

Here is, for example, how to set the `tcpsend-buffer-size` value to 64 KB:

```
[standalone@192.168.59.104:9990 /] /subsystem=messaging-
activemq/server=default/http-connector=http-connector/:write-
attribute(name=params,value={"tcp-send-buffer-size" => "65536"})
    {
```

```
    "outcome" => "success",
    "response-headers" => {
        "operation-requires-reload" => true,
        "process-state" => "reload-required"
    }
}
[standalone@192.168.59.104:9990 /]
```

You need to reload your server for changes to take effect.

If you want to see how Artemis internal components are configured, by issuing the tab key while specifying the `child-type` property, you can see which one is available, as follows:

```
[standalone@192.168.59.104:9990 /] /subsystem=messaging-
activemq/server=default:read-children-resources(include-
runtime=true,include-defaults=true,recursive=true,child-type=Tab key
acceptor    broadcast-group connector discovery-group    ha-policy in-vm-
acceptor    jms-topic pooled-connection-factory remote-connector
address-setting    cluster-connection    connector-service divert    http-
acceptor    in-vm-connector    legacy-connection-factoryqueue    runtime-queue
bridge connection-factory    core-address grouping-handler
http-connector jms-queue    path    remote-acceptor    security-setting
```

Then complete the command using the proper name:

```
[standalone@192.168.59.104:9990 /] /subsystem=messaging-
activemq/server=default:read-children-resources(include-
runtime=true,include-defaults=true,recursive=true,child-type=jms-queue)
    {
        "outcome" => "success",
        "result" => {
            "DLQ" => {
                "consumer-count" => 0,
                "dead-letter-address" => "jms.queue.DLQ",
                "delivering-count" => 0,
                "durable" => true,
                "entries" => ["java:/jms/queue/DLQ"],
                "expiry-address" => "jms.queue.ExpiryQueue",
                "legacy-entries" => undefined,
                "message-count" => 0L,
                "messages-added" => 0L,
                "paused" => false,
                "queue-address" => "jms.queue.DLQ",
                "scheduled-count" => 0L,
                "selector" => undefined,
                "temporary" => false
            },
            "ExpiryQueue" => {
```

```
                "consumer-count" => 0,
                "dead-letter-address" => "jms.queue.DLQ",
                "delivering-count" => 0,
                "durable" => true,
                "entries" => ["java:/jms/queue/ExpiryQueue"],
                "expiry-address" => "jms.queue.ExpiryQueue",
                "legacy-entries" => undefined,
                "message-count" => 0L,
                "messages-added" => 0L,
                "paused" => false,
                "queue-address" => "jms.queue.ExpiryQueue",
                "scheduled-count" => 0L,
                "selector" => undefined,
                "temporary" => false
            }
        },
        "response-headers" => {"process-state" => "reload-required"}
    }
    [standalone@192.168.59.104:9990 /]
```

Configuring persistence

By configuring message persistence you gain message reliability. ActiveMQ Artemis persists its messages using its high-performance journal, which, in a Linux environment (kernel 2.6), can also benefit from using Linux's Asynchronous IO library (AIO).

The ActiveMQ Artemis journal is based on a set of files on a disk, instead of a database. Each file is pre-created and of a fixed size (configurable). Every time a message arrives, the operation is recorded, appended, on the journal. When a journal file is full, the broker automatically creates a new one.

A complete list of properties related to message persistence is as follows:

```
    [standalone@192.168.59.104:9990 /] /subsystem=messaging-
activemq/server=default:read-resource(attributes-only=true)
    {
        "outcome" => "success",
        "result" => {
            "async-connection-execution-enabled" => true,
            "cluster-password" => "CHANGE ME!!",
            "cluster-user" => "ACTIVEMQ.CLUSTER.ADMIN.USER",
            "connection-ttl-override" => -1L,
            "create-bindings-dir" => true,
            "create-journal-dir" => true,
            "id-cache-size" => 20000,
```

```
        "incoming-interceptors" => undefined,
        "jmx-domain" => "org.apache.activemq.artemis",
        "jmx-management-enabled" => false,
        "journal-buffer-size" => undefined,
        "journal-buffer-timeout" => undefined,
        "journal-compact-min-files" => 10,
        "journal-compact-percentage" => 30,
        "journal-file-size" => 10485760,
        "journal-max-io" => undefined,
        "journal-min-files" => 2,
        "journal-pool-files" => -1,
        "journal-sync-non-transactional" => true,
        "journal-sync-transactional" => true,
        "journal-type" => "ASYNCIO",
        "log-journal-write-rate" => false,
        "management-address" => "jms.queue.activemq.management",
        "management-notification-address" => "activemq.notifications",
        "memory-measure-interval" => -1L,
        "memory-warning-threshold" => 25,
        "message-counter-max-day-history" => 10,
        "message-counter-sample-period" => 10000L,
        "message-expiry-scan-period" => 30000L,
        "message-expiry-thread-priority" => 3,
        "outgoing-interceptors" => undefined,
        "override-in-vm-security" => true,
        "page-max-concurrent-io" => 5,
        "perf-blast-pages" => -1,
        "persist-delivery-count-before-delivery" => false,
        "persist-id-cache" => true,
        "persistence-enabled" => true,
        "run-sync-speed-test" => false,
        "scheduled-thread-pool-max-size" => 5,
        "security-domain" => "other",
        "security-enabled" => true,
        "security-invalidation-interval" => 10000L,
        "server-dump-interval" => -1L,
        "statistics-enabled" => false,
        "thread-pool-max-size" => 30,
        "transaction-timeout" => 300000L,
        "transaction-timeout-scan-period" => 1000L,
        "wild-card-routing-enabled" => true
    }
}
[standalone@192.168.59.104:9990 /]
```

We have lots of properties to look at; the first is obviously `persistence-enabled`, which determines if messages are persisted on the journal, according to the `journaltype` parameter, which can have the following values: `NIO` or `ASYNCIO`. When NIO is chosen, the Java NIO journal is used. When `ASYNCIO` is chosen, the Linux asynchronous IO journal is used. If you use the Linux journal and you are running on a different operating system, the messaging system will automatically fallback to the Java journal.

`journalminfiles` specifies the minimum number of files the journal will maintain. When ActiveMQ Artemis starts, there is no data at all, and ActiveMQ Artemis will the journal files as per the number of `journalminfiles`.

`journalfilesize` specifies the maximum size (in bytes) for the journal file.

All persistence parameters can be set via the CLI, as follows:

```
[standalone@192.168.59.104:9990 /] /subsystem=messaging-
activemq/server=default/:write-attribute(name=journal-file-
size,value=102400)
    {
        "outcome" => "success",
        "response-headers" => {
            "operation-requires-reload" => true,
            "process-state" => "reload-required"
        }
    }
[standalone@192.168.59.104:9990 /]
```

Although ActiveMQ Artemis supports a huge amount of messages, when the system is getting low in memory you have the option to page them to disk (just like an OS has the swap partition to handle more memory than RAM). The parameter that specifies whether you are handling paging or not is `maxsizebytes`, and its default is around 10 MB:

```
[standalone@192.168.59.104:9990 /] /subsystem=messaging-
activemq/server=default/address-setting=#:read-attribute(name=max-size-
bytes)
    {
        "outcome" => "success",
        "result" => 10485760L
    }
[standalone@192.168.59.104:9990 /]
```

By increasing this value, you allow a larger set of data in memory, thus reducing the pagination. For example, to increase it to around 15 MB, do as follows:

```
[standalone@192.168.59.104:9990 /] /subsystem=messaging-
activemq/server=default/address-setting=#:write-attribute(name=max-size-
```

```
bytes,value=15728640L)
    {"outcome" => "success"}
    [standalone@192.168.59.104:9990 /]
```

On the other hand, when `maxsizebytes` is set to `1`, pagination will be disabled.

The pagination policy is governed by the `addressfullpolicy` parameter, which can have the following values: `PAGE`, `BLOCK`, `DROP`, and `FAIL`. The following table summarizes them all:

Pagination policy	Description
PAGE	When `maxsizebytes` is exceeded, incoming messages will be paged.
BLOCK	When `maxsizebytes` is exceeded, incoming messages will be blocked and the client will block until there is enough room to store the new messages.
DROP	When `maxsizebytes` is exceeded, incoming messages will just be dropped silently, without reporting any exception to the client side.
FAIL	When `maxsizebytes` is exceeded, incoming messages will be dropped, raising an exception to the client producer.

Each address has an individual folder where messages are stored in multiple files (page files). By default, the page folder is configured to be placed under (that is, relative to) "jboss.server.data.dir". To read the configuration, invoke the following commands:

```
    [standalone@192.168.59.104:9990 /] /subsystem=messaging-
activemq/server=default/path=paging-directory:read-attribute(name=path)
    {
        "outcome" => "success",
        "result" => "pagingdir"
    }
    [standalone@192.168.59.104:9990 /] /subsystem=messaging-
activemq/server=default/path=paging-directory:read-attribute(name=relative-
to)
    {
        "outcome" => "success",
        "result" => "jboss.server.data.dir"
    }
    [standalone@192.168.59.104:9990 /]
```

To change the above settings, issue the following commands:

```
[standalone@192.168.59.104:9990 /] /subsystem=messaging-
activemq/server=default/path=paging-directory:write-
attribute(name=path,value=pagingdir)
{"outcome" => "success"}
[standalone@192.168.59.104:9990 /] /subsystem=messaging-
activemq/server=default/path=paging-directory:write-
attribute(name=relative-to,value="jboss.server.data.dir")
{
    "outcome" => "success",
    "response-headers" => {
        "operation-requires-reload" => true,
        "process-state" => "reload-required"
    }
}
[standalone@192.168.59.104:9990 /]
```

Each file will contain messages up to a max-configured size (pagesizebytes). The system will navigate the files as needed, and it will remove the page file as soon as all the messages are acknowledged up to that point.

Configuring destinations

Configuring and creating destinations is quite easy. You can rely on the Web console, or the CLI. As already mentioned in previous chapters, knowing CLI commands gives you more flexibility and a deeper knowledge of the entire platform. For these same reasons, we will see how to configure your destinations using the CLI.

To create a destination named `testQueue`, do as follows:

```
[standalone@192.168.59.104:9990 /] jms-queue add --queue-
address=jms.queue.TestQueue --entries=java:/jms/queue/testQueue
```

If running in domain mode, just add the `--profile` directive, specifying the profile name to use, as follows:

```
[domain@192.168.59.104:9999 /] jms-queue add --queue-
address=jms.queue.TestQueue --entries=java:/jms/queue/testQueue --
profile=full
```

In case you want to create a topic, there is a command analogous to `jms-queue`, as follows:

```
[standalone@192.168.59.104:9990 /] jms-topic add --topic-
address=jms.topic.TestTopic --entries=java:/jms/topic/testTopic
```

If running in domain mode, just add the `--profile` directive, specifying the profile name to use, as follows:

```
[domain@192.168.59.104:9999 /] jms-topic add --topic-
address=jms.topic.TestTopic --entries=java:/jms/topic/testTopic --
profile=full
```

So far, we have seen how to add a destination; now we will see how to customize a destination. Let's first see which parameters we can act on, by invoking the following command within the CLI:

```
[standalone@192.168.59.104:9990 /] /subsystem=messaging-
activemq/server=default/address-setting=#:read-resource()
    {
        "outcome" => "success",
        "result" => {
            "address-full-policy" => "PAGE",
            "auto-create-jms-queues" => false,
            "auto-delete-jms-queues" => false,
            "dead-letter-address" => "jms.queue.DLQ",
            "expiry-address" => "jms.queue.ExpiryQueue",
            "expiry-delay" => -1L,
            "last-value-queue" => false,
            "max-delivery-attempts" => 10,
            "max-redelivery-delay" => 0L,
            "max-size-bytes" => 15728640L,
            "message-counter-history-day-limit" => 10,
            "page-max-cache-size" => 5,
            "page-size-bytes" => 2097152L,
            "redelivery-delay" => 0L,
            "redelivery-multiplier" => 1.0,
            "redistribution-delay" => -1L,
            "send-to-dla-on-no-route" => false,
            "slow-consumer-check-period" => 5L,
            "slow-consumer-policy" => "NOTIFY",
            "slow-consumer-threshold" => -1L
        }
    }
```

The **#** symbol is a wildcard indicating all destinations, both queues and topics. This means that, when applying a setting to #, this will be settled for all destinations, if not specified differently.

By the way, the parameters to take care of while dealing with messaging systems are:

- `dead-letter-address` – The dead letter address
- `expiry-address` – Defines where to send a message that has expired

- `redelivery-delay` – Defines how long to wait before attempting redelivery of a cancelled message
- `max-delivery-attempts` – Defines how many time a cancelled message can be redelivered before sending to the dead-letter-address
- `max-size-bytes` – The max bytes size

All the properties can be fully described, in the CLI itself, by invoking the following command:

```
[standalone@192.168.59.104:9990 /] /subsystem=messaging-
activemq/server=default/address-setting=#/:read-resource-description()
```

Routing messages to other destinations

A common use case for messaging systems is to route messages to other destinations or servers. ActiveMQ Artemis offers the following options:

- Divert messages from one destination to another on the same server
- Bridge messages between two JMS Brokers

Although both options can be used for the same purpose, the difference between them is that a Bridge implies a connection between two ActiveMQ Artemis servers, whilst a message Divert operates on the same ActiveMQ Artemis server.

Diverting messages to other destinations

So basically diverting is used for internal routing. With this in mind, diverting can be very helpful if you want to change the body of a message. It can also apply filters to messages and add some transformation by delegating all the transformations to a class.

Once the messages are selected they can be diverted to other destinations.

A divert to get in action needs the following mandatory attributes:

- `routingname`: This is the name associated with the Divert
- `divertaddress`: This is the source of JMS Messages
- `forwardingaddress`: This is the target destination for JMS Messages

So, to create a diversion, do as follows:

```
[standalone@192.168.59.104:9990 /] /subsystem=messaging-
activemq/server=default/divert=DivertTest:add(divert-
address=jms.queue.TestQueue,forwarding-address=jms.queue.NextQueue,routing-
name=DivertTest)
   {"outcome" => "success"}
```

Furthermore, you can set additional attributes such as:

- `exclusive`: This option determines if the divert is exclusive, meaning that the message is diverted to the new address, and does not go to the old address at all. If the divert is qualified as nonexclusive, the message continues to go to the old address, and a copy of it is also sent to the new address.
- `filter`: This is an optional filter string. If specified, only messages that match the filter expression specified will be diverted. The filter string follows the ActiveMQ Artemis filter expression syntax described in the ActiveMQ Artemis documentation (`http://activemq.apache.org/artemis/docs/1.0.0/filter-expressions.html`).
- `transformer classname`: The name of a class used to transform the message's body or properties before it is diverted.

Creating a bridge between two ActiveMQ Artemis servers

The concept behind a bridge is similar to divert, with one main difference: the bridge physically consumes messages from a destination on an ActiveMQ Artemis server, and reproduces and sends the same messages to another remote ActiveMQ Artemis server. Nonetheless, the bridge can connect to any JMS 1.1- compliant broker.

In order to set up a bridge between two JMS Servers you should define:

- On your Source JMS Broker: a JMS Bridge along with a source destination, and also with a connector to connect to the target destination
- On your Target JMS Broker: a JMS destination

ActiveMQ Artemis source configuration

Log into your CLI shell and execute the following script, which will create the source JMS destination and define the Remote Connection Factory used for transport and the connector used by the factory:

```
batch
/subsystem="messaging-activemq"/server="default"/jms-
queue="JMSBridgeSourceQueue":add(entries=["queue/JMSBridgeSourceQueue","jav
a:jboss/exported/jms/queues/JMSBridgeSourceQueue"])
    /socket-binding-group=standard-sockets/remote-destination-outbound-
socket-binding=messaging-remote/:add(host=localhost,port=8180)
    /subsystem=messaging-activemq/server=default/http-connector=bridge-
connector/:add(endpoint=http-acceptor,socket-binding=messaging-remote)
    /subsystem=messaging-activemq/server=default/connection-
factory=RemoteConnectionFactory:write-
attribute(name=connectors,value=["bridge-connector"])
    /subsystem=messaging-activemq/server=default/connection-
factory=RemoteConnectionFactory:write-
attribute(name=entries,value=["java:jboss/exported/jms/RemoteConnectionFact
ory"])
    /subsystem="messaging-activemq"/jms-bridge="simple-jms-
bridge":add(failure-retry-interval="10000",max-batch-size="10",max-batch-
time="100",max-retries="1",quality-of-service="AT_MOST_ONCE",source-
connection-factory="ConnectionFactory",source-
destination="queue/JMSBridgeSourceQueue",target-connection-
factory="jms/RemoteConnectionFactory",target-
context={"java.naming.factory.initial" =>
"org.jboss.naming.remote.client.InitialContextFactory","java.naming.provide
r.url" => "http-remoting://localhost:8180"},target-
destination="jms/queues/JMSBridgeTargetQueue",target-
password="password",target-user="jmsuser")
    run-batch
```

The following server definition will be created for the messaging subsystem:

```
<subsystem xmlns="urn:jboss:domain:messaging-activemq:1.0">
    <server name="default">
        <journal file-size="102400" />
        <paging-directory path="pagingdir" />
        <security-setting name="#">
            <role name="guest" delete-non-durable-queue="true"
              create-non-durable-queue="true" consume="true" send="true"
/>
        </security-setting>
        <address-setting name="#"
            message-counter-history-day-limit="10" page-size-
bytes="2097152"
```

```
                    max-size-bytes="15728640" expiry-
address="jms.queue.ExpiryQueue"
                dead-letter-address="jms.queue.DLQ" />
        <http-connector name="http-connector" endpoint="http-acceptor"
                socket-binding="http">
                <param name="tcp-receive-bu er-size" value="65536" />
        </http-connector>
        <http-connector name="http-connector-throughput"
                endpoint="http-acceptor-throughput" socket-binding="http">
                <param name="batch-delay" value="50" />
        </http-connector>
        <http-connector name="bridge-connector" endpoint="http-acceptor"
                socket-binding="messaging-remote" />
        <in-vm-connector name="in-vm" server-id="0" />
        <http-acceptor name="http-acceptor" http-listener="default" />
        <http-acceptor name="http-acceptor-throughput"
                http-listener="default">
                <param name="batch-delay" value="50" />
                <param name="direct-deliver" value="false" />
        </http-acceptor>
        <in-vm-acceptor name="in-vm" server-id="0" />
        <divert name="DivertTest" forwarding-address="jms.queue.NextQueue"
                address="jms.queue.TestQueue" routing-name="DivertTest" />
        <jms-queue name="ExpiryQueue"
entries="java:/jms/queue/ExpiryQueue" />
        <jms-queue name="DLQ" entries="java:/jms/queue/DLQ" />
        <jms-queue name="jms.queue.TestQueue" entries=
          "java:/jms/queue/testQueue" />
        <jms-queue name="JMSBridgeSourceQueue"
         entries="queue/JMSBridgeSourceQueue java:
         jboss/exported/jms/queues/JMSBridgeSourceQueue" />
        <jms-topic name="jms.topic.TestTopic" entries=
          "java:/jms/topic/testTopic" />
        <connection-factory name="InVmConnectionFactory"
         entries="java:/ConnectionFactory" connectors="in-vm" />
        <connection-factory name="RemoteConnectionFactory"
         entries="java:jboss/exported/jms/
         RemoteConnectionFactory" connectors="bridge-connector" />
        <pooled-connection-factory name="activemq-ra"
         transaction="xa" entries="java:/JmsXA
         java:jboss/DefaultJMSConnectionFactory"
         connectors="in-vm" />
    </server>
    <jms-bridge name="simple-jms-bridge" max-batch-time="100"
        max-batch-size="10" max-retries="1" failure-retry-interval="10000"
        quality-of-service="AT_MOST_ONCE">
        <source destination="queue/JMSBridgeSourceQueue"
         connection-factory="ConnectionFactory" />
```

```
            <target password="password" user="jmsuser"
                destination="jms/queues/JMSBridgeTargetQueue"
                connection-factory="jms/RemoteConnectionFactory">
                <target-context>
                        <property name="java.naming.factory.initial"
                            value=
        "org.jboss.naming.remote.client.InitialContextFactory" />
                        <property name="java.naming.provider.url" value=
                    "http-remoting://localhost:8180" />
                </target-context>
            </target>
        </jms-bridge>
    </subsystem>
```

Additionally, the following network definition will be created on the `socket-binding-group` configuration:

```
<socket-binding-group name="standard-sockets"
    default-interface="public" port-offset="${jboss.socket.binding.port-
offset:0}">
    ...
    <outbound-socket-binding name="messaging-remote">
        <remote-destination host="localhost" port="8180" />
    </outbound-socket-binding>
</socket-binding-group>
```

ActiveMQ Artemis target configuration

Target configuration is much easier as it just requires the Queue configuration. Here's the Queue configuration:

```
/subsystem="messaging-activemq"/server="default"/jms-
queue="JMSBridgeTargetQueue":add(entries=["queue/JMSBridgeTargetQueue","jav
a:jboss/exported/jms/queues/JMSBridgeTargetQueue"])
```

That's all you need to create a bridge configuration between two ActiveMQ Artemis servers.

Bridging messages to another JMS broker

In order for the bridge to connect to a different remote broker, we need to specify, via the `resource-adapters` subsystem, a `resource-adapter` component (RA).

The RA needs a lot of parameters to be set, so we will edit the XML file directly. In our example, we will use ActiveMQ as the external ActiveMQ broker.

Here is the configuration that we need to properly connect to the ActiveMQ broker:

```
<subsystem xmlns="urn:jboss:domain:resource-adapters:3.0">
    <resource-adapters>
        <resource-adapter id="activemq">
            <archive>activemq-rar-5.12.0.rar</archive>
            <transaction-support>XATransaction</transaction-support>
            <config-property name="UseInboundSession">false
            </config-property>
            <config-property name="Password"> defaultPassword
            </config-property>
            <config-property name="UserName"> defaultUser</config-
property>
            <config-property name="ServerUrl">tcp://localhost:61616
            </config-property>
            <connection-de nitions>
                <connection-definition class-name=
"org.apache.activemq.ra.ActiveMQManagedConnectionFactory"
                jndi-name="java:/MQConnectionFactory" enabled=
                "true" pool-name="ConnectionFactory">
                    <xa-pool>
                        <min-pool-size>1</min-pool-size>
                        <max-pool-size>20</max-pool-size>
                        <prefill>false</prefill>
                        <is-same-rm-override>false</is-same-rm-override>
                    </xa-pool>
                </connection-de nition>
            </connection-de nitions>
            <admin-objects>
                <admin-object class-name=
                "org.apache.activemq.command.ActiveMQQueue"
                jndi-name="java:jboss/activemq/queue/TestQueue"
                use-java-context="true" pool- name="TestQueue">
                    <config-property name="PhysicalName">activemq/
                    queue/TestQueue</config-property>
                </admin-object>
            </admin-objects>
        </resource-adapter>
    </resource-adapters>
</subsystem>
```

Now, we can configure the bridge to consume the message on `JMSBridgeSourceQueue`, and to connect to the target destination bound in the JNDI name `activemq/queue/TestQueue`, using the ActiveMQ Connection factory `MQConnectionFactory`, as follows:

```
<jms-bridge name="simple-jms-bridge" max-batch-time="100" max-batch-
size="10" max-retries="1"
    failure-retry-interval="10000" quality-of-service="AT_MOST_ONCE">
    <source destination="queue/JMSBridgeSourceQueue"
     connection-factory="ConnectionFactory"/>
    <target destination="activemq/queue/TestQueue"
     connection-factory="MQConnectionFactory"/>
</jms-bridge>
```

We will now see how to get clustering failover capabilities to our messaging system.

Clustering

A cluster of messaging clusters allows groups of JBoss EAP 7 servers to be grouped together in order to balance the incoming messages. The advantage of using a cluster is that, by distributing the load across different servers, a higher throughput of messages can be achieved. You can also achieve high availability by configuring backup servers that will be used as a fallback solution if one active server fails.

In order to learn how to configure clustering for ArtemisMQ servers, we will go through the following list of topics:

- At first we will learn how server discovery happens so that messaging clients or other servers are able to propagate connection details
- Then we will learn how to configure a cluster for high availability

Configuring server discovery

Server discovery is a mechanism by which messaging servers can propagate the Cluster Topology to other servers and messaging clients.

The first step in server discovery is obviously establishing the initial first connection to the messaging server. In terms of protocol, the connection can be carried out either using UDP or by means of JGroups channels.

The core discovery process relies on two key components named **Broadcast groups** and **Discovery groups**, which are strictly related to the backbone of ArtemisMQ: Acceptors and Connectors.

Broadcast groups

As we know, a connector configures the way in which a server or a client can make connections to the server. Hence, a broadcast group uses the available connectors and broadcasts them on the network. The following is the default broadcast group available in a clustered configuration:

```
<broadcast-group name="bg-group1" connectors="http-connector" jgroups-
channel="activemq-cluster"/>
```

Here is a short description of the attributes:

- `connectors`: Specifies the names of connectors that will be broadcast
- `jgroups-channel`: Specifies the name used by a JGroups channel to join a cluster

Other attributes that can be set on the broadcast-group are:

- `broadcast-period`: The period in milliseconds between consecutive broadcasts
- `jgroups-stack`: The name of a stack defined in the jgroups subsystem used to form a cluster
- `socket-binding`: The broadcast group socket binding

The `jgroups-stack` attribute is a handy option if you want to rely on the JGroup protocol stack defined in your jgroups configuration. For example, here is how to switch to the tcp stack:

```
/subsystem=messaging-activemq/server=default/broadcast-group=bg-
group1:write-attribute(name=jgroups-stack,value=tcp)
```

If you don't want to rely on the default `jgroups-channel` mechanism, you can specify the broadcast group via `socket-binding`. The following batch script defines the socket binding to be used by UDP multicast communication. Next we need to set the binding at the `broadcast-group` level and finally unset the `jgroups-channel` attribute, which is mutually exclusive with the `socket-binding` attribute. Here is our batch CLI script:

```
batch
/socket-binding-group=standard-sockets/socket-binding=udp-messaging-
group:add(interface=private,port=5432,multicast-
address=231.7.7.7,multicast-port=9876)
/subsystem=messaging-activemq/server=default/broadcast-group=bg-
group1:write-attribute(name=socket-binding,value=udp-messaging-group)
/subsystem=messaging-activemq/server=default/broadcast-group=bg-
group1:undefine-attribute(name=jgroups-channel)
run-batch
```

As a result, the following configuration will be created in the messaging-activemq subsystem:

```
<broadcast-group name="bg-group1" connectors="http-connector" socket-
binding="udp-messaging-group"/>
```

Discovery groups

A discovery group is the second key component in server discovery: it defines how the connector information is received from a multicast address.

If the discovery group has not received a broadcast from a particular server for a configurable length of time it will remove that server's entry from its list.

The default configuration of the discovery groups relies on a `jgroups-channel`, just like its `broadcast-group` counterpart:

```
<discovery-group name="dg-group1" jgroups-channel="activemq-cluster"/>
```

The meaning of the attributes is exactly the same in the `broadcast-group` configuration. The following CLI script will let you revert the `discovery-group` configuration to use the UDP multicast address 231.7.7.7 and port 9876:

```
batch
/socket-binding-group=standard-sockets/socket-binding=messaging-
group:add(interface=private,port=5432,multicast-
address=231.7.7.7,multicast-port=9876)
    /subsystem=messaging-activemq/server=default/discovery-group=dg-
group1:write-attribute(name=socket-binding,value=udp-messaging-group)
    /subsystem=messaging-activemq/server=default/discovery-group=dg-
group1:undefine-attribute(name=jgroups-channel)
    run-batch
```

Here is the messaging-activemq configuration after the execution of the batch:

```
<discovery-group name="dg-group1" socket-binding="udp-messaging-group"/>
```

The discovery group contains the following additional properties:

- `initial-wait-timeout`: This is the period, in milliseconds, to wait for an initial broadcast to give us at least one node in the cluster
- `refresh-timeout`: This is the period, in milliseconds, the discovery group waits after receiving the last broadcast from a server before removing its connector from the list

Configuring high availability

The foundation of messaging high availability relies on the concept of a backup pair. In a clustered messaging environment, all running JMS servers (called live servers) are linked together with backup servers. A backup server is a passive server which does nothing until the live server fails.

> A backup server is also not able to process deployments until it becomes a live server. For this reason, special care must be taken if you are deploying a messaging-dependent application (for example, containing message-driven beans) cluster-wide. In fact, if you are deploying an application to a server group that also includes backup servers, the deployment will be rolled back. So either define your backup servers in separate Server Groups or switch off the backup servers before deploying JMS applications to the single Server Group.

In order for high availability to work it is imperative that the following requirements are met:

- Both the live and backup server must be part of the same cluster
- Their cluster user and password must match

JBoss EAP 7 supports two different strategies for backing up a server: Shared Store and Replication. Let's see both of them in detail.

HA with shared-store

When using a shared store, both live and backup servers share the same data using a shared file system. This means the paging folder, journal folder, large messages, and binding directory. When failover occurs and a backup server takes over, it will load the persistent storage from the shared file system and clients can connect to it.

For performance reasons it is highly recommended to use Fiber Channel or HyperSCSI to share the journal directory, instead of a file-based protocol such as NFS or SMB/CIFS.

Here is a sample configuration that declares a messaging server to be an active server, also called shared-store-master:

```
<server>
    <shared-store-master />
    <cluster-connection name="my-cluster">
    . . .
    </cluster-connection>
</server>
```

You can add the shared-store-master attribute via CLI as follows:

```
/subsystem=messaging-activemq/server=default/ha-policy=shared-store-
master:add(cluster-name="my-cluster")
```

Configuration of the backup server would need to use the shared-store-slave element to declare its role:

```
<server>
    <shared-store-slave />
    <cluster-connection name="my-cluster">
    . . .
    </cluster-connection>
</server>
```

Here is the corresponding command to create the shared-store-slave element in your configuration:

```
/subsystem=messaging-activemq/server=default/ha-policy=shared-store-
slave:add(cluster-name="my-cluster")
```

A common configuration pattern that can be adopted in Domain mode is to define a Profile for master servers and a Profile for slave servers.

The location of the shared storage can be defined through the following elements, which define respectively, the directory locations of message bindings, the journal file, large messages, and the paging directory:

```
<bindings-directory path="/sharedpath/activemq/bindings" />
<journal-directory path="/sharedpath/activemq/journal" />
```

```
<large-messages-directory path="/sharedpath/activemq/largemessages" />
<paging-directory path="/sharedpath/activemq/paging" />
```

Restoring the master node

A common requirement is to allow the master node to retain its active role once it returns online. This can be achieved by restarting the slave node (which has been elected as master) or rather by setting allow-fail-back to true on the slave, which will cause it to automatically stop once the master returns online. Here is a sample configuration to achieve this:

```
<server>
    ...
    <shared-store-slave
        allow-failback="true" />
    ...
</server>
```

HA with data replication

When using data replication, the live and the backup servers do not share the same storage and all data is synchronized through network traffic. Therefore, all the messages received by the live server will be duplicated to the backup.

Unlike the shared store HA, when using data replication the backup server will first need to synchronize all existing data from the live server before becoming an active server, so that it will eventually be capable of replacing the live server should it fail.

Here is a sample configuration that declares a messaging server to be an active server, also called replication-master:

```
<server>
    <replication-master cluster-name="my-cluster" />
    <cluster-connection name="my-cluster">
        ...
    </cluster-connection>
</server>
```

You can add the replication-master attribute via CLI as follows:

```
/subsystem=messaging-activemq/server=default/ha-policy=replication-
master:add(cluster-name="my-cluster")
```

The configuration of the backup server will need to use the replication-slave element to declare its role:

```
<server>
    <replication-slave cluster-name="my-cluster" />
    <cluster-connection name="my-cluster">
        . . .
    </cluster-connection>
</server>
```

You can add the replication-slave attribute via CLI as follows:

```
/subsystem=messaging-activemq/server=default/ha-policy=replication-
slave:add(cluster-name="my-cluster")
```

Shared-store versus replication

Both HA use cases have some advantages and disadvantages. Using a shared-store for high availability is convenient as no replication occurs between the live and backup nodes; this in turn means that you will not suffer any performance penalties due to the overhead of replication.

On the other hand, a shared-store requires that, once the backup server is activated, it needs to load the journal from the shared store, which can be time-consuming depending on the amount of data in the store. For this reason, unless you have a very fast and reliable io channel in your network, shared-store is discouraged.

Summary

In this chapter, you learned how to configure the messaging subsystem and the embedded component made of ActiveMQ Artemis.

You learned how to configure the transport layer, which is made up of the http acceptor and connector, and the invm acceptor and connector.

You also learned how to create destinations, both queues and topics. Additionally, you learned how to provide message reliability by properly configuring the persistence layer, which relies on a journal filesystem.

You learned about Bridge and how to integrate your messaging system with ActiveMQ Artemis and other brokers, such as ActiveMQ.

Last, but not least, you learned how to provide failover using clustering capabilities, provided by shared-store and replication configuration.

In the next chapter, you will learn how to configure the application server to provide security to your application using security-domains and different login-module components.

11
Securing the Application Server

Security is a fundamental element of any IT environment. You must be able to control access to your systems, also known as authentication, and manage access to resources based on the rights of users or groups. The latter process is also known as authorization. Additionally, in order to prevent disclosure of critical information to unauthorized individuals or systems, you have to use a protocol that provides encryption of the information.

After this short preamble, let's see how security is implemented in the application server. At the time of writing, release 7.0 of the application server ships with the **Picketbox** framework (`http://picketbox.jboss.org/`), which provides the authentication, authorization, auditing, and mapping capabilities to Java applications.

> In the upcoming 7.1 release, a new framework named **Elytron** will be the core security subsystem of the application server, although compatibility with former Picketbox implementation will be maintained.
> Additionally, another framework named **Red Hat Single Sign-On (SSO)** can be plugged into the application server to provide single sign-on and identity manager functionalities.
> As many users will retain their current security, this chapter will be based on Picketbox, while the new upcoming features of EAP 7.1 will be discussed in the next chapter.

We will cover in detail the following topics:

- Creating security domains
- Securing your management instruments
- Applying role-based access control
- Encrypting the HTTP interfaces

Creating security domains

The legacy security subsystem provides security to the application server via the `org.jboss.as.security` extension:

```
<extension module="org.jboss.as.security"/>
```

This subsystem is designed around the concept of a **security domain,** which is a set of **Java Authentication and Authorization Service (JAAS)** declarative security configurations. By defining security domains, your applications can control authentication, authorization, auditing, and mapping. Within each security domain, you can define **login modules,** which are the building blocks of your server security.

> A login module in the JBoss security model is derived from the Java interface `javax.security.auth.spi.LoginModule`, which contains some basic methods for authenticating a subject accessing your applications.

The list of available login modules is broad enough that we cannot discuss them all in detail. Generally speaking, the login modules are split into two main categories, depending on the location of the **identity store**:

- Internal based login modules, such as the `RealmDirect` login module
- External based login modules, such as database, LDAP, or Kerberos

Let's look at both options in more detail.

Internal based login modules

The default server configuration contains the definition of the `RealmDirect` login module as part of the other security domain:

```
<security-domains>
    <security-domain name="other" cache-type="default">
        <authentication>
            <login-module code="Remoting" flag="optional">
                <module-option name="password-stacking" value=
                "useFirstPass" />
            </login-module>
            <login-module code="RealmDirect" flag="required">
                <module-option name="password-stacking" value=
                "useFirstPass" />
            </login-module>
```

```
    </authentication>
  </security-domain>
</security-domains>
```

The default login module can be used for web applications that rely on file-based security storage which records management users in `mgmt-users.properties` and `mgmt-groups.properties`, and application users in `application-users.properties` and `application-groups.properties`.

You can add an application user via the `add-user.sh` script, as in the following example which creates `demouser1` as part of the `Admin` group:

$ ./add-user.sh -a -u demoser1 -p password1! -g Admin

You can then authenticate and authorize the user in the `web.xml` file of your application as in the following fragment:

```
<security-role>
    <role-name>Admin</role-name>
</security-role>
```

In an Enterprise context, however, robust security policies that are based on external storage are required. For your reference, you can check the official server documentation to learn about all the login module options at: `https://access.redhat.com/documentation/en/re d-hat-jboss-enterprise-application-platform/7..beta/login-module-reference/c hapter-1-login-module-overview`.

External based login modules

Here we will show two security domains which rely on external stores such as the **Database** and the **Kerberos** login modules. The first one is obviously simpler as it can reuse an existing connection pool definition from the server toward the database. The second approach is often used in enterprise contexts where authentication relies on a directory service and is secured via SSL. Kerberos authentication can be further augmented to use the **Simple and Protected Negotiation (SPNEGO)** mechanism to negotiate a single sign-on mechanism for users.

Database login module

A database login module is a JDBC-based login module which relies on a relational database where usernames, passwords, and roles are stored in a database. The login module which can be used is `DatabaseServerLoginModule`, which requires the following information as an argument:

- `dsJndiName`: The name of the datasource to reach the database
- `principalsQuery`: A query which verifies the password for a user login attempt
- `rolesQuery`: A query verifying the role for a user login attempt

For this purpose, we will use the datasource connection which we have created in Chapter 8, *Configuring Database Connectivity*. So, connect to your database with a MySQL client:

```
use mysql
```

Now create the tables to be used for storing the user credentials and their roles:

```
CREATE TABLE USERS(login VARCHAR(64) PRIMARY KEY,
passwd VARCHAR(64));
CREATE TABLE USER_ROLES(login VARCHAR(64), role VARCHAR(32));
```

Let's insert some users with a `Role`:

```
INSERT into USERS values('admin', 'admin');
INSERT into USER_ROLES values('admin', 'Admin');
```

From the CLI, execute the following commands to create a security domain named `DBSecurityDomain`:

```
/subsystem=security/security-domain=DBSecurityDomain:add()
/subsystem="security"/security-
domain=DBSecurityDomain/authentication="classic":add()
/subsystem=security/security-
domain=DBSecurityDomain/authentication="classic"/login-
module="Database":add(code="Database",flag="required",module-
options={"dsJndiName" =>"java:jboss/MySQLDS","principalsQuery" => "select
passwd from USERS where login=?","rolesQuery"=> "select role,'Roles' from
USER_ROLES where login=?"})
```

Now, from the CLI, reload your configuration:

```
reload
```

You should now be able to perform authentication and authorization in your applications by specifying the roles in the application JEE file (for example, `web.xml` in a web application):

```
<web-app>
    . . . .
    <security-constraint>
        <web-resource-collection>
            <web-resource-name>HtmlAuth</web-resource-name>
            <description>
              application security constraints
            </description>
            <url-pattern>/*</url-pattern>
            <http-method>GET</http-method>
            <http-method>POST</http-method>
        </web-resource-collection>
        <auth-constraint>
            <role-name>Admin</role-name>
        </auth-constraint>
    </security-constraint>
    <login-config>
        <auth-method>BASIC</auth-method>
        <realm-name>UserRoles simple realm</realm-name>
    </login-config>
    <security-role>
        <role-name>Admin</role-name>
    </security-role>
</web-app>
```

In the application server descriptor file (for example, `jboss-web.xml` in a web application) specify the security domain to be used by the application:

```
<jboss-web>
    <security-domain>DBSecurityDomain</security-domain>
</jboss-web>
```

Troubleshooting security domains

Many variables are involved in the authentication and authorization process, hence it can require some investigation to find an issue. The simplest way to get around it is by increasing the logging level of the `org.jboss.security` logger:

```
/subsystem=logging/logger=org.jboss.security/:add(handlers=["FILE"],level=T
RACE,use-parent-handlers=false)
```

Once done, check your server logs for details about the raised login exception.

Let's see how to deal with some common use cases. Here is an example stack trace you will find if you have entered an incorrect combination of user/password:

```
LoginModule Class: org.jboss.security.auth.spi.DatabaseServerLoginModule
ControlFlag: LoginModuleControlFlag: required
Options:
name=dsJndiName, value=java:jboss/MySQLDS
name=principalsQuery, value=select passwd from USERS where login=?
name=rolesQuery, value=select role,'Roles' from USER_ROLES where login=?
2016-03-22 15:45:47,976 TRACE [org.jboss.security] (myworker task-5)
PBOX00236: Begin initialize method
2016-03-22 15:45:47,976 TRACE [org.jboss.security] (myworker task-5)
PBOX00262: Module options [dsJndiName: java:jboss/MySQLDS, principalsQuery:
select passwd from USERS where login=?, rolesQuery: select role,'Roles'
from USER_ROLES where login=?, suspendResume: true]
2016-03-22 15:45:47,977 TRACE [org.jboss.security] (myworker task-5)
PBOX00240: Begin login method
2016-03-22 15:45:48,230 TRACE [org.jboss.security] (myworker task-5)
PBOX00263: Executing query select passwd from USERS where login=? with
username myuser
2016-03-22 15:45:48,240 TRACE [org.jboss.security] (myworker task-5)
PBOX00244: Begin abort method, overall result: false
2016-03-22 15:45:48,240 DEBUG [org.jboss.security] (myworker task-5)
PBOX00206: Login failure: javax.security.auth.login.FailedLoginException:
PBOX00062: No matching username found in principals
  at
org.jboss.security.auth.spi.DatabaseServerLoginModule.getUsersPassword(Data
baseServerLoginModule.java:188)
```

As you can clearly see, the datasource actually used for the login is printed (java:jboss/MySQLDS) along with the query issued. As evident from the last DEBUG information, no match was found for the username/password with the principalsQuery.

Another common issue is a mismatch between the database schema and the principalsQuery/rolesQuery. In some databases, such as MySQL/MariaDB, the case of the tables and fields matters, so here is what you will see if you attempt to reference a table which does not exist in your schema:

```
2016-03-22 15:52:36,748 DEBUG [org.jboss.security] (myworker task-8)
PBOX00206: Login failure: javax.security.auth.login.LoginException:
PBOX00065: Error processing query
. . . .
Caused by: com.mysql.jdbc.exceptions.jdbc4.MySQLSyntaxErrorException: Table
'mysqlschema.USER_ROLES' doesn't exist
  at sun.reflect.NativeConstructorAccessorImpl.newInstance0(Native Method)
```

Finally, a database that is unavailable, maybe because of a network issue, can be recognized by a `CommunicationsException` which is at the end of the stack trace:

```
2016-03-22 15:48:40,372 TRACE [org.jboss.security] (myworker task-2)
PBOX00263: Executing query select passwd from USERS where login=? with
username ddddd
2016-03-22 15:48:40,390 WARN
[org.jboss.jca.core.connectionmanager.listener.TxConnectionListener]
(myworker task-2) IJ000305: Connection error occured:
org.jboss.jca.core.connectionmanager.listener.TxConnectionListener@d5649a2[
state=NORMAL managed
connection=org.jboss.jca.adapters.jdbc.local.LocalManagedConnection@897c3ab
connection handles=1 lastReturned=1458657948240 lastValidated=1458657948230
lastCheckedOut=1458658120372 trackByTx=false
pool=org.jboss.jca.core.connectionmanager.pool.strategy.OnePool@61befdef
mcp=SemaphoreConcurrentLinkedQueueManagedConnectionPool@623672cb[pool=MySql
DS] xaResource=LocalXAResourceImpl@5d37319[connectionListener=d5649a2
connectionManager=7c34857a warned=false currentXid=null productName=MySQL
productVersion=5.5.5-10.0.23-MariaDB jndiName=java:jboss/MySQLDS]
txSync=null]: com.mysql.jdbc.exceptions.jdbc4.CommunicationsException:
Communications link failure
```

Hardening the database login modules

As it is, the database login modules use clear text passwords in the password field. Obviously, this needs to be hardened with some encryption mechanisms. The simplest way to do it is to hash the sensitive strings. The database login module includes the `hashAlgorithm` property to specify the `java.security.MessageDigest` algorithm to use to hash the password.

> The recommended hash for storing sensitive strings is `SHA-256`, which generates an almost-unique, fixed-size 256-bit (32-byte) hash.

You can create a security domain which includes a `base64 SHA-256` encoded password as follows:

```
/subsystem=security/security-
domain=DBSecurityDomain/authentication="classic"/login-
module="Database":add(code="Database",flag="required",module-
options={"dsJndiName" =>"java:jboss/MySQLDS","principalsQuery" => "select
passwd from USERS where login=?","rolesQuery"=> "select role,'Roles' from
USER_ROLES where login=?","hashAlgorithm"=> "SHA-256","hashEncoding"=>
"base64"})
```

That being said, you have to replace your clear text passwords with the hashed ones. You can do it in many ways:

Natively: Most databases support hashing functions, therefore you can delegate to the database the storage of the password. For example, the following INSERT statement would store a user's password with a hash compatible with DBSecurityDomain:

```
INSERT into USERS values('admin', TO_BASE64(UNHEX(SHA2('admin',256))));
```

Otherwise, you can use external tools to generate the hash and pass the hashed string to the INSERT string. Some examples: here is the same hash calculated using openssl:

```
$ echo -n "admin" | openssl dgst -sha256 -binary | openssl base64
jG125bVBBBW96Qi9Te4V37Fnqchz/Eu4qB9vKrRIqRg=
```

Or, if you prefer, using one utility class named org.jboss.security.Base64Encoder included in Picketbox's library JAR file:

```
java -classpath
./system/layers/base/org/picketbox/main/picketbox-4.9.6.Final-redhat-1.jar
org.jboss.security.Base64Encoder admin SHA-256
    [jG125bVBBBW96Qi9Te4V37Fnqchz/Eu4qB9vKrRIqRg=]
```

Since you have formerly inserted the passwords in clear text, you should obviously replace them with the hashed ones:

```
update USERS set passwd =
'jG125bVBBBW96Qi9Te4V37Fnqchz/Eu4qB9vKrRIqRg=' where login = 'admin';
```

Creating a Kerberos security domain

Kerberos is a strong authentication protocol, network which can be used for client/server applications by using secret-key cryptography. Kerberos relies on a trusted third party, the **Key Distribution Center(KDC)**, which is aware of all systems in the network and is trusted by all of them. In terms of software components, a directory service performs the functions of the KDC with two main functions:

- It acts as a **ticket-granting server** (TGS): a client that wishes to use a service has to receive a ticket – a time-limited cryptographic message – giving it access to the server
- It uses its authentication service to authenticate clients

Kerberos was originally created to authenticate desktop users on networks; however, with the use of additional tools, it can be used to authenticate users to web applications and to provide SSO for a set of web applications. This concept is known as **desktop-based SSO** since the user is being authenticated via a desktop-based authentication mechanism, and their authentication token (or ticket) is being used by the web application as well.

We will approach this complex area in three steps:

1. First, we will learn how to create a basic Kerberos configuration.
2. Next, we will show how to apply this configuration to JBoss EAP.
3. Finally, we will configure the SSO mechanism in EAP through the SPNGO module.

Basic Kerberos configuration

The installation steps of Kerberos can be quite different, depending on your operating system, hence we will not cover a standard Kerberos installation here; to get up to speed quickly, we will use a quicker approach, that is, running an ApacheDS server. ApacheDS (`http://directory.apache.org/apacheds/`) is commonly used as an LDAP server, but it also supports the Kerberos protocol and is a KDC, containing a TGS and an **authentication server** (**AS**).

The project we will use is available on GitHub at the following address: `https://github.com/mjbeap7/ch11` (please note this project is a refactoring of the demo provided by Josef Cacek at `https://github.com/kwart/spnego-demo`, to whom we credit the effort of building this quickstart).

The steps for setting up the environment are detailed on the readme page (`https://github.com/mjbeap7/ch11/blob/master/README.md`). We will just summarize the core part of it. First of all, once you have downloaded or cloned the Git project, build the `projects` with Maven as follows:

```
$ mvn clean install
```

This will build in turn the two subprojects:

- `kerberos-using-apacheds`: This project contains an implementation of ApacheDS featuring a Kerberos server
- `kerberos-spnego`: This project contains a demo application to test Kerberos

Let's enter into the first project, which will start our Kerberos server!

Running the Kerberos server

Move into the `kerberos-using-apacheds` folder:

```
$ cd kerberos-using-apacheds
```

The JAR file produced from the build, named `kerberos-using-apacheds.jar`, contains a minimal LDAP and Kerberos implementation which can be started up as follows:

```
$ java -jar target/kerberos-using-apacheds.jar test.ldif
```

Please note that the main application class accepts an LDIF file as an argument which contains the default realms, user, and organization. The server will start in debug mode, as you can see from the console log:

```
Starting Kerberos controll process.
. . . .
11:24:13.953 [main] INFO org.jboss.test.kerberos.KerberosSetup - Generating
kerberos configuration file 'krb5.conf'
Starting KDC
11:24:14.004 [main] DEBUG
org.apache.directory.server.kerberos.kdc.KdcServer - initializing the
kerberos replay cache
11:24:14.032 [main] INFO org.apache.directory.server.kerberos.kdc.KdcServer
- Kerberos service started.
Starting LDAP server
```

In order to connect to the Kerberos server, a configuration file is needed. By default, our application will create a file named `krb5.conf` in the current working directory. Here is the `krb5.conf` file created:

```
[libdefaults]
    default_realm = JBOSS.ORG
    default_tgs_enctypes = des-cbc-md5 des3-cbc-sha1-kd rc4-hmac
    default_tkt_enctypes = des-cbc-md5 des3-cbc-sha1-kd rc4-hmac
    kdc_timeout = 5000
    dns_lookup_realm = false
    dns_lookup_kdc = false
    dns_canonicalize_hostname = false
    rdns = false
    ignore_acceptor_hostname = true
    allow_weak_crypto = yes

[realms]
    JBOSS.ORG = {
        kdc = localhost:6088
    }
```

```
[domain_realm]
    localhost = JBOSS.ORG
```

This file contains Kerberos configuration information, such as locations of KDCs and admin servers for the Kerberos realms of interest. As you can see, the KDC for the realm JBOSS.ORG is available on localhost on port 6088. In order to use this configuration file, you can either copy it into the Kerberos default location, that is, in /etc/krb5.conf, or define the KRB5_CONFIG system variable. Let's follow the second pattern, assuming you have started the Kerberos server in the folder /home/jboss/mjbeap7/ch11/kerberos-using-apacheds:

$ export KRB5_CONFIG=/home/jboss/mjbeap7/ch11/kerberos-using-apacheds/krb5.conf

The next step will be creating a **keytab**. This file is used to store pairs of Kerberos principals and encrypted keys. You can use a keytab file to authenticate to various remote systems using Kerberos without entering a password. Our kerberos-using-apacheds.jar is also capable of doing that; you just need to run the org.jboss.test.kerberos.CreateKeytab class passing the principal name, its password, and the name of the keytab file as an argument as follows:

$ java -classpath target/kerberos-using-apacheds.jar org.jboss.test.kerberos.CreateKeytab HTTP/localhost@JBOSS.ORG httppwd http.keytab

As a result, the following output should be displayed:

Adding principal HTTP/localhost@JBOSS.ORG with passphrase httppwd
Keytab file was created: /home/jboss/mjbeap7/ch11/kerberos-using-apacheds/http.keytab

In terms of EAP configuration, what we need is to define a Kerberos security domain containing a reference to the principal name, the keytab file, and the main krb5 configuration file. Start the application server and execute the following commands through the CLI:

```
/subsystem=security/security-domain=host:add(cache-type=default)
/subsystem=security/security-
domain=host/authentication=classic:add(login-modules=[{"code"=>"Kerberos",
"flag"=>"required", "module-options"=>[
("debug"=>"true"), ("storeKey"=>"true"), ("refreshKrb5Config"=>"true"), ("useK
eyTab"=>"true"), ("doNotPrompt"=>"true"), ("keyTab"=>"/home/jboss/mjbeap7/ch1
1/kerberos-using-
apacheds/http.keytab"), ("principal"=>"HTTP/localhost@JBOSS.ORG")]}])
{allow-resource-service-restart=true}
```

Next, we will execute some additional commands to set some system properties:

```
/system-
property=java.security.krb5.conf:add(value="/home/jboss/mjbeap7/
    ch11/kerberos-using-apacheds/krb5.conf")
/system-property=java.security.krb5.debug:add(value=true)
```

The first property, named `java.security.krb5.conf`, is a pointer to the Kerberos configuration file. The second one, `java.security.krb5.debug`, enables debugging of the ticket exchange procedure.

> Please remember to replace the absolute paths contained in the CLI commands with the path of your local files.

Once executed, the following security domain configuration will be included in your server's configuration file:

```
<security-domain name="host" cache-type="default">
   <authentication>
     <login-module code="Kerberos" flag="required">
       <module-option name="debug" value="true"/>
      <module-option name="storeKey" value="true"/>
      <module-option name="refreshKrb5Config" value="true"/>
      <module-option name="useKeyTab" value="true"/>
    <module-option name="doNotPrompt" value="true"/>
    <module-option name="keyTab" value="/home/jboss/mjbeap7/ch11/
     kerberos-using-apacheds/http.keytab"/>
    <module-option name="principal" value="HTTP/localhost@JBOSS.ORG"/>
    </login-module>
    </authentication>
</security-domain>
```

Right now, what we can do to test our Kerberos security domain is to connect the management interfaces to the Keytab we have just created. The following CLI commands will do exactly that:

```
/core-service=management/security-realm=ManagementRealm/
  server-identity=kerberos:add
/core-service=management/security-realm=ManagementRealm/
  server-identity=kerberos/keytab="HTTP/localhost@JBOSS.ORG":
  add(path="/home/jboss/mjbeap7/ch11/kerberos-using-apacheds/
  http.keytab",debug=true)
/core-service=management/security-realm=ManagementRealm
/authentication=kerberos:add
```

The first command will add a new server's identity definition based on Kerberos. The second line will link the Kerberos identity to the Keytab file, while the last command will set Kerberos as the default management authentication.

The following configuration will now be included in your server's XML file:

```
<security-realm name="ManagementRealm">
   <server-identities>
     <kerberos>
       <keytab principal="HTTP/localhost@JBOSS.ORG"
path="/home/jboss/mjbeap7/
         ch11/kerberos-using-apacheds/http.keytab"
         debug="true"/>
     </kerberos>
   </server-identities>
 . . .
</security-realm>
```

Testing the Kerberos login against management interfaces

We will now test the Kerberos authentication against the web management interface. Before doing that, we will need to obtain an initial ticket for a principal of our realm.

The recommended package to do that is the `krb5-workstation package`, which can be installed on a RHEL or Fedora operating system as follows:

```
$ sudo yum install krb5-workstation
```

Now you can use the `kinit` command to collect a ticket for authentication. In the LDIF file we have imported, there are a couple of users for that purpose. One of them is `hnelson@JBOSS.ORG`, whose password is secret. Execute from the shell:

```
$ kinit hnelson@JBOSS.ORG
```

Enter `secret` as the password. You can check ticket availability through the `klist` command as follows:

```
$ klist
Ticket cache: FILE:/tmp/krb5cc_1000
Default principal: hnelson@JBOSS.ORG
Valid starting      Expires             Service principal
08/06/16 12:41:32   09/06/16 12:41:32   krbtgt/JBOSS.ORG@JBOSS.ORG
```

Now, from within the same shell, execute your browser pointing to the admin console:

```
$ firefox http://localhost:9990
```

> Please check the README file of the project, as some properties should be enabled on your browser in order to allow ticket negotiation between the browser and the Kerberos server.

You should be able to connect automatically (as `hnelson@JBOSS.ORG`) to the management interface, as depicted in the following screenshot:

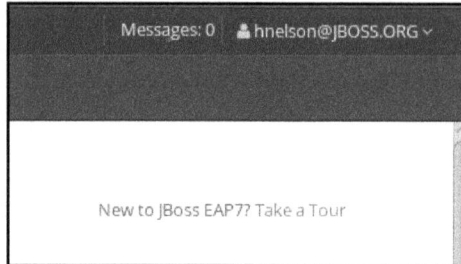

Using Kerberos to provide SSO

As we said, by combining Kerberos authentication with the **SPNEGO mechanism**, it is possible to extend the desktop-based authentication mechanism to web applications. The process, which is depicted in the following diagram, works like that: first, the user logs in to a desktop, which is governed by Kerberos, and completes an authentication exchange with the KDC. The user then attempts to access a secured resource contained in a web application; the server responds that authorization is required. The application then requests a service ticket from the Kerberos KDC. After the ticket is obtained, the application wraps it in a request formatted for SPNEGO, and sends it back to the web application, via the browser. The web container running the deployed web application unpacks the request and authenticates the ticket. Upon successful authentication, access is granted:

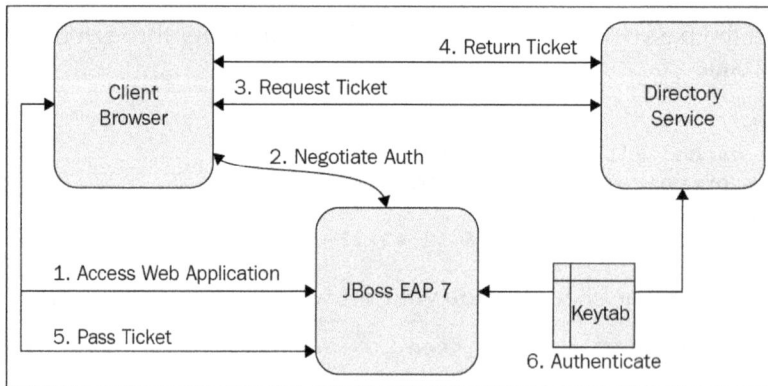

Let's see how to add it in practice. The following script can be used to add a SPNEGO login module based on the Kerberos security domain we have formerly created:

```
/subsystem=security/security-domain=SPNEGO:add(cache-type=default)
/subsystem=security/security-
domain=SPNEGO/authentication=classic:add(login-modules=[{"code"=>"SPNEGO",
"flag"=>"required", "module-options"=>[("serverSecurityDomain"=>"host")]}])
{allow-resource-service-restart=true}
/subsystem=security/security-domain=SPNEGO/mapping=classic:add(mapping-
modules=[{"code"=>"SimpleRoles", "type"=>"role", "module-
options"=>[("jduke@JBOSS.ORG"=>"Admin"),("hnelson@JBOSS.ORG"=>"User")]}])
{allow-resource-service-restart=true}
```

This will translate in practice into the following XML output:

```
<security-domain name="SPNEGO" cache-type="default">
    <authentication>
        <login-module code="SPNEGO" flag="required">
            <module-option name="serverSecurityDomain" value="host" />
        </login-module>
    </authentication>
    <mapping>
        <mapping-module code="SimpleRoles" type="role">
            <module-option name="jduke@JBOSS.ORG" value="Admin" />
            <module-option name="hnelson@JBOSS.ORG" value="User" />
        </mapping-module>
    </mapping>
</security-domain>
```

The first authentication block links the SPNEGO security domain to the host security domain which wraps the Kerberos authentication system. The second part, which includes the mapping modules, contains some basic user/role mappings that will be used by our sample application.

In order to test the SPNEGO authentication, you can use the application which is contained in the folder kerberos-spnego:

```
$ cd kerberos-spnego
```

As we have formerly built the parent project, you should have a war archive named spnego-demo.war available in the target folder. Simply copy it into the deployments folder of the application server:

```
$ cp target/spnego-demo.war $JBOSS_HOME/standalone/deployments
```

Now, if your ticket created with `kinit` is still valid, simply execute from the shell:

> **$ firefox http://localhost:8080/spnego-demo/**

You should land in the home page of the application. Click on the **User page** to negotiate a Kerberos authentication. The expected result is that you will be fully authorized to access this page without any extra login and your role will be printed in the page:

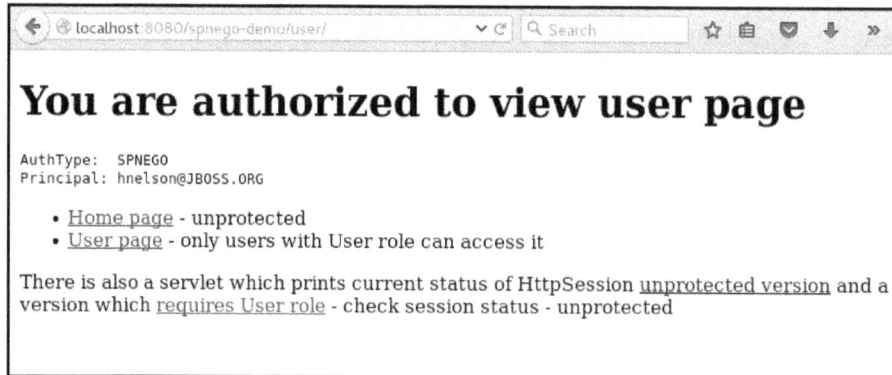

Under the hood, we had to add some configuration tweaks in our application to enable SPNEGO authentication. First of all, what we needed to include in the web application is a dependency towards the module `org.jboss.security.negotiation`. This can be done through the `jboss-deployment-structure.xml` as follows:

```
<jboss-deployment-structure>
  <deployment>
    <dependencies>
      <module name="org.jboss.security.negotiation"/>
    </dependencies>
  </deployment>
</jboss-deployment-structure>
```

Next, the `jboss-web.xml` file needs to reference the security domain which we have formerly added, named SPNEGO:

```
<jboss-web>
  <security-domain>SPNEGO</security-domain>
  <jacc-star-role-allow>true</jacc-star-role-allow>
</jboss-web>
```

The `jacc-star-role-allow` allows you to use the asterisk (*) character to match multiple role names.

Finally, we needed to include in the `web.xml` configuration file a restriction to some URL patterns specifying the roles which are enabled to access the page (in our case, the user `hnelson@JBOSS.ORG` belongs to the user group):

```
<web-app>
  <security-constraint>
    <display-name>Security Constraint on Conversation</display-name>
    <web-resource-collection>
      <web-resource-name>SpnegoDemo</web-resource-name>
      <url-pattern>/user/*</url-pattern>
    </web-resource-collection>
   <auth-constraint>
      <role-name>User</role-name>
      </auth-constraint>
  </security-constraint>
  <!-- Define the Login Configuration for this Application -->
  <login-config>
    <auth-method>SPNEGO</auth-method>
    <realm-name>SPNEGO</realm-name>
  </login-config>
  <!-- Security roles referenced by this web application -->
  <security-role>
    <description>Role required to log in to the Application</description>
    <role-name>User</role-name>
  </security-role>
</web-app>
```

Securing the management interfaces with LDAP

In the *Testing the Kerberos login against management interfaces* section, we discussed how to secure the management interfaces using the Kerberos ticketing system.

If you don't need that level of complexity in your infrastructure, but you still want to provide an adequate level of security, the recommended approach is to use a **directory service**. The directory service can be used both for authenticating the user and for granting a role to the user. If your management users will be all `SuperUsers` then it's enough to configure just the **authentication** layer. On the other hand, if you want to apply **Role-Based Access Control** (**RBAC**) on your management users then you have to configure the **authorization** part.

To get you started quickly with this topic, we can continue using the `ApacheDS` server contained in the `kerberos-using-apacheds` project, which contains some LDAP users along with the Kerberos configuration. Otherwise, you can download the full ApacheDS studio from `https://directory.apache.org/studio/downloads.html` and import the `test.ldif` file available in the project folder.

Out of the box, the `test.ldif` file contains the following users and groups:

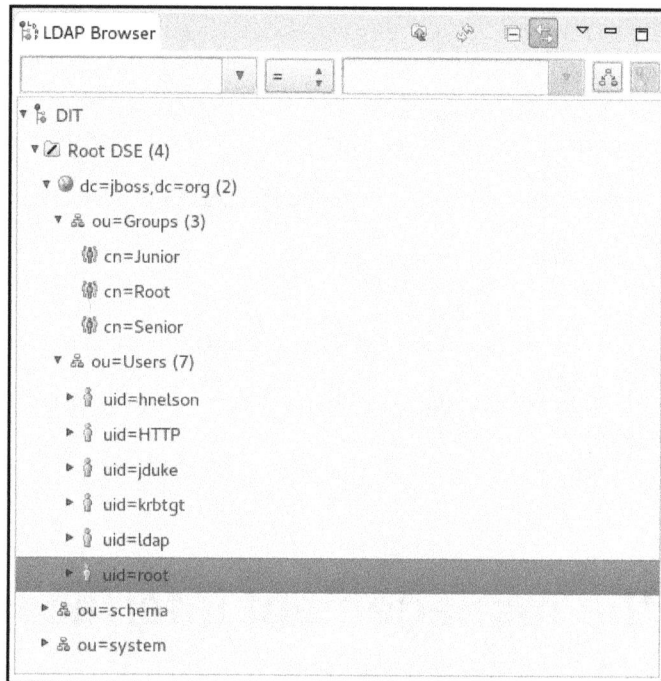

In the next section, we will configure EAP to connect with the users which are in the `OrganizationUnit` named users.

Setting up LDAP authentication

In order to set up authentication with LDAP, we will need to define a **security realm**. A security realm is responsible for the authentication and authorization of users allowed to administer JBoss EAP via the management interfaces.

In our case, the security realm will include a reference to our LDAP connection, which uses the following default settings:

LDAP URL	`ldap://127.0.0.1:10389`
Base dn	`ou=Users,dc=jboss,dc=org`
Default login user	`uid=hnelson,ou=Users,dc=jboss,dc=org`
Default password	`secret`

In order to create the security realm, execute the following commands from the EAP CLI:

```
/core-service=management/ldap-connection=ldap_connection/:add(search-
credential=secret, url=ldap://127.0.0.1:10389, search-dn="
uid=hnelson,ou=Users,dc=jboss,dc=org")
/core-service=management/security-realm=LDAPRealm:add(map-groups-to-
roles=true)
/core-service=management/security-
realm=LDAPRealm/authentication=ldap:add(base-
dn="ou=Users,dc=jboss,dc=org",connection=ldap_connection,username-
attribute=uid)
```

As a result, a new realm will be defined at the top of your configuration:

```
<security-realm name="LDAPRealm">
    <authentication>
        <ldap connection="ldap_connection" base-dn="ou=Users,
        dc=jboss,dc=org ">
            <username-filter attribute="uid" />
        </ldap>
    </authentication>
</security-realm>
```

> Some information about the above parameters will help: `base-dn` is the distinguished name (DN) of the context that searches for the user should begin from. The `username-filter` can be used to specify the attribute of the LDAP entries that should be searched to match against the supplied username.

Additionally, an **outbound connection** will be included with the LDAP connection String we have used to authenticate to the LDAP server:

```
<outbound-connections>
    <ldap name="ldap_connection" url="ldap://127.0.0.1:10389" search-
    dn="uid=hnelson,ou=Users,dc=jboss,dc=org" search-credential="secret"/>
```

```
</outbound-connections>
```

In order to switch to this realm for your management interfaces, you have to set the `security-realm` attribute from the management interface as follows:

```
/core-service=management/management-interface=http-interface:write-
attribute(name=security-realm,value=LDAPRealm)
```

This will result in the following change in your configuration:

```
<management-interfaces>
    <http-interface security-realm="LDAPRealm" http-upgrade-enabled="true">
        <socket-binding http="management-http"/>
    </http-interface>
</management-interfaces>
```

Now reload the server configuration and attempt to access the management interface at `localhost:9990`. A login prompt will inform you that you need to authenticate through the `LDAP Realm`:

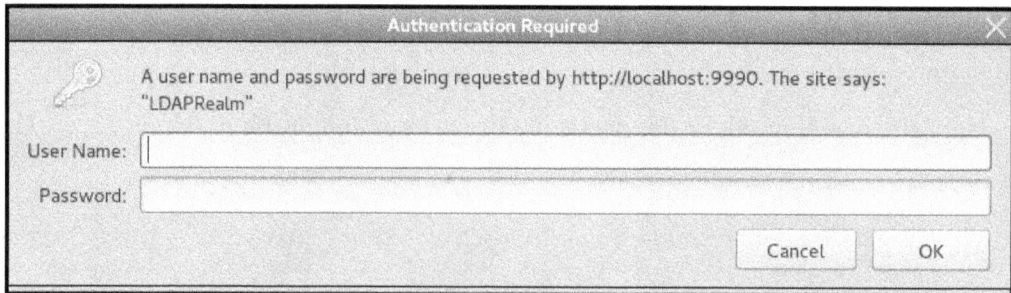

Enter the username/password of any of the users in the users loaded with the LDIF script (for example, root and secret as password). If you have followed the preceding steps, you should be able to access the management interfaces as depicted by this screenshot:

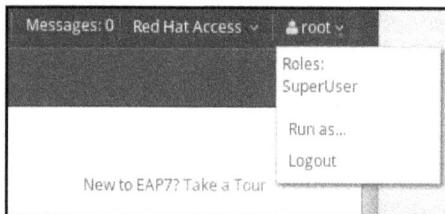

HA LDAP

As it is, the LDAP server represents a single point of failure in your architecture. The outbound connection is able to handle a failover scenario anyway, in case you have multiple LDAP servers. In the case of the failure of one server, the connection will be handled by survivor nodes. You can simply include the list of servers as part of the URL connection string as follows:

```
<outbound-connections>
    <ldap name="ldap" url="ldap://172.17.0.4:10389 ldap://172.17.0.5:10389"
search-
    dn="uid=hnelson,ou=Users,dc=jboss,dc=org" search-credential="secret"/>
</outbound-connections>
```

Configuring RBAC

Role-Based Access Control (RBAC) is a mechanism for configuring a set of permissions for EAP management users. It allows multiple users to share responsibility for managing EAP servers without requiring unrestricted access to them. By providing *separation of duties* for management users, JBoss EAP makes it easy for an organization to divide responsibility between administrators or groups without granting unnecessary privileges. This ensures the maximum possible level of security of your servers while still providing flexibility for management, configuration, and deployment.

Out of the box, the following roles are predefined in EAP 7, covering most common use cases:

Role	Description
Monitor	This role has the fewest permissions and can only read the current configuration and state of the server. Typically used for end users that need to watch the server metrics and availability.
Deployer	This role extends the Monitor permission, enabling the deployment of application resources. Typically used for end users that are in the delivery area of your IT.
Operator	This role extends the Monitor role, including the ability to modify the runtime state of the server. Fit for administrators in charge of starting/stopping/restarting servers or JMS destinations.

Maintainer	This role extends the Operator, including the ability to modify the configuration and execute operations, except for sensitive data and operations. Typically used for administrators, such as external consultants, that have full control over the server except for sensitive data, such as a company's passwords.
Administrator	This role has full access to the application server configuration and operations except for the audit logging system. Administrator is the only role (except SuperUser) that has access to sensitive data and operations. This role can also configure the access control system. The Administrator role is only required when handling sensitive data or configuring users and roles.
SuperUser	This role has complete access to all server configuration and operations. This is equivalent to the root user of an operating system.
Auditor	This role extends the Monitor role with two abilities: reading sensitive data and having full access to the audit logging system. Typically used for administrators in charge of overseeing the operations executed on the application server.

By default, RBAC is not enabled, so every management user, by default, is granted a SuperUser role. You need to enable RBAC through the management core service as follows:

```
/core-service=management/access=authorization:write-
attribute(name=provider, value=rbac)
```

A reload is required in order to enable the changes:

```
reload
```

Let's check the roles which are defined by default:

```
/core-service=management/access=authorization:read-children-
names(child-type=role-mapping)
{
    "outcome" => "success",
    "result" => ["SuperUser"],
}
```

As you can see, so far only the SuperUser has been included as a role. We will be using two additional roles, such as Deployer and Maintainer, hence we will add them as follows:

```
    /core-service=management/access=authorization/role-
mapping=Deployer/:add
    /core-service=management/access=authorization/role-
mapping=Maintainer/:add
```

As a proof of concept, check the list of roles which have been enabled:

```
    /core-service=management/access=authorization:read-children-
names(child-type=role-mapping)
    {
        "outcome" => "success",
        "result" => [
            "Deployer",
            "Maintainer",
            "SuperUser"
        ]
    }
```

Now that you have enabled RBAC and some of the default roles, we need to map our management users. This can be done in two ways: you can either map **individual** users or **groups** of users and their corresponding roles.

Mapping individual users

Mapping individual users requires that you obviously provide a role for each user that you have created. Let's first create a couple of users using the add-user script as follows:

```
    ./add-user.sh -m -u luigi -p password123!
    ./add-user.sh -m -u francesco -p password123!
```

Now let's assign some role to our users. First, we will make the SuperUser the administrator1 management user we created in Chapter 1, *Installation and Configuration*:

```
    /core-service=management/access=authorization/role-
mapping=SuperUser/include=administrator1/:add(type=USER,name=
administrator1)
```

Next, we will elect the users francesco and luigi as, respectively, deployer and maintainer:

```
    /core-service=management/access=authorization/role-
mapping=Deployer/include=francesco/:add(type=USER,name=francesco)
    /core-service=management/access=authorization/role-
mapping=Maintainer/include=luigi/:add(type=USER,name=luigi)
```

Reload the configuration to apply the changes:

```
reload
```

The simplest way to test RBAC is by means of the web console, hence point the browser to `localhost:9990` and log in with one of the user credentials we have just added.

As you can see from the following screenshot, the user francesco is a **Deployer**:

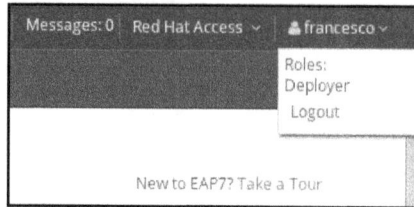

Hence, this user is able to deploy applications or resources on the server, as you can see from the following screenshot:

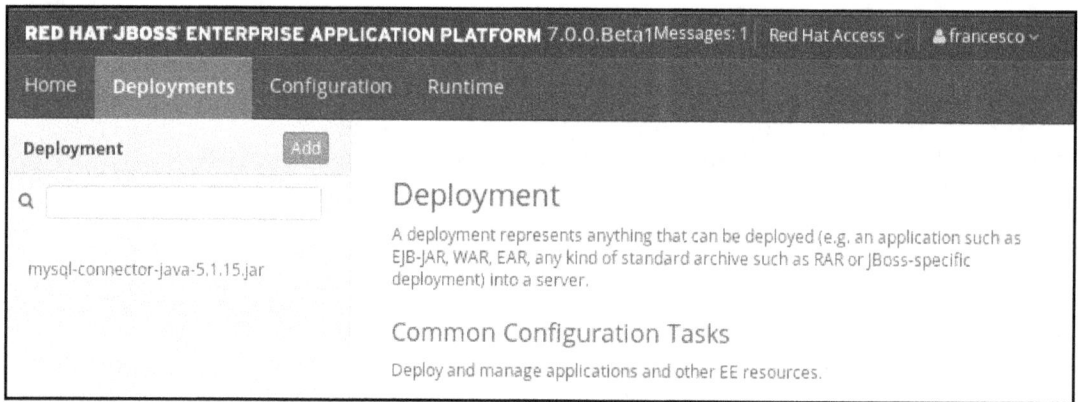

On the other hand, a deployer is not able to manage the server state (stop/suspend/reload), as you can see from the following screenshot:

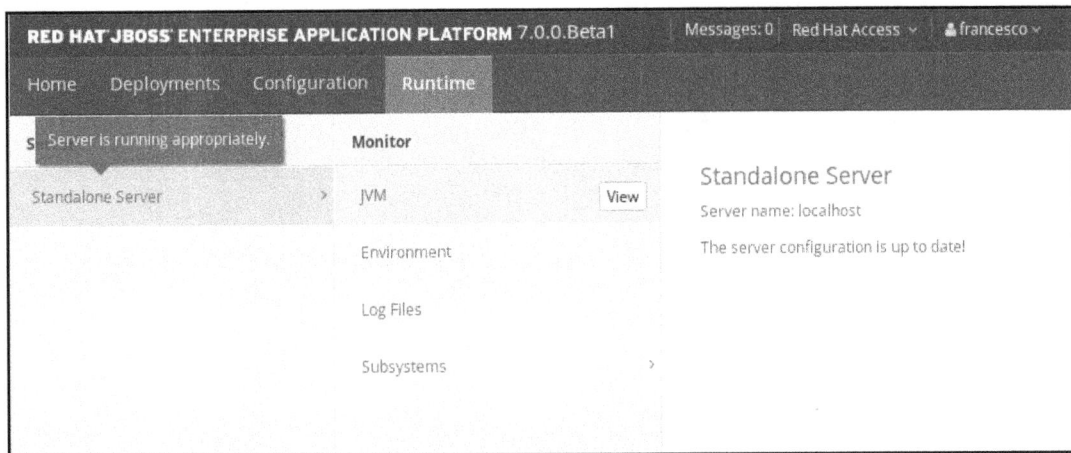

Conversely, if you try to log in with the user luigi, you will be a **Maintainer**:

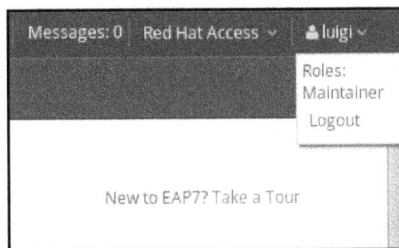

As Maintainer, you are able to manage the server state, as you can see from this screenshot:

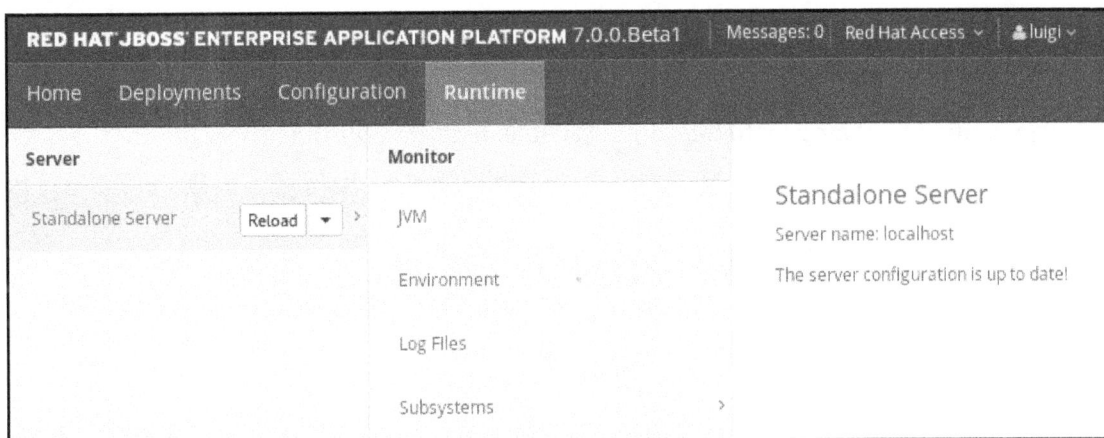

Mapping groups to roles

Groups are the most convenient way to use RBAC for large organizations, since entire groups can be associated with a role in a single mapping. Mapping groups with roles is currently supported for the following authentication store types:

- Properties file
- LDAP (via `directory-server-specific` configuration)

Let's first look at the simpler case.

Mapping groups with property files

When using property files, you can specify through the `add-user` shell script the group which the user belongs to. Here it is with one liner shell:

```
./add-user.sh -m -u jim -p password123! -g Admins
```

The user jim belongs to the admins group. This group needs to be mapped with the server's roles in order to work. First of all, if you haven't done it before, enable the Administrator Role Mapping:

```
/core-service=management/access=authorization/role-
mapping=Administrator/:add
```

Now, you can map this role to a Group. In our case, we will map it with the administrator group list with the following CLI command:

```
/core-service=management/access=authorization/role-
mapping=Administrator/include=grp-
administrators:add(name=Admins,type=GROUP)
```

You can verify, by logging on to the admin console, that the user **jim** is now an EAP **Administrator**:

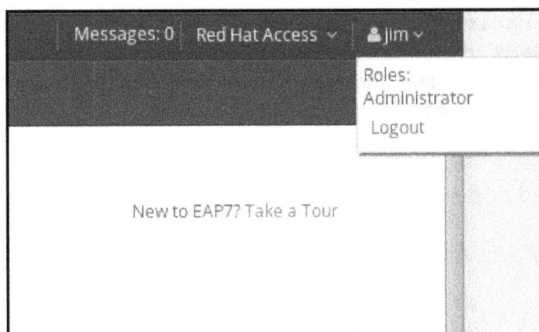

Mapping groups with LDAP

A directory service contains entries both for user accounts and groups, cross-referenced by their attributes. Using LDAP for handling RBAC authorization is thus a perfect match since users can be both authenticated and authorized to access the management interfaces based on their LDAP role. The only challenge for us will be mapping the LDAP roles with the application server roles.

There are two different styles that can be used when searching for group membership information:

- **Principal to group mapping,** which means that the user's entry contains a reference to the group(s) it is a member of (for example, using the memberOf attribute)
- **Group to principal mapping,** which means that the group's entry contains a reference to the user(s) who are members of it (for example, using the uniqueMember).

We will show here how to implement the latter case. If you have already defined an outbound connection toward LDAP, all you have to do is include in the LDAPRealm the authorization element which contains the group-search toward the LDAP group.

The following CLI batch script will create an authorization element in the LDAPRealm containing the group-to-principal configuration:

```
batch
/core-service=management/security-
realm=LDAPRealm/authorization=ldap:add(connection=ldap_connection)
/core-service=management/security-realm=LDAPRealm/authorization=ldap/group-
search=group-to-principal:add(base-dn="ou=Groups,dc=jboss,dc=org",group-
name-attribute=cn,group-name="SIMPLE",group-dn-
```

```
attribute="dn",iterative="true",search-
by=DISTINGUISHED_NAME,recursive=true,principal-attribute=uniqueMember)
/core-service=management/management-interface=http-interface:write-
attribute(name=security-realm,value=LDAPRealm)
run-batch
```

The following highlighted code contains the outcome in your LDAP realm security realm:

```
<security-realm name="LDAPRealm">
   <authentication>
      <ldap connection="ldap_connection" base-
dn="ou=Users,dc=example,dc=com">
         <username-filter attribute="uid" />
      </ldap>
   </authentication>
   <authorization>
    <ldap connection="ldap_connection">
       <group-search group-name="SIMPLE" iterative="true"
         group-dn-attribute="dn" group-name-attribute="cn">
       <group-to-principal base-dn="ou=Groups,dc=jboss,dc=org"
        recursive="true" search-by="DISTINGUISHED_NAME">
           <membership-filter principal-attribute="uniqueMember" />
       </group-to-principal>
       </group-search>
    </ldap>
  </authorization>
</security-realm>
```

As you can see, in this case the group membership is searched by distinguished name through the ou=Groups,dc=jboss,dc=org dn. Members of the group will need to use the uniqueMember attribute at the group level.

Before finishing off, we need to map the roles defined in LDAP with some EAP 7 roles. We will set the root group to be an Administrator, the Senior to be a Maintainer and the Junior to be a deployer.

Run the following CLI script to complete this action:

```
    /core-service=management/access=authorization/role-
mapping=Administrator/include=Root/:add(type=GROUP,name=Root)
    /core-service=management/access=authorization/role-
mapping=Deployer/include=Junior/:add(type=GROUP,name=Junior)
    /core-service=management/access=authorization/role-
mapping=Maintainer/include=Senior/:add(type=GROUP,name=Senior)
```

Finally, make sure that the `LDAPRealm` is set as the security realm for the management interfaces:

```
/core-service=management/management-interface=http-interface:write-
attribute(name=security-realm,value=LDAPRealm)
```

Now reload your configuration and verify that your roles are assigned based on membership to the LDAP group. For example, here is the `jduke` user elected as **Maintainer**:

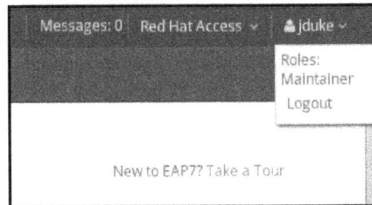

If you navigate through the **Access Control** UI, you should be able to see the list of **Groups** added and the matching role we have defined:

Scoped roles

When running in domain mode, you can apply the server roles we have described so far to a limited portion of the domain. In practice, you can define roles either to a set of server groups or to a set of hosts. This translates into the following two options:

- **Server group scoped roles**: The privileges on the server resources are constrained to one or more Server groups of your domain
- **Host scoped roles**: The privileges on the server resources are constrained to one or more hosts of your domain

Both options are activated in the same way. Before trying them, remember that you need to enable RBAC on you domain configuration as well. This can be done, as usual, through the management core service as follows:

```
/core-service=management/access=authorization:write-
attribute(name=provider, value=rbac)
```

Now, let's see the first case: we want to define a new `server-group-scoped-role` for the `main-server-group`. First, we need to create our scoped role:

```
/core-service=management/access=authorization/server-group-scoped-
role=MainG-Role:add(base-role=administrator, server-groups=[main-server-
group])
```

Next, we need to map users to the scoped role. For this purpose, we can just create a demo user named domain-user with the add-user script:

```
./add-user.sh -m -u domain-user -p password123!
```

Next, we will map it with the `MainG-Role`:

```
/core-service=management/access=authorization/role-mapping=MainG-Role:add
/core-service=management/access=authorization/role-mapping=MainG-
Role/include=domain-user:add(name=domain-user, type=user)
```

Now, if you log in to the admin console with this user, you will see that you only have access to the **main-server-group** in your domain, whereas the other **Server Groups** will be out of your scope:

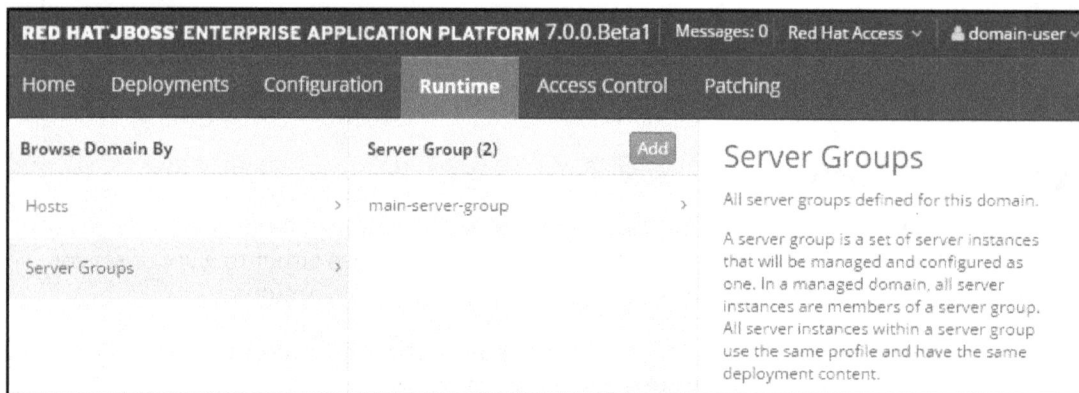

In much the same way, you can define a host scoped role to restrict the access of an user or group to one host of your domain. The following CLI can be used to demonstrate how to restrict the user domain-user to the Host Controller named master:

```
    /core-service=management/access=authorization/host-scoped-
role=MasterH:add(base-role=administrator,hosts=[master])
    /core-service=management/access=authorization/role-mapping=MasterH:add
    /core-service=management/access=authorization/role-
mapping=MasterH/include=domain-user:add(name=domain-user, type=user)
```

As a proof of concept, logging in again with the user will restrict its view to the host controller named master, as shown in the following screenshot:

In order to prevent disclosure of critical information to unauthorized individuals or systems, you have to use a protocol that provides encryption of the information. **Encryption** is the conversion of data into a form that cannot be understood by unauthorized people.

> The protocols that are used to secure the communication are SSL and TLS, the latter being considered a replacement for the older SSL.

To make sure that the encrypted information is not disclosed to unauthorized parties, Enterprises negotiate between them **digital certificates** or public key certificates. A digital certificate consists of a formatted block of data that contains the name of the certificate holder (which may be either a user or a system name) and the holder's public key, as well as the digital signature of a **certification authority** (**CA**) for authentication.

The tool that we will use for setting up digital certificates is **keytool**, which is a key and certificate management utility that ships with the Java SE. It enables users to administer their own public/private key pairs and associated certificates for use in self-authentication (where the user authenticates himself or herself to other users or services) or data integrity and authentication services, using digital signatures.

Keytool also allows users to cache the public keys (in the form of certificates) of their communicating peers. The keytool stores the keys and certificates in a file termed a **keystore**, a repository of certificates used for identifying a client or a server. Typically, a keystore contains one client or one server's identity, which is protected by using a password.

As far as communication is concerned, it can happen in two distinct ways:

- **One-way SSL**: In this scenario, the only party that needs to prove its identity is the server, which is required to present a certificate to the client in order to verify its identity.
- **Two-way SSL** (also called client or two-way authentication): This is where the server also requests a client certificate in X509 format during the SSL handshake over the network. Hence both parties need to prove their identities.

In the following section, we will show how to create both server and client certificates, which are needed for a mutual two-way authentication. You will obviously need just the server-side part if you are going to configure one-way SSL.

Generating certificates

Start by generating a public/private key pair for the entity whose alias is serverkey and has a distinguished name with a common name of Server Administrator, organization of Acme and two-letter country code of GB:

```
$ keytool -genkeypair -alias eap7book -keyalg RSA -keysize 2048 -validity
7360 -keystore server.keystore -keypass mypassword -storepass mypassword -
dname " cn=Francesco Marchioni,o=RedHat,c=COM "
```

Now, if you want mutual SSL authentication, generate a key pair also for the client, using the alias clientkey and registering a common name for it as well:

```
$ keytool -genkeypair -alias clientkey -keyalg RSA -keysize 2048 -validity
7360 -keystore client.keystore -keypass mypassword -storepass mypassword -
dname "cn=Client user,o=Example,c=IT"
```

Next, we will export both the server's and client's public key into certificates named, respectively, `server.crt` and `client.crt`:

```
$ keytool -export -alias eap7book -keystore server.keystore -rfc
-file server.crt -keypass mypassword -storepass mypassword
$ keytool -export -alias clientkey -keystore client.keystore  -rfc -file
client.crt -keypass mypassword -storepass mypassword
```

Now, in order to complete the SSL handshake successfully, we need to first import the client's public key into the server's truststore:

```
$ keytool -import -file server.crt -keystore client.truststore -keypass
mypassword -storepass mypassword
```

The keytool will dump the certificate on your terminal and ask if it is to be considered trustworthy:

```
Trust this certificate? [no]: y
```

Answer yes and move on. As a final step, the server certificate also needs to be trusted by the client. Therefore, we will import it into the client `truststore`:

```
$ keytool -import -file client.crt -keystore server.truststore -keypass
mypassword -storepass mypassword
```

Again, state that you are going to trust the certificate. Well done, you have completed the certificate installation. Now copy the server keystore and truststore files into a folder reachable by the application server, for example, its configuration folder:

```
$ cp server.keystore $JBOSS_HOME/standalone/configuration
$ cp server.truststore $JBOSS_HOME/standalone/configuration
```

Creating an SSL realm

The certificates that we have created so far will be included in a security realm that can be used by other subsystems requiring a SSL transmission (such as Undertow). The following CLI commands will create a realm named `SSLRealm`:

```
/core-service=management/security-realm=SSLRealm/:add()
/core-service=management/security-realm=SSLRealm/server-
identity=ssl/:add(keystore-path=server.keystore, keystore-relative-
to=jboss.server.config.dir, keystore-password=mypassword, alias=eap7book,
key-password=mypassword)
```

The result on your configuration will be the following XML excerpt:

```xml
<management>
  <security-realms>
    <security-realm name="SSLRealm">
      <server-identities>
        <ssl>
          <keystore path="server.keystore"
            relative-to="jboss.server.config.dir"
            keystore-password="mypassword"
```

```
                    alias="eap7book"/>
               </ssl>
            </server-identities>
         </security-realm>
             . . . .
   </management>
```

Next, if you are going to use this realm in your web server configuration, execute this command as well, which adds the HTTPS listener to Undertow's configuration:

```
/subsystem=undertow/server=default-server/https-
listener=https/:add(socket-binding=https, security-realm=SSLRealm)
```

The following XML contains, in the highlighted section, the element which has been added:

```
<subsystem xmlns="urn:jboss:domain:undertow:1.0">
 . . .
   <server name="default-server">
       <http-listener name="default" socket-binding="http" />
       <https-listener name="default-https"
        socket-binding="https"
        security-realm="SSLRealm" />
       <host name="default-host" alias="localhost">
           <location name="/" handler="welcome-content" />
       </host>
   </server>
 . . .
</subsystem>
```

On the other hand, if you are implementing mutual SSL authentication, you will also need to include the truststore information in your SSLRealm by executing this CLI:

```
/core-service=management/security-
realm=SSLRealm/authentication=truststore/:add(keystore-
password="mypassword", keystore-path="server.truststore", keystore-
relative-to="jboss.server.config.dir")
```

The following is the highlighted truststore information which has been added to your configuration:

```
<management>
   <security-realms>
       <security-realm name="SSLRealm">
           <server-identities>
               <ssl>
                   <keystore path="server.keystore"
                    relative-to="jboss.server.config.dir"
                    keystore-password="mypassword"
```

```
                                alias="eap7book"/>
                    </ssl>
            </server-identities>
            <authentication>
             <truststore path="server.truststore"
              relative-to="jboss.server.config.dir"
              keystore-password="mypassword"/>
            </authentication>
        </security-realm>
            . . . .
</management>
```

Lastly, you need to set the attribute verify-client to REQUESTED in your Undertow configuration in order to request the certificate from the client. Execute this command from the CLI:

```
/subsystem=undertow/server=default-server/https-
listener=https:write-attribute(name=verify-client,value="REQUESTED")
```

Securing the management interfaces

The certificates that you have created so far can also be used for securing your management interfaces. It needs two steps to be implemented:

1. Include the ssl definition in the realm used for authentication
2. Set http-interface to use HTTPS communication

We will include the ssl definition in the LDAPRealm which was previously created – if that's not your case, just change the target realm to the one you are using.

Update the LDAPRealm by executing the following command:

```
/core-service=management/security-realm=LDAPRealm/server-
identity=ssl/:add(keystore-path=server.keystore, keystore-relative-
to=jboss.server.config.dir, keystore-password=mypassword, alias=eap7book,
key-password=mypassword)
```

The LDAPRealm will be updated accordingly:

```
<security-realm name="LdapRealm">
    <server-identities>
        <ssl>
            <keystore path="server.keystore" relative-to=
            "jboss.server.config.dir" keystore-password=
            "mypassword" alias="eap7book" />
```

```
    </ssl>
 . . .
</security-realm>
```

Finally, set `management-interface` to use the HTTPS socket bindings with the following command:

```
/core-service=management/management-interface=http-interface:write-
attribute(name=secure-socket-binding,value=management-https)
```

And that is the outcome on the management-https socket binding configuration:

```
<management-interfaces>
    <http-interface security-realm="LDAPRealm"
     http-upgrade-enabled="true">
        <socket-binding http="management-https"/>
    </http-interface>
</management-interfaces>
```

Summary

This chapter has covered the most significant aspects of JBoss EAP 7 legacy security using the Picketbox framework. In the first part, we learnt how to configure security domains, while in the latter part, we discussed RBAC and communication encryption.

In the next chapter, we are going to uncover the new upcoming features that will be included in the upcoming release EAP 7.1.

12
New Security Features of EAP 7

The security concepts exposed in `Chapter 11`, *Securing the Application Server* have been consolidated across several releases of the application server. Although in the near future they will be usable as a legacy solution to secure EAP7, some new projects are being actively developed by Red Hat engineers to provide a brand new security model.

In this chapter, we will introduce an **elytron** project, which is going to replace the current PicketBox and JAAS security model. Next, we will show you how to delegate security concerns of web applications to **Red Hat Single Sign-On (SSO)**, which can centrally manage permissions for applications and services acting as an SAML or OpenID Provider.

We will cover the following topics in this chapter:

- An introduction to the new EAP security model
- The core building blocks of the elytron subsystem
- Creating realms and linking them to the new security domain
- Installing RH SSO and integrating it with EAP 7
- How to delegate a Web application authentication to RH SSO

EAP 7 new security model

Since the earliest releases of the application server, the security requirements were met by means of **Java Authentication and Authorization Service (JAAS)** which provided a **subject-based authorization** on authenticated identities. In modern IT, however, the simple caller principal and credential combination provided by JAAS is not in line with current security standards.

Additionally, the JAAS approach, which has been initially developed as a client based API, has never been finalized in the Java EE specification, thus leaving the choice of using it or not to the application servers' vendors.

Along with JAAS, other security layers have been introduced in the application server, based on **Simple Authentication and Security Layer** (**SASL**). By using SASL, you can decouple the authentication mechanisms from application protocols, in theory allowing any authentication mechanism supported by SASL to be used by the application server. An example of this is contained in the *remoting* subsystem which allows different kinds of authentication mechanisms for remote EJB connections, simply requiring at least one to succeed.

At the end of the day, the security stack of the application server includes several components working on the same requirement, but from different perspectives, which are however incompatible. This raised the need of a unified solution to handle all security aspects of the application server.

Introducing elytron

Elytron is a new subproject, developed for the upstream version of the application server (WildFly) which will completely replace the combination of **PicketBox** and **JAAS** as the application server's client and server security system.

In terms of features, a non-exhaustive list of elytron features, include:

- A set of API that you call and use to achieve your security goals, and a set of SPI that you can extend and implement to achieve custom security implementations
- A unified security solution across the application server, which is now fragmented into several parts of your configuration
- Support for secure server-side authentication mechanisms based on HTTP, SASL, and TLS, as well as supporting other authentication protocols in the future without change (such as RADIUS, for example)
- Support for password credential types using the standard Java cryptography extension structure (such as DES, MD5, SHA, bcrypt, and so on)
- Propagation of identities to remote application servers as well as within different deployments in the same application server

Elytron building blocks

In the elytron subsystem, the building blocks are still called **security realms** and **security domains**. However, in this context, they will be closely related to **identity stores**, which are the places where your identities, and the security data associated with them, are persisted. Let's look at them in more detail:

An **elytron security realm** encapsulates and integrates the application server with an identity store or repository (such as an LDAP server or a database). Hence, they are mainly responsible for obtaining or verifying credentials, obtaining the attributes associated with a given identity and last, but also important, creating an internal representation based on this information that will be used by a security domain to authenticate and perform role and permission mappings for a given principal.

> **Security realms and Identity Managers**:
> A security realm is not, however, an **Identity Management (IdM)** solution or API. In order to provide these features, another building block can be plugged into the application server named Red Hat SSO, which is an integrated SSO and IDM solution built on top of the OAuth 2.0, Open ID Connect, JSON Web Token (JWT), and SAML 2.0 specifications. See the section *Introducing Red Hat SSO* later in this chapter for more information about it.

A security realm can be compared to the legacy login modules, which we have learnt about in `Chapter 11`, *Securing the Application Server*. Unlike the JAAS login modules, however, elytron also provides the concept of *modifiable* realms, which are also capable of performing very basic and simple write operations against a specific repository. Here is, for example, the `FileSystemSecurityRealm` which, by default, stores the identities on a local filesystem, extending the `ModifiableSecurityRealm` interface:

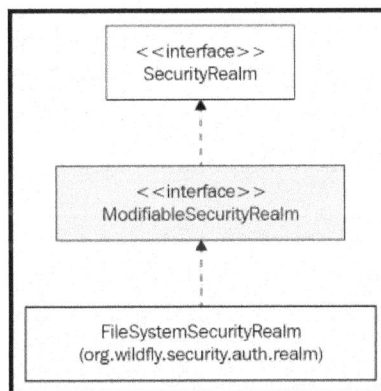

By default, elytron provides some built-in implementations of security realms that are capable of managing your identities. Here are some examples:

- **JDBCSecurity realm** : The class `org.wildfly.security.auth.realm.jdbc.JdbcSecurityRealm` is a security realm implementation backed by a database
- **File system security realm**: The class `org.wildfly.security.auth.realm.FileSystemSecurityRealm` is a simple filesystem-backed security realm
- **LDAP security realm** : The class `org.wildfly.security.auth.realm.ldap.LdapSecurityRealm` is a security realm implementation backed by LDAP
- **Property security realm**: The class `org.wildfly.security.auth.realm.LegacyPropertiesSecurityRealm` is an implementation that makes use of the legacy property files
- **Java KeyStores security realm**: The class `org.wildfly.security.auth.realm.KeyStoreBackedSecurityRealm` is a Keystore-backed security realm
- **Token security realm**: The class `org.wildfly.security.auth.realm.token.TokenSecurityRealm` is a security realm capable of building identities based on different security token formats based on a TokenValidator

The API also allows you to write your own custom security realm implementation if none of these are enough to satisfy your requirements.

The **security domain** is the entry point to all security operations available in your server infrastructure. It contains a high-level view of security policies and resources associated with your IT domain. The term *domain* should not be confused with an **Internet Protocol (IP)** resource. An elytron domain can be composed of a single application or multiple applications which share the same security policies. In terms of responsibilities, a security domain is in charge of:

- Mapping a principal to its corresponding identity on a specific security realm
- Permission mapping
- Role mapping
- Obtain the current and authorized identity and all information associated with it such as roles, permissions, and attributes
- A high-level view of the resources and configurations supported by a specific domain

The following diagram shows the relation between a security domain and realms:

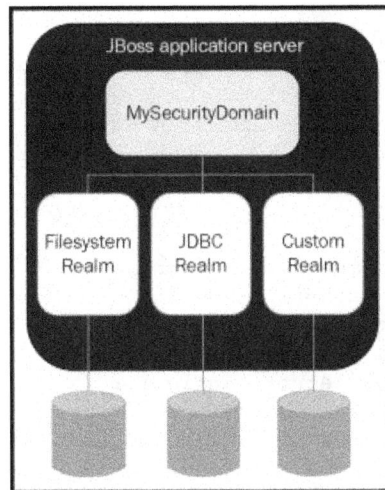

As you can see, a single security domain can reference multiple security realms and can manage multiple identities that are available on different repositories. In other words, from a single domain you can manage identities from different repositories. Elytron provides some very nice features that allow you to identify which realm a principal belongs to by using a mapper. In this regard, elytron can be very useful in multi-tenancy architectures, where you need to serve multiple applications and map their identities to different security realms.

An overview of the elytron subsystem

At the time of writing, the elytronsubsystem is still not included in the EAP 7 configuration. We can, however, preview the upcoming configuration (that will be part of EAP 7.1) thanks to the source code of its module which is available at:

`https://github.com/wildfly-security/elytron-subsystem`.

Although the content of the subsystem is going to evolve further, the following XML snippet will give you an idea of its core configuration:

```
<subsystem xmlns="urn:wildfly:elytron:1.0">
  <provider-loaders>
    <provider-loader name="test"/>
  </provider-loaders>
  <security-domains>
    <security-domain name="ApplicationDomain" default-realm=
```

```
       "ApplicationRealm">
       <realm name="ApplicationRealm" role-decoder="groups-
        to-roles"/>
       </security-domain>
       <security-domain name="ManagementDomain" default-realm=
           "ManagementRealm">
        <realm name="ManagementRealm" role-decoder="groups-
        to-roles"/>
       </security-domain>
      </security-domains>
      <security-realms>
        <properties-realm name="ApplicationRealm">
        <users-properties path="application-users.properties"
         relative-to="jboss.server.config.dir"/>
        <groups-properties path="application-roles.properties"
         relative-to="jboss.server.config.dir"/>
        </properties-realm>
        <properties-realm name="ManagementRealm">
        <users-properties path="mgmt-users.properties" relative-
         to="jboss.server.config.dir"/>
        <groups-properties path="mgmt-groups.properties"
         relative-to="jboss.server.config.dir"/>
        </properties-realm>
      </security-realms>
      <mappers>
       <simple-role-decoder name="groups-to-roles" attribute=
       "groups"/>
      </mappers>
      <http>
       <http-server-authentication name="management-http
        -authentication" http-server-factory="global" security-
        domain="ManagementDomain">
         <mechanism-configuration>
           <mechanism mechanism-name="BASIC">
           <mechanism-realm realm-name="Management Realm"/>
          </mechanism>
          </mechanism-configuration>
         </http-server-authentication>
        <http-server-authentication name="application-http-
         authentication" http-server-factory="global" security-
         domain="ApplicationDomain">
         <mechanism-configuration>
           <mechanism mechanism-name="BASIC">
           <mechanism-realm realm-name="Application Realm"/>
          </mechanism>
         </mechanism-configuration>
         </http-server-authentication>
           <provider-http-server-factory name="global"/>
```

```
    </http>
    <sasl>
      <sasl-server-authentication name="management-sasl-
       authentication" sasl-server-factory="global" security-
       domain="ManagementDomain"/>
      <sasl-server-authentication name="application-sasl
       -authentication" sasl-server-factory="global" security-
       domain="ApplicationDomain"/>
      <provider-sasl-server-factory name="global"/>
    </sasl>
  </subsystem>
```

From a bird's eye view, the subsystem contains two core security domains, as highlighted in the above code:

- The `ApplicationDomain` security domain, which is bound to the `ApplicationRealm`, is a property-based security realm used to govern application security. This realm uses the same configuration files as the legacy `ApplicationRealm`.
- The `ManagementDomain` security domain, which is bound to the `ManagementRealm`, is a property-based security realm used to govern access to the application server. This realm uses the same configuration files as the legacy `ManagementRealm`.

The next part of the subsystem configuration deals with the authentication mechanisms, that show multiple authentication mechanisms can be made available at the same time for different protocols. Out of the box, the two core authentication mechanisms available are the **HTTP** Server authentication and **SASL** Server authentication through their respective Factories. In order to integrate the authentication mechanisms with their target services (for example, Undertow Web server) a set of API and SPI have been added to elytron to allow a clean separation between elytron and the target services. This will allow the support of other authentication protocols in the future (such as RADIUS) without changes in the elytron core subsystem.

In the next section of this chapter, we will learn how to define some examples of security realms, which can be used to replace the current JAAS login modules.

Creating a FileSystem security realm

The most basic example of a security realm is the FileSystem Realm, which stores the identity information on a filesystem, by paging each identity in an XML file containing credentials and Roles.

Start the application server and connect to it from a CLI. Within the CLI, first define a new `filesystem-realm` named `fsRealm` and its respective path on the file system:

```
/subsystem=elytron/filesystem-realm=fsRealm:add(path="fs-
realm",relative-to="jboss.server.config.dir")
```

Next, you can start adding some users and their corresponding roles. As an example, let's add the `user` which will belong to the `User` role:

```
/subsystem=elytron/filesystem-realm=fsRealm/identity=user:add
/subsystem=elytron/filesystem-realm=fsRealm/identity=user:set-
password(clear={password="UserPassword1!"})
/subsystem=elytron/filesystem-realm=fsRealm/identity=user:add-
attribute(name=Roles,value=["User"])
```

The file system realm will be referenced by a new security domain that will be named `fsdomain`:

```
/subsystem=elytron/security-domain=fsdomain:add(default-
realm=fsRealm,realms=[{realm=fsRealm}])
```

Finally, since this security domain will use **HTTP Basic authentication**, we will define a new **HTTP Server Authentication policy** based on the `fsdomain` security domain and named `http-auth`:

```
/subsystem=elytron/http-server-authentication=http-auth:add(http-
server-factory=global,security-domain=fsdomain,mechanism-
configurations=[{mechanism-name=BASIC,mechanism-realm-
configurations=[realm-name="Secured by Elytron"]}])
```

In order to propagate the HTTP Authentication policy with Undertow, which governs your web applications, a component named **HTTP Authenticating factory** is needed. This will eventually trigger the `HttpServerAuthenticationMechanism` from within the Undertow web server. Here is the command needed to create an HTTP Authenticating factory:

```
/subsystem=undertow/application-security-domain=web-security:add(http-
authentication-factory=http-auth)
```

Reload your server configuration for the changes to take effect. In terms of configuration, the following XML section will be included in your elytron subsystem:

```
<subsystem xmlns="urn:wildfly:elytron:1.0">
  <security-realms>
    . . . .
    <filesystem-realm name="fsRealm">
     <file path="fs-realm" relative-to="jboss.server.config.dir"/>
    </filesystem-realm>
```

```
    </security-realms>
    <security-domain name="fsdomain" default-realm="fsRealm">
     <realm name="fsRealm"/>
    </security-domain>
     . . . . . .
    <http-server-authentication name="http-auth" http-server-
      factory="global" security-domain="fsdomain">
    <mechanism-configuration>
     <mechanism mechanism-name="BASIC">
     <mechanism-realm realm-name="Secured by Elytron"/>
     </mechanism>
    </mechanism-configuration>
   </http-server-authentication>
</subsystem>
```

Within the configuration of Undertow, the following XML will be included:

```
<subsystem xmlns="urn:jboss:domain:undertow:3.0">
   <application-security-domains>
      <application-security-domain security-domain="web-security" http-
authentication-factory="http-auth"/>
   </application-security-domains>
</subsystem>
```

So, within our Undertow subsystem we have included an application security domain which binds our `http-auth` Authentication Factory with the `web-security` security domain:

> In this case, the element security domain refers to the legacy security domain, which you can specify in your `jboss-web.xml`, so that your applications will retain compatibility in the new Security Model

```
<jboss-web>
  <security-domain>web-security</security-domain>
</jboss-web>
```

Finally, in the `web.xml` file, define the constraints on some URIs for one or more roles available to your application (see `Chapter 11`, *Serving the Application Server* section *Database login module* for an example of the `Admin` role).

Now if you try to deploy an application bound to this security domain, you will receive a BASIC HTTP Authentication challenge, as displayed by this screenshot:

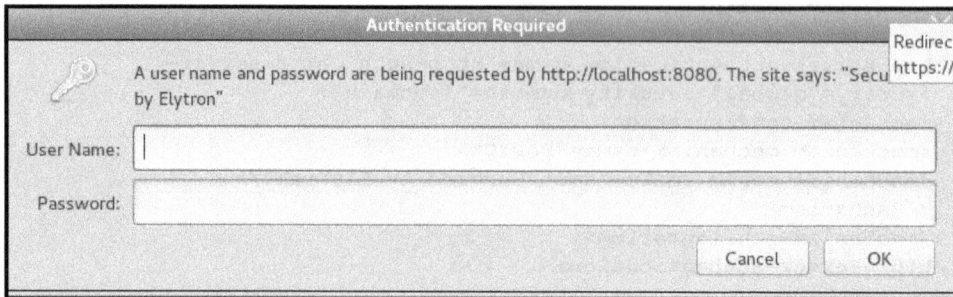

Enter one of the user names credentials that you have saved in the FileSystem realm and you will be granted the correct role in your application.

Developing a JDBC realm

An adequate level of security can be applied through the JDBC realm, which uses a relational database as storage. Assuming that you have started the application server and connected the Command Line, we will at first add a new `jdbc-realm` which contains the principal query definition and the `Datasource` object that we will reference. In this example, we will be using the datasource named `MySQLPool` as the resource for our data:

```
/subsystem="elytron"/jdbc-realm="jdbcRealm":add(principal-
query=[{sql="SELECT passwd from USERS where login = ? ",data-
source="MySQLPool",clear-password-mapper={password-index="1"}}])
    /subsystem="elytron"/security-domain="jdbcdomain":add(default-
realm="jdbcRealm",realms=[{realm="jdbcRealm"}])
```

Now, repeat the same steps we have discussed earlier, in order to add the `HttpServerAuthentication` mechanism to elytron and reference it from Undertow:

```
/subsystem=elytron/http-server-authentication=http-db-auth:add(http-
server-factory=global,security-domain=jdbcdomain,mechanism-
configurations=[{mechanism-name=BASIC,mechanism-realm-
configurations=[realm-name="Secured by Elytron"]}])
```

The HTTP authenticating factory will then trigger the `HttpServerAuthenticationMechanism` from within the Undertow web server:

```
/subsystem=undertow/application-security-domain=web-security:add(http-
authentication-factory=http-db-auth)
```

In terms of configuration, the relevant part for us is the `jdbc-realm`, which will be included in the elytron subsystem:

```
<subsystem xmlns="urn:wildfly:elytron:1.0">

    <jdbc-realm name="jdbcRealm">
      <principal-query sql="SELECT passwd from USERS where login =
      ? " data-source="MySQLPool">
      <clear-password-mapper password-index="1"/>
      </principal-query>
    </jdbc-realm>
    <security-domain name="jdbcdomain" default-realm="jdbcRealm">
      <realm name="jdbcRealm"/>
    </security-domain>
</subsystem>
```

As you can see, queries are defined using a `principal-query` element containing the `sql` and `data-source` attributes. Both are mandatory attributes as they allow you to specify the SQL `SELECT` statement and the datasource used to execute the access control list query, respectively. The next element, the `clear-password-mapper`, is responsible for mapping a specific column, or set of columns, to a password.

When mapping passwords, there is a specific element for each one of the supported password types. For example, in the following snippet, we're using a `bcrypt-mapper` to map a `BCRYPT` password:

```
<subsystem xmlns="urn:wildfly:elytron:1.0">
    . . . .
    <jdbc-realm name="JdbcRealmWithMultipleQueries">
      <principal-query sql="SELECT hashedpassword, salt, cost
        FROM USERS WHERE login = ?" data-source=" MySQLPool ">
          <bcrypt-mapper password-index="1" salt-index="2"
            iteration-count-index="3"/>
      </principal-query>
    </jdbc-realm>
    . . . .
</subsystem>
```

> Please note that in the above example you have to also provide the columns for the `#salt` index and an iteration count. (See this article for more details on crypting passwords with elytron: http://planet.jboss.org/post/using_a_database_to_authenticate_and_authorize_your_users_in_elytron)

Developing an LDAP realm

The last example we will include in this chapter is about the LDAPRealm, which defines the standard set of elements we have seen in the earlier chapter to secure the management interfaces with LDAP. To keep it pretty simple, we will use the default attributes available in an ApacheDS server, which are:

LDAP URL	`ldap://127.0.0.1:10389`
Base dn	`ou=Users,dc=example,dc=com`
Default login user	`uid=admin,ou=system`
Default password	`secret`

In order to create the `ldap-realm`, execute the following statement from the CLI:

```
/subsystem="elytron"/ldap-realm="LdapRealm":add(dir-context={"url" =>
"ldap://127.0.0.1:10389","principal" => "uid=admin,ou=system","credential"
=> "serverPassword","enable-connection-pooling" => "true"},identity-
mapping={"rdn-identifier" => "uid","use-recursive-search" =>
"true","search-base-dn" => "ou=Users,dc=example,dc=com"})
```

As usual, create a security domain for this realm or, re-use one of the preceding security domains that we have created so far. The following statement will create a SecurityDomain named `ldapdomain`, which references the LdapRealm:

```
/subsystem="elytron"/security-domain="ldapdomain":add(default-
realm="LdapRealm",realms=[{realm="LdapRealmWithoutAttributeMapping"}])
```

Expect the following configuration changes in your elytron subsystem:

```
<subsystem xmlns="urn:wildfly:elytron:1.0">
    . . . .
    <ldap-realm name="LdapRealm">
     <dir-context url="ldap://127.0.0.1:10389" principal=
     "uid=admin,ou=system" credential="secret" enable-connection-
      pooling="true"/>
     <identity-mapping rdn-identifier="uid" use-recursive-search
      ="true" search-base-dn="ou=Users,dc=example,dc=com"/>
    </ldap-realm>
    <security-domain name="ldapdomain" default-realm="LdapRealm">
      <realm name="LdapRealm"/>
    </security-domain>

</subsystem>
```

You can make this security domain available to Undertow through the `HttpServerAuthentication` mechanism, as shown in the earlier sections.

Introducing Red Hat SSO

The last part of this chapter will discuss the Red Hat SSO project, which is derived from the Keycloak upstream project (`http://www.keycloak.org/`). In short, RedHat SSO adds to your application SSO capabilities based on industry standards such as SAML 2.0, OpenID Connect, and OAuth 2.0. The SSO Server can centrally manage fine-grained permissions for applications and services acting as an SAML or OpenID Connect-based Identity Provider.

Red Hat SSO is not included by default in the EAP 7 stack; however, we will show here how you can integrate it with EAP through the following steps:

1. First of all, we will download the SSO server and the EAP client adapter.
2. Next, we will install the components and create a management user.
3. Finally, we will show how to create a Federation policy on the SSO to restrict access to client EAP applications.

Installing Red Hat SSO server

Once you have successfully logged into the Red Hat portal (`https://access.redhat.com/`), you can access the SSO Product from the following location: `https://access.redhat.com/jbossnetwork/restricted/listSoftware.html?product=core.service.rhsso`.

From there, download the `rh-sso-7.0.0.zip`, which is the SSO server, and the client adapter, `rh-sso-7.0.0-eap7-adapter.zip`.

Once you have downloaded the package, unzip it in a folder:

```
$ unzip rh-sso-7.0.0.zip
```

Then move to the directory `rh-sso-7.0/bin`:

```
$ cd rh-sso-7.0.0/bin
```

You can start the server, which contains the same core structure of the EAP:

```
$ standalone.sh
```

Once the server has started, open your browser at this location:
`http://localhost:8080/auth`. You will be requested to create a management user, as
you can see from the following screenshot:

Once done, click on the `Administration Console` link which will take you to
`http://localhost:8080/auth/admin` where you will have to enter the credentials of
your management user:

Great! Now you are logged into the EAP 7 SSO server:

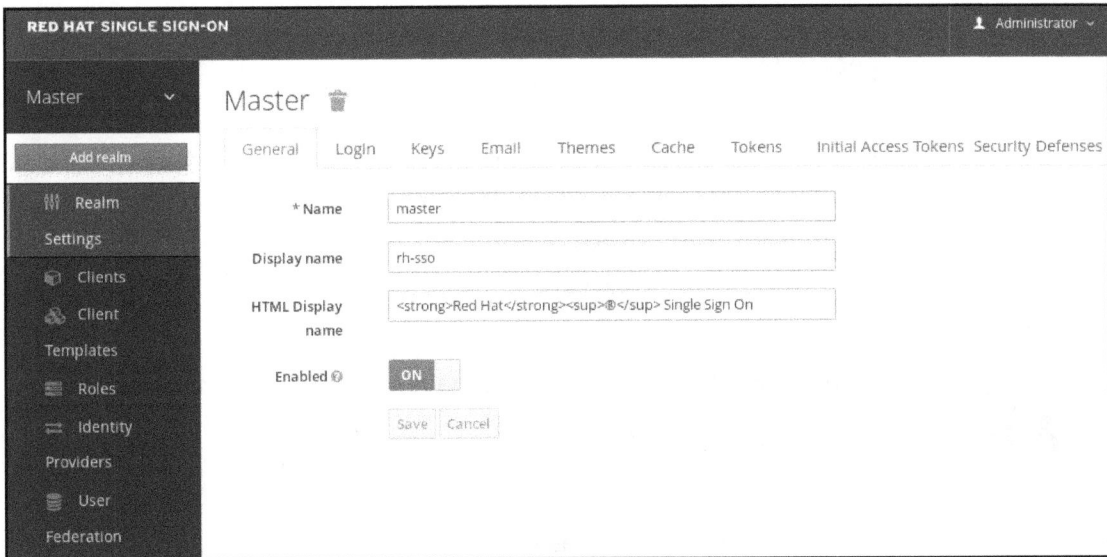

In the next section, we will learn how to create a new realm and use it to define your security policies.

Creating a new realm

A realm secures and manages the security data for a set of users, applications, and registered clients. As you can see from the home page, a built-in security realm named **Master** has been created for you. Users that are defined in this realm have permissions to view and manage any other realm created on the server instance, so they are de facto super users.

To keep things clean; however, it is not recommended that you use the master realm to manage the users and applications in your organization. For this reason we will create a new realm. In order to do that, point to the top-left corner, which contains a drop-down menu with the master realm. Click on `Add Realm` to add a new realm.

In the **Add realm** UI, which is shown in the following screenshot, specify the realm name you want to add and click the **Create** button:

As an alternative to creating realms from scratch, you can import existing realms (See the following link for some examples of ready to use realms: `https://github.com/keycloak/keycloak/tree/master/examples`)

We have named our new realm `ldap-demo` as we are supposed to federate the users available on a directory service. The next step will be to federate an external repository of users. Out of the box, we have support for LDAP and active directory.

To add a storage provider, go to the `User Federation` left menu item in the admin console. From the User Federation window, there is an `Add Provider` list box. Choose the provider you want to add and you will be redirected to the configuration page of that provider. In our case, we will choose an **LDAP Provider**.

Within the LDAP window you can specify the required LDAP settings. We will stick to the ApacheDS LDAP settings that we used in the `Chapter 11`, *Securing the Application Server* settings, therefore set the Connection URL to `ldap://localhost:10389`, the base DN to `ou=Users,dc=jboss,dc=org`, the BindDN to `uid=hnelson,` `ou=Users,dc=jboss,dc=org`, and its password to `secret`, as shown in the following screenshot:

Console Display Name ⊘	ldap-apacheds
Priority ⊘	1
Edit Mode ⊘	WRITABLE
Sync Registrations ⊘	ON
* Vendor ⊘	
* Username LDAP attribute ⊘	uid
* RDN LDAP attribute ⊘	uid
* UUID LDAP attribute ⊘	entryUUID
* User Object Classes ⊘	inetOrgPerson, organizationalPerson
* Connection URL ⊘	ldap://localhost:10389
* Users DN ⊘	ou=Users,dc=jboss,dc=org
* Authentication Type ⊘	simple
* Bind DN ⊘	uid=hnelson,ou=Users,dc=jboss,dc=org
* Bind Credential ⊘	●●●●●●
Custom User LDAP Filter ⊘	LDAP Filter

Now let's verify that both connectivity and authentication works. Before that, start the LDAP server with our sample LDIF file (See `Chapter 11`, *Securing the Application Server* for more details about it):

```
$ java –jar target/kerberos–using–apacheds.jar test.ldif
```

That will start the LDAP server. Verify that the connection with the LDAP server works through the **Test Connection** button and its authentication as well as through the `Test authentication`. Once done, click on **Save** at the bottom of the UI.

Now that we are done with the authentication, we will now map the LDAP roles with the LDAP provider roles so that we can authorize users accessing our application. From the User Federation UI, displayed in the following screenshot, select the `Mappers` tab and click on `Create`:

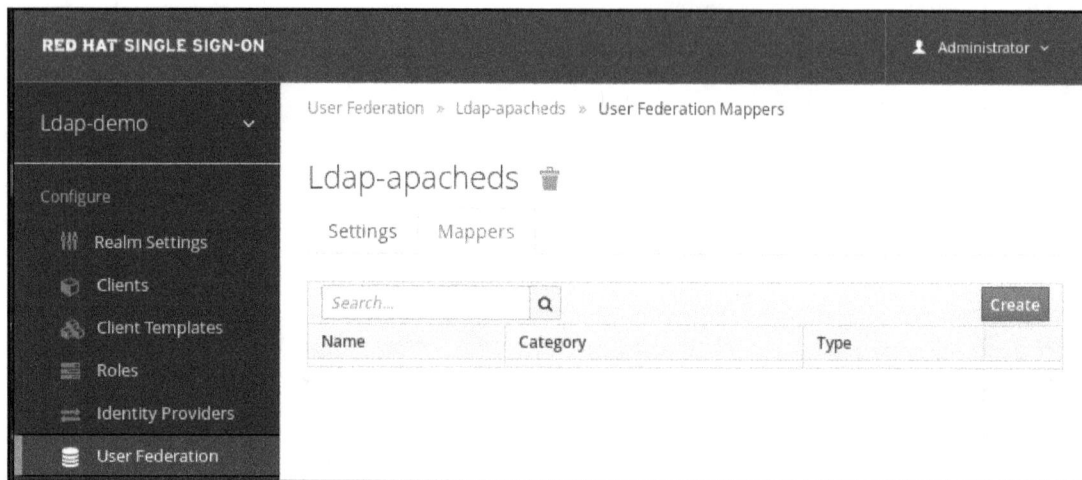

Based on the role definition contained in the `test.ldif` file, you will need the following settings:

Group 🗑

ID	01950565-8d21-4753-8b4e-b111a444711f
Name * ❓	Group
Mapper Type ❓	Role mappings
LDAP Roles DN ❓	ou=Groups,dc=jboss,dc=org
Role Name LDAP Attribute ❓	cn
Role Object Classes ❓	groupOfUniqueNames
Membership LDAP Attribute ❓	uniqueMember
Membership Attribute Type ❓	DN ▾
LDAP Filter ❓	
Mode ❓	LDAP_ONLY ▾
User Roles Retrieve Strategy ❓	LOAD_ROLES_BY_MEMBER_ATTRIBUTE ▾
Use Realm Roles Mapping ❓	ON
Client ID ❓	Select One... ▾

Save Cancel Sync LDAP Roles To Keycloak Sync Keycloak Roles To LDAP

As you can see, we have specified the DN of the roles (ou=Users,dc=jboss,dc=org), the role name attribute (cn), its class (groupOfUniqueNames), and the membership identifier (uniqueMember). As we will retrieve our roles through the uniqueMember attribute of the user, choose the appropriate selection in the combo box. Leave the other options with the default value and save your configuration.

Configuring client applications

Our SSO Server now contains a realm and a user federation policy. Obviously, we need some applications to use them.

In order to do that, we will first need an EAP server which is capable of using our security policies. That can be done through the `rh-sso-7.0.0-eap7-adapter.zip` that we have previously downloaded. Move this file to the folder where you have an EAP 7 installation and unzip it so that the SSO modules will be merged with the EAP 7 modules:

```
$ unzip rh-sso-7.0.0-eap7-adapter.zip -d /home/jboss/jboss-eap-7.0
```

Now, move to the `bin` folder, and execute the `adapter-install-offline.cli` script, which will register the `keycloak` subsystem in your configuration:

```
$ ./jboss-cli.sh --file=adapter-install-offline.cli
```

Now start the EAP server. If you are running EAP on the same machine as the SSO server, choose an offset, as in the following example:

```
$ standalone.sh -Djboss.socket.binding.port-offset=100
```

The next step will be registering a client application through the SSO console, so switch to your SSO admin console (`http://localhost:8080/auth/admin`) and select **Clients** in the left side menu. This will bring you to the clients page.

Click on the **Create** button, which is on the right-hand side, as you can see from the following screenshot:

Clients ❓

Client ID	Enabled	Base URL	Actions		
account	True	/auth/realms/ldap-demo/account	Edit	Export	Delete
admin-cli	True	Not defined	Edit	Export	Delete
broker	True	Not defined	Edit	Export	Delete
realm-management	True	Not defined	Edit	Export	Delete
security-admin-console	True	/auth/admin/ldap-demo/console/index.html	Edit	Export	Delete

In the **Add Client** UI, we have set the `ldap-portal` root URL for our client application named `ldap-app`. You can leave the other fields with default settings and click on **Save**:

Add Client

Import	Select file ⬑
Client ID * ❓	ldap-app
Client Protocol ❓	openid-connect ▾
Client Template ❓	▾
Root URL ❓	ldap-portal

Save Cancel

Back in the clients UI, we will need to refine some configuration properties of our client. Click on the **Edit** button for the **ldap-app**:

Clients ❓

Search... 🔍   Create

Client ID	Enabled	Base URL	Actions		
account	True	/auth/realms/ldap-demo/account	Edit	Export	Delete
admin-cli	True	Not defined	Edit	Export	Delete
broker	True	Not defined	Edit	Export	Delete
ldap-app	True	/ldap-portal	Edit	Export	Delete
realm-management	True	Not defined	Edit	Export	Delete
security-admin-console	True	/auth/admin/ldap-demo/console/index.html	Edit	Export	Delete

In our case, since the client application server will be running on port `8180`, we have set the `Redirect URI` accordingly, as shown in the following screenshot:

Now you will need to install your client policy on your client environment. You can obtain a template for the configuration through the `Installation` tab in the client UI:

Your template can be imported in two ways:

- As a `keycloak.json` file to be packaged in your web application
- As an element of your EAP client configuration

Just in case you have selected the first option, you will be able to download the following `keycloak.json` file, which will need to be placed in the `WEB-INF` folder of your application:

```
{
 "realm": "ldap-demo",
 "realm-public-key":
"MIGfMA0GCSqGSIb3DQEBAQUAA4GNADCBiQKBgQCrVrCuTtArbgaZzL1hvh0xtL5mc7o0NqPVnY
XkLvgcwiC3BjLGw1tGEGoJaXDuSaRllobm53JBhjx33UNv+5z/UMG4kytBWxheNVKnL6GgqlNab
MaFfPLPCF8kAgKnsi79NMo+n6KnSY8YeUmec/p2vjO2NjsSAVcWEQMVhJ31LwIDAQAB",
 "auth-server-url": "http://localhost:8080/auth",
 "ssl-required": "external",
 "resource": "ldap-app",
```

```
  "credentials": {
    "secret": "password"
  }
}
```

Within your `web.xml` descriptor, you will restrict access to one or more URIs of your application:

```
<security-constraint>
        <web-resource-collection>
            <web-resource-name>LDAPApp</web-resource-name>
            <url-pattern>/*</url-pattern>
        </web-resource-collection>
        <auth-constraint>
            <role-name>Junior</role-name>
        </auth-constraint>
</security-constraint>

<login-config>
        <auth-method>KEYCLOAK</auth-method>
        <realm-name>does-not-matter</realm-name>
</login-config>

<security-role>
        <role-name>Junior</role-name>
</security-role>
```

In the preceding example, we have specified `security-role` as the role `Junior`; hence, only users belonging to the `Junior` role will be allowed to enter your application. Notice the `auth-method` which is set to `KEYCLOAK`: that will instruct the SSO to handle the Authentication. Here is the content of your application's `WEB-INF` folder:

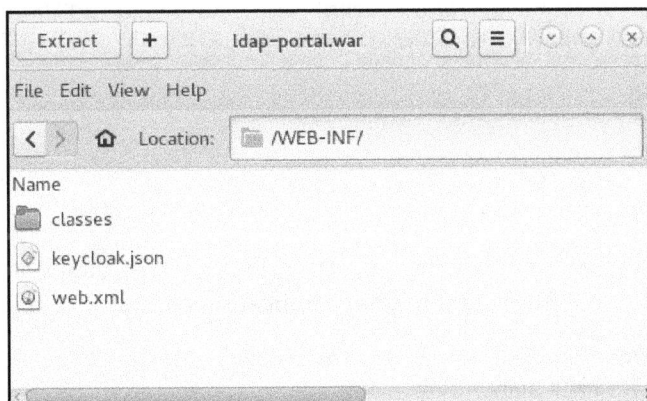

Now deploy your application on the EAP client server. When you try to access any resources within it, you will be redirected to the SSO which will display the realm against which you are challenged for the authentication:

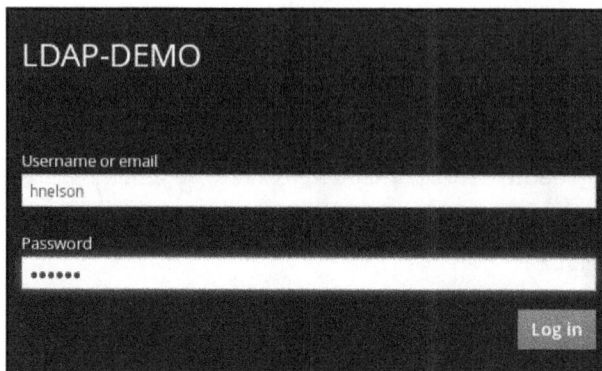

Enter the name of a user which is a junior role (such as `hnelson`) and you will be redirected back to your application.

Installing the client template on the server

If you prefer not to install the JSON file in your applications, from the Installation menu of the SSO, choose to export it as a subsystem. The following XML snippet will be generated:

```
<secure-deployment name="WAR MODULE NAME.war">
    <realm>ldap-demo</realm>
    <realm-public-
key>MIGfMA0GCSqGSIb3DQEBAQUAA4GNADCBiQKBgQCrVrCuTtArbgaZzL1hvh0xtL5mc7o0NqP
VnYXkLvgcwiC3BjLGw1tGEGoJaXDuSaRllobm53JBhjx33UNv+5z/UMG4kytBWxheNVKnL6Ggql
NabMaFfPLPCF8kAgKnsi79NMo+n6KnSY8YeUmec/p2vjO2NjsSAVcWEQMVhJ31LwIDAQAB</rea
lm-public-key>
    <auth-server-url>http://localhost:8080/auth</auth-server-url>
    <ssl-required>EXTERNAL</ssl-required>
    <resource>ldap-app</resource>
    <credential name="secret">password</credential>
</secure-deployment>
```

The preceding snippet needs to be included within the `keycloak` subsystem. You just need to change the `WAR MODULE NAME` text to your application name:

```
<subsystem xmlns="urn:jboss:domain:keycloak:1.1">
    <secure-deployment name="ldap-app">
        <realm>ldap-demo</realm>
```

```
        <realm-public-key>
MIGfMA0GCSqGSIb3DQEBAQUAA4GNADCBiQKBgQCrVrCuTtArbgaZzL1hvh0xtL5mc7o0NqP
VnYXkLvgcwiC3BjLGw1tGEGoJaXDuSaRllobm53JBhjx33UNv+5z/UMG4kytBWxheNVKnL6Ggq1
NabMa
FfPLPCF8kAgKnsi79NMo+n6KnSY8YeUmec/p2vjO2NjsSAVcWEQMVhJ31LwIDAQAB
        </realm-public-key>
        <auth-server-url>http://localhost:8080/auth</auth-server-url>
        <ssl-required>EXTERNAL</ssl-required>
        <resource>ldap-app</resource>
        <credential name="secret">password</credential>
    </secure-deployment>
</subsystem>
```

Summary

This chapter has covered the most recent aspects of application server security, including upcoming EAP 7.1 features (namely the elytron subsystem), and the integration with the SSO Server, which will let you centralize authentication and authorization of your web applications with minimum fuss.

We will now focus on the container technology, starting with the Docker framework whose interaction with EAP 7 is covered in detail in the following chapter.

13
Using EAP 7 with Docker

Today there is quite a buzz around the words Docker and containers. In short, Docker is a containerization engine that allows you to package up an application along with all the configuration and software required to run it and deploy it to a machine with the minimum of effort.

For some aspects, there are relevant advantages over a standard **Virtual Machine(VM)**. As a matter of fact, a VM, takes up quite a lot of system resources as it embeds a virtual copy of all the hardware and software that the operating system needs to run. This requires a lot, in terms of RAM and CPU cycles.

On the other hand, container technology requires a minimal operating system, supporting libraries, and system resources to run a specific program. There is no doubt that starting a container is much faster than a Virtual Machine.

Another important characteristic of containers is that they are designed to be *immutable* in terms of library versions, configurations, and applications. You can guarantee that one container can be reused in different environments. Later on in this chapter, we will discuss how we can mix and match the concept of *immutable* with an application that is *mutable* in terms of configuration.

Within this chapter, we will learn how to deliver EAP 7 using Docker containers. We will cover its advantages and challenges, setting the roadmap for the next chapter where we will discuss **OpenShift** technology which is solidly based on Docker. More in detail, here is our checklist:

- Introduction to Docker
- Running Docker images
- Managing multiple Docker containers

Getting to grips with Docker

As we learned from the introduction, Docker containers use shared operating systems. This means a much more efficient usage of system resources compared to Virtual Machines. The following diagram summarizes the concepts exposed so far, giving you an idea of the infrastructure of containers compared with VMs:

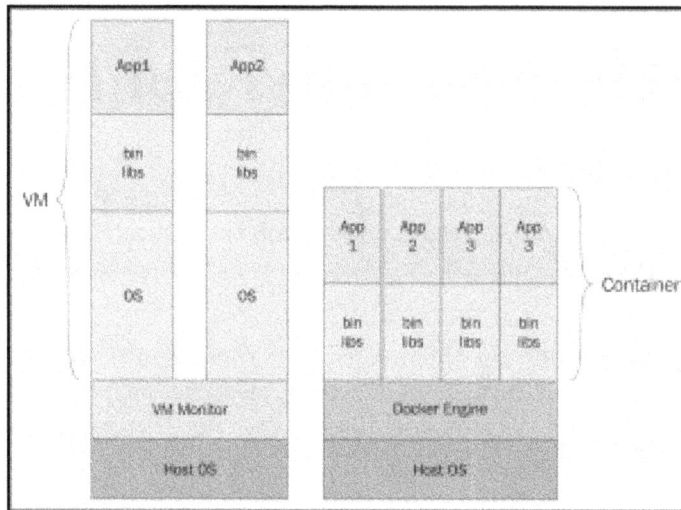

As you can see from the preceding diagram, instead of virtualizing hardware, containers rest on top of a single host operating system. This in turn, means that you can leave behind all the unneeded VM features, leaving you with a small, neat capsule containing your applications.

Basic components of containers

In order to get started with Docker, it is important to have a solid grasp of the main components that make up the Docker ecosystem. In detail, Docker is composed of the following elements:

- **Images**: A Docker image is, in a nutshell, an immutable file which contains some software such as operating systems, databases, or application servers. Images can be downloaded or built from existing images. From images you can produce containers.

- **Containers**: This is the running component of Docker. Using a programming metaphor, if the images can be compared to a class file, then the container is an instance of that class. Each container is isolated from the host that is running it and, by default, from other containers as well.
- **Registries**: These are the places where images are stored. There is a public registry where you can pull your image, called Docker hub (`http://hub.docker.com`) but private registries can be created as well.

To get started with Docker, we will need to first install it on our machine, then we will learn how to build and execute some images on top of it.

Installing Docker

Installing Docker can be done mostly in two ways:

Using a generic script approach, which will detect your Linux version and install Docker accordingly. In order to do that, download and execute with curl the following script as root user:

```
# curl -sSL https://get.docker.com/ | sh
```

Another option, suggested for Fedora and RHEL distribution, is through the yum package manager:

```
# yum -y install docker-io
```

Once you have completed the installation, if you want to start Docker at boot time, you can use the following command:

```
# systemctl enable docker
```

Now start Docker as a service:

```
# service docker start
```

As a quick test, verify the Docker version by executing your first command, which will also print the version of the software:

```
# docker version
Client:
 Version:       1.8.2-fc22
 API version:   1.20
 Package Version: docker-1.8.2-7.gitcb216be.fc22.x86_64
 Go version:    go1.5.1
 Git commit:    cb216be/1.8.2
```

```
    Built:
    OS/Arch:       linux/amd64
Server:
    Version:       1.8.2-fc22
    API version:   1.20
    Package Version:
    Go version:    go1.5.1
    Git commit:    cb216be/1.8.2
    Built:
    OS/Arch:       linux/amd64
```

As you can see from the last commands, we had to run Docker as `root user`.

> **TIP**
>
> It is generally not recommended to use Docker as root user. Unlike in a VM, the kernel is shared among all containers and the host, aggravating any vulnerabilities present in the kernel.

To avoid using Docker as root user, you can follow the following procedure which will allow you to run Docker as a non-root user. First of all, create a group called `docker`, by running as root the following command:

```
# groupadd docker
```

Next, add a user that will be part of the `docker` group:

```
# useradd jboss
```

Now add the user to the docker group:

```
# usermod -aG docker jboss
```

Now, change to the `jboss` user and check that you can run Docker commands also with non-root user:

```
root@localhost ~]# su - jboss
[jboss@localhost ~]$ docker version
Client:
 Version:       1.8.2-fc22
 API version:   1.20
 Package Version: docker-1.8.2-7.gitcb216be.fc22.x86_64
 Go version:    go1.5.1
 Git commit:    cb216be/1.8.2
 Built:
 OS/Arch:       linux/amd64
 . . . .
```

Running your first container

Right now we have the engine of Docker ready to run. Your first test drive will be running an operating system shell, which will be picked up from the Docker Hub (`https://hub.docker.com/`). For our purposes, we will use a Fedora image, which is the backbone of the next images used in this chapter.

The docker `pull` command will be the first one we will use. This command actually downloads an image from the current list of repositories:

```
$ sudo docker pull fedora
```

The download process will begin. When all the pulls are complete, we will be notified that the latest release of Fedora has been added to your local repository:

```
fedora:latest: The image you are pulling has been verified
511136ea3c5a: Pull complete
00a0c78eeb6d: Pull complete
834629358fe2: Pull complete
Status: Downloaded newer image for fedora:latest
```

What we want to do now is run a shell into the Fedora image that we have just downloaded. We will execute the docker run command with some parameters:

```
$ sudo docker run -it --rm fedora /bin/bash
```

> The `-it` parameters allow interactive processes, like a shell, to allocate a `tty` for the container process. The `--rm` parameter, on the other hand, will automatically clean up the container and remove the file system when the container exits.

You will instantly reach the bash shell of your Fedora image as a root user:

```
[root@935376c573f9 /]# ls
bin    dev  home  lib64       media  opt   root  sbin  sys  usr
boot   etc  lib   lost+found  mnt    proc  run   srv   tmp  var
```

Now open another shell on your Host machine, to check the docker processes which are running. The command docker ps can be used for this purpose:

```
$ sudo docker ps | awk '{print $1 $2}'
CONTAINER ID        IMAGE
935376c573f9        fedora
```

Please note that we are using `awk` to restrict the number of arguments to display for typographic reasons. On a sufficiently wide terminal you will not need it.

The first argument displayed (the `CONTAINER_ID`) is a key attribute as it's the one identified assigned to your container. We will use it across our examples to interact with our container. In this case, we will stop the container by issuing the `docker stop <ContainerId>` command:

```
$ sudo docker stop 935376c573f9
```

Another way to stop the container process is terminating the process attached to it, in our case typing `exit` at the command prompt of the container's shell

Congratulations! Your first container is running in good health. Now it's time to move on to creating a container with EAP 7 features.

Creating your Docker images

So far we have used a pre-built image with an operating system image. We will now show you how to create your own Docker image, containing EAP 7 and its required dependencies, such as the JDK environment.

In order to do that, we will use a `Dockerfile`, which is a text file that contains all the commands needed in order to build a specific image.

The available set of commands are described in depth in the site's documentation: `https://docs.docker.com/engine/reference/builder/`.

Here we will discuss the set of commands required to create an EAP 7 image: create a file named `Dockerfile` and include the following content:

```
### Set the base image
FROM jboss/base-jdk:8

### File Author / Maintainer
MAINTAINER "Francesco Marchioni" "fmarchio@redhat.com"
```

```
### Install EAP 7.0.0
ADD build/jboss-eap-7.0.0.zip /tmp/
RUN unzip /tmp/jboss-eap-7.0.0.zip

### Set Environment
ENV JBOSS_HOME /opt/jboss/jboss-eap-7.0

### Create EAP User
RUN $JBOSS_HOME/bin/add-user.sh admin Password1! --silent

EXPOSE 8080 9990


CMD ["/opt/jboss/jboss-eap-7.0/bin/standalone.sh", "-b", "0.0.0.0","-
bmanagement","0.0.0.0"]
```

Let's explain the syntax contained in this file: The first element is the FROM command. This command sets the base image to be used in your container.

FROM must be the first non-comment instruction in the Dockerfile.

In our case, we are using the jboss/base-jdk:8 image. This image extends a Fedora image adding the OpenJDK distribution for the selected version. Additionally, a JAVA_HOME environment variable will be set out of the box.

The second command we meet is MAINTAINER. This command simply tells us the name and e-mail of the person who has created the image.

The third command is where we nail the installation process of EAP. The ADD command is used to add files from our local system to our container. In our case, we have previously downloaded the ZIP file of the application server and copied it into the build folder. Once we are done with that, we will use the RUN command to unzip the application server into a temporary directory. The RUN command is a very versatile option that can be used for provisioning your container by running any command that you would typically run from the command line.

Next, we use the ENV command to set the JBOSS_HOME environment variable into the container. The environment variable is used in the next RUN command to create a management user so that you will be able to connect to the CLI when the image will be running.

The EXPOSE command informs Docker that the container listens on the specified network ports (in our case 8080 and 9990) at runtime. This will be mapped by Docker to an external port on the container, and finally forwarded when they are accessed externally.

The last command, CMD is the default argument to the container. In our case, we set it as default, the standalone mode exposing the public and management interfaces to all available IP addresses. This will be, in practice, the entry point of your container.

Building our image

Once you have created the Dockerfile, make sure you have placed the application server in the build folder that is located in the same path as the Dockerfile. Next, you will build the image by running the following command from the same folder as your Dockerfile:

```
$ sudo docker build --rm -t packt/eap-7.0 .
```

The build process will start, pulling images from the available Docker repositories. As for the Fedora image, the first time you execute this command it will require some time to complete this step as all required images need to be pulled. Once it is done, you can check for the available images with the docker image command, as follows:

```
$ sudo docker images
REPOSITORY   TAG   IMAGE ID CREATED     VIRTUAL SIZE
packt/eap-7.0   latest   374824a968f9  3 minutes ago    755.9 MB
docker.io/jboss/base-jdk   8      07a2bc8bddd5
35 hours ago          419.2 MB
fedora    latest  ded7cd95e059   3 months ago   186.5 MB
```

Once the image has completed building, you can run it. In order to run the image, you will need to reference it by its name, which in our case is packt/eap7.0:

```
$ sudo docker run -it packt/eap-7.0
```

The CMD command contained in the Dockerfile will start the application server using the default attributes.

> If you want to start the container in detached mode you can use the -d mode which will execute the container in the background. Example:
> docker run -d packt/eap-7.0

You can verify that the process is running by issuing the docker ps command, as follows:

```
$ sudo docker ps | awk '{print $1 $2}'
CONTAINER ID        IMAGE
1b2d77f52f84        packt/eap-7.0
```

The last information we need to acquire is the IP address which has been assigned to the Docker network interface. The docker inspect command can be used for that. As its output is quite verbose, we can focus just on the attribute we are interested in, that is the NetworkSettings.IPAddress. The inspect command needs the CONTAINER ID attribute which we already discovered using the docker ps command. Here is our IP address:

```
$ sudo docker inspect -f '{{ .NetworkSettings.IPAddress }}' 1b2d77f52f84
172.17.0.4
```

Now, you can try connecting to the public interface of the server at http://172.17.0.4:8080:

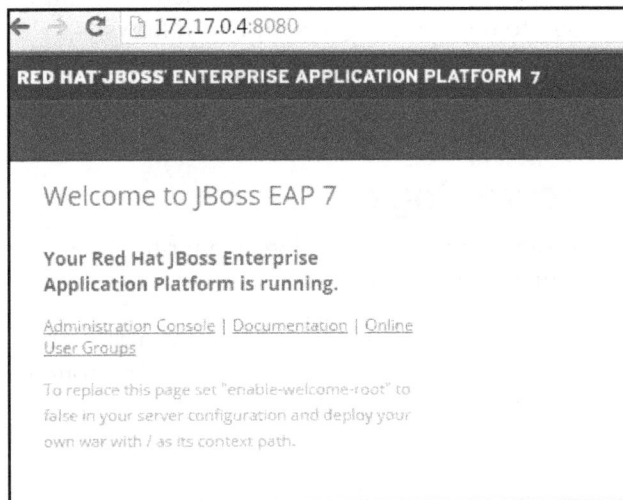

You can verify the connectivity with the management instruments through the Web console: http://172.17.0.4:9990. You can also try connecting with the CLI. You can use the locally installed CLI from your host machine:

```
$ /home/jboss/jboss-eap-7.0/bin/jboss-cli.sh
You are disconnected at the moment. Type 'connect' to connect to the
server or 'help' for the list of supported commands.
[disconnected /] connect 172.17.0.4
Authenticating against security realm: ManagementRealm
```

```
Username: admin
Password:
[standalone@172.17.0.4:9999 /]
```

Having verified the connectivity, you can shutdown the server from the CLI. This will terminate the container as well:

```
[standalone@172.17.0.4:9999 /] shutdown
[disconnected /] exit
```

Check from the shell that no Docker processes are active now:

```
[root@localhost book]# docker ps
CONTAINER ID        IMAGE            COMMAND            CREATED
STATUS              PORTS            NAMES
```

> **More about the entry point**:
> The Dockerfile CMD command is quite versatile: in fact, it can be overridden at runtime with a new entry point. For example, suppose you want to start the server in domain mode, then you simply need to specify the entrypoint to the domain.sh script, as follows:
> ```
> docker run -it packt/eap-7.0 /opt/jboss/jboss-
> eap-7.0/bin/domain.sh -b 0.0.0.0 -bmanagement 0.0.0.0
> ```

Inspecting the server logs

Docker features a built-in command to read the logs from processes running inside the container, which are printing to standard output (or error).

> Reading the container logs is a handy feature, although in production you will consider separating your server logs from the container image, which should be as *ephemeral* as possible.

You can retrieve the server logs for the container ID 1b2d77f52f84 with the following command:

```
$ sudo docker logs 1b2d77f52f84
```

As a result, the console logs will be printed in the standard output

Managing the server storage

One of the critical aspects of container management relates to the storage. So far we have started and executed a container which could be further enhanced by deploying applications on top of it and eventually adding specific configurations. You might be surprised, however, that when restarting the Docker image the changes you have applied are not included in your image.

This is not a defect of your container- Docker aims to preserve your containers data so that you can, at any time, restart them with minimal overhead. There are, of course, many strategies to handle changes happening to your container data. The cheapest solution could be to use the `docker commit` command, which as the name suggests, can be used to commit a container's file changes or settings into a new image. You need to provide it the container ID and the image to create (or update).

For example:

```
$ sudo docker commit 1b2d77f52f84 packt/eap-7.0:version2
```

Although useful for development purposes, it is not a good strategy in production to alter your base images as it defeats the purpose of the container's immutability which helps to provision a common base of your server environment. This introduces us to the concept of storage management in Docker. Basically, you have two main alternatives to deal with storage when you are using Docker:

- Mounting a host's volume as storage: This means mounting the variable part of your image in the host machine
- Using a data container as volume: This option uses a Docker container as volume for your storage

Let's see both options and their advantages and their challenges.

Mounting a volume from the host machine

Mounting a volume from your host machine is a simple way to deal with storage as it simply uses the host machine as an external volume for your container. A good candidate for local volume could be `jboss.server.base.dir` which corresponds, in standalone mode, to the `JBOSS_HOME/standalone` directory. In domain mode the equivalent is `jboss.server.base.dir`, which maps to the `JBOSS_HOME/domain` directory.

Let's see how to do it in practice: we will store `jboss.server.base.dir` in the host machine on the `/tmp/eap7` path. In order to do that, we need to prepare our host machine with a blank installation of the application server.

If you attempt to mount a non-existing directory, the directory will be created in the host with root as owner and permissions 755, making it not writable for any other user than root. The EAP image will run with the `jboss` user, so it will fail writing to this directory.

Let's create our host volume, as follows:

```
$ mkdir -r /tmp/eap7
```

Now copy a base standalone folder to the host volume:

```
$ cp -r /home/jboss/jboss-eap-7.0/standalone /tmp/eap7
```

Now we are ready to mount our EAP7 with a host mount point:

```
$ sudo docker run --rm -it -v /tmp/eap7:/opt/jboss/jboss-
eap-7.0/standalone:rw packt/eap-7.0
```

The syntax of the volume parameter (`-v`) is quickly explained: the first argument (`/tmp/eap7/standalone`) is the path in the host machine that will be mounted. The other argument, separated by a column (`/opt/jboss/jboss-eap-7.0/standalone:rw`) corresponds to the path of the container that will be locally mounted.

You can check that log files, for example, are being written to the mount point that we have specified:

```
$ tail -f /tmp/eap7/log/server.log
2016-02-27 09:48:20,800 INFO
[org.jboss.as.connector.subsystems.datasources] (MSC service thread 1-6)
WFLYJCA0001: Bound data source [java:jboss/datasources/ExampleDS]
2016-02-27 09:48:20,883 INFO [org.jboss.as.server.deployment.scanner] (MSC
service thread 1-2) WFLYDS0013: Started FileSystemDeploymentService for
directory /opt/jboss/jboss-eap-7.0/standalone/deployments
. . . . .
2016-02-27 09:48:21,291 INFO [org.jboss.as] (Controller Boot Thread)
WFLYSRV0060: Http management interface listening on
http://0.0.0.0:9990/management
2016-02-27 09:48:21,293 INFO [org.jboss.as] (Controller Boot Thread)
WFLYSRV0051: Admin console listening on http://0.0.0.0:9990
2016-02-27 09:48:21,293 INFO [org.jboss.as] (Controller Boot Thread)
WFLYSRV0025: EAP 7.0.0.Beta1 (WildFly Core 2.0.3.Final-redhat-1) started in
5642ms - Started 261 of 509 services (332 services are lazy, passive or on-
demand)
```

Although being a handy solution, this approach contains a big issue, which is your images will not be portable, as the variable part of your container will be spread in other file systems. In some cases, this might be acceptable; however, in larger company infrastructures this might introduce more complexity than simplicity.

For the sake of completeness, we will mention as option mounting the host directories over NFS as an option. This will not make your images truly portable, but it can still centralize the location of your configurations. A detailed treatment of this option is beyond the scope of the book, however, some more details are available in this book extract available here: `ht tps://jaxenter.com/how-to-share-docker-volumes-across-hosts-11962.html`.

Troubleshooting mounting volumes from the host machine

A common requirement for this approach to work is that you need a user with the same `uid/gid`, both in the container and on the host. This can happen automatically if the EAP 7 ZIP files belong to the same user that created the host mount point, otherwise you need to create a local user with the same `uid/gid` in the host machine.

Let's first check the `uid/gid` in the container. Retrieve the CONTAINER ID with `docker ps`:

```
$ sudo docker ps
CONTAINER ID        IMAGE
222c93543d52        packt/eap-7.0
```

Now use the `docker exec` command to enter into the container's bash:

```
$ sudo docker exec -it 222c93543d52 bash
[jboss@222c93543d52 ~]$ id
uid=1000(jboss) gid=1000(jboss) groups=1000(jboss)
```

Great, we found out that the eap7 process is executed in the container with uid/gid 1000-.

Now add the `jboss` group in the host machine with the same identifier:

```
# groupadd -r jboss -g 1000
```

Finally, add the `jboss` user in the host machine as well:

```
# useradd -u 1000 -r -g jboss -s /sbin/nologin -c "EAP7 container user" jboss
```

Now change the ownership of the directory that we have formerly created, by assigning it to the jboss user:

```
# chown -R jboss:jboss /tmp/eap7
```

Using a data container

The second approach that we will describe is the most recommended one, as it abstracts completely from the location where you are running Docker. In this case, instead of mounting a physical directory from the host, we use another container's feature called data containers. In short, a data container is a special kind of container solely responsible to hold some data. This is a much more effective way to organize your data as it decouples volumes from other potential concerns of the system.

First of all, create a new `Dockerfile` with the volume definition:

```
FROM packt/eap-7.0
VOLUME /space/jboss/jboss-eap-7.0/standalone
ENTRYPOINT /usr/bin/tail -f /dev/null
```

In this example, we have defined in the `Dockerfile` the `VOLUME` instruction which creates a mount point with a specified name. The Volume can point to an external resource available in the host machine or to other containers, as in our case.

We have specified `ENTRYPOINT` as the command `tail -f /dev/null`. By doing this, even if your main command runs in the background, your container doesn't stop because tail is kept running in the foreground. Now build your data image and tag it as `data`:

```
$ sudo docker build --tag="data" .
```

As you can see from the command log, the Docker daemon will start creating intermediate containers, until the `ENTRYPOINT` is reached:

```
Sending build context to Docker daemon 2.048 kB
Step 0 : FROM packt/eap-7.0
 ---> a1d60f8ebd06
Step 1 : VOLUME /space/jboss/jboss-eap-7.0/standalone
 ---> Running in 06313c03e7f3
 ---> 5e15d47be1c8
Removing intermediate container 06313c03e7f3
Step 2 : ENTRYPOINT /usr/bin/tail -f /dev/null
 ---> Running in 02afac65649c
 ---> 245cf996e17c
Removing intermediate container 02afac65649c
Successfully built 245cf996e17c
```

At this point, the data container should be enlisted among your images:

```
$ sudo docker images
REPOSITORY      TAG    IMAGE ID    CREATED      VIRTUAL SIZE
data      latest  245cf996e17c  56 seconds ago      758.6 MB
```

Now you can run the data container with `dockerrun`:

```
$ sudo docker run --name data data
```

You can expect at this point to see the Docker image enlisted in your Docker processes:

```
$ sudo docker ps | awk '{print $1 $2}'
CONTAINER ID         IMAGE
304211ce30b0         data
```

The last step will be connecting our former image `packt/eap-7.0`:

```
$ sudo docker run --rm -h eap7-v01 --name eap7-v01 --volumes-from data
packt/eap-7.0
```

The server process will start in the foreground, displaying the boot logs in the shell:

```
. . . . . .
08:41:40,148 INFO [org.jboss.as] (Controller Boot Thread) WFLYSRV0060: Http
management interface listening on http://0.0.0.0:9990/management
08:41:40,149 INFO [org.jboss.as] (Controller Boot Thread) WFLYSRV0051:
Admin console listening on http://0.0.0.0:9990
08:41:40,150 INFO [org.jboss.as] (Controller Boot Thread) WFLYSRV0025: EAP
7.0.0.Beta1 (WildFly Core 2.0.3.Final-redhat-1) started in 4881ms - Started
261 of 509 services (332 services are lazy, passive or on-demand)
```

Now verify that the server process started as well, with `docker ps`:

```
[root@localhost ~]# docker ps | awk '{print $1 $2}'
CONTAINER ID         IMAGE
bdac80792b7d         packt/eap-7.0
304211ce30b0         data
```

You can also inspect the location where the data image has been stored in your machine using the docker inspect command. In this case, we will filter through the Mounts element of the JSON data retuned by the command:

```
$ sudo docker inspect -f "{{json .Mounts}}" data
[{"Name":"2cc2f4a9d3509518c780f2c6f243e9545941b0fd5a23b6b7a90457cd12d418fe"
,"Source":"/var/lib/docker/volumes/2cc2f4a9d3509518c780f2c6f243e9545941b0fd
5a23b6b7a90457cd12d418fe/_data","Destination":"/space/jboss/jboss-
eap-7.0/standalone","Driver":"local","Mode":"","RW":true}]
```

Hence, the location selected by Docker to mount the container volume is
`/var/lib/docker/volumes/2cc2f4a9d3509518c780f2c6f243e9545941b0fd5a23b6b`
`7a90457cd12d418fe`

Managing multiple containers

In the first part of this chapter, we covered how to use Docker to run containers and build images. If you've mastered these fundamentals, you are ready to jump into high-level concepts and more complete tasks. The last part of this chapter will introduce you to Docker compose which is a tool for defining, launching, and managing services running in Docker containers.

Compose lets you stop focusing on single containers and instead describe full environments and service component interactions using a simple syntax contained in a YAML file (`http://yaml.org/`) and managed with the Command Line program Docker-compose.

Using Docker compose

We will first install docker compose which is available on GitHub. At the time of writing, the latest stable build is 1.6.2, and so the following command will download and install it:

```
curl -L
https://github.com/docker/compose/releases/download/1.6.2/docker-compose-`u
name -s`-`uname -m` > /usr/local/bin/docker-compose
```

Assign the required permission to the `docker-compose` command, as follows:

```
chmod +x /usr/local/bin/docker-compose
```

We will now show two examples of integration between different containers.

In the first one, we will orchestrate a PostgreSQL database with EAP 7 linking the database to the application server; this way the datasource connection will work no matter what IP address gets assigned to the database.

In the second example, we will show how to scale a cluster of EAP nodes fronted by `mod_cluster`; this second example will require setting up a custom image of `mod_cluster`.

Composing EAP 7 with a Database

Now we will create a YAML file to orchestrate two containers: an EAP 7 container and a PostgreSQL database container.

> The syntax of a YAML file is pretty much a human readable one, composed of a list of items; each item in the list has a list of key/value pairs, commonly called a *hash* or a *dictionary*.

Create a file named docker-compose.yml with the following content:

```
postgredb:
image: postgres
ports:
    - "5432:5432"
  environment:
    - POSTGRES_USER=user
    - POSTGRES_PASSWORD=password
eap7:
image:   packt/eap-7.0
links:
- postgredb:db
ports:
- 8080:8080
- 9990:9990
```

In this file, we have highlighted two items: the images that will be linked by docker compose. The first one is postgres which is not yet in our repository and the second is packt/eap-7.0 which we have formerly used.

The other items in the file are pretty intuitive: ports can be used to expose ports. Either both ports (HOST:CONTAINER) as in our case, or just the container port. The environment item can be used to override some specific settings of a container via environment variables. In our case, POSTGRES_USER will create the specified user with superuser rights and a database with the same name. Much the same way as POSTGRES_PASSWORD will set the password for our user.

The other image, packt/eap-7.0, contains the same port settings used so far. Finally, pay attention to the links item which links the two containers using the alias db. Containers for the linked service will be reachable at a hostname identical to the alias; in our case, we will be able to see the other container from EAP 7 using the db hostname.

Now you can start `docker-compose` in detached mode, as follows:

```
$ sudo docker-compose up -d
```

The `postgres` image will be downloaded and next the two images will be created. Now you can check that the two Docker processes are active:

```
$ sudo docker ps | awk '{print $1 $2}'
CONTAINER ID        IMAGE
1d501840ba83        packt/eap-7.0:latest
222b31b9dfc6        postgres:latest
```

At first, check out the IP address which has been assigned to the container:

```
$ sudo docker inspect -f '{{ .NetworkSettings.IPAddress }}'
1d501840ba83
172.17.0.4
```

As a test, we will try to install a datasource for connecting EAP 7 with the Postgres database. Start by downloading the Postgres JDBC driver from `https://jdbc.postgresql.org/download.html`.

Save the JDBC Driver on a local path, for example, on `/tmp`. Next, deploy the JDBC Driver by connecting to the application server using the command line interface:

```
$ /home/jboss/jboss-eap-7.0/bin/jboss-cli.sh
You are disconnected at the moment. Type 'connect' to connect to the
server or 'help' for the list of supported commands.
[disconnected /] connect 172.17.0.5
Authenticating against security realm: ManagementRealm
Username: admin
Password:
[standalone@172.17.0.4:9999 /] deploy /tmp/postgresql-9.4.1208.jre6.jar
```

Now create a datasource named PostgreSQL with the following command:

```
[standalone@172.17.0.4:9999 /] data-source add --name=PostgreSQL --
connection-url=jdbc:postgresql://db:5432/user --user-name=user --
password=password --driver-name=postgresql-9.4.1208.jre6.jar --jndi-
name=java:/PostgreSQL
```

Please notice that we have used, instead of the database IP address (which might vary) the hostname alias `db`, as defined in the YAML file.

You can check for connectivity with the database, as follows:

```
[standalone@172.17.0.4:9999 /] /subsystem=datasources/data-
source=PostgreSQL:test-connection-in-pool
{
    "outcome" => "success",
    "result" => [true]
}
```

Composing a cluster of EAP 7 nodes

The second example will be slightly more complex as we will build up a `mod_cluster`
image. Some `mod_cluster` images do exist in the DockerHub, however, just to make sure
the configuration meets our needs, we will assemble our own image.

Create a `Dockerfile` in a new folder with the following content:

```
FROM fedora
####### Base installation ###################
RUN yum install -y httpd mod_cluster
RUN yum clean all
####### Adapt configuration ##############
# Disable mod_proxy_balancer module to allow mod_cluster to work
RUN sed -i 's|LoadModule proxy_balancer_module|# LoadModule
proxy_balancer_module|' /etc/httpd/conf.modules.d/00-proxy.conf
RUN sed -i '1,4d' /etc/httpd/conf.d/mod_cluster.conf
RUN sed -i 's/^#//g' /etc/httpd/conf.d/mod_cluster.conf
RUN sed -i -e 's/Require host 127.0.0.1/Require all granted/g'
/etc/httpd/conf.d/mod_cluster.conf
RUN echo 'ServerAdvertise On' >> /etc/httpd/conf.d/mod_cluster.conf
####### Open Port 80 ##############
EXPOSE 80
####### Execute
CMD ["/usr/sbin/apachectl", "-D", "FOREGROUND"]
```

At this point of the chapter, the preceding configuration should be quite intuitive. With the
first block of code we are setting our base image for our container. Next, we are installing
the RPM files of `mod_cluster` through `yum`.

The following lines (9-16) are just used to adjust the configuration of `mod_cluster` to allow
a basic default policy so that all hosts connections are accepted and **Node Advertising** is
enabled. Finally, the `httpd` service is started.

You can build your image as usual with:

```
$ sudo docker build --rm -t modcluster .
```

The next step will be extending our EAP 7 image so that it uses an HA profile and deploys a clusterable Web application on top of it. Create the following Dockerfile in a new folder with the following content:

```
FROM packt/eap-7.0
ADD build/cluster-demo.war "$JBOSS_HOME/standalone/deployments/cluster-
demo.war"
# Start JBoss using the HA Profile
CMD ["/opt/jboss/jboss-eap-7.0/bin/standalone.sh", "-c","standalone-
ha.xml","-b", "0.0.0.0","-bmanagement","0.0.0.0"]
```

As you can see, we are extending the packt/eap-7.0 image we have created so far, adding the cluster-demo.war application we have already used in Chapter 5, *Load Balancing*. This application basically includes a distributable stanza in web.xml, so that the JGroups web channel is activated. The application is packaged in the build folder of the current directory. Finally, we have set the startup options to include the standalone-ha.xml file.

We will tag this image as packt/eap-7.0/ha so that it differentiates from the EAP 7 base image:

```
$ sudo docker build --rm -t packt/eap-7.0/ha .
```

Now it's about time to create the YAML file which orchestrates the two containers we have built so far. Here is our new docker-compose.yml:

```
modcluster:
  image: modcluster
  ports:
   - 80:80
eap7:
  image: packt/eap-7.0/ha
  links:
    - modcluster:httpd
```

Let's now start and attach the containers with:

```
$ sudo docker-compose up -d
```

The output will indicate that containers are being created (or re-created if you have already built them):

```
Creating compose_modcluster_1...
Recreating compose_eap7_10...
```

If you check the process list, you will see that the two containers are now running:

```
$ sudo docker ps | awk '{print $1 $2}'
CONTAINER ID        IMAGE
0e8794a3f99e             packt/eap-7.0/ha:latest
dd5d0afbe967         modcluster:latest
```

Most interesting for us, is the option to scale our environment. By using the `scale` option with `docker-compose` you will be able to set the number of containers to run for a service. Suppose we want three instances of the EAP 7 cluster, then execute the following command from the shell:

```
$ sudo docker-compose scale eap7=3
```

At this point, we have three instances of EAP 7 running and one instance of modcluster, as evident from the docker process list:

```
$ sudo docker ps | awk '{print $1 $2}'
CONTAINER ID    IMAGE
0e8794a3f99e             packt/eap-7.0/ha:latest
968edeb13e1c             packt/eap-7.0/ha:latest
2a082ae80794             packt/eap-7.0/ha:latest
dd5d0afbe967         modcluster:latest
```

You can check the connectivity of your servers, through the `mod_cluster`'s manager application. For example, if your `mod_cluster` server was bound on the IP address `172.17.0.10`, then you can reach it at the following address: `http://172.17.0.10/mod_cluster_manager`:

---

mod_cluster/1.2.6.Final

Auto Refresh show DUMP output show INFO output

Node c1eb2b80a623 (ajp://0.0.0.0:8009):

Enable Contexts Disable Contexts
Balancer: mycluster,LBGroup: ,Flushpackets: Off,Flushwait: 10000,Ping: 10000000,Smax: 2,Ttl: 60000000,

Node 37e9a81897a9 (ajp://0.0.0.0:8009):

Enable Contexts Disable Contexts
Balancer: mycluster,LBGroup: ,Flushpackets: Off,Flushwait: 10000,Ping: 10000000,Smax: 2,Ttl: 60000000,

Node a941a7fb1928 (ajp://0.0.0.0:8009):

Enable Contexts Disable Contexts
Balancer: mycluster,LBGroup: ,Flushpackets: Off,Flushwait: 10000,Ping: 10000000,Smax: 2,Ttl: 60000000,

---

As you can see, our cluster of three servers has been correctly balanced through `mod_cluster`.

Summary

This chapter has covered the most significant aspects of Docker technology applied to the JBoss EAP middleware. Throughout it, we have seen how Docker can help system administrators and developers to solve some common problems while simplifying the installation, execution, and publishing of applications.

In the next chapter, we will see how to evolve this technology by using OpenShift Enterprise which will take your container productivity to the next level.

14
Running EAP 7 on the Cloud Using OpenShift

This final chapter continues the journey from a container point of view. In this chapter, you will learn what **OpenShift** is. We will not go into depth about how you can install OpenShift, because it's out of the scope of the book. Installing OpenShift requires a very deep knowledge of the Linux operating system, network ninja skills, and all that comes with it.

In this chapter, you will learn how to configure and run your application using OpenShift Online.

The following are the topics we will take a dive into:

- Introduction to OpenShift Online
- Registering with OpenShift Online
- Developing and deploying your first OpenShift application on the cloud

Introducing OpenShift

OpenShift is a **PaaS**, which stands for **Platform as a Service**. OpenShift is Red Hat's PaaS, and you can find it in three different versions:

- **OpenShift Origin**: This one is the free and open source version of OpenShift. You can find its code stream on GitHub at `https://github.com/openshift/origin`.

- **OpenShift Online (OSO)**: OpenShift Online is the version that we will use in this chapter. For the moment, you just need to know that it's a free PaaS, where you can deploy your application based on your favorite environment. We will discuss it later in the chapter. OpenShift Online is available for free at `https://www.openshift.com`.
- **OpenShift Enterprise (OSE)**: OpenShift Enterprise is the version for which Red Hat provides support at the enterprise level.

> The latest version of OpenShift is 3. It has been entirely rewritten and is now based on a Linux container, using a Docker image format, Kubernetes, and much more.

Linux containers (in the middle of 2016, you should know about them) are a virtualization method at the operating system level. They allow you to run multiple isolated Linux systems and control them from within the host.

OpenShift uses the Docker container image format for its ease of use and its wide adoption.

If you want to know more about Docker, please refer to `Chapter 13`, *Using EAP 7 with Docker*, or have a look at the following site: `https://www.docker.com/`.

Kubernetes is an orchestrator for containers, for a containerized environment. It comes with a lot of features such as service discovery, load balancing, horizontal scaling, self-healing, and much more.

OpenShift leverages Kubernetes, capabilities, providing you an automated platform to work with.

If you want to know more about Kubernetes, please refer to the following site: `http://kubernetes.io/docs/`.

Let's discover the OpenShift Online world together.

OpenShift Online

To begin, we need a valid internet connection to register to the OpenShift Online platform, brought to you freely by Red Hat:

1. Open your favorite browser and point it to the following URL: `https://www.openshift.com/devpreview/register.html`. You should see a page similar to the following:

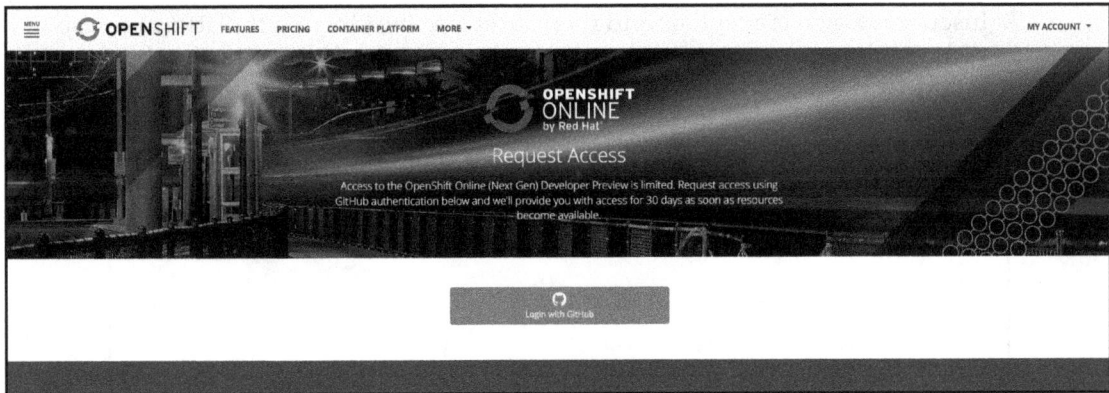

OpenShift login page

2. As you can see, you need a **GitHub** account to authenticate to OpenShift; click on the blue GitHub login button. You will be asked to log in to your GitHub account, as follows:

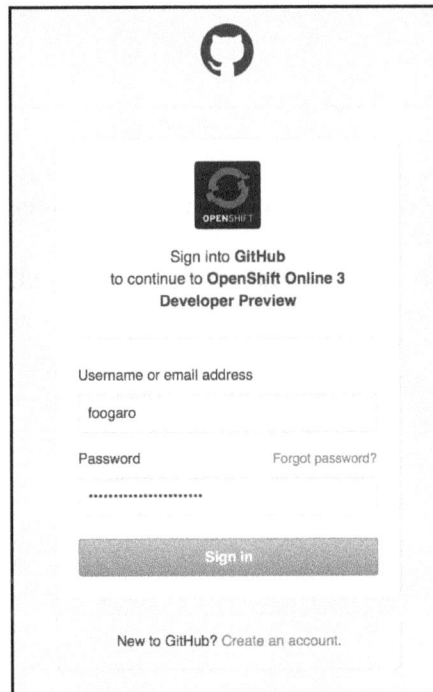

GitHub login page

3. Insert your own credentials and then authorize the OpenShift platform to use your GitHub account by clicking on the green **Authorize application** button, as follows:

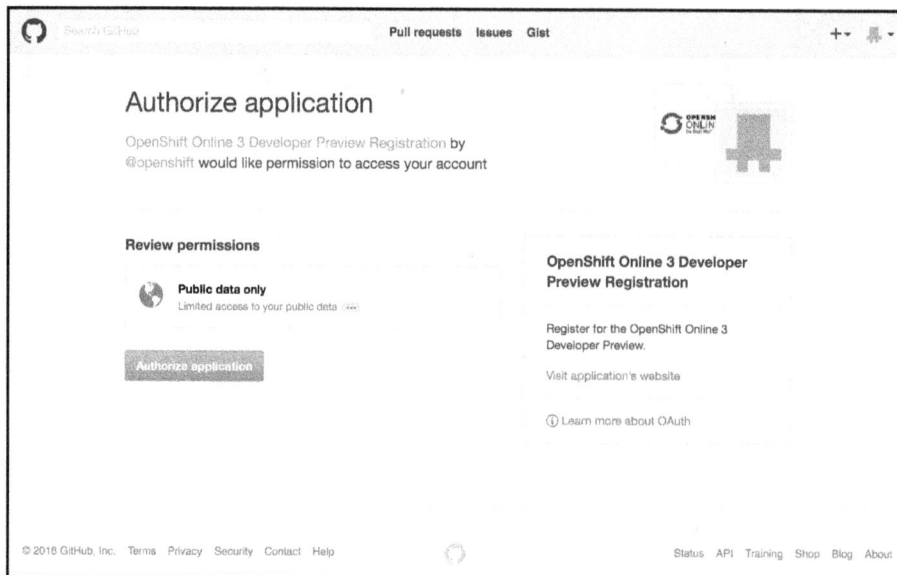

GitHub OpenShift authorization page

4. OpenShift will be able to identify you and read public information; it will not have any write permission.
5. Once the authorization process is completed, you will have to fill in the following form in OpenShift, as follows:

OpenShift registration form

6. Keep in mind that access to the developer preview of OpenShift Online based on Docker is limited; you will then need to wait for your request to be approved, as shown in the screenshot here:

OpenShift Online developer preview request access

7. But guess what? It will not take much time, just have a coffee and come back; an email is already waiting for you, just like the following:

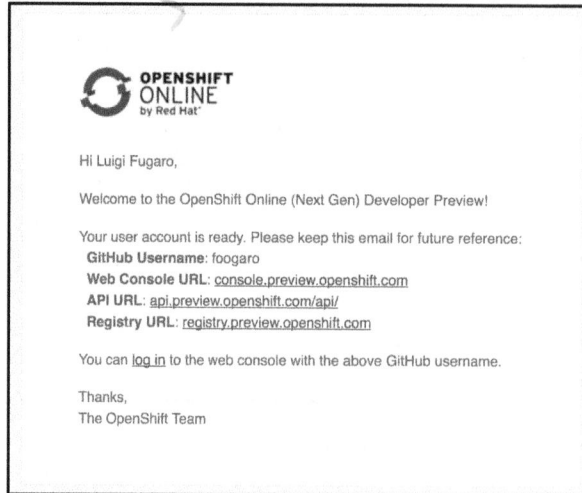

OpenShift Online Developer preview welcome email

Now we are ready to fully operate on the best platform as a service, OpenShift.

Developing and deploying your first OpenShift application in the cloud

To begin, follow these steps:

1. Open your browser and point it to the following URL:
   `https://console.preview.openshift.com/console/`

2. Log in with your GitHub account and you will be ready to create your first project. Just click on the blue **New Project** button, as depicted in the following screenshot:

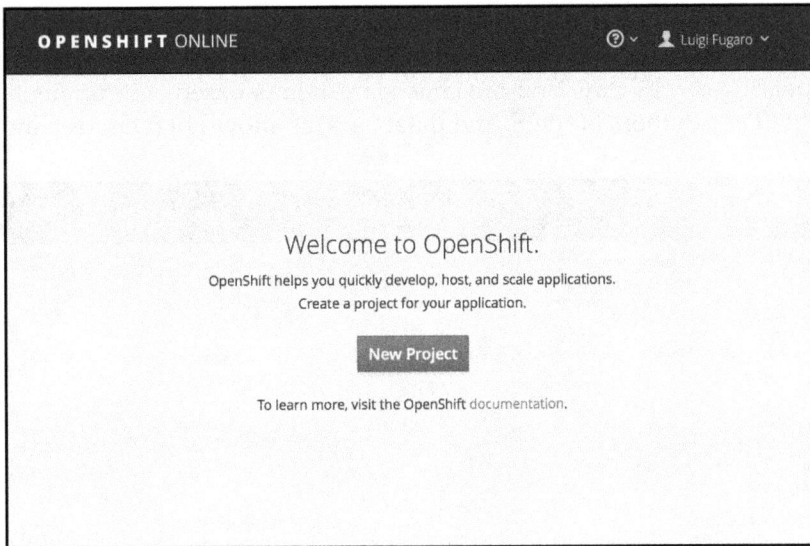

OpenShift welcome page

3. When you click on the blue **New Project** button, you will have to fill in the form to create your own project. For reference, here is my form:

OpenShift project creation form

4. Once done, you have to choose your application environment. In OpenShift, you have dozens of runtime environments to choose from, and more and more are appearing day by day. You can choose from Java-based environments to PHP, Ruby, Perl, Python, NodeJS, and databases, as shown in the screenshot here:

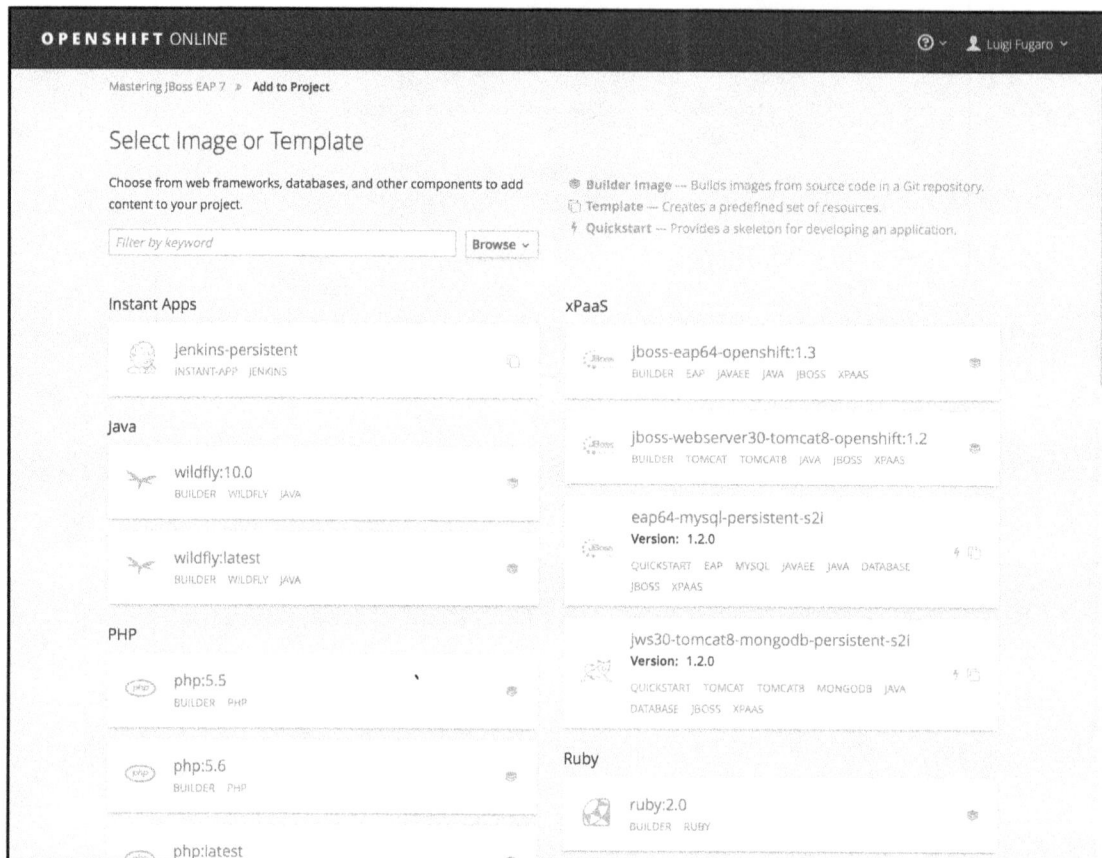

OpenShift template page

5. While writing this book, JBoss EAP 7 (just announced at *Red Hat Summit 2016*) is not available yet on the OpenShift platform, but at this time we can easily and confidently go for **WildFly 10**, which is the community version that EAP 7 is based on.

6. Just click on the **wildfly:10.0** box button, and fill in the form regarding the GitHub application you want to deploy using WildFly 10.0 on OpenShift, as shown here:

Hooking OpenShift to a GitHub repository

7. If you don't have an application ready to be built and deployed, you can easily choose mine, by forking it on GitHub at the following URL: `https://github.com/mjbeap7/openshift.git`.

> When creating a project, apart from the required information, such as the name and GitHub's repository URL, you can configure a lot of other settings, such as routing, build, and deployment.

8. To view these options, click on the blue link **Show advanced routing, build, and deployment options**, before hitting the blue **Create** button. The first setting is about **Routing**, as shown in the following screenshot:

Routing   ⑦ About Routing

☑ Create a route to the application

Hostname

    www.example.com

Public hostname for the route. If not specified, a hostname is generated.

Path

    /

Path that the router watches to route traffic to the service.

Target Port

    8080/TCP   ▼

Target port for traffic.

Show options for secured routes

Routing setting configuration

Routing is a way to make your application publicly visible. Otherwise you may only be able to access your application by its IP address, if allowed by the system administrator.

9. Next is the **Build Configuration**, as depicted here:

Build Configuration   ⑦ About Build Configuration

☑ Configure a webhook build trigger ⑦
☑ Automatically build a new image when the builder image changes ⑦
☑ Automatically build a new image when the build configuration changes

Environment Variables (Build and Runtime) ⑦

    Name   Value   Add

Build Configuration

The Build Configuration describes how to build your deployable image. This includes your source, the base builder image, and when to launch new builds.

10. Next is the **Deployment Configuration**, as depicted here:

Deployment Configuration

The deployment configuration describes how your application is configured by the cluster and under what conditions it should be recreated (for example, when the image changes).

11. Next is **Scaling**, as shown here:

Scaling configuration

Scaling defines the number of running instances of your built image.

12. Next is **Resource Limits**, as depicted here:

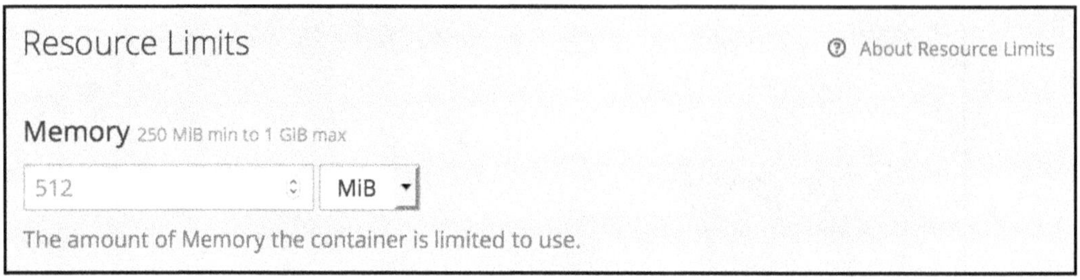

Resource Limits

Resource Limits control compute resource usage by a container on a node.

13. Next is **Labels**, as shown here:

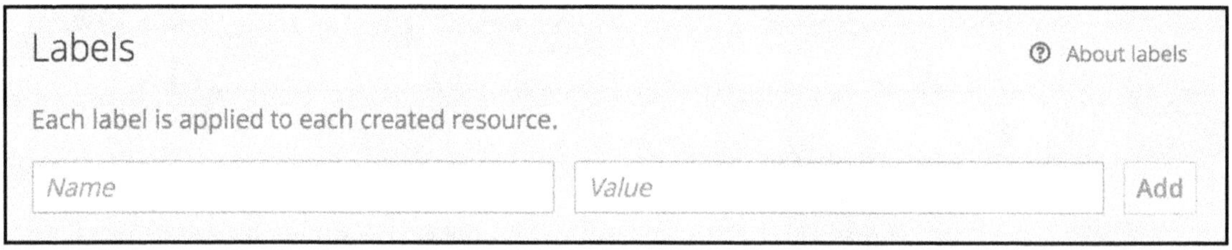

Labels configuration

Labels are used to organize, group, or select objects and resources, such as pods.

14. Now we are ready to create our first project. Click on the blue **Create** button and your project will be created, as shown in the following screenshot:

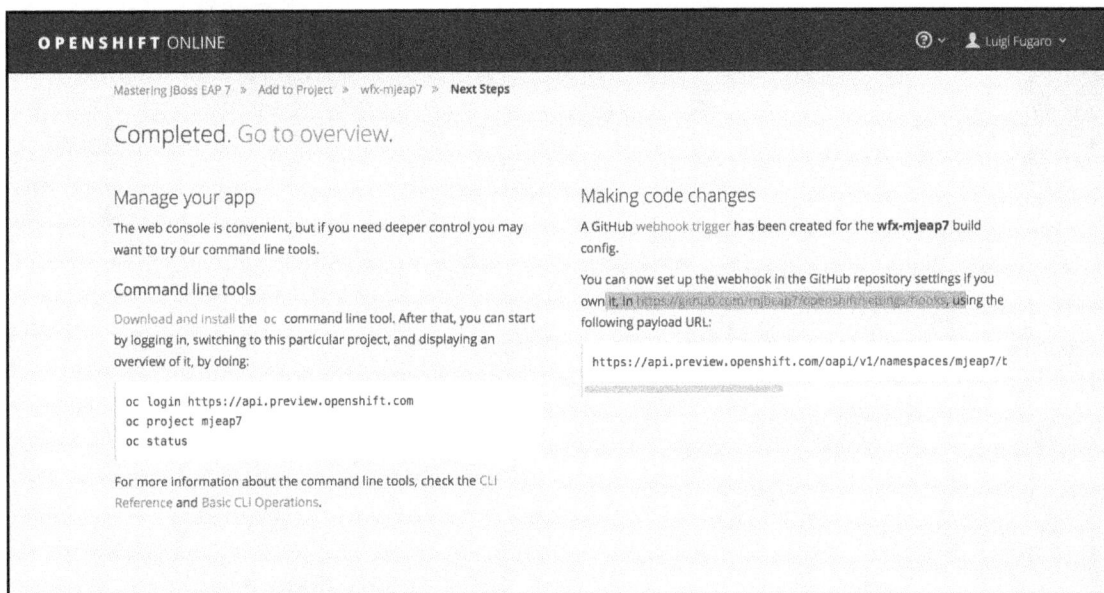

OpenShift project created

Despite the project and its environment, OpenShift has created for us a GitHub webhook trigger, which allows us to trigger a new build by sending a request to the OpenShift API endpoint. GitHub webhooks handle the call made by GitHub when a repository is updated in a few words when a `push` occurs.

Let's keep a note of this, as we will test the GitHub webhook later on in the chapter (use your own):

- GitHub webhook: `https://github.com/mjbeap7/openshift/settings/hooks`
- Webhook payload URL:
  `https://api.preview.openshift.com/oapi/v1/namespaces/mjeap7/buildconfigs/wfx-mjeap7/webhooks/b146e71dd5cfa5ff/github`

We can now have a look at the overview of our project by clicking on the **Overview** link, as follows:

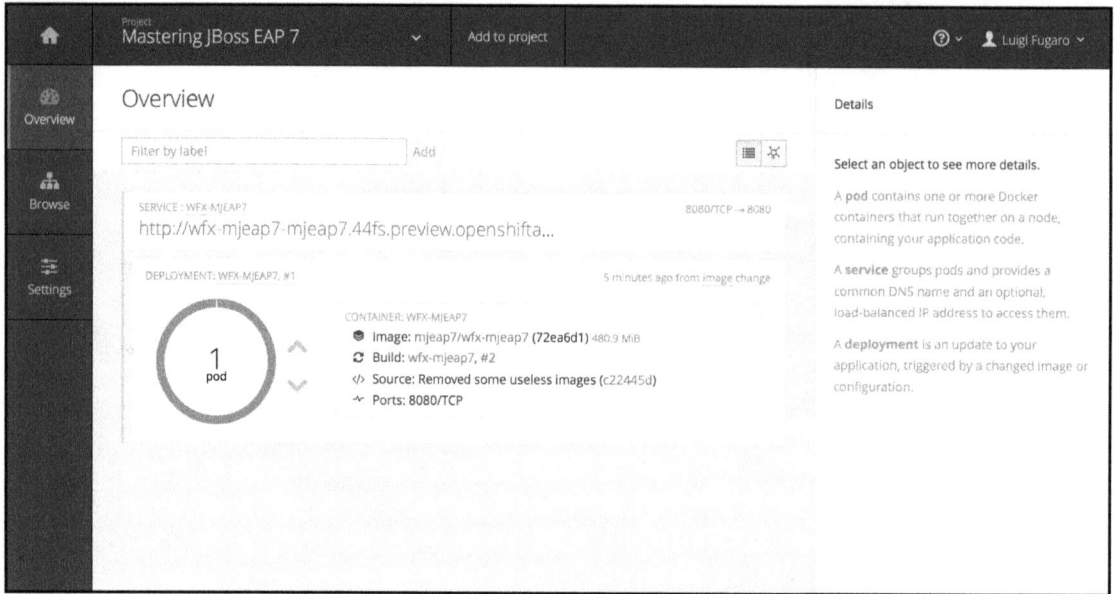

Project overview

We can see our project shown in the previous screenshot, along with its URL. Try to open it. You should see the following:

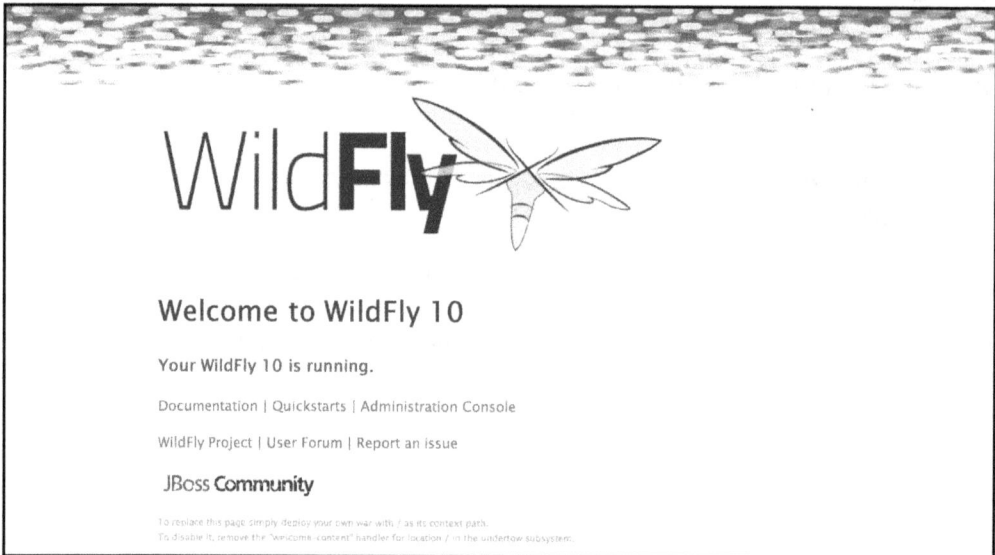

WildFly welcome page

This is not our application, but the platform environment we chose at the beginning when creating our first project.

If, by opening the project link, we want our application to be shown, we need to give a forward slash (/) as the context path of our application. To achieve this, we need to add the `jboss-web.xml` file to our code in the `WEB-INF` folder, with the following code:

```
<jboss>
    <context-root>/</context-root>
</jboss>
```

As we will need to push our new code to GitHub and rebuild our image from within OpenShift, we can take advantage of GitHub webhooks and have a push do the whole thing.

Let's try this by going back to the note we made earlier in the chapter:

1. Open the link that describes your application hooks it in your browser. You should find a page similar to the following:

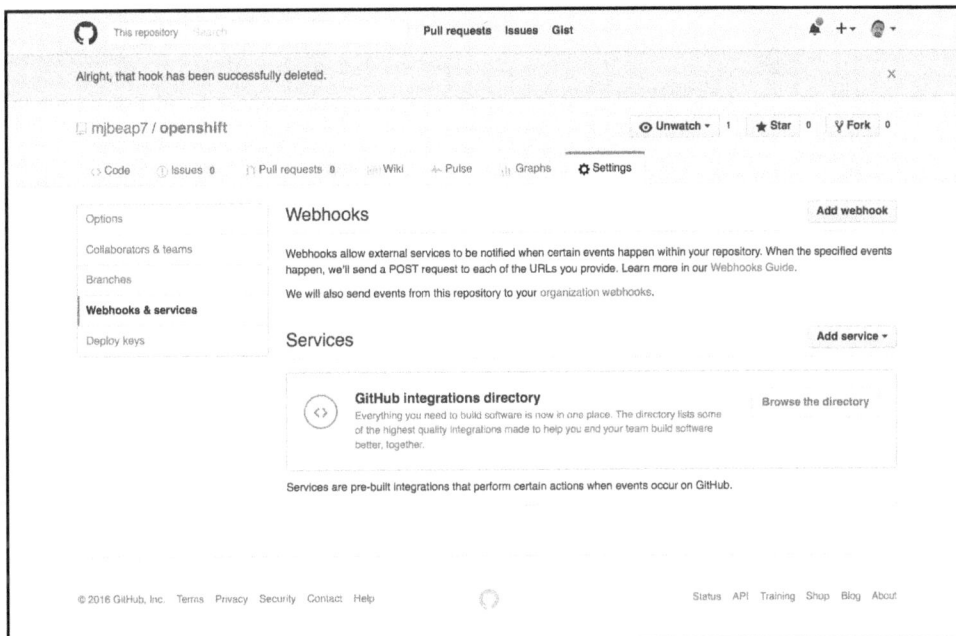

GitHub webhooks configuration

2. Click on the **Add webhook** button and fill in the form with the payload URL and the secret value, which makes your webhook URL unique, then press the green **Add webhook** button, as follows:

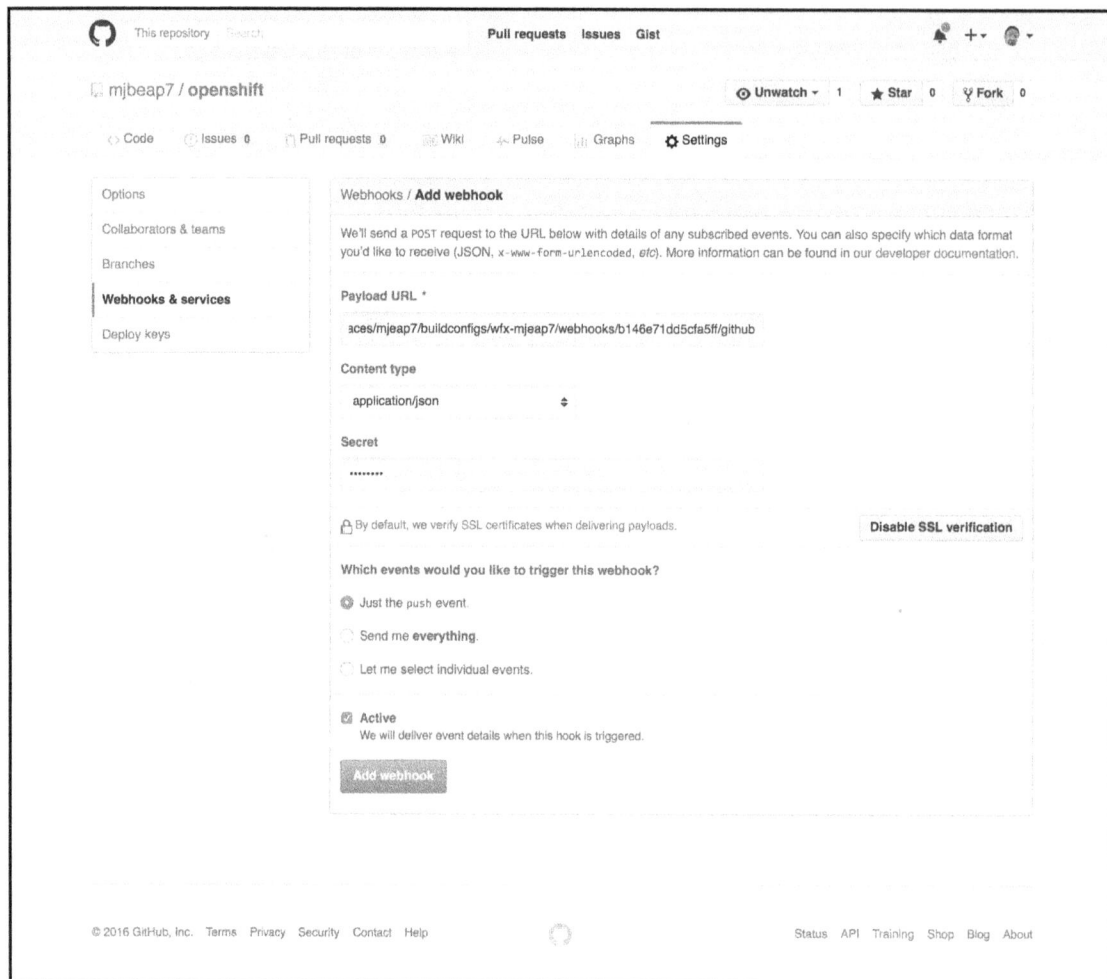

Webhook creation

3. Once the **webhook** is created, we can go back to our code, add the changes to the GitHub repository, and commit and push them, as shown in the following screenshot:

```
Luigis-MacBook-Pro:openshift foogaro$ vim src/main/webapp/WEB-INF/jboss-web.xml
Luigis-MacBook-Pro:openshift foogaro$ git status
On branch master
Your branch is up-to-date with 'origin/master'.
Untracked files:
  (use "git add <file>..." to include in what will be committed)

        src/main/webapp/WEB-INF/jboss-web.xml

nothing added to commit but untracked files present (use "git add" to track)
Luigis-MacBook-Pro:openshift foogaro$ git add .
Luigis-MacBook-Pro:openshift foogaro$ git commit -m "Added jboss-web.xml file to change applicaiton's context path to root"
[master a326f10] Added jboss-web.xml file to change applicaiton's context path to root
 1 file changed, 3 insertions(+)
 create mode 100644 src/main/webapp/WEB-INF/jboss-web.xml
Luigis-MacBook-Pro:openshift foogaro$ git push
Username for 'https://github.com': foogaro
Password for 'https://foogaro@github.com':
Counting objects: 7, done.
Delta compression using up to 8 threads.
Compressing objects: 100% (5/5), done.
Writing objects: 100% (7/7), 604 bytes | 0 bytes/s, done.
Total 7 (delta 1), reused 0 (delta 0)
To https://github.com/mjbeap7/openshift.git
   c22445d..a326f10  master -> master
Luigis-MacBook-Pro:openshift foogaro$ █
```

Committing changes to GitHub

4. Right after pushing everything to the GitHub repository, switch back to the browser and without any action at all, you can already see our project building a new image, as shown in the following screenshot:

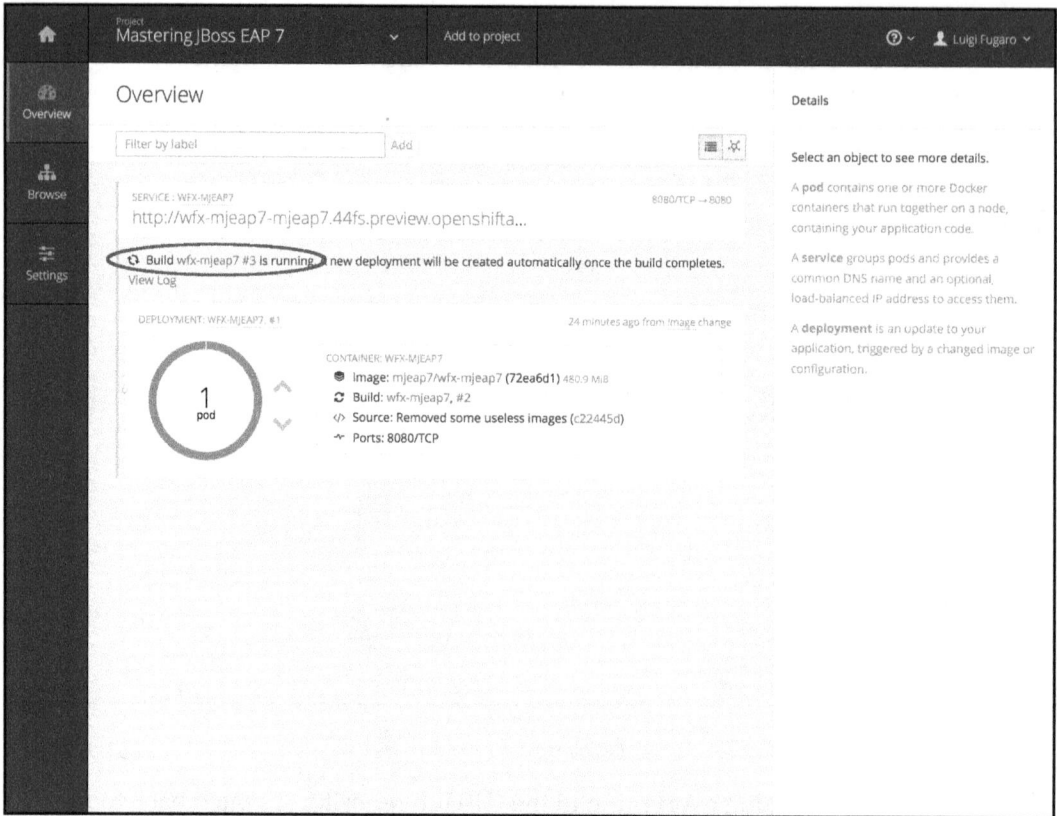

OpenShift triggered by GitHub to build a new image

That's because of the GitHub webhook! Sweet!

5. Once the build image process is terminated, go back to the URL of our application, and now you should see it working, just like mine, as follows:

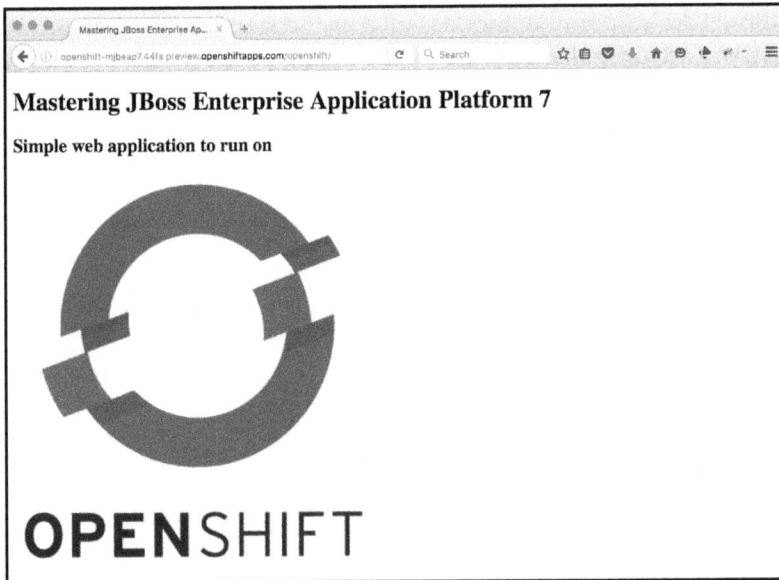

Showing the application

That was just a sip of OpenShift. Since you are registered for free, you have no excuse not to play around with it, just keep the following URLs handy:

```
https://docs.openshift.com/online/dev_guide/index.html
https://console.preview.openshift.com/console/command-line
```

Summary

In this chapter, you learned how to use the OpenShift Online web UI. OpenShift has changed a lot since its first release. Now everything is based on the Linux container.

You learned how to configure GitHub's webhook, which automatically triggers your OpenShift project image rebuild based on the new code.

This was the last chapter of the book. We really hope you liked the book and that your skills have grown to transform you into a real JBoss EAP 7 master.

It was a long journey, where you learned the basis of the Red Hat middleware platform and a lot of advanced topics.

We have seen JBoss EAP's operative modes, such as the standalone domain. We have seen the differences (there are only management differences) between the two modes. You learned how to configure your environment via the Web console and the CLI, which is the one we suggest for its potentiality and its support for automation (it can be invoked as script).

We have seen how to use the JBoss EAP 7 platform as message oriented middleware, using the embedded Apache Artemis broker server.

And finally, you learned about database connectivity, high availability, clustering, security, Docker, and much, much more.

Index

* 9 7 8 1 7 8 6 4 6 3 6 3 0 *